ANNUAL EDITIONS

Health

Twenty-ninth Edition

08/09

W9-AVA-448

EDITOR

Eileen L. Daniel

SUNY at Brockport

Eileen Daniel, a registered dietitian and licensed nutritionist, is a Professor in the Department of Health Science and Associate Dean of Professions at the State University of New York at Brockport. She received a B.S. in Nutrition and Dietetics from the Rochester Institute of Technology in 1977, an M.S. in Community Health Education from SUNY at Brockport in 1987, and a Ph.D. in Health Education from the University of Oregon in 1986. A member of the American Dietetics Association, and other professional and community organizations, Dr. Daniel has published more than 40 journal articles on issues of health, nutrition, and health education. She is the editor of *Taking Sides: Clashing Views on Controversial Issues in Health and Society, 7th edition,* (Dushkin, 2006).

Boston   Burr Ridge, IL   Dubuque, IA   New York   San Francisco   St. Louis
Bangkok   Bogotá   Caracas   Kuala Lumpur   Lisbon   London   Madrid   Mexico City
Milan   Montreal   New Delhi   Santiago   Seoul   Singapore   Sydney   Taipei   Toronto

Higher Education

ANNUAL EDITIONS: HEALTH, TWENTY-NINTH EDITION

This book is printed on recycled, acid-free paper containing 10% postconsumer waste.

1 2 3 4 5 6 7 8 9 0 QPD/QPD 0 9 8 7

ISBN 978–0–07–339759–7
MHID 0–07–339759–8
ISSN 0278–4653

Managing Editor: *Larry Loeppke*
Production Manager*: Beth Kundert*
Developmental Editor*: Jade Bennedict*
Editorial Assistant: *Nancy Meissner*
Production Service Assistant: *Rita Hingtgen*
Permissions Coordinator: *Lenny Behuke*
Senior Marketing Manager: *Julie Keck*
Marketing Communications Specialist: *Mary Klein*
Marketing Coordinator: *Alice Link*
Project Manager: *Jean Smith*
Design Specialist: *Tara McDermott*
Senior Administrative Assistant: *DeAnna Dausener*
Senior Operations Manager: *Pat Koch Krieger*
Cover Graphics: *Maggie Lytle*

Compositor: Laserwords Private Limited
Cover Image: Getty Images and Jupiterimages/Image Source

Library in Congress Cataloging-in-Publication Data
Main entry under title: Annual Editions: Health. 2008/2009.
1. Health—Periodicals. I. Daniel, Eileen L., *comp.* II. Title: Health.
658'.05

www.mhhe.com

Editors/Advisory Board

Members of the Advisory Board are instrumental in the final selection of articles for each edition of ANNUAL EDITIONS. Their review of articles for content, level, currentness, and appropriateness provides critical direction to the editor and staff. We think that you will find their careful consideration well reflected in this volume.

Preface

In publishing ANNUAL EDITIONS we recognize the enormous role played by the magazines, newspapers, and journals of the public press in providing current, first-rate educational information in a broad spectrum of interest areas. Many of these articles are appropriate for students, researchers, and professionals seeking accurate, current material to help bridge the gap between principles and theories and the real world. These articles, however, become more useful for study when those of lasting value are carefully collected, organized, indexed, and reproduced in a low-cost format, which provides easy and permanent access when the material is needed. That is the role played by ANNUAL EDITIONS.

America is in the midst of a revolution that is changing the way millions of Americans view their health. Traditionally, most people delegated responsibility for their health to their physicians and hoped that medical science would be able to cure whatever ailed them. This approach to health care emphasized the role of medical technology and funneled billions of dollars into medical research. The net result of all this spending is the most technically advanced and expensive health care system in the world. In an attempt to rein in health care costs, the health care delivery system has moved from privatized health care coverage to what is termed "managed care." While managed care has turned the tide regarding the rising cost of health care, it has done so by limiting reimbursement for many cutting edge technologies. Unfortunately many people also feel that it has lowered the overall quality of care that is being given. Perhaps the saving grace is that we live at a time in which chronic illnesses rather than acute illnesses are our number one health threat, and many of these illnesses can be prevented or controlled by our lifestyle choices. The net result of these changes has prompted millions of individuals to assume more personal responsibility for safeguarding their own health. Evidence of this change in attitude can be seen in the growing interest in nutrition, physical fitness, dietary supplements, and stress management. If we as a nation are to capitalize on this new health consciousness, we must devote more time and energy to educating Americans in the health sciences so that they will be better able to make informed choices about their health.

Health is a complex and dynamic subject, and it is practically impossible for anyone to stay abreast of all the current research findings. In the past, most of us have relied on books, newspapers, magazines, and television as our primary sources for medical/health information, but today, with the widespread use of personal computers connected to the World Wide Web, it is possible to access vast amounts of health information any time of the day without ever leaving one's home. Unfortunately, quantity and availability does not necessarily translate into quality, and this is particularly true in the area of medical/health information. Just as the Internet is a great source for reliable timely information, it is also a vehicle for the dissemination of misleading and fraudulent information. Currently there are no standards or regulations regarding the posting of health content on the Internet, and this has led to a plethora of misinformation and quackery in the medical/health arena. Given this vast amount of health information, our task as health educators is twofold: (1) To provide our students with the most up-to-date and accurate information available on major health issues of our time and (2) to teach our students the skills that will enable them to sort out fact from fiction in order to become informed consumers. *Annual Editions: Health 07/08* was designed to aid in this task. It offers a sampling of quality articles that represent the latest thinking on a variety of health issues, and it also serves as a tool for developing critical thinking skills.

The articles in this volume were carefully chosen on the basis of their quality and timeliness. Because this book is revised and updated annually, it contains information that is not generally available in any standard textbook. As such, it serves as a valuable resource for both teachers and students. This edition of *Annual Editions: Health* has been updated to reflect the latest thinking on a variety of contemporary health issues. We hope that you find this edition to be a helpful learning tool filled with information and presented in a user-friendly format. The 10 topical areas presented in this edition mirror those that are normally covered in introductory health courses: Promoting Health Behavior Change, Stress and Mental Health, Nutritional Health, Exercise and Weight Control, Drugs and Health, Sexuality and Relationships, Preventing and Fighting Disease, Health Care and the Health Care System, Consumer Health, and Contemporary Health Hazards. Because of the interdependence of the various elements that constitute health, the articles selected were written by authors with diverse educational backgrounds and expertise including: naturalists, environmentalists, psychologists, economists, sociologists, nutritionists, consumer advocates, and traditional health practitioners.

Annual Editions: Health 08/09 was designed to be one of the most useful and up-to-date publications currently available in the area of health. Please let us know what you think of it by filling out and returning the postage paid *article rating form* on the last page of this book. Any anthology can be improved. This one will be—annually.

Eileen L. Daniel

Eileen L. Daniel
Editor

Contents

UNIT 1
Promoting Healthy Behavior Change

Unit Overview   **xviii**

The concepts in bold italics are developed in the article. For further expansion, please refer to the Topic Guide.

UNIT 2
Stress and Mental Health

UNIT 3
Nutritional Health

The concepts in bold italics are developed in the article. For further expansion, please refer to the Topic Guide.

UNIT 4
Exercise and Weight Management

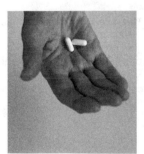

UNIT 5
Drugs and Health

The concepts in bold italics are developed in the article. For further expansion, please refer to the Topic Guide.

UNIT 6
Sexuality and Relationships

The concepts in bold italics are developed in the article. For further expansion, please refer to the Topic Guide.

UNIT 7
Preventing and Fighting Disease

UNIT 8
Health Care and the Health Care System

The concepts in bold italics are developed in the article. For further expansion, please refer to the Topic Guide.

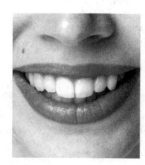

UNIT 9
Consumer Health

The concepts in bold italics are developed in the article. For further expansion, please refer to the Topic Guide.

UNIT 10
Contemporary Health Hazards

The concepts in bold italics are developed in the article. For further expansion, please refer to the Topic Guide.

Correlation Guide

The **Annual Editions** series provides students with convenient, inexpensive access to current, carefully selected articles from the public press. **Annual Editions: Health 08/09** is an easy-to-use reader that presents articles on important topics such as *health behaviors, exercise, sexuality, and many more.* For more information on **Annual Editions** and other **McGraw-Hill Contemporary Learning Series** titles visit **www.mhcls.com.** This convenient guide matches the units in **Annual Editions: Health 08/09** with the corresponding chapters in two of our best-selling **McGraw-Hill Health** textbooks by Paul M. Insel and Walton T. Roth.

Annual Editions: Health 08/09	Core Concepts in Health, Brief Update, 10/e by Insel/Roth	Core Concepts in Health, 10/e by Insel/Roth
Unit 1: Promoting Healthy Behavior Change	Chapter 1: Taking Charge of Your Health	Chapter 1: Taking Charge of Your Health
Unit 2: Stress and Mental Health	Chapter 2: Stress: The Constant Challenge Chapter 3: Psychological Health	Chapter 2: Stress: The Constant Challenge Chapter 3: Psychological Health
Unit 3: Nutritional Health	Chapter 9: Nutrition Basics	Chapter 12: Nutrition Basics
Unit 4: Exercise and Weight Management	Chapter 10: Exercise for Health and Fitness Chapter 11: Weight Management	Chapter 13: Exercise for Health and Fitness Chapter 14: Weight Management
Unit 5: Drugs and Health	Chapter 7: The Use and Abuse of Psychoactive Drugs Chapter 8: Alcohol and Tobacco	Chapter 9: The Use and Abuse of Psychoactive Drugs Chapter 10: The Responsible Use of Alcohol Chapter 11: Toward a Tobacco-free Society
Unit 6: Sexuality and Relationships	Chapter 4: Intimate Relationships and Communication Chapter 5: Sexuality, Pregnancy, and Childbirth Chapter 6: Contraception and Abortion	Chapter 4: Intimate Relationships and Communication Chapter 5: Sex and Your Body Chapter 6: Contraception Chapter 7: Abortion Chapter 8: Pregnancy and Childbirth
Unit 7: Preventing and Fighting Disease	Chapter 12: Cardiovascular Disease and Cancer Chapter 13: Immunity and Infection	Chapter 15: Cardiovascular Health Chapter 16: Cancer Chapter 17: Immunity and Infection Chapter 18: Sexually Transmitted Diseases
Unit 8: Health Care and the Health Care System	Chapter 15: Conventional and Complementary Medicine	Chapter 21: Conventional and Complementary Medicine
Unit 9: Consumer Health	Chapter 8: Alcohol and Tobacco	Chapter 10: The Responsible Use of Alcohol Chapter 11: Toward a Tobacco-free Society
Unit 10: Contemporary Health Hazards	Chapter 16: Personal Safety Chapter 17: Environmental Health	Chapter 22: Personal Safety Chapter 23: Environmental Health

Topic Guide

This topic guide suggests how the selections in this book relate to the subjects covered in your course. You may want to use the topics listed on these pages to search the Web more easily.

On the following pages a number of Web sites have been gathered specifically for this book. They are arranged to reflect the units of this *Annual Edition*. You can link to these sites by going to the student online support site at *http://www.mhcls.com/online/*.

ALL THE ARTICLES THAT RELATE TO EACH TOPIC ARE LISTED BELOW THE BOLD-FACED TERM.

AIDS
30. Sex, Drugs, Prisons, and HIV
33. How AIDS Changed America

Alcoholism
1. The Perils of Higher Education
22. Drinking Too Much, Too Young

Behavior change
1. The Perils of Higher Education
2. Is Health Promotion Relevant Across Cultures and the Socioeconomic Spectrum?
3. Putting a Premium on Health
4. Health: The New Sex Symbol
5. On the Road to Wellness

Birth control
35. Pharmacist Refusals: A Threat to Women's Health

Breastfeeding
14. Suck on This

Cancer
32. Why We Are Still Losing the Winnable Cancer War

Consumer health
12. When It Pays to Buy Organic
13. This Package May Say Healthy, But This Grocer Begs to Differ
14. Suck on This
39. Dentists Frown at Overuse of Whiteners
41. How to Ease Your Pain
42. Deep into Sleep

Controversies
2. Is Health Promotion Relevant Across Cultures and the Socioeconomic Spectrum?
35. Pharmacist Refusals: A Threat to Women's Health
39. Dentists Frown at Overuse of Whiteners

Decision making
3. Putting a Premium on Health
5. On the Road to Wellness

Diabetes
14. Suck on This
29. 'Diabesity,' a Crisis in an Expanding Country

Dieting and weight loss
18. How Sleep Affects Your Weight
19. "Fat Chance"

Drug use and abuse
1. The Perils of Higher Education
20. Rx for Fraud

21. Some Cold Medicines Moved Behind the Counter
22. Drinking Too Much, Too Young
23. The Changing Face of Teenage Drug Abuse—The Trend toward Prescription Drugs
24. The Price of Pain

Environmental health hazards
12. When It Pays to Buy Organic
44. In Katrina's Wake
45. Facing an Uncertain Future

Exercise and fitness
4. Health: The New Sex Symbol
16. Exercise Abuse

Food safety
12. When It Pays to Buy Organic

Gender issues
14. Suck on This
25. You, Me and Porn Make Three
28. Girl or Boy? As Fertility Technology Advances, So Does an Ethical Debate
35. Pharmacist Refusals: A Threat to Women's Health

Global warming
45. Facing an Uncertain Future

Health behavior
1. The Perils of Higher Education
2. Is Health Promotion Relevant Across Cultures and the Socioeconomic Spectrum?
3. Putting a Premium on Health
4. Health: The New Sex Symbol
5. On the Road to Wellness
38. The Silent Epidemic—The Health Effects of Illiteracy

Health care issues
35. Pharmacist Refusals: A Threat to Women's Health
36. A System in Crisis
37. Medicine's Turf Wars
38. The Silent Epidemic—The Health Effects of Illiteracy

Heart disease
6. Love Is Real Medicine

Immunity and infections
33. How AIDS Changed America
34. A Mandate in Texas

Mental health
6. Love Is Real Medicine
7. Stressed Out Nation
8. Seasonal Affective Disorder
9. Dealing with Demons
10. Attacking the Myths

Internet References

The following Internet sites have been carefully researched and selected to support the articles found in this reader. The easiest way to access these selected sites is to go to our student online support site at *http://www.mhcls.com/online/*.

AE: Health 08/09

The following sites were available at the time of publication. Visit our Web site—we update our student online support site regularly to reflect any changes.

General Sources

National Institute on Aging (NIA)
http://www.nia.nih.gov/

The NIA, one of the institutes of the U.S. National Institutes of Health, presents this home page to lead you to a variety of resources on health and lifestyle issues on aging.

U.S. Department of Agriculture (USDA)/Food and Nutrition Information Center (FNIC)
http://www.nal.usda.gov/fnic/

Use this site to find nutrition information provided by various USDA agencies, to find links to food and nutrition resources on the Internet, and to access FNIC publications and databases.

U.S. Department of Health and Human Services
http://www.os.dhhs.gov

This site has extensive links to information on such topics as the health benefits of exercise, weight control, and prudent lifestyle choices.

U.S. National Institutes of Health (NIH)
http://www.nih.gov

Consult this site for links to extensive health information and scientific resources. Comprising 24 separate institutes, centers, and divisions, the NIH is one of eight health agencies of the Public Health Service, which, in turn, is part of the U.S. Department of Health and Human Services.

U.S. National Library of Medicine
http://www.nlm.nih.gov

This huge site permits a search of a number of databases and electronic information sources such as MEDLINE. You can learn about research projects and programs and peruse the national network of medical libraries here.

World Health Organization
http://www.who.int/en

This home page of the World Health Organization will provide links to a wealth of statistical and analytical information about health around the world.

UNIT 1: Promoting Healthy Behavior Change

Ask Dr. Weil
http://www.drweil.com/u/Home/index.html

Dr. Weil, a Harvard-trained physician, is director of the Center for Integrative Medicine at the University of Arizona. He offers a comprehensive Web site that addresses alternative medicine. Look for research, FAQs, and links to related sites.

Columbia University's Go Ask Alice!
http://www.goaskalice.columbia.edu/index.html

This interactive site provides discussion and insight into a number of personal issues of interest to college-age people and those younger and older. Many questions about physical and emotional health and well-being are answered.

The Society of Behavioral Medicine
http://www.sbm.org/

This site provides listings of major, general health institutes and organizations as well as discipline-specific links and resources in medicine, psychology, and public health.

UNIT 2: Stress and Mental Health

The American Institute of Stress
http://www.stress.org

This site provides comprehensive information on stress: its dangers, the beliefs that build helpful techniques for overcoming stress, and so on. This easy-to-navigate site has good links to information on anxiety and related topics.

National Mental Health Association (NMHA)
http://www.nmha.org/index.html

The NMHA is a citizen volunteer advocacy organization that works to improve the mental health of all individuals. The site provides access to guidelines that individuals can use to reduce stress and improve their lives in small yet tangible ways.

Self-Help Magazine
http://www.selfhelpmagazine.com/index.html

Reach lots of links to self-help resources on the Net at this site, including resources on stress, anxiety, fears, and more.

UNIT 3: Nutritional Health

The American Dietetic Association
http://www.eatright.org

This organization, along with its National Center of Nutrition and Dietetics, promotes optimal nutrition, health, and well-being. This easy-to-navigate site presents FAQs about nutrition and dieting, nutrition resources, and career and member information.

Center for Science in the Public Interest (CSPI)
http://www.cspinet.org/

CSPI is a nonprofit education and advocacy organization that focuses on improving the safety and nutritional quality of our food supply and on reducing the health problems caused by alcohol. This agency also evaluates the nutritional composition of fast foods, movie popcorn, and chain restaurants. There are also good links to related sites.

Food and Nutrition Information Center
http://www.nalusda.gov/fnic/index.html

An official Agriculture Network Information Center web site. The FNIC is one of several information centers at the National Agriculture Library, the Agricultural Research Service, and the U.S. Department of Agriculture. The web site has information on nutrition-related publications, an index of food and nutrition-related Internet resources, and an on-line catalog of materials.

UNIT 4: Exercise and Weight Management

American Society of Exercise Physiologists (ASEP)
http://www.asep.org

The ASEP is devoted to promoting people's health and physical fitness. This extensive site provides links to publications related to exercise and career opportunities in exercise physiology.

Eating Disorders Awareness and Prevention, Inc.
http://www.edap.org

This site offers information on eating disorders, including suggestions for families and friends of sufferers, details for professionals, and general information on eating disorders for the interested public.

Cyberdiet
http://www.cyberdiet.com/reg/index.html

This site, maintained by a registred dietician, offers CyberDiet's interactive nutritional profile, food facts, menus and meal plans, and exercise and food-related sites.

Shape Up America!
http://www.shapeup.org

At the Shape Up America! Web site you will find the latest information about safe weight management, healthy eating, and physical fitness.

UNIT 5: Drugs and Health

Food and Drug Administration (FDA)
http://www.fda.gov/

This site includes FDA news, information on drugs, and drug toxicology facts.

National Institute on Drug Abuse (NIDA)
http://www.nida.nih.gov/

Use this site index for access to NIDA publications and communications, information on drugs of abuse, and links to other related Web sites.

Prescription Drugs: The Issue
http://www.opensecrets.org/news/drug/

This site offers information on a variety of prescription drugs, including interactions, side effects, and related material.

UNIT 6: Sexuality and Relationships

Planned Parenthood
http://www.plannedparenthood.org/

This home page provides links to information on contraceptives (including outercourse and abstinence) and to discussions of other topics related to sexual health.

Sexuality Information and Education Council of the United States (SIECUS)
http://www.siecus.org/

SIECUS is a nonprofit private advocacy group that affirms that sexuality is a natural and healthy part of living. This home page offers publications, what's new, descriptions of programs, and a listing of international sexuality education initiatives.

UNIT 7: Preventing and Fighting Disease

American Cancer Society
http://www.cancer.org

Open this site and its various links to learn the concerns and lifestyle advice of the American Cancer Society. It provides information on tobacco and alternative cancer therapies.

American Heart Association
http://www.amhrt.org

This award-winning comprehensive site of the American Heart Association offers information on heart disease, prevention, patient facts, eating plans, what's new, nutrition, smoking cessation, and FAQs.

National Institute of Allergy and Infectious Diseases (NIAID)
http://www3.niaid.nih.gov/

Open this site and its various links to learn the concerns and lifestyle advice of the National Institute of Allergy and Infectious Diseases.

American Diabetes Association Home Page
http://www.diabetes.org

This site offers information on diabetes including treatment, diet, and insulin therapy.

UNIT 8: Health Care and the Health Care System

American Medical Association (AMA)
http://www.ama-assn.org

The AMA offers this site to find up-to-date medical information, peer-review resources, discussions of such topics as HIV/AIDS and women's health, examination of issues related to managed care, and important publications.

MedScape: The Online Resource for Better Patient Care
http://www.medscape.com

For health professionals and interested consumers, this site offers peer-reviewed articles, self-assessment features, medical news, and annotated links to Internet resources. It also contains the Morbidity & Mortality Weekly Report, which is a publicatiobn of the Centers for Disease Control and Prevention.

UNIT 9: Consumer Health

FDA Consumer Magazine
http://www.fda.gov/fdac

This site offers articles and information that appears in the FDA Consumer Magazine.

Global Vaccine Awareness League
http://www.gval.com

This site addresses side effects related to vaccination. Its many links are geared to provide copious information.

UNIT 10: Contemporary Health Hazards

Centers for Disease Control: Flu
http://www.cdc.gov/flu

This CDC site provides updates, information, key facts, questions and answers, and ways to prevent influenza (the flu). Updated regularly during the flu season.

National Sleep Foundation
http://www.sleepfoundation.org

The National Sleep Foundation (NSF) is an independent nonprofit organization dedicated to improving public health and safety by achieving public understanding of sleep and sleep disorders.

Center for the Study of Autism
http://www.autism.org

This site provides resources for both professionals and family members of individuals with autism. The site includes interventions, family support, and stories of persons with the condition.

Food and Drug Administration Mad Cow Disease Page
http://www.fda.gov/oc/opacom/hottopics/bse.html

This Food and Drug Administration page includes information, articles, and updates about Bovine Spongiform Encephalopathy (BSE) also known as "Mad Cow Disease."

Environmental Protection Agency
http://www.epa.gov

Use this site to find environmental health information provided by various EPA agencies.

We highly recommend that you review our Web site for expanded information and our other product lines. We are continually updating and adding links to our Web site in order to offer you the most usable and useful information that will support and expand the value of your Annual Editions. You can reach us at: *http://www.mhcls.com/annualeditions/.*

UNIT 1

Promoting Healthy Behavior Change

Unit Selections

Key Points to Consider

- Why do you think that people continue to engage in negative health behaviors when they know that these behaviors will have a negative impact on their health? Have you ever done so? If so, why?

- What negative behaviors practiced by college students contribute to academic difficulties?

- What is the relationship between health behaviors and sexuality?

- What behaviors do you wish you could undo?

- What factors contribute to successful lifestyle change?

- What personal health behaviors would you like to improve? What prevents you from making these changes? How can you overcome these obstacles?

- Should companies charge employees more for health insurance if they continue to engage in unhealthy behaviors?

- What social and economic issues affect health behaviors?

Student Web Site
www.mhcls.com/online

Internet References
Further information regarding these Web sites may be found in this book's preface or online.

Ask Dr. Weil
  http://www.drweil.com/u/Home/index.html
Columbia University's Go Ask Alice!
  http://www.goaskalice.columbia.edu/index.html
The Society of Behavioral Medicine
  http://www.sbm.org/

"That hose of us who protect our health daily and those of us who put our health in constant jeopardy have exactly the same mortality: 100 percent. The difference, of course, is the timing." This quotation from Elizabeth M. Whelan, ScD, MPH, reminds us that we must all face the fact that we are going to die sometime. The question that is decided by our behavior is when and, to a certain extent, how. This book and especially this unit are designed to assist students in the development of cognitive skills and knowledge that when put to use help make the moment of our death come as late as possible in our lives and to maintain our health as long as possible. While we cannot control many of the things that happen to us, we must all strive to accept personal responsibility for, and make informed decisions about, things that we can control. This is no minor task, but it is one in which the potential reward is life itself.

Perhaps the best way to start this process is by educating ourselves on the relative risks associated with the various behaviors and lifestyle choices we make. To minimize all risk to life and health would be to significantly limit the quality of our lives, and while this might be a choice that some would make, it certainly is not the goal of health education. A more logical approach to risk reduction would be to educate the public on the relative risk associated with various behaviors and lifestyle choices so that they are capable of making informed decisions. While it may seem obvious that certain behaviors, such as smoking, entail a high level of risk, the significance of others such as toxic waste sites and food additives are frequently blown out of proportion to the actual risks involved. The net result of this type of distortion is that many Americans tend to minimize the dangers of known hazards such as tobacco and alcohol and focus attention, instead, on potentially minor health hazards over which they have little or no control.

Educating the public on the relative risk of various health behaviors is only part of the job that health educators must tackle in order to assist individuals in making informed choices regarding their health. They also must teach the skills that will enable people to evaluate the validity and significance of new information as it becomes available. Just how important informed decision making is in our daily lives is evidenced by the numerous health-related media announcements and articles that fill our newspapers, magazines, and television broadcasts. Rather than inform and enlighten the public on significant new medical discoveries, many of these announcements do little more than add to the level of confusion or exaggerate or sensationalize health issues. Why is this so? While there is no simple explanation, there appear to be at least two major factors that contribute to the confusion. The first has to do with the primary goals and objectives of the media itself. One only has to scan the headlines on the cover pages of magazines or newspapers to realize that the primary goal of these publications is to entice the potential reader into purchasing their product. How better to

Thinkstock Images/Jupiter Images

capture the readers' attention than to sensationalize and exaggerate scientific discoveries. This is not to blame the media but rather to remind the reader that given the economic realities of the competitive world in which we live, sometimes the methodical plodding of the scientific method takes second place to the marketing needs of a publisher.

Let's assume for a minute that the scientific community is in general agreement that certain behaviors clearly promote our health while others damage our health. Given this information, are you likely to make adjustments to your lifestyle to comply with the findings? Logic would suggest that of course you would, but experience has taught us that information alone isn't enough to bring about behavioral change in many people. Why is it that so many people continue to make bad choices regarding their health behaviors when they are fully aware of the risks involved? There may be many reasons, but two possible explanations are presented in the article "On the Road to Wellness." According to the author, the underlying motivation behind many of our behavioral decisions is our desire to receive immediate gratification, and in their article they suggests a strategy that can be use to counter the psychological appeal of immediate gratification which can help us live to 100! John Dorschner's article "Putting a Premium on Health," suggests that we can empower ourselves to change our behavior and benefit both physically and financially. We can vow to make changes to try and undo or minimize negative health behaviors of our past. While strategies such as these may work for those who feel they are at risk, how do we help those who do not feel that they are at risk or those who feel that it is too late in their lives for the changes to matter? In "The Perils of Higher Education," the author maintains that while college is a place to learn and grow, for many students it becomes four years of a bad diet, too little sleep, and too much alcohol. These negative health behaviors affect not the students' health, but may impact their grades. In addition to the negative impact on grades, a healthy lifestyle may increase sexiness! In "Health: The New Sex Symbol," Pilar Gerasimo maintains that positive personal health factors such as exercise and good nutrition increase both healthiness and sexuality.

Another viewpoint is demonstrated in Alexandra Garcia's article which addresses whether or not health promotion is relevant across cultures and among different socioeconomic groups. The author maintains that health promoters should consider the social issues relevant to their patient's health and develop programs based on these issues.

While the goal of health education is to promote healthy behaviors that lead to healthy lifestyles, this objective will not be reached unless, or until, the public is armed with the knowledge and skills necessary to make informed decisions regarding their health. Even then, there is no guarantee that the information gleaned will serve as motivation. In a free society such as ours, the choice is, and must remain, up to the individual.

The Perils of Higher Education

Can't remember the difference between declensions and derivatives? Blame college. The undergrad life is a blast, but it may lead you to forget everything you learn.

STEVEN KOTLER

We go to college to learn, to soak up a dazzling array of information intended to prepare us for adult life. But college is not simply a data dump; it is also the end of parental supervision. For many students, that translates into four years of late nights, pizza banquets and boozy week ends that start on Wednesday. And while we know that bad habits are detrimental to cognition in general—think drunk driving—new studies show that the undergrad urges to eat, drink and be merry have devastating effects on learning and memory. It turns out that the exact place we go to get an education may in fact be one of the worst possible environments in which to retain anything we've learned.

Dude, I Haven't Slept in Three Days!

Normal human beings spend one-third of their lives asleep, but today's college students aren't normal. A recent survey of undergraduates and medical students at Stanford University found 80 percent of them qualified as sleep-deprived, and a poll taken by the National Sleep Foundation found that most young adults get only 6.8 hours a night.

All-night cramfests may seem to be the only option when the end of the semester looms, but in fact getting sleep—and a full dose of it—might be a better way to ace exams. Sleep is crucial to declarative memory, the hard, factual kind that helps us remember which year World War I began, or what room the French Lit class is in. It's also essential for procedural memory, the "know-how" memory we use when learning to drive a car or write a five-paragraph essay. "Practice makes perfect," says Harvard Medical School psychologist Matt Walker, "but having a night's rest after practicing might make you even better."

Walker taught 100 people to bang out a series of nonsense sequences on a keyboard—a standard procedural memory task. When asked to replay the sequence 12 hours later, they hadn't improved. But when one group of subjects was allowed to sleep overnight before being retested, their speed and accuracy improved by 20 to 30 percent. "It was bizarre," says Walker. "We were seeing people's skills improve just by sleeping."

For procedural memory, the deep slow-wave stages of sleep were the most important for improvement—particularly during the last two hours of the night. Declarative memory, by contrast, gets processed during the slow-wave stages that come in the first two hours of sleep. "This means that memory requires a full eight hours of sleep," says Walker. He also found that if someone goes without sleep for 24 hours after acquiring a new skill, a week later they will have lost it completely. So college students who pull all-nighters during exam week might do fine on their tests but may not remember any of the material by next semester.

Walker believes that the common practice of back-loading semesters with a blizzard of papers and exams needs a rethink. "Educators are just encouraging sleeplessness," says Walker. "This is just not an effective way to force information into the brain."

Who's Up for Pizza?

Walk into any college cafeteria and you'll find a smorgasbord of French fries, greasy pizza, burgers, potato chips and the like. On top of that, McDonald's, Burger King, Wendy's and other fast-food chains have been gobbling up campus real estate in recent years. With hectic schedules and skinny budgets, students find fast food an easy alternative. A recent Tufts University survey found that 50 percent of students eat too much fat, and 70 to 80 percent eat too much saturated fat.

But students who fuel their studies with fast food have something more serious than the "freshman 15" to worry about: They may literally be eating themselves stupid. Researchers have known since the late 1980s that bad eating habits contribute to the kind of cognitive decline found in diseases like Alzheimer's. Since then, they've been trying to find out exactly how a bad diet might be hard on the brain. Ann-Charlotte Granholm, director of the Center for Aging at the Medical University of South Carolina, has recently focused on trans fat, widely used in fast-food cooking because it extends the shelf life of foods. Trans fat is made by bubbling hydrogen through unsaturated fat, with copper or zinc added to speed the chemical reaction along. These metals are frequently found in the brains of people with Alzheimer's, which sparked Granholm's concern.

To investigate, she fed one group of rats a diet high in trans fat and compared them with another group fed a diet that was just as greasy but low in trans fat. Six weeks later, she tested the animals in a water maze, the rodent equivalent of a final exam in organic chemistry. "The trans-fat group made many more errors," says Granholm, especially when she used more difficult mazes.

When she examined the rats' brains, she found that trans-fat eaters had fewer proteins critical to healthy neurological function. She also saw inflammation in and around the hippocampus, the part of the brain responsible for learning and memory. "It was alarming," says Granholm. "These are the exact types of changes we normally see at the onset of Alzheimer's, but we saw them after six weeks," even though the rats were still young.

Students who fuel their studies with fast food have something serious to worry about: They may literally be eating themselves stupid.

Her work corresponds to a broader inquiry conducted by Veerendra Kumar Madala Halagaapa and Mark Mattson of the National Institute on Aging. The researchers fed four groups of mice different diets—normal, high-fat, high-sugar and high-fat/high-sugar. Each diet had the same caloric value, so that one group of mice wouldn't end up heavier. Four months later, the mice on the high-fat diets performed significantly worse than the other groups on a water maze test.

The researchers then exposed the animals to a neurotoxin that targets the hippocampus, to assess whether a high-fat diet made the mice less able to cope with brain damage. Back in the maze, all the animals performed worse than before, but the mice who had eaten the high-fat diets were most seriously compromised. "Based on our work," says Mattson, "we'd predict that people who eat high-fat diets and high-fat/high-sugar diets are not only damaging their ability to learn and remember new information, but also putting themselves at much greater risk for all sorts of neurodegenerative disorders like Alzheimer's."

Welcome to Margaritaville State University

It's widely recognized that heavy drinking doesn't exactly boost your intellect. But most people figure that their booze-induced foolishness wears off once the hangover is gone. Instead, it turns out that even limited stints of overindulgence may have long-term effects.

Less than 20 years ago, researchers began to realize that the adult brain wasn't just a static lump of cells. They found that stem cells in the brain are constantly churning out new neurons, particularly in the hippocampus. Alcoholism researchers, in turn, began to wonder if chronic alcoholics' memory problems had something to do with nerve cell birth and growth.

In 2000, Kimberly Nixon and Fulton Crews at the University of North Carolina's Bowles Center for Alcohol Studies subjected lab rats to four days of heavy alcohol intoxication. They gave the rats a week to shake off their hangovers, then tested them on and off during the next month in a water maze. "We didn't find anything at first," says Nixon. But on the 19th day, the rats who had been on the binge performed much worse. In 19 days, the cells born during the binge had grown to maturity—and clearly, the neurons born during the boozy period didn't work properly once they reached maturity. "[The timing] was almost too perfect," says Nixon.

While normal rats generated about 2,500 new brain cells in three weeks, the drinking rats produced only 1,400. A month later, the sober rats had lost about half of those new cells through normal die-off. But all of the new cells died in the brains of the binge drinkers. "This was startling," says Nixon. "It was the first time anyone had found that alcohol not only inhibits the birth of new cells but also inhibits the ones that survive." In further study, they found that a week's abstinence produced a twofold burst of neurogenesis, and a month off the sauce brought cognitive function back to normal.

What does this have to do with a weekend keg party? A number of recent studies show that college students consume far more alcohol than anyone previously suspected. Forty-four percent of today's collegiates drink enough to be classified as binge drinkers, according to a nationwide survey of 10,000 students done at Harvard University. The amount of alcohol consumed by Nixon's binging rats far exceeded intake at a typical keg party—but other research shows that the effects of alcohol work on a sliding scale. Students who follow a weekend of heavy drinking with a week of heavy studying might not forget everything they learn. They just may struggle come test time.

Can I Bum a Smoke?

If this ledger of campus menaces worries you, here's something you really won't like: Smoking cigarettes may actually have some cognitive benefits, thanks to the power of nicotine. The chemical improves mental focus, as scientists have known since the 1950s. Nicotine also aids concentration in people who have ADHD and may protect against Alzheimer's disease. Back in 2000, a nicotine-like drug under development by the pharmaceutical company Astra Arcus USA was shown to restore the ability to learn and remember in rats with brain lesions similar to those found in Alzheimer's patients. More recently Granholm, the scientist investigating trans fats and memory, found that nicotine enhances spatial memory in healthy rats. Other researchers have found that nicotine also boosts both emotional memory (the kind that helps us *not* put our hands back in the fire after we've been burned) and auditory memory.

There's a catch: Other studies show that nicotine encourages state-dependent learning. The idea is that if, for example, you study in blue sweats, it helps to take the exam in blue sweats. In other words, what you learn while smoking is best recalled while smoking. Since lighting up in an exam room might cause problems, cigarettes probably aren't the key to getting on the dean's list.

Nonetheless, while the number of cigarette smokers continues to drop nationwide, college students are still lighting up: As many as 30 percent smoke during their years of higher education. The smoking rate for young adults between the ages of 18 and 24 has actually risen in the past decade.

All this news makes you wonder how anyone's ever managed to get an education. Or what would happen to GPAs at a vegetarian university with a 10 P.M. curfew. But you might not need to go to such extremes. While Granholm agrees that the excesses of college can be "a perfect example of what you shouldn't do to yourself if you are trying to learn," she doesn't recommend abstinence. "Moderation," she counsels, "just like in everything else. Moderation is the key to collegiate success."

STEVEN KOTLER, based in Los Angeles, has written for *The New York Times Magazine, National Geographic, Details, Wired* and *Outside.*

Is Health Promotion Relevant Across Cultures and the Socioeconomic Spectrum?

Is health promotion a White middle-class phenomenon that people from other cultures and classes do not regard as important? When implementing health-promotion initiatives, are healthcare providers making assumptions that are not valid for other cultural or socioeconomic groups? How do people of various cultures and classes perceive health and health promotion? To explore these questions, this article reviews some of the relevant literature on culture and class in relation to health promotion, exploring issues foundational to the effectiveness of health-promotion programs and pertinent to delivering health-promotion interventions to ethnic, racial, and cultural minorities and poor populations. Health promoters are encouraged to consider the social determinants of their patients' health and tailor programs on the basis of their patients' motivations and resources.

ALEXANDRA GARCÍA, PhD, RN

The relevance of health promotion to heterogeneous populations is an important issue for healthcare practitioners, researchers, and policy makers who are interested in developing and delivering inclusive, culturally appropriate interventions and evaluating their outcomes. Researchers and providers have implemented health-promoting interventions for diverse groups of people for many years and have reported mixed degrees of success. They have also been aware that unequal distributions of disease and disability disproportionately affect racial and ethnic minorities and impoverished peoples.[1] These disproportionate impacts are called health disparities. To address these disparities, healthcare providers have been directed by the *Healthy People 2010* guidelines to increase the quality and years of healthy life by promoting health and preventing disease, disability, and premature death,[2] thereby attempting to eliminate health disparities.

In the purest sense, health promotion is associated with wanting to improve one's health via "behavior motivated by the desire to increase well-being and actualize human health potential."[3] Such behavior changes might include engaging in more physical activity or getting more sleep. Health promotion, consistent with the *Healthy People 2010* mandate, also includes health protection, or "behavior motivated by a desire to actively avoid illness, detect it early, or maintain functioning within the constraints of illness."[3(p7)] Health protection might include incorporating more hygienic or safer practices into daily routines, participating in disease screenings, or obtaining immunizations and vaccinations.

Sociocultural factors, such as ethnic or racial identity, culturally based practices, and socioeconomic standing, are acknowledged in several health-promotion models[3] but are viewed as relatively fixed and not amenable to healthcare providers' interventions. These factors deserve closer attention because they may be the key to improving health-promotion efforts and resolving health disparities.

We should not build on the assumption that health is a universal value that can be uniformly promoted to all populations because much of what healthcare deliverers assume about health promotion may not hold for many patients. The ineffectiveness of some health-promotion interventions may be the result of unarticulated incongruence of social and cultural assumptions between the health-promotion intervention deliverers and the targeted group. To explore questions related to issues of relevance that seem to be crucial to developing the next stage of health-promotion interventions, this article reviews literature on health promotion with respect to culture and social class.

Culture

Culture is a term that refers to the inherited set of implicit and explicit rules guiding how a group's members view, feel about, and interact with the world. Cultural expressions and, to a lesser extent, cultural values change over time and are influenced by others. Individual and group beliefs about personal control, individualism, collectivism, spirituality, familial roles, and communication patterns contribute to cultural expression.[4] Even so, cultures are heterogeneous so that there are few, if any, constants among all members.[5]

Most people belong to more than one culture based on their ethnicity or where they live and work. Healthcare professionals themselves comprise a particular culture.[6] The notion that healthcare providers and people outside the healthcare culture (including those who are ill or have a disability, live in rural or underserved areas, are of low education levels, or who are impoverished) may have differing beliefs, values, or perspectives on health, illness, and how to manage health has been well documented by medical anthropologists.[7,8] Ethnomedicine and emic approaches have been used to understand how people conceptualize their health, diseases, illnesses, treatments, and symptoms in the context of their culture and experience. For instance, Hunt and Arar[9] reported that though patients and physicians were usually compatible in their beliefs about the cause and course of diabetes, they differed strongly in their goals, strategies, and evaluations of care.

In fact, although researchers have focused on how people of various cultures define illness, they focus less often on how people define their health and maintain it according to their definition. Several studies have quantified behaviors believed by healthcare providers to promote health (eating a diet high in fiber and low in cholesterol, eg) but few have explored which behaviors people of other cultures (ie, minority, disabled, rural, underserved, chronically ill) consider important or the meanings ascribed to those behaviors. Arcury et al[10] explored these questions with rural-dwelling elderly Anglo-Americans, Blacks, and Native Americans and found agreement in several domains and themes of health-promoting behaviors across the groups. For instance, balance and moderation were themes common among members of all 3 ethnic groups.

On the basis of an awareness of the importance of culture, program developers have made considerable efforts to make interventions that are culturally relevant.[11] The following 5 questions arise from a concern for cultural relevance and health promotion.

First, is health promotion not relevant because of differences in cultural norms? For instance, is health promotion too individualistic for a member of a collectivist culture? Strong group or family-oriented values can create a predisposition not to engage in activities when they are for the exclusive benefit of an individual, especially when they interfere with that person's obligations.[12] Health-promotion efforts would be more successful if based on the understanding that for many participants personal fulfillment comes from satisfying group rather than individual needs.

Second, does the Anglo American emphasis on efficiency create a barrier to people who are used to more personal healthcare systems? In Hispanic cultures, *personalismo,* characterized by a trusting close relationship, is an important element for Hispanics'

interactions with their healthcare providers. Does *personalismo* have a counterpart in non-Hispanic cultures? Perhaps so, for even Anglo-Americans reminisce about the "good old days" when physicians made house calls and were intimate members of their patients' societies. Health-promotion programs might incorporate more *personalismo* in order to attract and retain Hispanic clients and others preferring friendly and intimate interactions.[12,13]

Third, if the culture is oriented more in the present than in the future, is a focus on disease prevention relevant? Is promoting health a goal for people who hold a fixed belief on their future health status? Some people seem governed by fatalism, which inhibits the seeking of medical help and possibly deters them from making lifestyle modifications.[12] For them, it can be extremely difficult to change from a sedentary lifestyle or a long accustomed harmful diet. As cited in Hunt and Arar,[9(p356)] one Mexican American said, "Well I have diabetes, what the hell, I'm gonna die anyways."

Fourth, could a group's pervasive low self-esteem and depression be to blame for some participants' reluctance to engage in health-promotion activities? Hunt and Arar[9(p356)] quoted an Anglo-American physician's assistant working in South Texas who said, *"Mi cuerpo es jonque* [my body is junk] is a typical comment [from Mexican American patients]. Their houses and cars are junk, too, so they accept the same for their bodies. . . . They don't see much to live for, so they want to die happy, eating."

Finally, some cultural beliefs may be inconsistent with the requirement to be proactive. Holland and Courtney[14] suggested that Hispanic immigrants tend to expect the healthcare provider to cure their ailments and are not accustomed to an emphasis on health promotion, disease prevention, and self-responsibility. So, are differences in expectations about responsibility for health based on differences in culture? These questions and others like them should be explored for people of various cultural groups.

Social Class

Certainly, not all behaviors and beliefs can be explained by culture; many other factors may determine behaviors and beliefs. For instance, individual factors (such as age, gender, intelligence, education, and experience), socioeconomic factors (such as social class, occupation, and sources of social support systems), and environmental factors (including the natural and built environments and exposures) may influence behavior at various times.

Social classes, or "hierarchically arranged, socially meaningful groupings linked to the structure of society,"[15(p377)] make up complex societies and have their own mores.[4] In the sociological literature, class relates to the economic and political power described by Marx. More commonly, social class is used interchangeably with socioeconomic status (SES),[16] referring to stratifications based on education, income, occupation, and property ownership.[15] As cited in 2 extensive reviews of patterns of SES and health,[15,17] many studies have demonstrated a clear relationship between SES and health during the latter half of the 20th century, reflecting rapid gains in health for those with high SES and worsening conditions for those with lower SES.

In general, health disparities are often attributed to low SES.[1,15] Higher levels of income and education are related to lower mortality rates.[18–22] Lower SES respondents were more likely to smoke cigarettes, not exercise or exercise less, and eat fewer fruits and vegetables. Furthermore, lower SES respondents were less likely to be future oriented, had lower expectations of longevity, and had stronger beliefs than higher SES respondents toward the importance of chance to health status.[23] These behaviors and beliefs begin in childhood. Children who have grown up in socially disadvantaged homes are less likely to have consistent daily mealtimes and bedtimes or eat lunch or dinner with their family.[24] Overall, people with lower SES die earlier than people with higher SES, partly because people with higher SES have healthier lifestyles.[25] Moreover, social inequalities lead to unequal exposures to environmental hazards.[26]

Although health-status differences between income groups are greater than differences between races, minority status is often used as a synonym for low SES in part because health indicators are rarely reported by income levels in the United States.[27] Poverty affects proportionately more women of color than White women and affects more women than men. Women are vulnerable because of their responsibilities as caretakers to children and elders. Minority women are affected more than White women because race is more likely than gender to influence quality of education, leaving a larger percentage of minority women ill prepared to earn a living wage.[28]

Long-term adherence to a healthy diet and exercise regimen is always challenging for patients in terms of motivation and self-control, but it is particularly challenging for the impoverished because of the necessary extra expenditures of money and the time needed. Health-promotion strategies, therefore, may not be effective for people with lower SES because of their bigger challenges to meet their basic needs, that is, to earn a living and provide a home for their family members. It is likely that some of what healthcare providers ask people to do for health promotion is not compatible with the essential demands upon their time and income, much less with their preferences for food or "leisure" activity. Furthermore, patients who are depressed (because of the effects of disease, poverty, or racism) may not feel they can make a significant difference or even begin to learn and practice new behaviors.

Access to, and quality of, medical care, though an important determinant of health status,[1,15] is not always readily available to low-SES persons. People who cannot get an appointment for illness care certainly will not try to make preventive or wellness visits.[29] This is unfortunate because when they do receive medical care that care seems to exert a greater impact on their health than on their more advantaged counterparts.[15] There is a definite need for creative health-promotion strategies to reach low-SES families.

For example, a low-SES Latina with diabetes could not justify time for medical visits, preparing healthy meals, or exercising because she worked 12 hours a day, 7 days a week, to care for her children. Only after her bilateral amputations when she could no longer work did she have the time (but not the income) to focus on her and her family's health.[30] Low-income Latinas declared that lack of time and money was a major barrier to attending preventive mental health programs[31] and health-promotion programs for new mothers and their families (B.S. Sterling et al, unpublished data).

Individuals identified as members of the middle-class described health as having "energy, positive attitudes, and the ability to cope well and be in control of one's life."[32(p171)] Crawford argued that middle-class samples were more likely than working-class samples to relate health to a sense of personal control.[33] Freund et al posited that because working-class people have less control over

their circumstances than do middle-class people, the concept of personal control may be remote or even inconceivable to them.[32] Accordingly, the amount of control people have may be the key determinant of their ability to be interested in wellness, its components, and aspects as well as their ability to follow healthcare recommendations. It stands to reason that those with some time to spare and interest in current affairs are likely to be the first to hear about the latest developments in healthcare. High-SES people also have the resources to put this information to work for them, whether in buying necessary products, changing routines or behaviors, or in accessing professional help.[34]

People with chronic illnesses may be viewed by the medical, government, and middle-class establishments as being in opposition to the model of a good citizen, that is, the citizen "who actively participates in social and economic life, makes rational choices and is independent, self-reliant and responsible."[35(p107)] Those lower SES persons who are also burdened with chronic illness usually lack the resources to be so responsible. They are not likely to engage in an active approach to healthy living, which necessitates engaging in time-consuming or costly health-promoting activities, or even to abstaining from risky health behaviors, which may provide a feeling of pleasure. The ability to benefit from health promotion seems to be related to one's autonomy and self-determination; therefore, people who lack either or both are likely not to respond as well to health-promotion interventions.

Control over one's circumstances allows one to consider following health-promotion advice, like choosing a health-promoting diet and engaging in regular physical activity. This "choice" seems far more real for those who actually have the ability and control necessary to opt for healthier living. Those who do not follow health promoters' advice appear to be choosing a lifestyle that jeopardizes their well-being and are labeled as noncompliant.[36]

No one wants to die of AIDS, lung cancer, cirrhosis of the liver, or injuries sustained in an automobile accident. The public policy debate is not over the desirability of avoiding illness, injury, or premature death, but over the individual and collective sacrifices we are willing to make to maximize our chances of living long and healthy lives. If those sacrifices were simply of a material nature, the personal and social dilemmas that life-style modification issues raise would be less intractable. The choice, however, is rarely limited to spending more or less money; it invariably involves allowing more or less personal freedom.[36(p249)]

Crossley[37] (building on Crawford[33]) explored the notion that health has become a moral phenomenon in that there is an expectation in Western society that people will do what is necessary to live long and well. She described a tension between the values of individual responsibility toward health and individual freedom for decision making. She suggested that the more extreme practices of actively resisting health messages by smoking, drinking more than modest quantities of alcohol, eating excessive amounts of fattening foods, and engaging in other risky health behaviors are a way for people to assert their rights, freedom, and independence from society at large and from what they perceive to be the government's interference in their personal lives.[38,39]

Her focus group participants expressed skepticism toward health-promotion messages and a distrust of the credibility of health-promotion authorities (scientists, government agencies, and healthcare providers) because of the frequent changing messages about particular health behaviors.[37] Rather, the participants embraced the popular philosophy that all things can be healthy in moderation and the notion that too strict a lifestyle is unhealthy, an echo of Williams's[40] explanation that lay beliefs embrace pleasure as part of being healthy. In a similar vein, Blaxter[41(p752)] noted that some working-class people "express[ed] scorn for those who need to engage in health-promoting activity [as] the mark of a self-indulgent life." For people of these opinions, Crossley's[39] solution was to engage them in a dialogue about the benefits of the suggested behaviors instead of giving them authoritative directives.

According to Blaxter,[41] members of the working class and middle class agreed that health depends on personal behaviors and that individuals are responsible for their own health. In fact, it seems that both classes have internalized the dominant Western cultural value of health as an individual's responsibility,[33,35,40] to the extent of blaming individuals for ill health. On the other hand, those in the middle class were more likely than those in the working class to attribute ill health to environmental and social causes.[41]

Most health-promotion messages seem to presume that lifestyles are controllable and disregard the possible effects of luck or chance and environmental circumstances.[42] Considering that most improvements in health and life expectancy have been the result of public health achievements, such as vaccinations, safer workplaces, motor vehicle safety, increased safety and improved nutritional content of food, family planning, safe-sex recommendations, and anti-smoking campaigns,[43] perhaps more health-promotion efforts should be aimed at the community level. By recognizing the multiple social determinants to health and safety, health-promotion strategies can be tailored according to the unique resources, circumstances, and concerns of the community.[44] Community-wide strategies that make health maintenance a normal way of living are of benefit to people of all cultures and classes and can make individual health messages more palatable to those who would benefit from behavioral changes.

Conclusion

Healthcare providers seem to be caught in the tension between the population's health perceptions and needs. In our Western society, health interventions are often targeted to individuals without taking into account important social determinants of their health status. Our current health-promotion model therefore is not necessarily relevant for people whose social determinants are so weighted against their health that they do not exercise control over their own behavior. Identification of these people and their particular frames of reference can more effectively market health-promotion efforts.

There is however a risk of paying too much attention to "culture." We must be careful that identifying members of particular cultures does not label them with a finite set of determinants that leaves out individual beliefs, feelings, and experiences that may turn out to be important for the success of health-promotion interventions. Effective healthcare provision addresses both individually focused strategies and broad policies to improve the economic and social environment and can be tailored to address the problem at hand.

Practitioners realize that placing blame upon patients and labeling them as noncompliant is not helpful. Instead, health promoters must intervene at the individual level on health behavior because they can recognize the barriers to compliance, such as overwhelming poverty, and also try to find reasonable and viable alternatives. Individual providers cannot remedy either SES or the environment and must, therefore, work harder to adapt the plan to the circumstances.

The lifestyle choices people make depend on their individual characteristics, their personal health circumstances, as well as the biases assimilated from their culture. The challenge for health promoters is to deliver healthcare messages in a way that all kinds of people find relevant and to enable all patients to practice the advice they are given. To that end, health-promotion interventions need to be based on knowledge of cultural effects and be personalized and adapted to patients' situations and SES.

References

1. Institute of Medicine. *Unequal Treatment: Confronting Racial and Ethnic Disparities in Healthcare.* Washington, DC: National Academies Press; 2003.
2. US Department of Health and Human Services. *Health People 2010: Understanding and Improving Health.* 2nd ed. Washington, DC: US Government Printing Office; 2000.
3. Pender NJ, Murdaugh CL, Parsons MA. *Health Promotion in Nursing Practice.* Upper Saddle River, NJ: Prentice Hall; 2002.
4. Kreuter MW, Lukwago SN, Bucholtz DC, Clark EM, Sanders-Thompson V. Achieving cultural appropriateness in health promotion programs: targeted and tailored approaches. *Health Education & Behavior.* 2002;30:133–145.
5. Helman CG. *Culture, Health, and Illness.* New York: Arnold Publishers; 2001.
6. Hahn RA. *Sickness and Healing: An Anthropological Perspective.* New Haven, CT: Yale University Press; 1995.
7. Kleinman A. Concepts and a model for the comparison of medical systems as cultural systems. *Social Science & Medicine.* 1978;12:85–93.
8. Kleinman A, Eisenberg L, Good B. Culture, illness, and care: clinical lessons from anthropologic and cross-cultural research. *Annals of Internal Medicine.* 1978;88:251–258.
9. Hunt LM, Arar NH. An analytical framework for contrasting patient and provider views of the process of chronic disease management. *Medical Anthropology Quarterly.* 2001;15:347–367.
10. Arcury TA, Quandt SA, Bell RA. Staying healthy: the salience and meaning of health maintenance behaviors among rural older adults in North Carolina. *Social Science & Medicine.* 2001;53:1541–1556.
11. Brown SA, Garcia AA, Winchell M. Reaching underserved populations and cultural competence in diabetes education. *Current Diabetes Reports.* 2002;2:166–176.
12. National Coalition of Hispanic Health and Human Services Organizations (COSSMHO). Meeting the health promotion needs of Hispanic communities. *American Journal of Health Promotion.* 1995;9:300–311.
13. Warda MR. Mexican Americans' perceptions of culturally competent care. *Western Journal of Nursing Research.* 2000;22:203–224.
14. Holland L, Courtney R. Increasing cultural competence with the Latino community. *Journal of Community Health Nursing.* 1998;15:45–53.

15. Williams DR, Collins C. US socioeconomic and racial differences in health: patterns and explanations. *Annual Review of Sociology.* 1995;21:349–386.

16. Kniepp SM, Drevdahl JJ. Problems with parsimony in research on socioeconomic determinants of health. *Advances in Nursing Science.* 2003;26:162–172.

17. Whitfield KE, Weidner G, Clark R, Anderson NB. Sociodemographic diversity and behavioral medicine. *Journal of Consulting and Clinical Psychology.* 2002;70:463–481.

18. Duleep HO. Measuring socioeconomic mortality differentials over time. *Demography.* 1989;26:345–351. Cited by: Williams DR, Collins C. US socioeconomic and racial differences in health: patterns and explanations. *Annual Review of Sociology.* 1995;21:349–386.

19. Feldman JJ, Makue DM, Kleinman JC, Coroni-Huntley J. National trends in educational differentials in mortality. *American Journal of Epidemiology.* 1989;129:919–933. Cited by: Williams DR, Collins C. US socioeconomic and racial differences in health: patterns and explanations. *Annual Review of Sociology.* 1995;21:349–386.

20. Haan M, Kaplan G, Camacho, T. Poverty and health: prospective evidence from the Alameda County Study. *American Journal of Epidemiology.* 1987;125:989–998. Cited by: Williams DR, Collins C. US socioeconomic and racial differences in health: patterns and explanations. *Annual Review of Sociology.* 1995;21:349–386.

21. Mare RD. Socio-economic careers and differential mortality among older men in the United States. In: Vallin J, D'Souza S, Palloni A, eds. *Measurement and Analysis of Mortality: New Approaches.* Oxford: Clarendon; 1990:362–387. Cited by: Williams DR, Collins C. US socioeconomic and racial differences in health: patterns and explanations. *Annual Review of Sociology.* 1995;21:349–386.

22. Pappas G, Queen S, Hadden W, Fisher, G. The increasing disparity in mortality between socioeconomic groups in the United States, 1960 and 1986. *The New England Journal of Medicine.* 1993;329:103–115. Cited by: Williams DR, Collins C. US socioeconomic and racial differences in health: patterns and explanations. *Annual Review of Sociology.* 1995;21:349–386.

23. Wardle J, Steptoe A. Socioeconomic differences in attitudes and beliefs about healthy lifestyles. *Journal of Epidemiology and Community Health.* 2003;57:440–443.

24. Flores G, Tomany-Korman SC, Olson L. Does disadvantage start at home? Racial and ethnic disparities in health-related early childhood home routines and safety practices. *Archives of Pediatrics & Adolescent Medicine.* 2005;159:158–165.

25. Isaacs SL, Schroeder SA. Class: the ignored determinant of the nation's health. *The New England Journal of Medicine.* 2004;351:1137–1142.

26. Schultz A, Northridge ME. Social determinants of health: implications for environmental health promotion. *Health Education & Behavior.* 2004;31:455–470.

27. Kawachi I, Daniels N, Robinson DE. Health disparities by race and class: why both matter. *Health Affairs.* 2005;24:343–352.

28. Starrels ME, Bould S, Nicholas LJ. The feminization of poverty in the United States: gender, race, ethnicity, and family factors. *The Journal of Family Issues.* 1994;15:590–607.

29. Elliott BA, Beattie K, Kaitfors SE. Health needs of people living below poverty level. *Family Medicine.* 2001;33:361–366.

30. García AA. *Diabetes Symptom Self-Care of Mexican Americans* [dissertation]. Austin: The University of Texas; 2002.

31. Mann A, Garcia AA. Characteristics of community interventions for Latinas with depression. *Hispanic Health Care International.* 2005;3:87–93.

32. Freund PES, McGuire MB, Podhurst LS. *Health, Illness, and the Social Body: A Critical Sociology.* Upper Saddle River, NJ: Prentice Hall; 2003.

33. Crawford R. A cultural account of "health": control, release and the social body. In: McKinlay JB, ed. *Issues in the Political Economy of Health Care.* London: Tavistock; 1984:60–103.

34. Syme SL. Control and health: a personal perspective. *Advances.* 1991;7:16–27. Cited by: Williams DR, Collins C. US socioeconomic and racial differences in health: patterns and explanations. *Annual Review of Sociology.* 1995;21:349–386.

35. Galvin R. Disturbing notions of chronic illness and individual responsibility: towards a genealogy of morals. *Health.* 2002;6:1007–1037.

36. Leichter HM. *Free to be Foolish: Politics and Health Promotion in the United States and Great Britain.* Princeton: Princeton University Press; 1991.

37. Crossley ML. "Would you consider yourself a healthy person?" Using focus groups to explore health as a moral phenomenon. *Journal of Health Psychology.* 2003;8:501–514.

38. Crossley M. Resistance and health promotion. *Health Education Journal.* 2001;60:197–204.

39. Crossley M. Health resistance: the limits of contemporary health promotion. *Health Education Journal.* 2002;61:101–112.

40. Williams S. Health as a moral performance: ritual, transgression, and taboo. *Health.* 1998;2:435–457.

41. Blaxter M. Whose fault is it? People's own conceptions of the reasons for health inequalities. *Social Science & Medicine.* 1997;44:747–756.

42. Davison C, Frankel S, Davey Smith G. The limits of lifestyle: re-assessing "fatalism" in the popular culture of illness prevention. In: Sidell M, Jones L, Katz J, Peberdy A, Douglas J, eds. *Debates and Dilemmas in Promoting Health: A Reader.* Houndmills, Great Britain: Palgrave MacMillan; 2003:84–93.

43. Centers for Disease Control and Prevention. Ten great public health achievements: United States, 1900–1999. *MMWR Morbidity and Mortality Weekly Report.* 1999;48:241–243.

44. Institute of Medicine. *Improving Health in the Community: A Role for Performance Monitoring.* Washington, DC: National Academies Press; 1997.

Putting a Premium on Health

Employers are looking to cut healthcare costs by charging less for those who maintain a healthy lifestyle—and charge more for those who don't

JOHN DORSCHNER

As healthcare costs soar, some experts are now asking tough questions: Should fat people pay more for health insurance? What about smokers? Should healthy people who go regularly to the gym pay less?

"We believe people should be given the tools to improve their health," says Howard Gruverman, a Fort Lauderdale consultant with Chapman Schewe who advises companies on their health plans. "To the extent they follow the tools, they shouldn't pay more. But if they don't take advantage of [the tools], then they *should* pay more."

Some major South Florida employers—Baptist Health, Ryder System, the University of Miami—already require smokers to pay more for health coverage. But that may be just the beginning.

"The relationship between employer and employee is going to change in the next five years," says Bruce Shanefield, a Miami healthcare specialist with Aon Consulting.

Some consumer advocates are wary.

"This is an area worthy of exploration, but it has to be done with great care," says Ron Pollack of Families USA. Charging smokers more "makes eminent sense, but there are other areas that could be questionable."

A few companies nationally, like Weyco in Michigan, have fired smokers and warned they will do random tests for nicotine, but large employers here are taking a more complex approach which, at least to begin with, involves more carrot than stick.

Would smokers pay more?

"The main point is to get people healthy," says Maribeth Rouseff, who handles Baptist Health's wellness program. "We have to get away from the notion of a pill to fix everything."

"Our system is based on illness, not wellness, and frankly we need to change that paradigm," says Andy Scibelli of Florida Power & Light. "There is no other place to go with shifting healthcare costs."

Surveys

What's happening is a multistep process. Many employers start with health-assessment surveys—a basic measure of an employee's health, including weight, blood pressure, and chronic conditions, such as diabetes.

Many consultants would like to see all employees who want health insurance be forced to complete the surveys, but those employers using the survey locally have made them voluntary. "We believe the carrot is stronger than the stick right now," says Pam Rothstein at Ryder.

Employees at the transportation company are invited to fill out a survey on the Internet about health status and "lifestyle choices" that is then analyzed by an independent third party that will not show the data to Ryder, says Pam Rothstein, who handles health benefits. About 20 percent of employees have done the survey in the several months that the program has been available.

As a reward, the employees who complete the survey get their names entered in a drawing, and 10 end up with six months of free health insurance.

Baptist Health offers free health screenings twice a year that include tests to measure for cholesterol, blood sugar, body fat and osteoporosis. About a third of Baptist employees have participated, says Rouseff, and 20 percent go on to complete the health assessment survey. Their reward: A $10,000 death benefit paid to the survivor.

At Florida Power & Light, about 30 percent fill out the survey. They're rewarded by getting their names entered in raffles for items like digital cameras and iPods.

Employers say that answers on the surveys will have no repercussions in the workplace, and they're assuming employee honesty in filling them out. But how many employees want to be honest about their penchant for Big Macs or Pinot Noir?

"A big question is how far you go before it's an invasion of privacy," says Pollack, the consumer advocate. "And how does it get monitored."

Step two: Giving employees advice based on the surveys. Those overweight may get pamphlets on diet and exercise. Diabetics can be instructed on the importance of having blood sugar levels measured regularly. Smokers can be told about a variety of programs to help them stop.

This advice is naturally linked to employers' growing use of wellness programs. Baptist Health and Ryder, for example, have free on-site gyms.

Florida Power & Light offers gyms at small monthly fees, and it gives extra raffle entries for those who make such health-driven steps.

Wellness Coaches

Baptist also has "wellness coaches" who are sometimes stationed outside employee parking garages during shift changes, to chat with employees and pass out brochures on healthy lifestyles. "The coach hopes to look hundreds of employees in the eyes," says Rouseff.

Baptist Health started the emphasis on this wellness program in 2001, after the 10,500-employee organization went mostly to self-insurance. Rouseff says the program has paid off. Instead of annual increases "in the mid-double digits" for healthcare expense, the five-hospital organization now sees changes of 6.5–8 percent annually—a noteable achievement.

FPL reports it has averaged 5 percent annual increases the past two years, but attributes that to a wide range of factors designed to make employees more careful consumers of healthcare. Hewitt Associates says the average increase in Florida runs about 12 percent.

Eventually, consultants believe employers need to use the stick: If your cholesterol is too high, start lowering it with statins or diets. If you're too overweight, sign in at the gym three times a week.

And if you don't take those steps, says Gruverman, then employers should have a right to raise your insurance rates, because the history of healthcare indicates you're likely to be costing your employer more.

Right now, the stick is seen only with smokers, and it's a minimal one. The University of Miami and Ryder charge smokers $10 a month more.

Baptist Health charges $10 per biweekly pay period, though Rouseff says studies show smokers really cost an employer an average of $1,200 to $1,500 a year more in health expenses.

UM was an early starter in the smoking field, beginning its surcharge more than a decade ago. "We had about 1,800 acknowledged smokers in 1992," of its 9,000 employees, says benefits manager Bill Walsh, "and now we're down to 600 or 700."

He says that "every dollar" of the extra money from smokers "is dedicated to assist employees who want to break the habit." That includes paying for stop-smoking classes and nicotine patches.

The issue of overweight persons paying extra is more problematic. Tommy Thompson, secretary of Health and Human Services in the first George W. Bush administration, suggested in 2003 that group health plans should be rewarded if they maintained a healthy weight.

Local employers, however, are concerned that weight issues could be what Walsh calls "a black hole."

He and other benefits managers point to complex issues: Is obesity a disease or a lifestyle choice?

What's the right borderline for obesity? What happens if a person slips from normal to obese during the year, or goes from obese to normal?

Exercise

"I'm all for promoting a healthier lifestyle," says Pollack, the consumer advocate. "Promoting more exercise, free membership in gyms. But when you start penalizing people and possibly invading their privacy, that could be a very questionable practice."

Walsh at UM doubts obesity will ever become an issue in premium payments. "I don't see this coming down the pike."

But many other things may be. Scibelli says FPL is considering contributing dollars to employees tax-free health accounts depending on how many steps employees take toward a health lifestyle.

As Shanefield of Aon Consulting says, "You're just seeing the beginning."

Health: The New Sex Symbol

From the biological basis for attraction to the underpinnings of head-turning good looks—an exploration into the compelling connections between vitality and sex appeal.

PILAR GERASIMO

To say that healthiness and sexiness are connected is, in many ways, to understate the obvious.

It's widely recognized, of course, that many conspicuous elements of physical attractiveness—things like shiny hair, clear eyes, smooth skin, a fit body—have their natural roots in physiological health. And yet, both the true depth and complexity of the connection between good health and perceived sexiness remain largely undersold.

In reality, it would be virtually impossible to *overstate* the profusion of health factors that play a role in what we think of as "sex appeal." Scientific studies have demonstrated that everything from miniscule variations in body symmetry to the concentrations of various hormones in our bloodstream can affect whether or not we are perceived as attractive to others.

In fact, there are whole realms of scientific inquiry around the theory of "sexual selection," which concerns itself primarily with establishing the ways in which the fitness-seeking mating habits of our own and other species have guided social behavior, sexual competition and genetic evolution.

Whether we like it or not, the state of our organ, endocrine and circulatory systems, our nervous and immune systems, our fertility—even the quality of our DNA—are constantly being broadcast to others by a variety of discernable (though sometimes invisible) physical characteristics. And we humans are far more sensitive at reading and responding to these variations, often on subconscious levels, than most of us would ever suspect.

To properly catalog and explain the myriad ways in which healthiness and sexiness intersect would be a giant and overwhelming endeavor. Charles Darwin only got a start on the fundamentals in his massive book, *The Descent of Man, and Selection in Relation to Sex* (originally published in 1871), and since then, the scientific literature has expanded significantly. In just the last 25 years, the fields of evolutionary biology and psychology have themselves evolved dramatically,

and our understanding of the dynamics of our own physiology has become considerably more detailed.

Of course, one doesn't need an encyclopedia of sexiness to observe and understand that good health is powerfully attractive. Still, it's a shame, really, that such a detailed and contemporary compendium isn't more accessible in a user-friendly format, because—let's face it—sex sells. If something promises to make us more appealing to others, in general, we want it.

Health sells, too, of course. But it sells along utilitarian lines—something like the appeal of Fruit of the Loom when compared to the appeal of Victoria's Secret.

Certainly, there's plenty to be said about the rewards of improving one's nutrition and digestion, of increasing one's immunity, or of reducing the risk of, say, heart disease, diabetes or osteoporosis. These are all important, worthy and potentially life-saving enterprises. Described in such "100 percent cotton" terms, however, these good-health endeavors sound far less sexy than they are. And it's arguable that if more people understood how being a bit healthier could render them, among other things, a bit sexier, then more people just might find themselves more deeply invested in achieving better health.

At least, that's the line of reasoning that inspired this article.

On the following pages, you'll find a quick glimpse into just a few of the personal-health factors that can render us sexy or unsexy on various levels. You'll also discover some very interesting facts about our instinctive attraction to health indicators of which we may not even be consciously aware.

At no point will this article argue that the quest for enhanced sexiness is necessarily the *very best* or *most meaningful* health motivation available to us. Certainly, the quest for health has a great many practical inspirations. And to be sure, there are some for whom sex *really* is the last thing on their minds.

But if the scientific observations are even remotely accurate, the dynamics of sexual attraction are a matter of some interest to most of us—whether or not we like to admit it.

And whether we happen to be casting about for a mate, polishing our self-image, searching out a wider range of compelling health motivations or pursuing deeper insight into our own species' most basic instincts, most of us can benefit from understanding the ways that sexiness and healthiness overlap.

So if you're interested—for whatever reason—in knowing more about healthiness, sexiness, or the best of both worlds, by all means, read on.

Sexual Selection 101

Darwin's "survival of the fittest" theory explained a lot about natural selection and evolutionary adaptations. But it didn't explain everything. Take, for example, the male peacock's flashy but hopelessly unwieldy tail. That tail, which makes the peacock an easy target for predators and presents a major metabolic inefficiency, would seem likely to have weeded him out of the evolutionary chain long ago.

Instead, it appears to have contributed to his evolutionary success. Specifically, it contributed to his *breeding* success—because that gorgeous tail apparently makes male peacocks more attractive to their female counterparts (known as peahens), who select their mates, at least in part, on the basis of the size and appearance of their rear-end appendages.

Now, before we criticize the peahen for judging the peacock's book by its iridescent cover, we should take note of an important fact—namely, that the beauty of a peacock's tail just so happens to be reliably correlated with the quality of a peacock's heritable genetic potential. The size, symmetry and splendor of that bird's feathers are not just visually impressive, they're indicators of good genetic stock—a marker of what evolutionary-science scholars refer to as the bird's "general fitness."

So yes, the peahen is making a selection on the basis of what she finds attractive. But what she finds *attractive* bears a strong relationship to what she knows, instinctively, to be *healthy*.

This aspect of sexual selection flies in the face of what we've been taught about tooth-and-nail "survival of the fittest." But it's a perfect illustration of the sexual-selection dynamic that University of New Mexico evolutionary psychologist Geoffrey Miller, PhD, refers to as "reproduction of the sexiest."

In his book, *The Mating Mind: How Sexual Choice Shaped the Evolution of Human Nature* (Anchor, 2001), Miller explains many fascinating intricacies of sexual selection, including this counterintuitive insight: The fact that a peacock's tail represents an *obstacle* to survival is, in fact, an essential component of the bird's perceived attractiveness. Specifically, that a given bird can survive in the wild—even with the "handicap" of his totally impractical tail—is an

indicator of that bird's above-average physical and mental fitness. Without them, presumably, he could not have outrun and outwitted the many potential predators that might otherwise have struck him down before his prime. All of which is to say that there's some very discerning instinctive logic behind the peahen's apparently superficial preference.

So yes, the peahen is making a selection on the basis of what she finds attractive. But what she finds *attractive* bears a strong relationship to what she knows, instinctively, to be *healthy*.

But, of course, we're not primarily concerned with peacocks and peahens here, and neither is Miller. In fact, his book deals mostly with subtler aspects of sexual selection in human beings, such as our preferences based on perceived intellectual, emotional and character traits. But we'll come back to that in a moment.

For now, let's return our attention to the matter of physical health and fitness, and the powerful roles they play in how we humans regard each other—and ourselves.

The Beguiling Body

In her book *Survival of the Prettiest: The Science of Beauty* (Anchor, 1999), psychologist Nancy Etcoff, PhD, explains why the pursuit of beauty is so deeply ingrained in all animal instinct (including human), and how it plays out in—among other things—a strong preference for symmetry in facial and body features. "Symmetry is tied to beauty," she writes, "because it acts as a measure of overall fitness."

In the world of evolutionary psychologists and biologists like Miller and Etcoff, the term "fitness" has a broader meaning than it does in the general culture. In the realm of sexual selection, Miller explains, it refers to "an organism's propensity to survive and reproduce in a particular environment." That propensity may include aspects of physical fitness, health and attractiveness, but also mental and emotional capacities—and the quality of the organism's underlying genetic material.

Symmetry is a reliable indicator of this "general fitness" because, as Etcoff explains, it speaks for an individual's resiliency against all kinds of potentially damaging stressors, "including inbreeding, parasites and exposure to radiation, pollutants, extreme temperatures or marginal habitats [that] can interfere with the precise expression of developmental design during the growth of symmetrical traits such as horns, antlers, petals, tails, wings, ankles, feet, faces or whole bodies."

In other words, whatever kind of animal you are, if you wind up as a symmetrical adult in decent condition, it suggests you've been successful in the face of all kinds of potential adversity. And if you've been successful, then there's a good chance you have some pretty decent genetics going for you. Thus, you make an attractive candidate for a mate.

Even in our modern society, of course, many of the same characteristics that represent good breeding potential still translate to basic sex appeal. This is why, at core, so many of the traits we think of as attractive equate with (or at least suggest) good health. It is also why the *absence* of apparent health can be such a powerful turn-off. "Skin and hair, so sexy and glorious when healthy, are repellent when not," writes Miller in *The Mating Mind*.

Of course, visible characteristics like feature symmetry, smooth skin, good muscle tone, clear eyes and shiny hair are only the beginning. But all speak loudly for the presence of adequate nutrition, good circulation and efficient detoxification—without which, a great variety of unattractive problems can ensue (see "Why Healthy Is Hot"). Consider the visual appeal of conditions such as toenail fungus, open sores, jaundiced skin, patchy hair and bloodshot eyes, and you have a sense of the health-equals-attractiveness dynamic.

But our vision is only one sense among many, and we also use our senses of hearing, taste, touch and smell to discern the markers of health in potential mates. Our brains are capable of processing all these channels of information simultaneously, and as Malcolm Gladwell demonstrates in *Blink: The Power of Thinking Without Thinking* (Little, Brown & Co., 2005), most of us are eminently capable of making decisions on the basis of such combined sensory information—without even batting an eye.

The Nose Knows

Our ability to quickly discern health and fitness indicators (including complex genetic and immune characteristics) on the basis of smell alone is quite astonishing. Take what's become affectionately known as the "Stinky T-shirt Study," conducted in 1996 by Claus Wedekind, a zoologist at the University of Bern in Switzerland.

The study involved 44 men, each of whom wore a single T-shirt for two nights in a row. Wedekind then supplied the T-shirts to a group of women and asked them to select the T-shirts that appealed to them.

The women reliably preferred the scents of men who—as demonstrated by genetic testing—had immune systems dissimilar to their own, and who would thus be likely to produce the broadest combined spectrum of immune function in the case of potential offspring. In other words, the women's noses led them to make what would be a healthy reproductive choice. (This was not true of the women taking hormonal contraceptives; they tended to choose the shirts of men whom they described as smelling like their father or brother.)

If we are naturally capable of discerning complex immune characteristics using only our sense of smell, it's not difficult to imagine how effectively we might sniff out other markers of health, disease and all kinds of other subtle states to boot. Many vegans, for example, swear they can smell meat-eaters from yards away. Some men assert they can identify an ovulating woman from the sweet smell of her breath. Studies in mice confirm an uncanny ability to make mate-selection choices on the basis of the presence of specific peptides in urine. And while human studies exploring our reactions to pheromones remain somewhat inconclusive, our responses to a vast variety of hormonal fluctuations leave little doubt about our ability to perceive equally subtle physiological fluctuations of all kinds.

While healthy and compatible bodily aromas are mightily attractive, of course, unhealthy and incompatible aromas can be downright repulsive. And while millions are spent on perfumes, colognes, deodorants, soaps and other fragranced products designed to enhance or mask our body's own olfactory signatures, none can effectively compensate for the very unsexy odors given off when our bodies are in a state of diminished health.

Bad breath, flatulence and offensive body odor can result from a variety of health conditions, including compromised digestion, inadequate detoxification, disrupted metabolism, endocrine imbalances, parasitic infections and the presence of necrotic (decaying) tissue.

In her book *Digestive Wellness: How to Strengthen the Immune System and Prevent Disease Through Healthy Digestion* (McGraw-Hill, 2005), Elizabeth Lipski, PhD, a clinical nutritionist, catalogs a multitude of such health conditions, laying out their underlying causes and unappealing symptoms, as well as their cures. Many of the symptoms of compromised digestion, she notes, lead to other health conditions—like gas and bloating, halitosis, and psoriasis — that negatively affect individuals' perceived attractiveness and self-esteem.

"Some chronic health problems, like irritable bowel syndrome, prevent many of my patients from dating altogether," says Lipski. "Others suffer social anxiety as the result of bad breath, excessive flatulence or eczema."

Lipski describes the case of a man suffering from a parasitic bowel infection that resulted in a chronic case of flatulence so bad it caused both coworkers and potential dates to keep their distance. She describes others for whom nutrient deficiencies contributed to everything from cheilosis (cracking at the corners of the mouth and lips) to premature aging of the skin.

The reversal of these problems can often be quickly and reliably accomplished only by resolving their underlying health issues (the man with the parasitic infection, for example, required only 10 days of treatment). "When our bodies present symptoms," notes Lipski, "they are trying to get our attention. So rather than covering up a symptom with mouthwash or moisturizer, it makes sense to look for and treat the underlying issues."

Going to the Source

"We're programmed to look for cosmetic camouflage for things like dull skin, brittle hair and thin, splitting nails," says certified nutritionist Ann Louise Gittleman, PhD, CNS, author of *The Living Beauty Detox Program: The Revolutionary Diet for Each and Every Season of a Woman's Life* (HarperCollins, 2001) and dozens of other health books. "But in reality, virtually all the things we think of as beautiful are essentially representative of an inner state of health and balance."

In Gittleman's view, becoming authentically healthy calls for a program of proper nutrition and exercise, detoxification, and hormone balancing, as well as careful management of stress, emotional wellness and other mind-body-spirit concerns. "You can't separate how you look from who you are," she says.

Indeed, what most of us think of as "a healthy glow" is rooted in a quality of radiance produced by, among other things, good capillary action and oxygenation of the blood, a translucent dewiness of the skin, a clarity and shininess of the eyes—all of which indicate the health of our organ, endocrine and circulatory systems. But that glow is also often rooted in personal demeanor of openness, optimism and approachability.

"That kind of radiance is partially the result of balanced hormones, adequate nutrients and a clean, resilient system," says Gittleman, "but it's also a certain quality of spirit and energy shining through."

This brings us to another interesting aspect of the healthy-equals-sexy equation: the way that markers of good health not only create an appealing physical container, but also represent the possession of other appealing internal qualities and characteristics.

Think back to the peacocks. Their robust tails are attractive not just for their visual beauty, but because they "advertise" other desirable traits—such as disease resistance and cleverness—that presumably contributed to their success in the face of environmental challenges.

It's not so different with us, except that our contemporary environmental challenges have less to do with natural dangers and more to do with lifestyle trends like unhealthy eating and lack of physical activity.

"In our culture, there's a major food surplus, and it's easy to get more than enough to eat," explains Miller. "Given the kinds of temptations and tendencies we all face on a daily basis, if a person makes it to 30 or 40 years old and *hasn't* developed some kind of obvious weight problem, we are inclined to conclude that he or she possesses certain personal characteristics, including self-restraint, willpower, discernment and self-esteem, for example."

We may also be inclined to make some assumptions about a person's mental health, Miller notes. "Being fit sends the message, 'I'm not depressed,'" he explains. "People with major psychosis tend not to be in good shape because they are preoccupied. They tend to gain excess weight, lose unhealthy amounts of weight or smoke."

Why Healthy Is Hot

Health factors	Good function supports . . .	When compromised, results in . . .
Nutritional intake	Smooth skin, shiny hair, clear eyes, general vitality, proper body composition, weight management, good energy and metabolism	Tissue and organ breakdown, dull hair, brittle nails, skin conditions, premature aging, undesirable weight gain or loss, susceptibility to disease
Digestion	Proper nutrient assimilation (see above), regular elimination, good detoxification (see below)	Gas and bloating; bad breath; body odor; rashes; nutritional deficiencies (see above); fatigue; reduced resistance to parasitic, fungal and bacterial infections
Detoxification	Clear complexion, radiant and smooth skin, shiny eyes, appealing aroma, proper body composition	Acne, rashes, dark circles, yellowed or bloodshot eye whites, dull skin, pallor, puffiness, blotchiness, bloating, fat accumulation and hormone disruption, indigestion, eczema, psoriasis, flora imbalances resulting in yeast infections
Endocrine function	Clear, smooth skin; good energy and metabolism; proper hormone balance and libido; appealing aroma; good mood	Weight gain, acne, body odor, hair loss, lethargy, reduction of libido and sexual function, depression
Circulatory function	Rosy, healthy skin; robust energy; healthy tissue; good support of muscle tone, nerve health and proper sexual function	Pallor, ruddiness, necrotic lesions, loss of sensation, low energy, muscle atrophy, nerve damage, sexual dysfunction

It is, perhaps, mostly in this respect that we can speak of health as a "new" sex symbol. Evidently, health has been sexy for a long, long time. But in the current cultural environment of rampant obesity and other "lifestyle-related" diseases, the achievement of good health and fitness has become an increasingly rare, desirable and differentiating trait.

Faking Fitness

Given how much we read into perceived well-being, it should come as no surprise that we invest deeply in goods and services that help us exaggerate our current state of health and fitness, or at least enhance our appearance of vitality. Of course, in many cases, these interventions (think cosmetics, tanning booths, hair plugs, plastic surgery and steroids) don't actually improve our condition in any meaningful way—and, in some cases, they can even put our true health and vitality at risk. But they advertise characteristics we *associate* with health and, thus, with desirability.

Miller is currently working on a new book, in fact, that explores how we use consumer goods and services to look younger, fitter and more attractive—in effect, as he says, "to give the impression that we are doing better than we are."

Such fitness-faking can only take us so far, though. Because when our underlying health suffers—as it does in the case of anorexia, poor cardiovascular health, diabetes or cancer—so does the vitality that makes sexual attraction interesting in the first place.

For better or for worse, our sexual function and desire are also dependent on our general health. Hormonal and neurological imbalances, chronic diseases, depression, fatigue, and health problems of all kinds can radically reduce both our desire for sex and our ability to enjoyably engage in it.

In her book, *I'm Not in the Mood: What Every Woman Should Know About Improving Her Libido* (HarperCollins, 1999), Judith Reichman, MD, describes the "Seven Sexual Saboteurs" that interfere with a satisfying sex life. The majority of them (four of the seven to be precise) are health-related—and that's if you don't count "psychological issues" as a health concern.

Late-night TV is awash in commercials for prescription drugs designed to reverse or mask the symptoms of various sexual "dysfunctions"—many of which prove to be circulatory or hormonal in nature. But even if this or that drug succeeds in resolving your or your partner's primary symptoms, there's another little problem to worry about: Before taking a certain erectile-dysfunction drug, the spokesperson cautions, you should check with your doctor to make sure "you're healthy enough to have sex."

It turns out that many of the chronic conditions and diseases that contribute to sexual dysfunction—things like diabetes and heart disease—can also contribute to your early demise should you suddenly over-exert yourself.

Making It Real

But let's leave questions of "faked fitness" aside now and return to the matter of real health and fitness. While we've only scratched the surface of the variables underlying our genetically preprogrammed tendencies toward sexual selection, it should by now be clear that what's perceived as sexy (and what's not) can very often be closely linked with what's healthy (and what's not).

It should also be clear that we're not talking exclusively about the health and soundness of the body, but rather, of the appeal of a person as a whole. Yes, unhealthy habits lead to distinctly unsexy signals (from tooth decay and yellowed eyes to flatulence and snoring), while healthy habits tend to engender sexiness (a vital, energetic body; attractive skin and hair; an appealing aroma). The deeper message, though, is that there's something inherently sexy about a person who *keeps* himself or herself healthy—not the least of which are the healthy values, disciplines and discernments their apparent health broadcasts on their behalf.

Naturally, physical health and fitness is by no means the best or only indicator of a potential mate's inherent qualities, and they are by no means the only things that attract us. One of Miller's chief areas of interest in *The Mating Mind*, in fact, concerns the mental and moral traits we seek out in potential mates—things like intelligence, humor, creativity and generosity.

"When people are initially attracted," asserts Miller, "it is often on the basis of predictable physical characteristics: ratios and symmetries of body parts and facial features; the healthy appearance of muscle, skin, hair; and so on. But when they fall in love, it tends to be with mental and moral traits."

And when they break up, he adds, "it's generally not because someone suddenly got physically ugly, but because someone is revealing that they have a bad personality, a personal vice, addiction, lack of honesty, or is less interesting than they originally seemed to be."

Well-adjusted individuals are inclined to seek out potential mates whom they intuit will be advantageous and enjoyable partners—generally as the result of possessing desirable mental, emotional, moral *and* physical traits. We are on the lookout, in other words, for potential mates who will enhance our *own* "general fitness"—our own "propensity to survive and reproduce in a particular environment."

When we encounter individuals willing and able to go through the steps it takes to keep themselves healthy (good nutrition, regular exercise, a decent sleep schedule, manageable priorities), it's understandable that we endow them with all kinds of presumed strengths. And whether we are right or wrong about our first impressions, those impressions act powerfully on our choices.

The Deeper Appeal

Ultimately, even though our quest for sexiness may be biologically preprogrammed, on a deeper level, it's really about developing and seeking out what's best in us as human beings—in our bodies, but also in our minds, emotions, spirits and traits of character.

When we encounter individuals willing and able to go through the steps it takes to keep themselves healthy (good nutrition, regular exercise, a decent sleep schedule, manageable priorities), it's understandable that we endow them with all kinds of presumed strengths.

We all face aging and health challenges that diminish our physical vitality over time. Some of us also face catastrophic injuries, diseases and health crises that make concerns with appearance and attraction seem out of reach or almost entirely inconsequential. But each of us can cultivate the qualities—from discernment and self-restraint to resiliency and self-esteem—that help engender good health and fitness. We can treat with care, respect and appreciation the miraculous bodies with which we all are blessed from birth. And very often, when we do this, our most unique and irresistible brand of beauty shines through.

In *The Living Beauty Detox Program,* Gittleman emphasizes this notion with a quote from the French artist Auguste Rodin, who observed: "Beauty is but the spirit breaking through the flesh."

The vagaries of sexual selection may never be entirely revealed to us, and many of us will never possess—or be able to "fake"—certain desirable physical attributes that might render us sexier to others. All of us, however, can become responsible and motivated stewards of the bodies, hearts, minds and spirits with which we are endowed. And in this way, we can cultivate the kind of uncategorizable appeal that will perhaps always reside beyond the decisive grasp of science, but that most of us would love to have forever within our own arms' reach.

PILAR GERASIMO is the editor in chief of *Experience Life.*

On the Road to Wellness

Lawmakers want Americans to eat better, stop smoking, exercise and relax.

AMY WINTERFELD

Dave Barry was kidding, but he was way ahead of the curve in 1985, when he advised everyone to "stay fit and healthy until you're dead." U.S. Secretary of Health and Human Services Mike Leavitt, however, was dead serious when he said, in October 2006, that he wants to make Americans healthier.

"Emphasis on the four pillars of the HealthierUS initiative—physical activity, good diet, healthy choices and preventive screening—is crucial for the nation's health," says Leavitt. "Changing the culture from one of treating sickness to staying healthy calls for small steps and good choices to be made each and every day. [The department's] physical activity guidelines will encourage the creation of a culture of wellness across America."

The California governor's plan for health care reform, announced last month, also gives a nod to wellness, leading off with a proposed Healthy Action Rewards/Incentives program for both publicly and privately insured Californians. It would provide incentives such as gym memberships, weight management programs and reductions in health insurance premiums to promote prevention, wellness and healthy lifestyles.

It's no wonder that Leavitt and other policymakers want to encourage Americans to adopt healthy habits and stay well. Treatment for chronic diseases accounts for 75 percent of what the country spends on health care each year. Rates continue to rise for one of the leading precursors to chronic disease, obesity. An estimated 66 million Americans are overweight or obese. More than 60 percent of American adults do not get enough physical activity, and 25 percent are not active at all.

Another 44.5 million U.S. adults continue to smoke cigarettes, even though this will result in death or disability for half of them.

Treatment for the consequences of these unhealthy behaviors is improving. But it costs—a lot. Preventing diseases and promoting good health for everyone can help control these costs. Making healthy food choices more available, designing environments to encourage physical activity, offering incentives for healthy behaviors and encouraging preventive screenings are strategies that work at lowering costs.

"We have a finite amount of resources to spend on health care," says Hawaii Representative Josh Green, an ER doctor who chairs the House Health Committee. "The only way to afford the things we must have is to focus on preventive health measures and screening. We'll always need trauma centers like the one where I work, but that means we need to be smart about other health costs."

Starting Young

During the past 30 years, obesity rates have more than quadrupled for children ages 6 to 11 and more than tripled for young people 12 to 19. Many lawmakers are enacting wellness policies for schools, where 98 percent of 5- to 17-year-olds can be found on any given school day in the United States.

Beginning this fall, federal law requires school districts participating in federally funded school meals programs—nearly every school district in the country—to establish a local wellness policy that includes goals for physical activity. School meals must meet nutrition standards set by the U.S. Department of Agriculture. And there must be a plan for measuring success.

Colorado, Florida, Illinois, Indiana, Kentucky, Mississippi, Ohio, Pennsylvania, Rhode Island, Tennessee and Washington have all enacted legislation in the past few years to support school and state wellness policies.

Legislators have worked to improve the nutritional quality of school foods, provide more opportunities for physical activity, and ensure that nutrition is part of the school curriculum. At the local level, 92 of the nation's 100 largest school districts—which educate 23 percent of American students—have developed a wellness policy.

Lawmakers are also looking at ways to encourage kids to get more exercise on the way to school. The federal Safe Routes to School program includes $612 million for grants over five years for communities to build bike lanes, sidewalks and trails that will make it safer and easier for children to bike and walk to school.

Getting Workers Healthy

Investing in employee health also pays off. Healthy workers are more productive. An analysis of 32 studies of workplace wellness initiatives found 28 with an average return on investment

Paying for Prevention for the Publicly Insured

States have recently begun to structure public insurance programs to cover more preventive care to help ward off chronic conditions, which account for 96 percent of Medicare spending and about 83 percent of Medicaid spending. Examples include the following:

- **Coverage for obesity prevention services.** In Connecticut, the state's Medicaid managed care plans pay for obesity related services if they are medically necessary. Nutritional counseling, exercise programs and behavioral health services are covered under Medicaid and SCHIP if they meet the necessity criteria. The state also covers gastric bypass surgery through Medicaid, if medically necessary.
- **Coverage for smoking cessation treatments.** In 2005, 38 states covered some tobacco-dependence counseling or medication for all Medicaid recipients. Four more states offered coverage only for pregnant women. Oregon is the single state offering all smoking cessation medication and counseling treatments recommended by the U.S. Public Health Service.
- **Wellness incentives.** West Virginia has some of the nation's highest rates of obesity, diabetes, heart disease and smoking. In three pilot counties, Medicaid patients will be asked to sign contracts agreeing to do their best to stay healthy by attending health improvement programs as directed, having routine checkups and health screenings, taking prescribed medicine, keeping appointments and limiting emergency room use. As an

incentive, they will receive antismoking and weight loss classes, home health visits as needed, mental health counseling, diabetes management assistance, cardiac rehabilitation and additional prescription medications. Over future years, Medicaid beneficiaries who stick to the plan will qualify for extra benefits, possibly orthodontic or other dental care. Medicaid recipients who do not sign or adhere to the contract will be limited to the standard benefits determined by the state. Critics say the plan may limit access to the enhanced benefits by those most likely to need them, for example, people with existing mental health or substance abuse problems that create difficulties in keeping scheduled appointments. It may also put doctors in an awkward position as administrative enforcers of factors that may be beyond patient control and may interfere with effective doctor-patient relationships.

- **Preventive services for those on Medicare.** In January, Medicare increased payments to doctors for face-to-face doctor-patient consultations about a patient's health and what needs to be done to maintain or improve health. The hope is to encourage more discussions about preventive services like controlling diabetes and get doctors to refer more patients to diabetes self-management training and medical nutrition therapy. Medicare will also now cover these services at federally qualified health centers, increasing access in rural and underserved areas.

of $3.48 per $1 in program costs, as reported in 2001 in the *American Journal of Public Health*. Citibank saved $8.9 million over two years after investing $1.9 million for wellness initiatives, translating into a return of $4.70 for each dollar spent on the wellness program. Motorola saw a return of $3.93 for every dollar spent on its wellness program, and saved nearly $10.5 million annually in disability expenses for program participants compared to non-participants.

State governments and other public employers are initiating workplace wellness programs as well. The U.S. Department of Health and Human Services awarded Hawaii an innovation in prevention award last November for promoting physical activity and nutrition at work. The state health department has outlined these ideas in an online Worksite Wellness Toolkit, so that other employers can start similar programs.

Delaware, Kentucky, Oklahoma, Rhode Island and South Dakota have launched health promotion initiatives for state employees. And Arkansas, North Dakota, Ohio and Vermont have statewide wellness programs for the whole population. In 2005, Nevada's legislature established a State Program for Fitness and Wellness and a state advisory council to raise awareness and create programs for physical fitness, nutrition and the prevention of obesity and chronic diseases. In Arizona, an executive order created a State Employee Wellness Advisory Council in 2005 that organizes wellness fairs and health screenings

for state employees, including blood pressure screenings, cholesterol checks, smoking cessation, weight management and diabetes screenings.

States have also had success by starting on a small scale, building on pilot programs. North Carolina's HealthSmart program started with nine local programs that identified employees with specific health conditions and provided them with intensive health advice on lifestyle changes. It was expanded to all state employees in 2005. Delaware launched the Health Rewards pilot study program for state employees in 2003, offering comprehensive health assessments, guidance, and fitness advice to state employees through their group health insurance programs.

State efforts to improve workplace wellness have also included smoking bans that cover all workplaces, including bars and restaurants. Hawaii's ban, effective in November 2006, is "essentially the end of the issue of secondhand smoke in public places," says Representative Green.

Building Healthy Communities

The way we design our communities can influence our health. Decisions about zoning, community design and land use affect the daily choices people make, whether it is to drive or walk to the store, exercise, or the buy healthy foods. Creating incentives can encourage cities and developers to take health and livability into account when retrofitting old developments or building new ones. The design of neighborhoods, transportation systems and biking or walking paths can encourage physical activity.

Healthy foods, such as fresh fruits and vegetables, which are accessible and affordable, are part of the equation. Encouraging schools and government agencies to buy local produce, providing fiscal incentives for locating grocery stores in all communities—especially underserved urban or rural communities—and setting school nutrition standards and school wellness policies can have a big impact on people's health.

Incentives for Wellness

Indiana Senator Beverly Gard wants to give employers incentives to create wellness programs. She sponsored legislation last year that will allow Indiana employers to offer financial incentives to reduce employee tobacco use.

"This seemed like something we could do that would give employers an opportunity to provide employees with incentives for healthy behavior," Gard says. Rather than penalize smokers, Indiana amended its smokers' bill of rights to allow employers to implement financial incentives related to employer-provided health benefits that are intended to reduce employee tobacco use. "We wanted to take a more positive approach," Gard says.

States have looked at a number of different ways to provide incentives for wellness and healthy behavior for individuals and for businesses, large and small. Some of the most popular are:

- **Insurance incentives such as premium discounts or rebates.** Michigan enacted legislation in 2006 that requires insurers, HMOs and nonprofits that offer group health insurance coverage to give premium rebates when a majority of employees or health plan members enroll and maintain participation in group wellness programs. The rebate applies for individuals and families with their own policies who participate in approved wellness programs too.
- **Insurance rating incentives.** New Hampshire lawmakers in 2004 permitted small group and individual insurers to use a rating factor to discount premium rates for plans, giving monetary incentives for participants in wellness or disease management programs.
- **Tax credits.** Over the past few years, wellness tax credits have been proposed in at least seven states including Hawaii, Iowa, Mississippi, New Jersey, New York, Rhode Island and Wisconsin. The idea is to provide employers—especially smaller businesses—with income, franchise or corporate tax credits for wellness programs

such as nutrition, weight management, smoking cessation or substance abuse counseling, or purchasing or maintaining fitness equipment.
- **Insurance benefits for screenings and early treatment.** According to Blue Cross-Blue Shield's "Survey of Health Plans" for 2005, specific preventive or screening benefits currently required by states include alcoholism treatment (44 states), blood lead screening (7 states), bone density screening (15 states), cervical cancer screening (29 states), colorectal cancer screening (24 states), diabetic supplies or education (47 states), mammography screening (50 states), morbid obesity care (4 states), prostate cancer screening (28 states) and well child care (32 states).
- **Task forces, advisory committees or studies.** States have considered creating task forces or advisory committees, or conducting studies exploring the benefits and feasibility of wellness programs or health promotion activities.
- **Raising awareness.** Legislators are sponsoring or participating in wellness events. For example, the Legislature declared May 2006 as Fitness Month in California and encouraged all Californians to enrich their lives through proper diet and exercise. Kentucky established the Governor's Council on Wellness and Physical Activity specifically to raise public awareness and promote citizen engagement.

Something Must Be Done

What if Americans don't get healthier? The costs could be shocking. Future cost of health care and other benefits could reach between $600 billion and $1.3 trillion for the nation's estimated 24.5 million active and retired state and local public employees.

Moving U.S. health policy toward a more preventive approach is key to containing health care costs. "The burden of chronic disease is increasingly making the U.S. health system unaffordable and causing much unnecessary pain and suffering," says former U.S. Surgeon General David Satcher. The solution? According to health experts at the Robert Wood Johnson Foundation it is "Leadership that informs and motivates, economic incentives that encourage change, and science that moves the frontiers."

NCSL's health care expert **AMY WINTERFELD** tracks wellness and obesity.

UNIT 2
Stress and Mental Health

Unit Selections

Key Points to Consider

- How have humankind's stressors changed over the last 5,000 years?

- What are the major stressors in your life? How do you manage your stress?

- What role do religion, love, and spirituality play in the progress of disease?

- Give examples that demonstrate the interaction between mental health and physical health.

- Explain how worry can be both a positive and a negative force in shaping one's life.

- Why were many predictions made about post traumatic stress disorders following the September 11 attacks?

Student Web Site
www.mhcls.com/online

Internet References
Further information regarding these Web sites may be found in this book's preface or online.

The American Institute of Stress
   http://www.stress.org
National Mental Health Association (NMHA)
   http://www.nmha.org/index.html
Self-Help Magazine
   http://www.selfhelpmagazine.com/index.html

The brain is the one organ that still mystifies and baffles the scientific community. While more has been learned about this organ in the last decade than in all the rest of recorded history, our understanding of the brain is still in its infancy. What has been learned, however, has spawned exciting new research and has contributed to the establishment of new disciplines such as psychophysiology and psychoneuroimmunology (PNI).

Traditionally, the medical community has viewed health problems as either physical or mental, treating each type separately. This dichotomy between the psyche (mind) and soma (body) is fading in light of scientific data that reveal profound physiological changes associated with mood shifts. Just what are the physiological changes associated with stress? Hans Selye, the father of stress research, described stress as a nonspecific physiological response to anything that challenges the body. He demonstrated that this response could be elicited by both mental and physical stimuli. Stress researchers have come to regard this response pattern as the "flight or fight" response, perhaps an adaptive throwback to our primitive ancestors. Researchers now believe that repeated and prolonged activation of this response can trigger destructive changes in our bodies and contribute to the development of several chronic diseases. So profound is the impact of emotional stress on the body that current estimates suggest that approximately 90 percent of all doctor visits are for stress-related disorders. If emotional stress elicits a generalized physiological response, why are there so many different diseases associated with it? Many experts believe that the answer may best be explained by what has been termed "the weak-organ theory." According to this theory, every individual has one organ system that is most susceptible to the damaging effects of prolonged stress.

Mental illness, which is generally regarded as a major dysfunction of normal thought processes, has no single identifiable etiology. One may speculate that this is due to the complex nature of the organ system involved. There is also mounting evidence to suggest an organic component to traditional forms of mental illness such as schizophrenia, chronic depression, and manic depression. The fact that certain mental illnesses tend to occur within families has divided the mental health community into two camps: those who believe there is a genetic factor operating and those who see the family tendency as more of a learned behavior. In either case, the evidence supports mental illness as another example of the weak-organ theory.

The reason one person is more susceptible to the damaging effects of stress than another may not be altogether clear, but evidence is mounting that one's perception or attitude plays a key role in the stress equation. A prime example demonstrating this relationship comes from research linking cardiovascular disease to stress. "Happier and Healthier" also discusses a mind/body connection and suggests that having a healthy perspec-

Ryan McVay/Getty Images

tive on life can positively impact one's health. The realization that our attitude has such a significant impact on our health has led to a burgeoning new movement in psychology termed "positive psychology." Dr. Martin Segilman, professor of psychology at the University of Pennsylvania and father of the positive psychology movement, believes that optimism is a key factor in maintaining not only our mental health but our physical health as well. Dr. Segilman notes that while some people are naturally more optimistic than others, optimism can be learned.

One area in particular that appears to be influenced by the "positive psychology movement" is the area of stress management. Traditionally stress management programs have focused on the elimination of stress, but that is starting to change as new strategies approach stress as an essential component of life and a potential source of health. It is worth noting that this concept, of stress serving as a positive force in a person's life, was presented by Dr. Hans Selye in 1974 in his book *Stress Without Distress.* Dr. Selye felt that there were three types of stress: negative stress (distress), normal stress, and positive stress (eustress). He maintained that positive stress not only increases a person's self-esteem but serves to inoculate the person against the damaging effects of distress. Only time will tell if this change of focus in the area of stress management makes any real difference in patient outcome. In "Stressed Out

Nation," author Zak Stambor indicates that while most people experience stress, it's necessary to know how to manage stress. He claims that negative responses to stress such overeating, smoking or alcohol abuse can lead to health problems that will actually increase stress.

The causes of stress are many, but for some individuals, the coming of winter is a very difficult time for them. Many of these folks experience periods of depression during the shorter days of winter. Other causes of stress include more global issues including armed conflicts and the fallout from September 11. In "Attacking the Myths", Roxane Cohen Silver discusses stress following the terrorist attacks in 2001. Fortunately, while we view the world differently since that day, most Americans have bounced back.

Researchers have made significant strides in their understanding of the mechanisms linking emotional stress to physical ailments, but they are less clear on the mechanisms by which positive emotions bolster one's health. One area in particular that is both difficult to study and appears to be getting increased scientific scrutiny is the area of humor and stress. While medical experts have known for years that hostility induces physiological changes that promote cardiovascular disease and appear to weaken the immune system, they are only beginning to explore the potential healing of mindfulness and spirituality. Dr. Dean Ornish in "Love is Real Medicine" claims that love and relationships can be an important component in wellness.

Although significant gains have been made in our understanding of the relationship between body and mind, much remains to be learned. What is known points to perception and one's attitude as the key elements in shaping our responses to stressors.

Love Is Real Medicine

Loneliness fosters cardiovascular disease. Fortunately, there's an antidote.

DEAN ORNISH, MD

People who survive a heart attack often describe it as a wake-up call. But for a 61-year-old executive I met recently, it was more than that. This man was in the midst of a divorce when he was stricken last spring, and he had fallen out of touch with friends and family members. The executive's doctor, unaware of the strife in his life, counseled him to change his diet, start exercising and quit smoking. He also prescribed drugs to lower cholesterol and blood pressure. It was sound advice, but in combing the medical literature, the patient discovered that he needed to do more. Studies suggested that his risk of dying within six months would be four times greater if he remained depressed and lonely. So he joined a support group and reordered his priorities, placing relationships at the top of the list instead of the bottom. His health has improved steadily since then, and so has his outlook on life. In fact he now describes his heart attack as the best thing that ever happened to him. "Yes, my arteries are more open," he says. "But even more important, *I'm* more open."

Medicine today focuses primarily on drugs and surgery, genes and germs, microbes and molecules. Yet love and intimacy are at the root of what makes us sick and what makes us well. If a new medication had the same impact, failure to prescribe it would be malpractice. Connections with other people affect not only the quality of our lives but also our survival. Study after study find that people who feel lonely are many times more likely to get cardiovascular disease than those who have a strong sense of connection and community. I'm not aware of any other factor in medicine—not diet, not smoking, not exercise, not genetics, not drugs, not surgery—that has a greater impact on our quality of life, incidence of illness and premature death.

In part, this is because people who are lonely are more likely to engage in self-destructive behaviors. Getting through the day becomes more important than living a long life when you have no one else to live for. As one patient told me, "I've got 20 friends in this pack of cigarettes. They're always there for me. You want to take away my 20 friends? What are you going to give me instead?" Other patients take refuge in food, alcohol or drugs: "When I feel lonely, I eat a lot of fat—it coats my nerves and numbs the pain." But loneliness is not just a barrier to fitness. Even when you eat right, exercise and avoid smoking, it increases your risk of early death.

Fortunately, love protects your heart in ways that we don't completely understand. In one study at Yale, men and women who felt the most loved and supported had substantially less blockage in their coronary arteries. Similarly, researchers from Case Western Reserve University studied almost 10,000 married men and found that those who answered "yes" to this simple question—"Does your wife show you her love?"—had significantly less angina (chest pain). And when researchers at Duke surveyed men and women with heart disease, those who were single and lacked confidants were three times as likely to have died after five years. In all three studies, the protective effects of love were independent of other risk factors.

Awareness is the first step in healing. When we understand the connection between how we live and how long we live, it's easier to make different choices. Instead of viewing the time we spend with friends and family as luxuries, we can see that these relationships are among the most powerful determinants of our well-being and survival. We are hard-wired to help each other. Science is documenting the healing values of love, intimacy, community, compassion, forgiveness, altruism and service—values that are part of almost all spiritual traditions as well as many secular ones. Seen in this context, being unselfish may be the most self-serving approach to life, for it helps free both the giver and recipient from suffering, disease and premature death. Rediscovering the wisdom of love and compassion may help us survive at a time when an increasingly balkanized world so badly needs it.

ORNISH, a clinical professor of medicine at the University of California, San Francisco, is founder and president of the Preventive Medicine Research Institute. His books include "Love and Survival" and "Dr. Dean Ornish's Program for Reversing Heart Disease." For more information, go to pmri.org or ornish.com.

Stressed Out Nation

Many Americans resort to unhealthy habits to help manage extreme stress, a new survey suggests.

ZAK STAMBOR

More than half of working adults—and 47 percent of all Americans—say they are concerned with the amount of stress in their lives, according to a new telephone survey conducted Jan. 12–24 by APA's Practice Directorate in partnership with the National Women's Health Resource Center and iVillage.com.

Moreover, the survey finds that people experiencing stress are more likely to report hypertension, anxiety, depression or obesity. The survey, which sampled 2,152 adults who are 18 years or older, is part of the Practice Directorate's "Mind/Body Health: For a Healthy Mind and Body, Talk to a Psychologist" campaign. The initiative aims to highlight psychology's role at the intersection between mental and physical well-being.

By focusing on the physical and mental toll of stress, the campaign is shining light on how many Americans react to both work- and family-related stress—by engaging in unhealthy behaviors, such as comfort eating, making poor diet choices, smoking and being inactive, says Helen Mitternight, assistant executive director of public relations in the Practice Directorate.

"Americans are stressed out, and they are dealing with that stress in an unhealthy way," says Mitternight.

However, on a positive note, she notes, nearly 20 percent of those most concerned about stress said that seeing a mental health professional could help them get back on track and relieve some of their stress.

Gender Differences

Stress is particularly prevalent for the primary decision-maker in the household for health issues, says Mitternight. Since 73 percent of women identify themselves as such, women feel the brunt of the health-care burden, she adds.

"Women are the health-care managers of their families," says Amber McCracken, director of communications for the National Women's Health Resource Center. "From taking care of their own health to serving as the caregivers for their children, partner and parents, each aspect of care brings stress. Unfortunately, too often women do not take the necessary steps to alleviate that stress, and their own physical health suffers."

Moreover, men and women exhibit their stress differently, the survey found. Women are more likely than men to report feelings of nervousness, wanting to cry or lacking energy. Men, 40 percent of whom consider themselves the primary health-care decision-maker, are prone to describing their stressed condition as sleepless, irritable or angry.

Those gender differences are magnified in men and women's coping mechanisms, the survey found. For instance, nearly 31 percent of women say they are comfort eaters, while only 19 percent of men report eating to deal with their problems. The urge to comfort-eat can have complex consequences, as the survey found that comfort eaters are more likely to exhibit higher levels of the most common stress symptoms, including fatigue, lack of energy, nervousness and sleeplessness.

The survey also found that 21 percent of participants who ate at a fast-food restaurant in the week prior to the survey reported being very concerned about stress, while only 13 percent of people who did not eat at a fast-food restaurant in the week prior to the survey were very concerned about stress. Not surprisingly, the fast-food-eaters were also more likely to experience more serious health problems like hypertension and high cholesterol.

Mind/Body Connection

The survey suggests that for most Americans stress results from a conglomeration of concerns. For instance, an office worker stressing out over a project deadline may quickly down a hamburger and fries while he or she works to save time. In turn, that stress-fueled decision may next lead to health worries.

"Everybody experiences stress," says Newman. "The key is how effectively people deal with and manage stress. People who turn to comfort food or smoking are starting a vicious cycle. Their attempts to reduce stress can actually lead to health problems that result in even more stress."

Russ Newman
APA Practice Directorate

The office worker's stressors are not unique, as more than half the survey respondents included concerns about money, work, family-member health problems or the state of the world today, as some of their leading sources of stress. More than 40 percent of participants also cited the health of immediate family members and caring for their children as common stressors.

An effective means of dealing with stress, suggests Russ Newman, PhD, JD, executive director of APA's Practice Directorate, is learning how to cope.

"Everybody experiences stress," says Newman. "The key is how effectively people deal with and manage stress. People who turn to comfort food or smoking are starting a vicious cycle. Their attempts to reduce stress can actually lead to health problems that result in even more stress."

To help break the cycle, Newman suggests that stressed people pay attention to their behaviors and lifestyle choices. Additionally, he notes that although some behaviors can be particularly difficult to change, working with a psychologist can help modify those actions.

The survey sponsors released the results at February press event in New York City that garnered national media attention on TV news shows such as "Good Morning America" and in newspapers such as *USA Today*. In addition to the media campaign, the sponsors are pairing the results with additional tips on how to manage stress. iVillage is also posting a Stress Smarts Quiz on its Web site to help readers understand the seriousness of their stress.

Seasonal Affective Disorder

Patients with seasonal affective disorder have episodes of major depression that tend to recur during specific times of the year, usually in winter. Like major depression, seasonal affective disorder probably is underdiagnosed in primary care settings. Although several screening instruments are available, such screening is unlikely to lead to improved outcomes without personalized and detailed attention to individual symptoms. Physicians should be aware of comorbid factors that could signal a need for further assessment. Specifically, some emerging evidence suggests that seasonal affective disorder may be associated with alcoholism and attention-deficit/hyperactivity disorder. Seasonal affective disorder often can be treated with light therapy, which appears to have a low risk of adverse effects. Light therapy is more effective if administered in the morning. It remains unclear whether light is equivalent to drug therapy, whether drug therapy can augment the effects of light therapy, or whether cognitive behavior therapy is a better treatment choice. (Am Fam Physician 2006;74:1521–24. Copyright © 2006 American Academy of Family Physicians.)

STEPHEN J. LURIE, MD, PHD; BARBARA GAWINSKI, PHD; DEBORAH PIERCE, MD, MPH; AND SALLY J. ROUSSEAU, MSW

The *Diagnostic and Statistical Manual of Mental Disorders,* 4th ed., (DSM-IV) categorizes seasonal affective disorder (SAD) not as a unique mood disorder, but as a specifier of major depression.[1] Thus, patients with SAD experience episodes of major depression that tend to recur at specific times of the year. These seasonal episodes may take the form of major depressive or bipolar disorders.

Epidemiology

The overall lifetime prevalence of SAD ranges from 0 to 9.7 percent.[2] This estimate depends on the specific population studied, as well as whether SAD is diagnosed by a screening questionnaire or a more rigorous clinical interview. In one U.S. study that used DSM-IV-based criteria, the lifetime prevalence of major depression with a seasonal pattern was 0.4 percent.[3] Prevalence may be higher at northern latitudes, and it may vary within ethnic groups at the same latitude.[4]

Patients with SAD are more likely to have family members with SAD, although this may be subject to reporting bias.[5] Twin studies have found that there may be a genetic component to susceptibility. Several genes code for serotonin transport, but the overall pattern of heritability likely is complex and polygenomic.[6]

Patients with SAD have more outpatient visits, more diagnostic testing, more prescriptions, and more referrals throughout the year compared with age- and sex-matched controls.[7] Patients with SAD visit their primary care physician more often in the winter than other patients, but rates between the groups are similar the rest of the year.[8]

Screening for SAD

Primary care physicians routinely fail to diagnose nearly one half of all patients who present with depression and other mental health problems.[9] Because SAD is a subtype of major depression, screening for depression should theoretically help identify patients with this disorder. The U.S. Preventive Services Task Force (USPSTF) concluded that there is good evidence that screening improves the accurate identification of patients with depression in primary care settings, and that treatment decreases clinical morbidity. The USPSTF concluded that the benefits of screening likely outweigh any potential harms.[10]

There are several instruments for detecting depression in primary care, ranging in length from one to 30 items with an average administration time of two to six minutes. Typically, the reading level of these instruments is between the third- and fifth-grade levels.[11] Some standardized instruments focus more narrowly on SAD. Reports on the sensitivity and specificity of these instruments can be difficult to interpret because of the small sizes and heterogeneity of patient samples tested, the possibility of differential recall bias (depending on the time of year the test is administered), and ongoing controversy over the criteria standard for SAD.

The Seasonal Pattern Assessment Questionnaire (SPAQ) is perhaps the most widely studied tool. It has been reported to have a high specificity (94 percent) for SAD but a low sensitivity (41 percent).[12] Other authors, however, have reported a much lower specificity.[13] The Seasonal Health Questionnaire has been reported to have higher specificity and sensitivity than the SPAQ,[14] but these results must be confirmed in larger and more diverse patient groups.

Sort: Key Recommendations for Practice

Clinical recommendation	Evidence rating	References
Standardized screening instruments for SAD probably are not sensitive enough to be used for routine screening.	C	12
Light therapy may be used for treating SAD, with effect sizes similar to those for antidepressant medications in treating depression. The total daily dosage should be approximately 5,000 lux, administered in the morning over 30 to 120 minutes.	A	23
Cognitive behavior therapy may be considered as an alternative to light therapy in the treatment of SAD.	B	28

SAD = seasonal affective disorder.

A = consistent, good-quality patient-oriented evidence; B = inconsistent or limited-quality patient-oriented evidence; C = consensus, disease-oriented evidence, usual practice, expert opinion, or case series. For information about the SORT evidence rating system, see page 1463 or http://www.aafp.org/afpsort.xml.

Although benefits from screening are less likely to be achieved without an accurate diagnostic work-up, effective treatment interventions, and close follow-up, it is unclear whether screening ultimately improves the care and outcomes of patients with major depression. When deciding to implement a screening instrument in a practice, office personnel should consider the administration time, scoring ease, reading level, and usefulness in identifying major depression and assessing change in the depression scores over time.[15]

Once patients have been identified as having major depression, questions must be asked to determine if the depression is linked to SAD. These questions concern the relationship between depression and time of year (if remission occurs during certain times of the year) and whether the depression has occurred at the same time during the past two years.

Associated Diagnoses

Because SAD is associated with serotonergic dysregulation and possibly with noradrenergic mechanisms, it may overlap with other diagnoses that share similar mechanisms, including generalized anxiety disorder, panic disorder, bulimia nervosa, late luteal phase dysphoric disorder, and chronic fatigue syndrome.[16] SAD also may be associated with attention-deficit/hyperactivity disorder (ADHD). Both conditions have been described as "disorders of central underarousal coupled with a heightened sensitivity to stimuli from the physical environment," and both are more common in women with a particular genotype for *HTR2A,* a gene that codes for a serotonin receptor.[17,18]

A pattern of seasonal alcohol use also may be associated with SAD. A summary of current research findings concluded that some patients with alcoholism may be self-medicating an underlying depression with alcohol or manifesting a seasonal pattern to alcohol-induced depression.[19] Such patterns appear to have a familial component and, like the link between ADHD and SAD, may be related to serotonergic functioning.

Treatment

Treatment options for SAD include light therapy, cognitive behavior therapy, and pharmacotherapy. Each option has been proven beneficial in treating SAD, but no large studies have found any treatment to be superior.

Light Therapy

Among susceptible persons, decreased seasonal exposure to light may mediate SAD through phase shifts in circadian rhythms, with resulting alterations in several aspects of serotonin metabolism. Thus, light replacement has been the most widely studied treatment for SAD.[20] In a review of studies of light therapy, an average dosage of 2,500 lux daily for one week was superior to placebo, as indicated by improvements on a depression rating scale.[21] The dosage most often found to be effective is 5,000 lux per day, given as 2,500 lux for two hours or 10,000 lux for 30 minutes.[22] A recent meta-analysis of 23 studies of light therapy found that the odds ratio for remission was 2.9 (95% confidence interval, 1.6 to 5.4); this ratio is similar to those of many pharmaceutical treatments for depression.[23] Like drug therapy for depression, light therapy carries some risk of precipitating mania.[24]

Light therapy generally is most effective when administered earlier in the day.[21,25,26] Early morning light therapy regulates the circadian pattern of melatonin secretion, whereas the use of light in the evening delays the normal melatonin phase shift.[27]

To ensure adequate response, patients should be treated with light therapy units that are specifically designed to treat SAD. Units that are not specifically designed for SAD treatment may not provide adequate brightness and may not have appropriate ultraviolet light filtration.[22]

Cognitive Behavior Therapy

Although cognitive behavior therapy (CBT) has some effectiveness in improving dysfunctional automatic thoughts and attitudes, behavior withdrawal, low rates of positive reinforcement, and ruminations in patients with major depression, few studies have assessed its effectiveness in the treatment of SAD. In one small clinical trial, patients with SAD were randomized to six weeks of treatment with CBT or light therapy, or CBT plus light therapy.[28] At the end of treatment, all three groups had significantly decreased levels of depression, but there was no difference between groups. However, this study only enrolled

26 subjects. To date, there have been no studies large enough to establish the effectiveness of CBT in the treatment of SAD.

Pharmacotherapy

Because patients with SAD also must fulfill criteria for depression, several randomized trials have assessed the use of antidepressants for this condition.[29-33] Most of these studies have compared pharmacotherapy with placebo rather than light therapy, making it difficult to determine if one treatment is superior. In the largest of these trials, patients with SAD had significantly better response on several measures of depression after eight weeks of sertraline (Zoloft) therapy compared with control patients.[29] Patients were excluded if they were receiving light therapy or other psychoactive medications, or if they had a history of alcoholism, drug abuse, or "emotional or intellectual problems."

A smaller study found that, in some statistical analyses, fluoxetine (Prozac) was better than placebo in the treatment of SAD.[30] Another small study found that the monoamine oxidase inhibitor moclobemide (not available in the United States) was similar to placebo in terms of changes on several general depression scales.[31]

Small trials of other agents (i.e., carbidopa/levodopa [Sinemet] and vitamin B_{12}) found no benefit over placebo.[34,35] Although there may be some theoretical justification for these treatments, there have not been trials of sufficient size to assess their effects.

Few randomized trials have assessed the effect of light therapy compared with pharmacotherapy.[32,36] These trials failed to find a difference between the effect of 6,000 lux and that of 20 mg of fluoxetine daily,[32] or between 10,000 lux and 20 mg of fluoxetine daily.[36] Larger trials will be required to establish whether there is a difference in effect size between light therapy and pharmacotherapy.

It is also possible that pharmacotherapy may preserve an initial therapeutic response to light therapy. Among 168 patients who had a positive response to light therapy, citalopram (Celexa) was found to be no more effective than placebo at preventing relapse; however, it was superior in terms of some secondary measures of depression.[33] In general, current evidence does not provide clear guidance as to whether antidepressant treatment is superior to light therapy, or whether antidepressants are useful as an adjunct to light therapy.

References

1. American Psychiatric Association. Task Force on DSM-IV. Diagnostic and Statistical Manual of Mental Disorders. 4th ed. Washington, D.C.: American Psychiatric Association, 1994.
2. Magnusson A. An overview of epidemiological studies on seasonal affective disorder. Acta Psychiatr Scand 2000;101:176–84.
3. Blazer DG, Kessler RC, Swartz MS. Epidemiology of recurrent major and minor depression with a seasonal pattern. The National Comorbidity Survey. Br J Psychiatry 1998;172:164–7.
4. Mersch PP, Middendorp HM, Bouhuys AL, Beersma DG, van den Hoofdakker RH. Seasonal affective disorder and latitude: a review of the literature. J Affect Disord 1999;53:35–48.
5. Sher L, Goldman D, Ozaki N, Rosenthal NE. The role of genetic factors in the etiology of seasonal affective disorder and seasonality. J Affect Disord 1999;53:203–10.
6. Sher L. Genetic studies of seasonal affective disorder and seasonality. Compr Psychiatry 2001;42:105–10.
7. Eagles JM, Howie FL, Cameron IM, Wileman SM, Andrew JE, Robertson C, et al. Use of health care services in seasonal affective disorder. Br J Psychiatry 2002;180:449–54.
8. Andrew JE, Wileman SM, Howie FL, Cameron IM, Naji SA, Eagles JM. Comparison of consultation rates in primary care attenders with and without seasonal affective disorder. J Affect Disord 2001;62:199–205.
9. Higgins ES. A review of unrecognized mental illness in primary care. Prevalence, natural history, and efforts to change the course. Arch Fam Med 1994;3:908–17.
10. U.S. Preventive Services Task Force. Screening for depression: recommendations and rationale. Ann Intern Med 2002;136:760–4.
11. Williams JW Jr, Pignone M, Ramirez G, Perez Stellato C. Identifying depression in primary care: a literature synthesis of case-finding instruments. Gen Hosp Psychiatry 2002;24:225–37.
12. Mersch PP, Vastenburg NC, Meesters Y, Bouhuys AL, Beersma DG, van den Hoofdakker RH, et al. The reliability and validity of the Seasonal Pattern Assessment Questionnaire: a comparison between patient groups. J Affect Disorder 2004;80:209–19.
13. Raheja SK, King EA, Thompson C. The Seasonal Pattern Assessment Questionnaire for identifying seasonal affective disorders. J Affect Disord 1996;41:193–9.
14. Thompson C, Thompson S, Smith R. Prevalence of seasonal affective disorder in primary care; a comparison of the seasonal pattern assessment questionnaire. J Affect Disord 2004;78: 219–26.
15. Nease DE Jr, Malouin JM. Depression screening: a practical strategy. J Fam Pract 2003;52:118–24.
16. Partonen T, Magnusson A. Seasonal Affective Disorder: Practice and Research. New York, N.Y.: Oxford University Press, 2001.
17. Levitan RD, Masellis M, Basile VS, Lam RW, Jain U, Kaplan AS, et al. Polymorphism of the serotonin-2A receptor gene (HTR2A) associated with childhood attention deficit hyperactivity disorder (ADHD) in adult women with seasonal affective disorder. J Affect Disord 2002;71:229–33.
18. Levitan RD, Jain UR, Katzman MA. Seasonal affective symptoms in adults with residual attention-deficit hyperactivity disorder. Compr Psychiatry 1999;40:261–7.
19. Sher L. Alcoholism and seasonal affective disorder. Compr Psychiatry 2004;45:51–6.
20. Partonen T, Lonnqvist J. Seasonal affective disorder. Lancet 1998;352:1369–74.
21. Terman M, Terman JS, Quitkin FM, McGrath PJ, Stewart JW, Rafferty B. Light therapy for seasonal affective disorder. A review of efficacy. Neuropsychopharmacology 1989;2:1–22.
22. Levitan RD. What is the optimal implementation of bright light therapy for seasonal affective disorder (SAD)? J Psychiatry Neurosci 2005;30:72.
23. Golden RN, Gaynes BN, Ekstrom RD, Hamer RM, Jacobsen FM, Suppes T, et al. The efficacy of light therapy in the treatment of mood disorders: a review and meta-analysis of the evidence. Am J Psychiatry 2005;162:656–62.
24. Sohn CH, Lam RW. Treatment of seasonal affective disorder: unipolar versus bipolar differences. Curr Psychiatry Rep 2004;6:478–85.
25. Eastman CI, Young MA, Fogg LF, Liu L, Meaden PM. Bright light treatment of winter depression: a placebo-controlled trial. Arch Gen Psychiatry 1998;55:883–9.

26. Terman M, Terman JS, Ross DC. A controlled trial of timed bright light and negative air ionization for treatment of winter depression. Arch Gen Psychiatry 1998;55:875–82.

27. Terman JS, Terman M, Lo ES, Cooper TB. Circadian time of morning light administration and therapeutic response in winter depression. Arch Gen Psychiatry 2001;58:69–75.

28. Rohan KJ, Lindsey KT, Roecklein KA, Lacy TJ. Cognitive-behavioral therapy, light therapy, and their combination in treating seasonal affective disorder. J Affect Disord 2004;80:273–83.

29. Moscovitch A, Blashko CA, Eagles JM, Darcourt G, Thompson C, Kasper S, et al., for the International Collaborative Group on Sertraline in the Treatment of Outpatients with Seasonal Affective Disorders. A placebo-controlled study of sertraline in the treatment of outpatients with seasonal affective disorder. Psychopharmacology (Berl) 2004;171:390–7.

30. Lam RW, Gorman CP, Michalon M, Steiner M, Levitt AJ, Corral MR, et al. Multicenter, placebo-controlled study of fluoxetine in seasonal affective disorder. Am J Psychiatry 1995;152:1765–70.

31. Lingjaerde O, Reichborn-Kjennerud T, Haggag A, Gartner I, Narud K, Berg EM. Treatment of winter depression in Norway. II. A comparison of the selective monoamine oxidase A inhibitor moclobemide and placebo. Acta Psychiatr Scand 1993;88:372–80.

32. Ruhrmann S, Kasper S, Hawellek B, Martinez B, Hoflich G, Nickelsen T, et al. Effects of fluoxetine versus bright light in the treatment of seasonal affective disorder. Psychol Med 1998;28:923–33.

33. Martiny K, Lunde M, Simonsen C, Clemmensen L, Poulsen DL, Solstad K, et al. Relapse prevention by citalopram in SAD patients responding to 1 week of light therapy. A placebo-controlled study. Acta Psychiatr Scand 2004;109:230–4.

34. Oren DA, Moul DE, Schwartz PJ, Wehr TA, Rosenthal NE. A controlled trial of levodopa plus carbidopa in the treatment of winter seasonal affective disorder: a test of the dopamine hypothesis. J Clin Psychopharmacol 1994;14:196–200.

35. Oren DA, Teicher MH, Schwartz PJ, Glod C, Turner EH, Ito YN, et al. A controlled trial of cyanocobalamin (vitamin B12) in the treatment of winter seasonal affective disorder. J Affect Disord 1994;32:197–200.

36. Lam RW, Levitt AJ, Levitan RD, Enns MW, Morehouse R, Michalek EE, et al. The Can-SAD study: a randomized controlled trial of the effectiveness of light therapy and fluoxetine in patients with winter seasonal affective disorder. Am J Psychiatry 2006;163:805–12.

STEPHEN J. LURIE, MD, PhD, is assistant professor of family medicine at the University of Rochester (N.Y.) School of Medicine and Dentistry. **BARBARA GAWINSKI,** PhD, is director of psychosocial curriculum in the Department of Family Medicine at the University of Rochester School of Medicine and Dentistry. **DEBORAH PIERCE,** MD, MPH, is clinical associate professor of family medicine at the University of Rochester School of Medicine and Dentistry. **SALLY J. ROUSSEAU,** MSW, is administrator of the Family Medicine Research Center at the University of Rochester School of Medicine and Dentistry.

Address correspondence to Stephen J. Lurie, MD, PhD, Dept. of Family Medicine, University of Rochester School of Medicine and Dentistry, 1381 South Ave., Rochester, NY 14620 (e-mail: Stephen_Lurie @urmcrochester.edu). Reprints are not available from the authors.

Dealing with Demons

Seen as a public health problem, suicide is preventable—at least that's an approach several states are starting to take.

CHRISTOPHER CONTE

In the mid-1990s, the United States Air Force was hit by a deadly epidemic: Every year between 1991 and 1996, about 60 airmen took their own lives, making suicide the second leading cause of death among the service's 350,000 members.

Eager to reduce the terrible toll, the service conducted "psychological autopsies" of the victims. These linked most of the suicides to problems airmen were having with the law, finances, intimate relationships, mental health, job performance and alcohol and drugs. The study also found most of the airmen were socially isolated and lacked the skills needed to cope with stress.

With these findings in hand, the service launched a counterattack. Top Air Force officials began urging airmen to seek assistance when they encountered personal difficulties, assuring them that doing so would not hurt their chances of promotion. he service also started training all its members in suicide risk-awareness and prevention, and it established "stress management" teams to help airmen and their families deal with potentially traumatic events.

These and other efforts worked. The suicide rate, which had been 14.1 per 100,000 active-duty service members from 1991 to 1996, fell to 9.1 per 100,000 from 1997 to 2002. Air Force officials attribute the improvement to the breadth of the program. "Suicide prevention," says one service manual, "is everyone's business."

The Air Force experience is getting a lot of attention these days in state capitols. At least 20 states have adopted suicide-prevention plans, most of them in the past few years, and many other states are working on the issue, too. Their efforts are driven by the belief that public health strategies, which involve looking for patterns that may point to the sources of disease and launching broad-based public information campaigns to encourage healthier living among the population at large, may hold the key to reducing suicide—just as they have been used to reduce heart attacks, strokes and lung cancer.

Public health campaigns to discourage smoking, bad diet or unsafe sexual practices have become a familiar and remarkably successful part of American life, but the use of such strategies against a psychological disorder represents a significant new departure. If successful, it could usher in one of the most fundamental shifts in thinking about the role of state mental health programs in decades—one in which mental health agencies increasingly offer their services to the entire population rather than to the small group of people diagnosed as having severe mental illness.

"We have been missing opportunities to use public health promotion and prevention in the mental health sector," notes Alan Radke, who, as medical director for the adult mental health division of Hawaii's Department of Health, has been spearheading a broad review of prevention strategies for the National Association of State Mental Health Program Directors. "If we can demonstrate that the use of health promotion and prevention strategies works with suicide, from those learnings we can address any number of other conditions."

An Ounce of Prevention

That's a big "if." The overall suicide rate has been stuck between 10 and 13 per 100,000 people annually for the past 50 years, and despite a handful of promising signs such as the Air Force program, there is no conclusive evidence that any strategy to reduce it will work. Indeed, suicide-prevention advocates sometimes seem to be acting more on faith than scientific proof. "When I started, I worried that this is too hard to fix and too big to understand," concedes Jerry Reed, executive director of the Suicide Prevention Action Network—USA, a lobby group that represents "suicide survivors," as family members of suicide victims call themselves. "But sometimes you have to act like a little bird, and hope when you leave the nest that you'll sprout wings before you hit the ground."

Although the prospects for success seem uncertain, advocates can offer some compelling reasons to tackle the problem. Suicide is the 11th leading cause of death in the United States, accounting for about 30,000 deaths a year. That's more than die from homicide (about 20,000 annually) or AIDS (14,000 a year). Moreover, researchers estimate that as many as 25 people attempt suicide for every one who actually kills himself. In 2002, some 250,000 people required medical treatment following suicide attempts, according to the Centers for Disease Control and Prevention. And surveys by the CDC show that 20 percent of teenagers have seriously considered killing themselves. (Much of the current push to combat suicide stems from a tripling of the rate among people aged 15 to 24 between 1950 and 1993, even though it has since leveled off.)

Suicide survivors have played a central role in planting the idea that suicide is a community problem, rather than a private, individual matter. That is no small step, because suicide has long carried a stigma. "It took me a couple of years before I could even talk about it," says Massachusetts state Senator Robert Antonioni, who lost a brother to suicide and has since persuaded the Massachusetts legislature to spend close to $1 million on suicide-prevention efforts over the past several years.

The important point, adds Kentucky state Senator Tom Buford, who steered a suicide-prevention bill through his state legislature this year partly in honor of his father who killed himself years ago, is that although "you feel you're living in sinful territory because somebody

Trail of Anguish

State-by-state suicide death rates, 2001

Between 14 and 23 Deaths per 100,000 People

- Alaska
- Arizona
- Arkansas
- Colorado
- Florida
- Idaho
- Montana
- Nevada
- New Mexico
- Oklahoma
- Oregon
- West Virginia
- Wyoming

Between 12 and 14 Deaths per 100,000 People

- Delaware
- Kentucky
- Maine
- Missouri
- New Hampshire
- North Carolina
- North Dakota
- South Dakota
- Tennessee
- Utah

Between 11 and 12 Deaths per 100,000 People

- Alabama
- Georgia

- Hawaii
- Indiana
- Mississippi
- South Carolina
- Vermont
- Virginia
- Washington
- Wisconsin

Between 6 and 11 Deaths per 100,000 People

- California
- Connecticut
- Illinois
- Iowa
- Kansas
- Louisiana
- Maryland
- Massachusetts
- Michigan
- Minnesota
- Nebraska
- New Jersey
- New York
- Ohio
- Pennsylvania
- Rhode Island
- Texas

Source: Suicide Prevention Action Network Inc.

in your family committed suicide, after a while you see it's just an illness that needs to be treated."

Because the majority of people who are suicidal go undiagnosed until it's too late to treat the illness, researchers say the only effective strategy may be to stress prevention in messages aimed at the entire population. "By reducing the risk for a lot of people, you get more bang for your buck than concentrating on the few who are at high risk," explains Kerry Knox, an assistant professor of preventive medicine at the University of Rochester.

The idea that broad strategies work more effectively than narrow ones against a hidden enemy is a fundamental tenet of public health. Epidemiologists liken society's approach to suicide today to its understanding of cardiovascular disease 30 years ago. Then, strokes, heart attacks and high blood pressure were treated largely on a case-by-case basis. The results were far from satisfactory because, as with suicide, these afflictions often went undetected until victims suffered crippling or fatal symptoms. But research in the 1970s and '80s showed that public information campaigns designed to promote low-cholesterol diets, exercise and screening for high blood pressure among the population at large were an effective way to prevent cardiovascular disease—even

though many of the people who hear such warnings probably face little risk.

At first blush, suicide seems different because it isn't a medical disease. But the latest research suggests that it may not be so different. Like cardiovascular disease, it apparently results from both biological and environmental causes. People who commit suicide or attempt it have abnormalities in the prefrontal cortex area of their brains, which controls "inhibitory" functioning. Because of this biological condition, "they are less able to restrain themselves and more likely to have strong feelings," observes J. John Mann, chief of neuroscience at the New York State Psychiatric Institute. "When they get depressed, they get more depressed than most people." He concludes that suicide may be the product of "stress-diathesis"—that is, a confluence of "stressors" arising from the environment and a "diathesis," or predisposition for suicidal behavior.

Knox and Mann both serve on a suicide-prevention working group convened by the New York State Office of Mental Health (the Psychiatric Institute, considered one of the foremost research institutions in its field, is part of the state agency). Although they come from a public health and a neurobiological background, respectively, they agree that, as Mann puts it, "You need a combination of strategies to have an impact on the suicide rate." While he believes the day isn't far off when doctors will be able to detect people who have suicidal proclivities by reading their brain scans, the technology will be of little value unless people are willing to seek help for themselves or recognize when people they know need it. "You need to educate the public to understand there are such things as psychiatric illnesses, and that they can lead to suicide," he says. "That requires the involvement of government."

The CPR Method

Most states have started their suicide-prevention efforts with broad-based educational campaigns. This spring, for instance, New York State issued "SPEAK," which stands for Suicide Prevention Education Awareness Kits—packets of materials that explain the connections between depression and suicide and encourage help-seeking among teens, men, women and older people. Some states also offer advice to the news media on how to report on suicide. Guidelines adopted by Maine, for instance, seek to minimize the danger of "suicide contagion" by encouraging the press to refrain from describing how a person killed himself, glorifying a suicide and using such phrases as "successful suicide."

Some states have gone beyond educational programs to concentrate on strengthening the bonds that make for more supportive communities. In Alaska, where religious disillusionment and social breakdown are believed to lie behind high suicide rates among some native peoples, the state provides funds for village elders to teach children about their heritage. "This builds pride and relationships, so that if a kid gets in trouble later, he'll have somebody to turn to," explains Susan Soule, Alaska's program coordinator for suicide prevention and rural human services.

In the lower 48, suicide-prevention programs seek to accomplish the same objective by training "gatekeepers"—clergy, doctors, teachers, social workers and others—who might come into contact with people who are suicidal. Paul Quinnett, president and chief executive of the QPR Institute in Spokane, Washington, believes that doctors, psychologists and social workers should be required to receive suicide-prevention training as a condition of being licensed. QPR, a deliberate take-off on the familiar emergency treatment CPR, stands for "Question, Persuade and Refer," a simple methodology for detecting people at risk of suicide and helping them get professional assistance.

North Dakota has provided its own version of suicide-prevention training to 28,000 people since 2000 on a budget of just $75,000 a year. The program seeks official gatekeepers as well as informal leaders—people who tend to pull communities together by force of personality rather than official position. "We go into schools and ask, 'Who is the person who makes things happen?'" says Mark Lomurray, the state's suicide-prevention project leader. "That's who we train." While Lomurray can't prove a causal connection, he notes that the number of suicide deaths in North Dakota has fallen by almost half since the program began.

A Broad Reach

It is too early to say if all the efforts surrounding suicide prevention will pay off, but if they do, state mental health programs may well need more money. "Right now, we do a good job identifying people who are suicidal, and we can refer them for services if there's a crisis," notes Cheryl DiCara, director of Maine's Youth Suicide Prevention Program. But for people who are troubled and haven't reached the crisis point, she says, "there's not a lot we can do."

Prevention advocates say that public health strategies may save money in the long run by reducing the need for acute care. But that implies new methods of serving people who don't need institutionalization. New York State offers some clues about where this more expansive orientation might lead. Traditionally, the Office of Mental Health has focused exclusively on helping people with severe mental disorders. After the September 2001 terrorist attacks, however, the department, with funding from the Federal Emergency Management Agency, began offering post-trauma counseling to the entire population of New York City and 10 surrounding counties. In two years, more than a million people availed themselves of these free counseling and educational services.

"We're reaching out to a much broader constituency than we ever did previously," notes Sharon Carpinello, New York's mental health commissioner. She expects the agency to become involved in a variety of new public health endeavors. In addition to suicide prevention, the agency is developing a disaster preparedness and "resiliency" campaign for the entire state and a separate campaign aimed at combating eating disorders in young women.

John Allen, who serves as the office's liaison with outside groups, says the new public health focus has brought enormous changes to his job. In the past, he mainly worked with a few small groups that represented patients in mental hospitals. But the post-9/11 project took him into the mainstream. One of his most important partnerships was with the New York State Thruway Authority, which helped the office distribute brochures to commuters. And the suicide-prevention program is bringing him into contact with major employers, local civic organizations and chambers of commerce.

As the department increasingly operates in a bigger arena, some prevention advocates hope it will start asserting itself on matters that previously have been beyond its ability to influence—including proposals to require insurance companies to offer the same coverage for mental illness treatments as they provide for medical care. The idea, of course, is very controversial because of the possible costs, but it's nothing compared with another issue that some prevention advocates have in their sights: gun control.

At the moment, there is no consensus even among suicide experts that stricter gun control would reduce the suicide rate over the long run. The best evidence is that making the leading instrument of suicide less available might have an impact for a while but that the improvement might dissipate over time as people switch to alternative methods to kill themselves. But the simple fact that the idea is even being discussed is a measure of how optimistic the mental health community is about the potential of public health strategies.

"I think we have to stay away from the more controversial strategies until society changes a little bit, but I don't feel totally hopeless," says Madelyn Gould, a research scientist at the New York State Psychiatric Institute who has participated in the state's suicide-prevention working group. "After all, who would have thought a couple of decades ago that anti-smoking campaigns would be so successful that today you can't even smoke anymore in bars in New York City?"

CHRISTOPHER CONTE can be reached at crconte@earthlink.net

From *Governing*, August 2004, pp. 28–31. Copyright © 2004 by Congressional Quarterly, Inc. Reprinted by permission.

Attacking the Myths

In the days following September 11, we were flooded with predictions of how individuals and communities would fare as they processed their darkest emotions. The passage of time has taught us that much of what we may believe about how people respond to sudden and traumatic loss needs to be torn apart and reconstructed.

ROXANE COHEN SILVER

It is now five years since the terrorist attacks that shattered our country's sense of invulnerability. Even those who did not personally know anyone who died that day have been touched by the deaths that occurred on 9/11. We are different now. Most of us willingly tolerate long lines at the airport. We remove shoes, belts, and jackets, and send them through X-ray machines without complaint. We open our bags and empty our pockets before entering sporting events, musical performances, and theaters. Sometimes, we gaze suspiciously at young men carrying backpacks on public transportation. How have we grieved this loss of innocence? Have we recovered from the loss of thousands of people, even if we knew them only through pictures?

We have not recovered if "recovery" means returning to the place we were on September 11, 2001. But we have "bounced back." People have returned to air travel and to Lower Manhattan. Many have come to terms with their losses. We are a resilient nation.

In this country, we make strong assumptions about how individuals respond to traumatic events. These assumptions are derived, in part, from clinical lore about coping with loss and from our cultural understanding of the experience. Yet many of our expectations about the coping process are wrong. How people are *supposed* to respond often stands in sharp contrast to the ways in which empirical data suggest they do.

Oftentimes, in fact, predictions about how people will respond to a community or personal trauma are made without the benefit of any data at all. Research in the natural environment—in the world as opposed to in a laboratory—is expensive, arduous, and time-consuming, and recruiting samples of traumatized populations can be challenging. We do, however, have enough data to know that "recovery" from loss rarely occurs after a few weeks or months, even though many lose patience with those who are unable to get back on their feet quickly. We should not look at the calendar and expect recovery for everyone by a certain point

in time. Research provides little support for the notion that there is a "right" or "wrong" way to respond to significant losses. There are only *different* ways.

More than two decades ago, I set out to understand the variety of ways people cope, to go beyond the assumptions and the clinical lore. I have studied the impact of community disasters, both natural and man-made. I have examined psychological responses over time. I have conducted studies on thousands of participants across a wide variety of victimizations, including physical disability, death of a spouse or child, childhood sexual assault, divorce, family violence, and war. In time, my research led me to uncover the "myths" of coping—and to challenge them.

There is no one, universal response to loss. It is a myth that psychological responses to loss are predictable. And it is a myth that everyone goes through an orderly sequence of reactions, or that there are "stages" of grief. Many clinicians, for example, expect that shortly after a significant loss, a person will have a negative emotional response, and they suspect that if a person does not have that kind of response—thus failing to confront the experience—he or she will be at high risk for "delayed onset" of psychological problems. But empirical support for that position has rarely been obtained. Indeed, not everyone will respond to traumatic events with early and intense emotional distress.

It is also a mistake to believe that people who have experienced a traumatic event will inevitably search for a way to "make sense" of their experience and that they will, over time, find some way to resolve their loss, find meaning in the outcome, and put the issue aside. What I found in prior research with parents who were coping with the death of their infants was strikingly different. Almost three-quarters of the parents we interviewed during the first year and a half after their loss were unable to make any sense of their baby's death, and more than eighty percent were unable to answer the question, "Why me?" or "Why my baby?" In another study, this one of adult survivors of childhood incest, ninety percent reported—twenty years after the experience had ended—that they were still searching for meaning in the abuse or trying to find a way to make sense of it. Time did not decrease the importance of finding meaning for the women in this study, and of those who were still actively searching for meaning in their abuse, more than half reported that they were unable to make any sense of what had happened to them during their childhood. Clearly, adjustment to a traumatic event does not mean one can simply find meaning in the experience and move on.

Obviously, the results of my research didn't take shape the way one might have predicted, and so we began to question the entire framework. Our long-held myths about how a person should respond to a traumatic event don't seem to account for variability of reactions, but variations do exist. In the aftermath of 9/11, many of us felt any number of emotions: shock or emotional numbness when we first saw or heard about the attacks; a sense that it could not be "real"; a calm, collected feeling that allowed us to "do what needed to be done"; intense fear or anxiety about the future; an overwhelming sense of sadness or depression. And these feelings may have continued and been exacerbated as world events unfolded—the initiation of military conflict, economic strain, heightened anxiety about subsequent terrorism at home and abroad. Physical symptoms, including nausea, loss of appetite, headaches, nervousness, and gastrointestinal distress or chest pains, also may have been quite common. Overall, some people experienced less distress than others might have expected; others responded with pronounced distress for far longer than might have been judged "normal" under the circumstances.

Almost immediately following 9/11, I began examining the impact of that day's attacks in the United States. This study was the only large-scale national longitudinal investigation of emotional, cognitive, and social responses to the attacks, and we surveyed several thousand people, repeatedly, from about two weeks after the attacks through the three-year anniversary.

We found that post-traumatic stress symptoms declined over the years after the attacks. We also found, though, that the degree of any one person's response was not proportional to that person's loss, degree of exposure to the attacks, or proximity to the World Trade Center. Our results demonstrated, quite clearly, that 9/11 had widespread consequences across the country: Psychological effects were not limited to the communities directly impacted.

Two months after the attacks, seventeen percent of subjects living outside of New York City reported symptoms of post-traumatic stress, including ongoing and intrusive ruminations

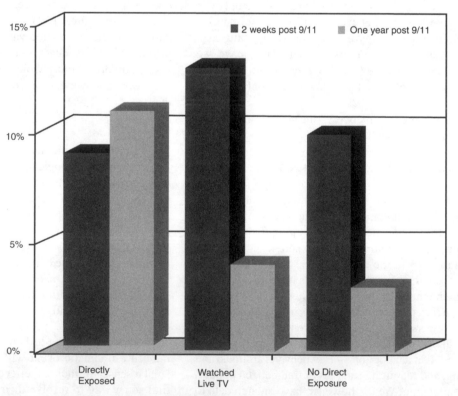

High Levels of Acute and Post-Traumatic Stress Symptoms Post-9/11. Based on data from "Exploring the myths of coping with a national trauma: A longitudinal study of responses to the September 11th terrorist attacks," by R.C. Silver, M. Poulin, E.A. Holman, D.N. McIntosh, V. Gil-Rivas, and J. Pizarro, *Journal of Aggression, Maltreatment & Trauma*, 2004.

and dreams about the attacks, and repeated attempts to avoid thoughts about them. Six months after 9/11, six percent continued to experience these problems. We also discovered, both immediately after the attacks and in the following years, that some of those who were only indirectly exposed to the attacks, meaning they watched them occur on live television and personally knew no one who died, reported symptoms at levels comparable to those who were directly affected or exposed to the trauma.

All across the country, we found people who wanted to be close to those they cared about—their families, friends, and neighbors—and many reported feeling a need to get in touch or "get back in touch" with important people in their lives. Many felt a need to talk about the trauma and their fears about the future. Many felt a sense of relief relative to those whose losses were greater than theirs, focusing on their own "luck" or "good fortune," but this sense of relief sometimes went hand in hand with a dose of "survivor guilt." Still others felt a need to do something, perhaps to regain a sense of control or simply to help in some small way. Accordingly, we saw an outpouring of donations—blood, money, time, goods and services for the recovery efforts or for survivors themselves. People who used active coping strategies, such as giving blood or attending a memorial service, showed lower levels of distress.

But beyond the post-traumatic stress symptoms, which are the typical focus of research after a catastrophic event, we also found that many people recognized unexpected positive consequences following the attacks. This was not totally surprising: Victims of spinal cord injuries, for example, often focus on the support they get from family and friends. Positive emotions can be quite prominent in the context of coping with loss.

For some of those we surveyed, the events of 9/11 actually had positive personal consequences: a change in their worldview, a new appreciation of the value of life, recognition of increased kindness and altruism among others ("People have put aside their differences"; "People went out of their way to help out, even risking their own lives"). Some saw benefits in the increase in religiosity that was apparent after the attacks ("Our nation has turned back to God and prayer") and in the increase in sociality ("People seem to put more value on family and friends now"). Others reported seeing political benefits as a result of the attacks, such as increased patriotism and a greater appreciation for the freedoms our country offers its residents. To some, there were benefits resulting from the increase in national security. A narrow focus on psychopathology that ignores these benefits devalues the resilience most people demonstrate when dealing with loss and keeps us mired in the same misunderstandings of how people cope with traumatic events.

Disasters like 9/11 cause physical damage and destruction, but they also disrupt life, alter routine patterns, and change our views of the world. Those who attacked us on 9/11 did far more than murder innocent civilians, shatter thousands of families, and destroy enormous buildings; they interrupted the rhythm, the cycle, the entire social fabric of our country. While the physical impact of this disaster may have been over in a few minutes, the psychological consequences are likely to extend over years and, for many of us, perhaps for the rest of our lives.

All of which makes inaccurate assumptions about the coping process even more devastating. Not only can such myths lead to the self-perception that we are not coping appropriately, but they also make it difficult for members of our social network to provide effective support. The best thing we can do to help our communities and ourselves is to recognize and respect people's need to respond to loss in their own ways and on their own timetables. Only in this way can we, as a country, expect to pull through traumatic events intact.

ROXANE COHEN SILVER is a professor in the department of psychology and social behavior and the department of medicine at the University of California, Irvine. A fellow of both the American Psychological Association and the Association for Psychological Science, she has spent the past twenty-five years studying reactions to stressful events, such as the loss of a loved one and the 9/11 attacks. Since 2003, she has served as a senior adviser to the U.S. Department of Homeland Security.

UNIT 3
Nutritional Health

Unit Selections

Key Points to Consider

- Why are trans fats unhealthy?

- What foods are considered healthy? Unhealthy?

- What dietary changes could you make to improve your diet? What is keeping you from making those changes?

- Do you think that fast food restaurants should be forced to limit the amount of fat and sodium in the food items they sell? Why or why not?

- What would you like to see on a food label?

- Should you consider buying the more expensive organic foods?

- What are the nutritional advantages of breastfeeding?

Student Web Site
www.mhcls.com/online

Internet References
Further information regarding these Web sites may be found in this book's preface or online.

The American Dietetic Association
  http://www.eatright.org
Center for Science in the Public Interest (CSPI)
  http://www.cspinet.org/
Food and Nutrition Information Center
  http://www.nalusda.gov/fnic/index.html

The McGraw-Hill Companies, Inc./Christopher Kerrigan, photographer

For years, the majority of Americans paid little attention to nutrition, other than to eat three meals a day and, perhaps, take a vitamin supplement. While this dietary style was generally adequate for the prevention of major nutritional deficiencies, medical evidence began to accumulate linking the American diet to a variety of chronic illnesses. In an effort to guide Americans in their dietary choices, the U.S. Dept. of Agriculture and the U.S. Public Health Service review and publish Dietary Guidelines every 5 years. The year 2000 Dietary Guidelines' recommendations are no longer limited to food choices; they include advice on the importance of maintaining a healthy weight and engaging in daily exercise. In addition to the Dietary Guidelines, the Department of Agriculture developed the *Food Guide Pyramid* to show the relative importance of food groups.

Despite an apparent ever-changing array of dietary recommendations from the scientific community, five recommendations remain constant: 1) eat a diet low in saturated fat, 2) eat whole grain foods, 3) drink plenty of fresh water daily, 4) limit your daily intake of sugar and salt, and 5) eat a diet rich in fruits and vegetables. These recommendations, while general in nature, are seldom heeded and in fact many Americans don't eat enough fruits and vegetables and eat too much sugar and saturated fat.

Of all the nutritional findings, the link between dietary fat and coronary heart disease remains the most consistent throughout the literature. The article "Fat City" addresses the recent New York City restaurant ban on trans fatty acids. These fats occur naturally in limited amounts in some meats and dairy products. The majority of these fats, however, enter the diet via a process known as hydrogenation. Hydrogenation causes liquid oils to harden into products such as vegetable shortening and margarine. In addition to these products, trans fats are found in many commercially prepared and restaurant foods. Current recommendations suggest that the types of fats consumed may play a much greater role in disease processes than the total amount of fat consumed. As it currently stands, most experts agree that it is prudent to limit our intake of trans fat which appears to raise LDLs, the bad cholesterol, and lower HDLs the good cholesterol and thus increases the risk of heart disease. There's also evidence that trans fats increase the risk of diabetes.

While the basic advice on eating healthy remains fairly constant, many Americans are still confused over exactly what to eat. Should their diet be low carbohydrate, high protein, or low fat? When people turn to standards such as the *Food Guide Pyramid,* even here there is some confusion. The *Pyramid,* designed by the Department of Agriculture over 20 years ago, recommends a diet based on grains, fruits and vegetables with several servings of meats and dairy products. It also restricts the consumption of fats, oils and sweets.

While the public continues to be confused over which foods are healthy, the media often contributes to the confusion. In "Food News Blues," Barbara Kantrowitz and Claudia Kalb address the many conflicting articles and how to make sense of the media hype surrounding nutritional recommendations. One of those controversies is whether organic food is worth the increased price. In "When It Pays to Buy Organic," the benefits of eating organic is discussed and which foods are better for you if they're grown organically. Finally, in "Suck on This," Pat Thomas addresses the benefits of breastfeeding on an infant's nutritional status. Formula increases the risks of babies developing diabetes, eczema and certain cancers as well as twice the overall risk of dying in the first six weeks of life.

Of all the topic areas in health, food and nutrition is certainly one of the most interesting, if for no other reason than the rate at which dietary recommendations change. Despite all the controversy and conflict, the one message that seems to remain constant is the importance of balance and moderation in everything we eat.

Fat City

Banning trans fats probably makes sense from a public-health standpoint—but will the doughnut survive?

CORBY KUMMER

In December, to the delight of many cardiologists and the dismay of many doughnut lovers, the New York City Board of Health voted to ban artificial trans fats from restaurants, school cafeterias, pushcarts, and almost every other food-service establishment it oversees, which includes most everything except hospitals. Trans fats don't occur naturally in the things people like but feel guilty eating, or at least not at high levels (there are small proportions in the fat in meat and dairy products). But artificial ones are plentiful in commercial foods, because they are easy to use, cheaper than natural fats, and keep practically forever. Trans fats are made by pumping hydrogen gas into liquid fats usually in the presence of nickel so that they will remain solid at room temperature, like butter and lard; and they have the same wonderful properties in pie crusts, cookies, and cakes. Crisco, still generic for solid shortening made by partial hydrogenation (of cottonseed oil), soon became the "sanitary" choice for pie crust and fried chicken, making pastry almost as flaky and skin almost as crisp as lard does.

But starting in the 1970s, a time of general fat panic related to heart disease, trans fats began to look as bad for cholesterol levels as the dreaded saturated fats, and in the 1990s the picture got worse. Trans fats, long-term studies reported, not only raise "bad" cholesterol (LDL); they also lower "good" cholesterol (HDL)—which not even saturated fats do. They look about as bad for the arteries as a fat can be. A 2002 consensus report from the National Academies of Sciences' Institute of Medicine called the relationship between trans-fat consumption and coronary heart disease "linear" and stated that the only acceptable level of trans fats in the diet was zero. The next year the Food and Drug Administration required food processors to list trans-fat levels on nutrition labels along with saturated fat. When the rule went into effect, in January 2006, public awareness of trans fats went up, and the stage was set for the New York City ban.

Thomas Frieden, New York's health commissioner, was already unpopular among libertarians. An epidemiologist and doctor whose speciality is infectious disease, he advocates the blunt instrument of regulation, often over the current public-health approach to most problems, which emphasizes education programs that encourage people to make healthy choices. Frieden

made international news by leading the charge to pass the city's comprehensive smoking ban, which has been duplicated across the country and the world. He believes that government should make the healthful choice the default, and that eliminating trans fats will do that, just as fluoridating water and getting the lead out of paint did.

Why an outright ban? Asking nicely didn't work. Starting in June of 2005, the city sent information on why and how to avoid trans fats to 30,000 restaurants and food-service establishments and to 200,000 clinics and community centers; it also provided training to 7,800 restaurant operators. A year later, the share of food-service establishments using trans fats—half—hadn't budged. With the support of Michael Bloomberg, Frieden's health-conscious boss, the city's board of health passed the proposed ban.

Libertarians were newly displeased, as legislators in California and Massachusetts began calling for similar bans. Chicago, which last summer enacted a widely ridiculed (and flouted) ban on foie gras, was also said to have trans fats in its sights. Columnists began asking exasperated what-next questions: Salt, a perennial runner-up to fat in the sin sweepstakes? Sugar? Whole milk? Alcohol, again?

Boston, with a similarly activist commissioner and a bold, public-healthminded mayor, Thomas M. Menino, was reported to be the next large city considering a ban. That commissioner, John Auerbach, is my spouse, so I followed the debate closely. I attended a meeting of the Boston Public Health Commission board (a meeting open to the public and press) and listened to the drafters of the New York ban narrate a PowerPoint presentation by conference call. The board was interested in the practicalities of enforcing the ban. I was interested in the practicalities of how small-business owners could follow the new rules—and how cooks could give customers the flavors and textures they were used to.

The New York presenters were reassuring, if short on details. Restaurant inspectors would simply add questions about trans fats to their normal checklist, scanning menus for items likely to contain them—say, cake mixes and frozen french fries—and asking to see labels for all cooking fats. It would add just a few

Doughnut Heaven

Since he began frying doughnuts in his East Village basement twelve years ago, using his North Carolina baker grandfather's recipe, Mark Isreal has made himself and his doughnuts New York City landmarks, selling to carriage-trade shops like Dean & Deluca and Zabar's and coyly (and correctly) refusing to ship them anywhere. What sets his doughnuts apart is the quality of the ingredients, particularly the butter—yes, doughnut batter has a lot of it—and the flavorings.

These days practically the first thing a visitor sees at the Doughnut Plant, Isreal's utilitarian Lower East Side shop, is a sign: NO TRANS FATS. Liquid oil (he fries in corn oil) is no problem for yeast doughnuts—airy, if very large, delights, which he makes in flavors like Valrhona chocolate and pistachio. But cake doughnuts are hard to make without trans-fat shortening, which thickens when it cools and gives Dunkin' Donuts' and other good commercial cake doughnuts the velvety, mouth-coating texture that virtuous cam oil can't quite match.

Isreal is as secretive about his recipes as he is talkative, so he wouldn't tell me which three milks he uses for "Ires Leches, the best of his cake doughnuts. But I suspect that condensed or evaporated milk, sweet and very thick, is his workaround for the mouthfeel challenge. None of his doughnuts ore ascetic, but these are lush.

Doughnut Plant, 379 Grand Street, New York City, 212-505-3700.

---

an artificial chemical in their food" that is killing them. A city trans-fat ban, he says, could prevent 500 premature deaths a year from heart disease.

I asked Frieden if he was trying to do what the federal government would not: force fast-food chains to remove trans fats. Kentucky Fried Chicken has already replaced its trans fats, as has Wendy's; Disney, Starbucks, and other companies have also gotten on the bandwagon. But McDonald's has been dragging its heels. It loudly announced, in 2002, that it would remove trans fats from all its food, but never got around to taking them out of its french fries—by far the biggest source, and the greatest challenge for texture (the original fat in McDonald's french fries was the lard-like beef tallow). Now it and every other chain unwilling to abandon the New York City market will have to reformulate their menus, and given research costs and economies of scale, the changes are likely to be national, not just regional. "Nothing like a deadline to focus the mind," Frieden said.

Wasn't New York's ban a case of governing the country from one city—and wasn't it really aimed at obesity? Frieden emphatically rejected the idea, saying that his fiduciary responsibility was solely to the citizens of New York City. The ban was meant to reduce premature deaths from heart disease, no more and no less. And he wasn't depriving people of pleasure. "We're not going to desalinate New York," he said, although he sounded as if he'd like to. "We're not going to ban eggs and ham." The science on trans fats, he said, had come clear slowly, as had the science on the effects of secondhand smoke. But once it did, it did decisively, and he had to act.

---

minutes to the usual hour-long inspection. As for telling restaurants how to substitute other fats and where to buy them, the health department planned to contract with culinary educators to teach at workshops and to staff technical-assistance help lines.

It seemed clear that restaurants would be left with plenty of questions, and I had a few of my own. I made an appointment to talk to Frieden, and to see several cooks whose businesses would be significantly affected by the ban. I also learned a lot about doughnuts—including that I like them more than can be good for me, whatever the fat.

A youthful forty-six, and thin, as you would expect, Frieden is both plainspoken and sure he is right. The morning I visited him, in the health department's WPA-era headquarters in Lower Manhattan, he told me that he and his communications director, Geoffrey Cowley, had just been wondering why his initiatives were so frequently "mis-spun" as the work of the "nanny state." He presents himself more as an emergency repairman. Little of what he does, he said, "would be necessary if our healthcare system worked—if every person had a doctor, continuity of care, and that doctor had access to their records." Better labels are all well and good, but "we don't want to exhort people to look at labels for trans fat," he said. "We want people to walk into a restaurant and not worry there's

So far, the chains that have initiated trans-fat removal have been the ones whose image depends on health or whose owners are concerned with health: the Tennessee-based Ruby Tuesday; the Boston-based Legal Sea Foods (whose owner, Roger Berkowitz, has long been ahead of every health curve); and Au Bon Pain, another Boston-based chain.

When I visited Au Bon Pain's headquarters and test kitchen, the head baker, Harold Midttun, told me that he had sold his family bakery after a heart attack at age thirty-nine. Once he got to Au Bon Pain, he took immediate interest in its mission to find substitutes for trans fats in cookies, muffins, and bagels; with Thomas John, the executive chef, and John Billingsley, the chief operating officer, he organized many tastings to sample new formulations alongside the originals. What were the tastings like? I asked the three men. Fattening, Billingsley replied.

Breads and even muffins were relatively simple; cookies were not. Chocolate-chip cookies, for instance, need the snap and solid texture that butter—or shortening, its much less expensive substitute—gives them when they cool. The company intended to "be zero trans fat" by April of this year, but not all the strudel problems (or the cream-soup ones, for that matter) had been solved.

I realized that saying trans fats are "totally replaceable," as Frieden repeatedly does—asserting that they are merely used for texture, not taste—is easier for a health official than for a product developer. It should be simple, yes, to get rid of an entirely artificial ingredient that is used mostly for the convenience of industry. Researchers have been working for decades on substitutes, which should by now be as plentiful and as cheap as trans fats.

But they're not. Midttun and John gave the example of their blueberry muffins, which used to be the highest in trans fats, as a challenge they had finally met. They did it by using a new fat and adding several other ingredients to mask its taste and still get the same mouthfeel. The ingredients, they told me, included oat bran, ground golden flaxseed, soy protein, and emulsifiers. Individual bakers, I thought, were sunk: They'd never be able to figure all that out, even with frequent calls to a city help line.

And the substitute fats have problems of their own. Earth Balance, a blend that Au Bon Pain uses, includes some palm-fruit oil, which is 50 percent saturated. Very highly saturated tropical oils, like coconut, were the target of a widely publicized 1994 expose of movie popcorn by the Center for Science in the Public Interest. Now, the current thinking runs, saturated fats are not quite as bad for you as trans fats—but they're still bad, and the American Heart Association has expressed concern about using them as a substitute for trans fats.

Dunkin' Donuts, another national chain based in the Boston area, says that it has tried twenty-two different fats in sixty-seven tests, hoping to get the same texture its doughnuts now have. Recognizing the difficulty posed by doughnuts and other fried doughs, New York modified its regulation to give doughnut makers eighteen months to come up with suitable alternatives. If Dunkin' has found a good substitute, it isn't saying.

Doughnut Plant, a cult fry shop on Manhattan's Lower East Side, is a poster child for the ban: It proudly announces that it fries only in corn oil (see "Doughnut Heaven," page 122). Mark Isreal, the eccentric, garrulous owner, certainly doesn't compromise on quality or expertise with his doughnuts. When I went to see him, I found myself following Frieden's example: He told me that at a health-department staff gathering after the ban was passed, he "couldn't stop eating" Isreal's doughnuts.

But when I tried similar favors at Dunkin' Donuts, I saw why lard and solid shortening have always been best for deep frying (Dunkin' has never used lard): The resolidified fat gives the interior a texture that oil simply cannot. Yeast-raised doughnuts are less problematic, because they should remain airy. But in a cake doughnut, the right texture is as unmistakable as the firm crumble of a butter cake—which, of course, requires a fat that solidifies at room temperature. A good cake doughnut has the substance of pound cake. It won't get that from corn or canola oil.

It's a confusing picture. Looking into trans fats got me hooked on an extremely fatty food I hadn't eaten since childhood (positively unpatriotic, as John T. Edge's monograph *Donuts: An American Passion* engagingly makes clear). Frieden readily admits that banning trans fats won't help reduce obesity. Posting calorie counts where you pay for your food—a less-noticed regulation he got passed at the same time as the trans-fat ban—might help. Or it might just make people eat more doughnuts: A Dunkin' Donuts glazed yeast doughnut has 180 calories, a glazed cake doughnut has 350, a reduced-fat blueberry muffin has 400, and a corn muffin has 510. Getting people to eat less fat and more fresh and unprocessed food—the real path to health—can't be done by any regulation yet proposed by the "food police."

Still, it does seem like a good idea to remove artificial substances from the food supply, especially if trans fats result in thousands of needless deaths a year. And the international headlines the initiative produced will most likely make people think more about the healthfulness of the food they eat, and restaurateurs about what they put into their food, all for a relatively modest expenditure on the city's part. As my spouse points out, regulations get headlines; education programs on the dangers of saturated fats and how to find, buy, and cook better food programs in which his department invests heavily—get yawns. I'll be watching follow-up studies to see whether the cure for trans fats, which in many cases is to replace them with highly saturated fats, is worse than the disease.

And when the beleaguered cooks at Dunkin' Donuts finally solve the riddle of removing trans fats, as New York City says they must by July of next year, I'll be eager to learn how they did it. At the risk of revealing a rival's trade secret, may I suggest oat bran and golden flaxseed?

CORBY KUMMER is an *Atlantic* senior editor.

When It Pays to Buy Organic

W hich apple? The decision doesn't end once you've figured out whether to buy, say, the McIntosh or the Red Delicious. In many food stores across the country, you're also faced with the more vexing question of buying organic or conventional, and not just at the apple bin. All kinds of organic fruits, vegetables, meats, poultry, eggs, cooking oils, even cosmetics are crowding store shelves.

For many shoppers, the decision often comes down to money. On average, you'll pay 50 percent extra for organic food, but you can easily end up shelling out 100 percent more, especially for milk and meat. Nevertheless, organic products are one of the fastest-growing categories in the food business. Nearly two-thirds of U.S. consumers bought organic foods and beverages in 2005, up from about half in 2004. While some buy organic to support its producers' environmentally friendly practices, most are trying to cut their exposure to chemicals in the foods they eat.

Critics argue that we're wasting our money because there's no proof that conventially produced foods pose significant health risks. Now, however, there are many new reasons to buy organic. First, a growing body of research shows that pesticides and other contaminants are more prevalent in the foods we eat, in our bodies, and in the environment than we thought. And studies show that by eating organic foods, you can reduce your exposure to the potential health risks associated with those chemicals.

Second, we found many ways to add more organic products to your shopping list without busting your budget. For one thing, you don't have to buy organic across the board. The truth is, not all organic-labeled products offer added health value. We found, for example, that it's worth paying more for organic apples, peaches, spinach, milk, and beef to avoid chemicals found in the conventionally produced versions of those items. But you can skip organic asparagus and broccoli because conventional varieties generally have undetectable pesticide levels. You can also pass on organic seafood and shampoo, which have labels that are often misleading. (See ShopSmart)

Moreover, we found that you need not pay a premium for organic foods if you know where to shop. See our tips for ways to cut your organic-food tab.

But you should also be aware that as more consumers are turning to organic products, some of the country's largest food producers are trying to chip away at what organic labels promise to deliver.

Organic Food Fight

If the organic label conjures up images of cackling chickens running free in a field and pristine vegetables without a trace of pesticides, keep reading. While the organic label indicates

---

CR Quick Take

Nearly two-thirds of consumers bought organic products in the past year, despite higher prices.

- The good news: New studies show that by eating organic food, you can greatly reduce your exposure to chemicals found in conventionally produced food.
- More good news: You don't have to clean out your wallet to buy organic foods if you know which ones to buy and where.
- The bad news: As more big players enter the organic market, government standards have come under attack. So it's more important than ever to understand food labeling and what's behind it.

---

that a product meets certain government standards, those standards are coming under pressure as big companies cash in on the growing demand for organic foods. H. Lee Scott Jr., chief executive of Wal-Mart Stores, has described organic as "one of the fastest-growing categories in all of food and in Wal-Mart."

During the past decade, U.S. organic sales have grown 20 percent or more annually. Organic food and beverage sales are estimated to have topped $15 billion in 2004, up from $3.5 billion in 1997. Sales are projected to more than double by 2009.

"Consumer spending on organic has grown so much that we've attracted big players who want to bend the rules so that they can brand their products as organic without incurring the expenses involved in truly living up to organic standards," says Ronnie Cummins, national director of the Organic Consumers Association, an advocacy group based in Finland, Minn.

Lobbying by large food companies to weaken organic rules started when the U.S. Department of Agriculture fully implemented organic labeling standards in October 2002. Food producers immediately fought the new rules. A Georgia chicken producer was ultimately able to persuade one of his state's congressional representatives to slip through a federal legislative amendment in a 2003 appropriations bill to cut its costs. The amendment stated that if the price of organic feed was more than twice the cost of regular feed—which can contain heavy metals, pesticides, and animal by-products—then livestock producers could feed their animals less costly, nonorganic feed but still label their products organic.

Did you know?
Food Labels Can Be Misleading

Organic-sounding labels can be confusing, or even meaningless. Below are examples of labels that are meaningful because there are government standards to back them up. You'll also find a couple of examples of meaningless labels. For more information on food labels, go to www.eco-labels.

Meaningful

"100% Organic." No synthetic ingredients are allowed by law. Also, production process must meet federal organic standards and must have been independently verified by accredited inspectors.

"Organic." At least 95 percent of ingredients are organically produced. The remainder can be nonorganic or synthetic ingredients. One exception: Organic labels on seafood are meaningless because the U.S. Department of Agriculture has no standards to back them up.

"Made with Organic Ingredients." At least 70 percent of ingredients are organic. The remaining 30 percent must come from the USDA's approval list.

Meaningless

"Free-range" or "free-roaming." Stamped on eggs, chicken, and other meat, this label suggests that an animal has spent a good portion of its life outdoors. But U.S. government standards are weak. The rule for the label's use on poultry products, for example, is merely that outdoor access be made available for "an undetermined period of each day." In other words, if a coop door was open for just 5 minutes a day, regardless of whether the chicken went outside, the animals' meat and eggs could legally be labeled "free-range."

"Natural" or "All Natural." This label does not mean organic. Their reason is that no standard definition for this term exists except when it's applied to meat and poultry products, which the USDA defines as not containing any artificial flavoring, colors, chemical preservatives, or synthetic ingredients. And the claim is not verified. The producer or manufacturer alone decides whether to use it.

That bizarre change in standards was repealed in April 2003 after consumers and organic producers protested, but the fight to maintain the integrity of organic labeling continues. In October 2005, Congress weakened the organic-labeling law despite protests from more than 325,000 consumers and 250 organic-food companies. The law overturns a recent court ruling that barred the use of synthetic ingredients in "organic" foods. It mostly affects processed products such as canned soups and frozen pizza.

The Massachusetts-based Organic Trade Association (OTA), which represents large and small food producers including corporate giants such as Kraft Foods and Archer Daniels Midland

Shopsmart

Know when it pays to buy organic food products to reduce your exposure to pesticides and other additives, when it might sometimes pay, and when it's a waste of your money. Use this section the next time you're making a grocery list.

Buy these items organic as often as possible

WHAT Apples, bell peppers, celery, cherries, imported grapes, nectarines, peaches, pears, potatoes, red raspberries, spinach, and strawberries.

WHY The U.S. Department of Agriculture's own lab testing reveals that even after washing, some fruits and vegetables consistently carry much higher levels of pesticide residue than others. Based on an analysis of more than 100,000 U.S. government pesticide test results, researchers at the Environmental Working Group (EWG), a research and advocacy organization based in Washington, D.C., have developed the "dirty dozen" fruits and vegetables, above, that they say you should always buy organic if possible because their conventionally grown counterparts tend to be laden with pesticides. Among fruits, nectarines had the highest percentage testing positive for pesticide residue. Peaches and red raspberries had the most pesticides (nine) on a single sample. Among vegetables, celery and spinach most often carried pesticides, with spinach having the highest number (10) on a single sample. (For more information on pesticide levels for other types of produce, go to www.foodnews.org.)

WHAT YOU'LL PAY About 50 percent more on average for organic produce, but prices vary based on the item and the time of year. A CONSUMER REPORTS price survey conducted in the New York City area in October 2005 found a premium of 24 percent on organic strawberries and 33 percent on grapes and spinach. Organic Idaho potatoes cost 101 percent more than conventional. When you buy organic produce in season at a farmer's market or directly from local providers, however, you might avoid paying a premium at all.

WHAT Meat, poultry, eggs, and dairy.

WHY You greatly reduce the risk of exposure to the agent believed to cause mad cow disease and minimize exposure to other potential toxins in nonorganic feed. You also avoid the results of production methods that use daily supplemental hormones and antibiotics, which have been linked to increased antibacterial resistance in humans.

WHAT Baby food.

WHY Children's developing bodies are especially vulnerable to toxins and they may be at risk of higher exposure. Baby food is often made up of condensed fruits or vegetables, potentially concentrating pesticide residues. Michelle Faist, a spokeswoman for Del Monte, says that even though its baby foods are not organic, pesticides and heavy metals are kept below government-recommended levels.

WHAT YOU'LL PAY Varies widely by store.

Buy these items organic if price is no object

WHAT Asparagus, avocados, bananas, broccoli, cauliflower, sweet corn, kiwi, mangos, onions, papaya, pineapples, and sweet peas.

WHY Multiple pesticide residues are, in general, rarely found on conventionally grown versions of these fruits and vegetables, according to research by the EWG. So if you're buying organic only for health reasons, you may not want to pay 22 percent extra for organic bananas, let alone more than 150 percent for organic asparagus—the premiums we found in our price survey of several New York City area supermarkets.

WHAT Breads, oils, potato chips, pasta, cereals, and other packaged foods, such as canned or dried fruit and vegetables.

WHY Although these processed products may have lower levels of contaminants in them, they offer limited health value because processing tends to wash away important nutrients. The process of milling organic whole grains into flour, for example, eliminates fiber and vitamins, though they are sometimes added back in. The more a food is processed, the less health value its organic version offers, especially in products such as cereals and pastas with labels that say "made with organic ingredients." Read the list of ingredients and you might find that while the flour is organic, the eggs aren't. The processed foods with the most added value are labeled "100% Organic" and "USDA organic." Price premiums vary. In our survey, organic Heinz ketchup cost 25 percent more than the conventional product; organic minestrone soup was only 8 percent more.

Don't Bother Buying these Items Organic

WHAT Seafood.

WHY Whether caught in the wild or farmed, fish can be labeled organic, despite the presence of contaminants such as mercury and PCBs. Some wild fish such as bluefish are very high in PCBs, and tuna and swordfish are laced with mercury. The USDA has not yet developed organic certification standards for seafood. In the meantime, producers are allowed to make their own organic claims as long as they don't use "USDA" or "certified organic" logos. California, however, recently passed a law that prohibits the use of any organic labeling on fish and other seafood until either state or federal certification standards are established.

WHAT Cosmetics.

WHY Unless a personal-care product consists primarily of organic agricultural ingredients, such as aloe vera gel, it's pointless to buy organic in this category. Most cosmetics contain a mix of ingredients, and USDA regulations allow shampoos and body lotions to carry an organic label if their main ingredient is "organic hydrosol," which is simply water in which something organic, such as a lavender leaf, has been soaked. While the USDA claims that organic labeled-cosmetics follow the same standards as food, we have found indiscriminate use of synthetic ingredients and violations of food-labeling standards. "Many of the ingredients in personal-care products didn't grow out of the ground but in test tubes—they're chemicals," says Lauren Sucher, director of public affairs at the EWG. Just because a product has the word "organic" or "natural" in its name doesn't necessarily mean it's safer. Only 11 percent of ingredients found in personal-care products, organic or not, have ever been screened for safety. In fact, when the EWG conducted its own safety rating of these products (available at www.ewg.org), scoring them on a scale of 0, for those posing lowest level of concern, to 5, for the highest concern due to potentially unsafe ingredients, those with scores of 4 or more included benign-sounding Naturessence All Day Moisture Cream.

Co., supported the amendment. "The issue is whether processed products could use a list of benign synthetic ingredients already approved by the National Organic Standards Board," says Katherine DiMatteo, executive director of the OTA, "and we do not believe standards will be weakened at all."

Not all organic producers agree, however. Executives at Earthbound Farm, which has been in the organic business for more than 20 years and is the nation's leading supplier of specialty organic salad greens, were startled to find their company's name on an OTA letter supporting the amendment. Earthbound objects to built-in "emergency exemptions" that would allow nonorganic ingredients in organically labeled food if the organic alternative is considered "commercially unavailable." As with the Georgia chicken-feed case, if organic corn is expensive because it's in short supply, a soup maker might argue that it is commercially unavailable and get an exemption to use nonorganic corn.

"This presents a risk to the integrity of the organic label that we would have preferred not to see," says Charles Sweat, chief operating officer at Earthbound Farm.

Other changes in the organic industry are occurring more quietly in the farm fields. Wal-Mart alone gobbles up so much of the organic dairy supply that some producers that have historically accounted for the bulk of organic products on the market haven't been able to meet the new demand. Suppliers filling the gap are doing so in part by exploiting loopholes in the organic rules, some consumer advocates say.

Organic Valley, a Wisconsin-based national cooperative of farmers that had been one of Wal-Mart's primary suppliers of organic milk, ended that direct relationship at the end of 2004. "When the first U.S. case of mad cow was discovered in a dairy cow at the end of 2003," says Theresa Marquez, chief marketing executive at Organic Valley, "demand for organic milk spiked and we've been in a short-supply situation ever since, with demand growing at 25 percent annually and supply growing at only 10 percent."

With supplies limited, Marquez says, the company decided to "stay true to our mission" and give top priority to filling orders from natural-food markets, its oldest customers, leaving it to Horizon Organic and other large competitors to "duke it out figuring out how to service Wal-Mart."

Horizon Organic is an organic dairy company that was acquired in 2003 by Dean Foods, the leading U.S. dairy processor. Its operations range in size from a 12-cow farm in Vermont to a 4,000-cow operation in Idaho, where animals may be confined in outdoor corrals and given organic feed, grasses, and hay. They graze in open pastures only on a rotating basis instead of primarily grazing in open pastures, as cows are required to do on farms that supply Organic Valley.

Current federal regulations state that organically raised animals must have access to pasture and may be "temporarily confined only for reasons of health, safety, the animal's stage of production, or to protect soil or water quality." But that vague language allows large producers to cut corners and compromise on what consumers expect from organic food, consumer advocates say.

The regulations also leave open questions about whether dairy animals could have been treated with antibiotics or consumed feed containing genetically modified grain or animal byproducts prior to becoming part of an organic dairy farm.

Horizon says it uses no antibiotics or growth hormones in its organic herd, though it can't control what animals eat before they arrive there. And the company says it plans to upgrade its Idaho farm to offer more pasture by 2007. In the meantime,

Horizon says, its cows are being kept in good health and treated humanely. "We permit cows to exercise and exhibit natural behaviors," says Kelly Shea, director of government and industry relations at Horizon. "We would never support lowering the standards."

What's in the Food

So what can you count on when you buy organic? No animals, except dairy cows prior to being moved to organic farms, can be given antibiotics, growth hormones, or feed made from animal byproducts, which can transmit mad cow disease. No genetic modification or irradiation is permitted, nor is fertilizer made with sewage sludge or synthetic ingredients, all of which are allowed in most conventional food production.

Organically raised animals must also have access to the outdoors, though it might simply mean that cattle are cooped up in outdoor pens. The rules governing poultry are even less stringent than for other livestock. Some "organic" chickens, for example, spend their short lives confined in coops with screen windows.

Organic fruits and vegetables are farmed with botanical or primarily nonsynthetic pest controls quickly broken down by

---

Healthwise

Chemical Health Risks of Conventionally Produced Foods

Here's what we know about those pesticides, hormones, antibiotics, and other chemicals used in the production of conventional meats, vegetables, and other foods:

Pesticides. More than a dozen formerly widely used pesticides have been banned, restricted, or voluntarily withdrawn by manufacturers since 1996, when a new federal law required pesticides to meet safety standards for children, whose developing immune, central-nervous, and hormonal systems are especially vulnerable to damage from toxic chemicals. Under that law, more pesticides are being investigated each year and banned or are undergoing lowering of limits on what can safely be tolerated, but consumers can still easily consume small amounts of more than 30 pesticides daily when eating a healthful variety of foods.

New evidence also shows that contrary to previous scientific belief, pesticides in a woman's bloodstream can be passed to a fetus in the womb. A study released in 2005 in which umbilical-cord blood of 10 children was collected by the Red Cross and tested for pollutants showed that 21 pesticides crossed the placenta.

Eating an organic diet can limit further exposure, however. A study supported by the Environmental Protection Agency and published in 2005 measured pesticide levels in the urine of 23 children in Washington State before and after a switch to an organic diet. Researchers found that after just five consecutive days on the new diet, specific markers for commonly used pesticides decreased to undetectable levels, and remained that way until conventional diets were reintroduced. The study's conclusion: "An organic diet

provides a dramatic and immediate protective effect" against such pesticide exposure.

"A lot of these pesticides are toxic to the brain," says Philip Landrigan, M.D., a professor of pediatrics and preventative medicine at Mount Sinai School of Medicine in New York City. "We have very good evidence that exposure of the fetus to organophosphorus pesticides produces babies with small head circumference, which is a risk factor for reduced intelligence and behavioral disturbances."

Hormones. Studies suggest that synthetic growth hormones may be carcinogenic and that exposure to them may be linked to the precocious onset of puberty in girls. The USDA bans the use of such hormones in all poultry (organic or not), but when it comes to hogs, beef, or dairy cattle, only organic producers are legally bound not to use them.

Antibiotics. Farmers' widespread use of antibiotics to speed up animals' growth and to deal with health issues that crop up from keeping animals in overcrowded and unsanitary pens has helped spawn antibiotic-resistant bacteria. This resistance increases the odds that a drug that might have saved your life if you were to be hit by, say, a life-threatening case of food poisoning will now do you no good.

Other toxins. Nonorganic foods can expose you to a range of other contaminants with potential health risks. Conventionally raised chicken, for example, eat feed that can contain neurotoxins, such as arsenic or heavy metals. And the animals' feet may be dipped in motor oil as a treatment for an ailment known as scaly leg mite.

sunlight and oxygen, instead of long-lasting synthetic chemicals. Organic produce sometimes carries chemical residues because of pesticides that are now pervasive in groundwater and rain, but their chemical load is much lower.

According to the Environmental Working Group (EWG), a research and advocacy organization in Washington, D.C., eating the 12 most contaminated fruits and vegetables exposes you to about 20 pesticides a day on average. If you eat the 12 least contaminated, you're exposed to about two pesticides a day.

Joseph Rosen, a professor of food science at Rutgers University, says that when it comes to pesticide exposure, "the amount in conventional foods is so low that it's not a health threat." Richard Wiles, senior vice president at the EWG, on the other hand, says that the cumulative effect of even low-level multiple pesticide exposures is both worrisome and little studied at this point.

Buying Organic on the Cheap

If you decide that you'd prefer fewer chemicals and other additives in your food, the choice isn't an easy one. Organic sticker shock can hit the most stalwart of organic shoppers. The fact is that organic farmers produce more labor-intensive products and don't enjoy the economies of scale or government subsidies that their big brothers in agribusiness do. But we found many ways to save on the cost of organic products.

Comparison shop. Do a price check among local grocery stores for often purchased organic items and shop where you find the lowest prices. In the New York City area, for example, we found a 4-ounce jar of Earth's Best organic baby food for as little as 69 cents and as much as $1.29. When it comes to fresh produce, remember that you'll save by buying it in season.

Go local. You can find organic growers at most farmer's markets, and a USDA study in 2002 found that about 40 percent of those farmers don't charge a premium. For listings of local farmer's markets and other sources, go to www.ams.usda .gov/farmersmarkets and www.localharvest.org.

Join the farm team. Buy a share in a community-supported organic farm and you'll get a weekly supply of produce from spring until fall. The cost to feed a family of four generally ranges from $300 to $500 for the season. (Some farms also require you to work a few hours a month distributing or picking produce.) The savings can be substantial. A price study by a community-supported farm in the Northeast showed that the average $10 weekly cost for a shareholder's produce supply almost always beat farmer's market organic prices and often cost less than the same nonorganic items at a supermarket. Go to www.sare.org for a list of community-supported farms.

Order by mail. National providers will ship items such as organic beef (www.mynaturalbeef.com). Some local businesses, such as FreshDirect (www.freshdirect.com) in the New York City area and Pioneer Organics (www.pioneerorganics.com) in the Pacific Northwest, offer home deliveries. Other helpful sites are at www.eatwellguide.org and www.theorganicpages.com.

Be a supermarket spy. Make sure you get what you pay for by watching where produce sits on shelves. All grocers are legally required to stack organic fruits and vegetables where they won't be exposed to water runoff from the misting of conventional produce, which could contaminate organic items with pesticide residue. If a store is not following that rule, you may be wasting your money by buying organic produce there.

The Package May Say Healthy, But This Grocer Begs to Differ

ANDREW MARTIN

For many grocery shoppers, the feeling is familiar: that slight swell of virtue that comes from dropping a seemingly healthful product into a shopping cart.

But at one New England grocery chain, choosing some of those products may induce guilt instead.

The chain, Hannaford Brothers, developed a system called Guiding Stars that rated the nutritional value of nearly all the food and drinks at its stores from zero to three stars. Of the 27,000 products that were plugged into Hannaford's formula, 77 percent received no stars, including many, if not most, of the processed foods that advertise themselves as good for you.

These included V8 vegetable juice (too much sodium), Campbell's Healthy Request Tomato soup (ditto), most Lean Cuisine and Healthy Choice frozen dinners (ditto) and nearly all yogurt with fruit (too much sugar). Whole milk? Too much fat—no stars. Predictably, most fruits and vegetables did earn three stars, as did things like salmon and Post Grape-Nuts cereal.

At a time when more and more products are being marketed as healthy, the fact that so many items seemed to flunk Hannaford's inspection raises questions about the integrity of the nutrition claims, which are regulated by the Food and Drug Administration—or possibly about whether Hannaford made its standards too prissy or draconian. Either way, the results do seem to confirm the nagging feeling that the benefits promoted by many products have a lot more to do with marketing than nutrition.

Furthermore, the rating system, introduced in September, puts the grocery store in the awkward position of judging the very products it is trying to sell, not to mention the companies that supply the foods. In fact, most of Hannaford's own store-branded products did not get stars.

Hannaford says it is not trying to be preachy or to issue a yes-or-no checklist, just to offer guidance to shoppers who want it—and if the average consumer's reliance on the United States Department of Agriculture's food pyramid system is any yardstick, many do not. Furthermore, the company said, there is a place for no-star foods in every balanced diet.

"We are saying there are no bad foods," said Caren Epstein, a Hannaford spokeswoman. "This is a good, better and best system."

Food manufacturers, she said, were apprehensive at first but relaxed when they learned that neither they nor their products would be penalized. "The people who represented salty snacks and cookies understood that they weren't going to get any stars," Ms. Epstein said.

Under a food chain's ratings, 78 percent of its products earn no stars for nutrition.

Hannaford's nutritionists acknowledge that their system is more stringent than the guidelines used by the F.D.A. The food agency sets standards that food manufacturers must use when they define a product as, say, low in fat or high in fiber, and companies may use those designations even if the product is loaded with less desirable ingredients. Hannaford's panelists said their formula was more balanced, taking into account all the positives and negatives.

The store chain, with 158 supermarkets in five states, is believed to be the first grocery retailer to have developed such a comprehensive assessment program, and it is trying to have its food-rating algorithm patented.

Not surprising, the food industry still is not entirely happy, and it disputes Hannaford's conclusions.

"We don't like the idea that there are good and bad foods out there, and these sort of arbitrary rating systems," said John Faulkner, director of brand communication at the Campbell Soup Company. The Healthy Request line of soup, he said, was "aligned with the government definition of what healthy is."

Similarly, a spokeswoman for ConAgra Foods, Stephanie Childs, said that her company would like to know how Hannaford concluded that many items in its Healthy Choice line did not merit any stars.

"This is surprising to us," Ms. Childs said. Healthy Choice, which offers a range of items from frozen meals to pasta sauces and deli meats, "has to use F.D.A.'s very stringent requirements for what is healthy."

Admirers of Guiding Stars say the ratings illustrate how nutrition claims on packages can mislead consumers even if they are technically true. Many packages trumpet the benefits of a few attributes—high fiber, for instance, or no trans fats—while ignoring negatives like too much sodium, they said.

"You look at a General Mills product and it looks like the bee's knees, but it may be nutritionally flawed," said Michael F. Jacobson, executive director of the Center for Science in the Public Interest, an advocacy group based in Washington. "It may be high in sugar even though it has fiber in it."

Many products that are marketed as healthy received zero stars from Hannaford because they contain too much salt or sugar or not enough nutrients, said Lisa A. Sutherland, an assistant professor of pediatrics and a nutrition scientist at Dartmouth Medical School who was part of the advisory panel that developed Hannaford's formula.

V8, for instance, which says it has "essential antioxidants" and is "vitamin rich," is "like drinking a vitamin with a lot of salt on it," she said. Ms. Sutherland said that the F.D.A.'s guidelines for labeling, including its definition of "healthy," were simply too lenient. Even the low-sodium version of V8 got no stars under the Hannaford system.

The F.D.A., for its part, points to its specific requirements for foods that make health claims as well as their labels. It also acknowledges that its policing abilities go only so far.

"The thing is, a lot of claims we see out there are puffery," said Joseph R. Baca, director of the office of compliance at the F.D.A.'s Center for Food Safety and Applied Nutrition. "But they don't get to the point where we can call them fake or misleading."

Although Hannaford's star ratings are posted on the same shelf tags that display prices, the chain has not changed the way it shelves products or markets them. This may have kept food manufacturers from rebelling, but it has not stopped them from questioning whether Hannaford is qualified to be the arbiter of healthiness.

"You end up with a lot of consumer confusion," said Mr. Faulkner of Campbell Soup, which makes V8 as well as Healthy Request. "Do you defer to the Hannaford Brothers? The federal government?"

The label of Campbell's Healthy Request Tomato soup, for instance, boasts that it is 98 percent fat-free, has zero grams of trans fat, low cholesterol and 30 percent less sodium than Campbell's standard tomato soup. "I don't know what their system is," Mr. Faulkner said, referring to Hannaford. "What are they calling too much salt?"

Hannaford, part of Delhaize America, a division of the Delhaize Group in Brussels, started Guiding Stars after customer surveys indicated that people were confused about the nutritional information available to them. Hannaford formed a seven-member advisory panel of nutritionists and a physician to develop a formula for evaluating the healthiness of food.

That algorithm evaluates a 100-calorie serving of each product using only the information that is available on the "nutrition facts" panel and the ingredients list. A product receives credit for vitamins, minerals, dietary fiber and whole grains, but is docked points for trans fat, saturated fat, cholesterol, added salt and added sugar.

People who choose to adhere closely to the Hannaford ratings will have Spartan diets indeed. Not only did cookies and potato chips rate poorly, but so did whole milk (although skim milk received three stars) and products with nourishing-sounding names like Healthy Choice Old-Fashioned Chicken Noodle Soup.

Indeed, the "three star" lunches and snacks recommended on Hannaford's Web site probably bear little relation to the meals most Americans are accustomed to eating. Hannaford suggests snacking on grapes, apple slices, raisins, plain yogurt, celery sticks, carrots and one to two ounces of popcorn—presumably without salt. A good lunch would be grilled chicken on a bed of spinach with a multigrain roll and an apple.

A. Elizabeth Sloan, president of Sloan Trends, which tracks the food industry, said that food manufacturers deserve credit for reformulating their products to make them healthier. But she said it was unrealistic for the manufacturers to remove all the fat, sugar and salt because nobody would buy the result.

"They have to keep the taste," she said. "Look at all those super-duper healthy products that are in those healthy food stores. They don't taste good."

She added, "Nothing is healthy if you get right down to it, except mother's milk, and that's probably got too much fat."

It is hard to tell whether Hannaford's nutrition index has had any impact on what consumers are buying. The chain declined to provide sales data.

At a Hannaford store in New Windsor, N.Y., several customers said they had heard about Guiding Stars in radio advertisements or seen it in the store, but that it had not influenced their purchasing. Several shoppers said they did not see the point.

"I buy whatever it is on my list," said Karen Wilson, 43. "If my kids want Cheerios, I buy them Cheerios and don't look at the stars."

LiseAnne Deoul, 34, said she liked the idea of Guiding Stars even though the system had not helped her narrow her choices during a quick stop last week to buy pasta.

"All of it was the same," she said. "They all had two stars."

Hannaford officials and members of the advisory panel emphasized that foods with no stars were not meant to be shunned.

"They are not everyday foods," said Ms. Sutherland. "They are great sometimes foods."

Nutritionists and food industry analysts said that Hannaford's findings highlight some unpleasant truths about Americans and their eating patterns. People want to be healthier but do not want to change their behavior, and so marketers have stepped in with products that improve on the originals but still leave something to be desired.

The poor marks doled out by Hannaford show "what happens when an independent group sets the criteria," said Marion Nestle, a professor of nutrition at New York University.

"As for health claims, expect to see more and more and more," she said. "It's the only thing that sells food these days."

Suck on This

**The human species has been breastfeeding for nearly half a million years.
It's only in the last 60 years that we have begun to give babies the highly
processed convenience food called 'formula'. The health consequences—
twice the risk of dying in the first six weeks of life, five times the risk of
gastroenteritis, twice the risk of developing eczema and diabetes and up to
eight times the risk of developing lymphatic cancer—are staggering. With UK
formula manufacturers spending around £20 per baby promoting this 'baby
junk food', compared to the paltry 14 pence per baby the government spends
promoting breastfeeding, can we ever hope to reverse the trend?
Pat Thomas uncovers a world where predatory baby milk manufacturers,
negligent health professionals and an ignorant, unsympathetic
public all conspire to keep babies off the breast and on the bottle.**

PAT THOMAS

All mammals produce milk for their young, and the human species has been nurturing its babies at the breast for at least 400,000 years. For centuries, when a woman could not feed her baby herself, another lactating woman, or 'wet nurse', took over the job. It is only in the last 60 years or so that we have largely abandoned our mammalian instincts and, instead, embraced a bottlefeeding culture that not only encourages mothers to give their babies highly processed infant formulas from birth, but also to believe that these breastmilk substitutes are as good as, if not better than, the real thing.

Infant formulas were never intended to be consumed on the widespread basis that they are today. They were conceived in the late 1800s as a means of providing necessary sustenance for foundlings and orphans who would otherwise have starved. In this narrow context—where no other food was available—formula was a lifesaver.

However, as time went on, and the subject of human nutrition in general—and infant nutrition, in particular—became more 'scientific', manufactured breastmilk substitutes were sold to the general public as a technological improvement on breastmilk.

'If anybody were to ask 'which formula should I use?' or 'which is nearest to mother's milk?', the answer would be 'nobody knows' because there is not one single objective source of that kind of information provided by anybody,' says Mary Smale, a breastfeeding counsellor with the National Childbirth Trust (NCT) for 28 years. 'Only the manufacturers know what's in their stuff, and they aren't telling. They may advertise special 'healthy' ingredients like oligosaccharides, long-chain fatty acids or, a while ago, beta-carotene, but they never actually tell you what the basic product is made from or where the ingredients come from.'

> **"There can be no food more locally
> produced, more sustainable or more
> environmentally friendly than a mother's
> breastmilk, the only food required by an
> infant for the first six months of life.
> It is a naturally renewable resource,
> which requires no packaging or transport,
> results in no wastage and is free."**

The known constituents of breastmilk were and are used as a general reference for scientists devising infant formulas.

But, to this day, there is no actual 'formula' for formula. In fact, the process of producing infant formulas has, since its earliest days, been one of trial and error.

Within reason, manufacturers can put anything they like into formula. In fact, the recipe for one product can vary from batch to batch, according to the price and availability of ingredients. While we assume that formula is heavily regulated, no transparency is required of manufacturers: they do not, for example, have to log the specific constituents of any batch or brand with any authority.

Most commercial formulas are based on cow's milk. But before a baby can drink cow's milk in the form of infant formula, it needs to be severely modified. The protein and mineral content must be reduced and the carbohydrate content increased, usually by adding sugar. Milk fat, which is not easily absorbed by the human body, particularly one with an immature digestive system, is removed and substituted with vegetable, animal or mineral fats.

Vitamins and trace elements are added, but not always in their most easily digestible form. (This means that the claims that formula is 'nutritionally complete' are true, but only in the crudest sense of having had added the full complement of vitamins and mineral to a nutritionally inferior product.)

Many formulas are also highly sweetened. While most infant formulas do not contain sugar in the form of sucrose, they can contain high levels of other types of sugar such as lactose (milk sugar), fructose (fruit sugar), glucose (also known as dextrose, a simple sugar found in plants) and maltodextrose (malt sugar). Because of a loophole in the law, these can still be advertised as 'sucrose free'.

Formula may also contain unintentional contaminants introduced during the manufacturing process. Some may contain traces of genetically engineered soya and corn.

The bacteria *Salmonella* and aflatoxins—potent toxic, carcinogenic, mutagenic, immunosuppressive agents produced by species of the fungus *Aspergillus*—have regularly been detected in commercial formulas, as has *Enterobacter sakazakii*, a devastating foodborne pathogen that can cause sepsis (overwhelming bacterial infection in the bloodstream), meningitis (inflammation of the lining of the brain) and necrotising enterocolitis (severe infection and inflammation of the small intestine and colon) in newborn infants.

The packaging of infant formulas occasionally gives rise to contamination with broken glass and fragments of metal as well as industrial chemicals such as phthalates and bisphenol A (both carcinogens) and, most recently, the packaging constituent isopropyl thioxanthone (ITX; another suspected carcinogen).

Infant formulas may also contain excessive levels of toxic or heavy metals, including aluminum, manganese, cadmium and lead.

Soya formulas are of particular concern due to the very high levels of plant-derived oestrogens (phytoestrogens) they contain. In fact, concentrations of phytoestrogens detected in the blood of infants receiving soya formula can be 13,000 to 22,000 times greater than the concentrations of natural oestrogens. Oestrogen in doses above those normally found in the body can cause cancer.

Killing Babies

For years, it was believed that the risks of illness and death from bottlefeeding were largely confined to children in developing countries, where the clean water necessary to make up formula is sometimes scarce and where poverty-stricken mothers may feel obliged to dilute formula to make it stretch further, thus risking waterborne illnesses such as diarrhoea and cholera as well as malnutrition in their babies. But newer data from the West clearly show that babies in otherwise affluent societies are also falling ill and dying due to an early diet of infant convenience food.

Because it is not nutritionally complete, because it does not contain the immune-boosting properties of breastmilk and because it is being consumed by growing babies with vast, ever-changing nutritional needs—and not meeting those needs—the health effects of sucking down formula day after day early in life can be devastating in both the short and long term.

Bottlefed babies are twice as likely to die from any cause in the first six weeks of life. In particular, bottlefeeding raises the risk of SIDS (sudden infant death syndrome) by two to five times. Bottlefed babies are also at a significantly higher risk of ending up in hospital with a range of infections. They are, for instance, five times more likely to be admitted to hospital suffering from gastroenteritis.

Even in developed countries, bottlefed babies have rates of diarrhoea twice as high as breastfed ones. They are twice as likely (20 per cent vs 10 per cent) to suffer from otitis media (inner-ear infection), twice as likely to develop eczema or a

Breastmilk vs Formula: No Contest

Breastmilk is a 'live' food that contains living cells, hormones, active enzymes, antibodies and at least 400 other unique components. It is a dynamic substance, the composition of which changes from the beginning to the end of the feed and according to the age and needs of the baby. Because it also provides active immunity, every time a baby breastfeeds it also receives protection from disease.

Compared to this miraculous substance, the artificial milk sold as infant formula is little more than junk food. It is also the only manufactured food that humans are encouraged to consume exclusively for a period of months, even though we know that no human body can be expected to stay healthy and thrive on a steady diet of processed food.

Breast Milk	Formula	Comments
Fats		
Rich in brain-building omega-3s, namely, DHA and AA. Automatically adjusts to infant's needs; levels decline as baby gets older. Rich in cholesterol; nearly completely absorbed. Contains the fat-digesting enzyme lipase	No DHA. Doesn't adjust to infant's needs. No cholesterol. Not completely absorbed. No lipase	The most important nutrient in breastmilk; the absence of cholesterol and DHA may predispose a child to adult heart and CNS diseases. Leftover, unabsorbed fat accounts for unpleasant smelling stools in formula-fed babies
Protein		
Soft, easily digestible whey. More completely absorbed; higher in the milk of mothers who deliver preterm. Lactoferrin for intestinal health. Lysozyme, an antimicrobial. Rich in brain- and body-building protein components. Rich in growth factors. Contains sleep-inducing proteins	Harder-to-digest casein curds. Not completely absorbed, so more waste, harder on kidneys. Little or no lactoferrin. No lysozyme. Deficient or low in some brain and body-building proteins. Deficient in growth factors. Contains fewer sleep-inducing proteins	Infants aren't allergic to human milk proteins
Carbohydrates		
Rich in oligosaccharides, which promote intestinal health	No lactose in some formulas. Deficient in oligosaccharides	Lactose is important for brain development
Immune-boosters		
Millions of living white blood cells, in every feeding. Rich in immunoglobulins	No live white blood cells or any other cells. Has no immune benefit	Breastfeeding provides active and dynamic protection from infections of all kinds. Breastmilk can be used to alleviate a range of external health problems such as nappy rash and conjunctivitis
Vitamins & Minerals		
Better absorbed. Iron is 50–75 per cent absorbed. Contains more selenium (an antioxidant)	Not absorbed as well. Iron is 5–10 per cent absorbed. Contains less selenium (an antioxidant)	Nutrients in formula are poorly absorbed. To compensate, more nutrients are added to formula, making it harder to digest
Enzymes & Hormones		
Rich in digestive enzymes such as lipase and amylase. Rich in many hormones such as thyroid, prolactin and oxytocin. Taste varies with mother's diet, thus helping the child acclimatise to the cultural diet	Processing kills digestive enzymes. Processing kills hormones, which are not human to begin with. Always tastes the same	Digestive enzymes promote intestinal health; hormones contribute to the biochemical balance and wellbeing of the baby
Cost		
Around £350/year in extra food for mother if she was on a very poor diet to begin with	Around £650/year. Up to £1300/year for hypoallergenic formulas. Cost for bottles and other supplies. Lost income when parents must stay home to care for a sick baby	In the UK, the NHS spends £35 million each year just treating gastroenteritis in bottlefed babies. In the US, insurance companies pay out $3.6 billion for treating diseases in bottlefed babies

wheeze if there is a family history of atopic disease, and five times more likely to develop urinary tract infections. In the first six months of life, bottlefed babies are six to 10 times more likely to develop necrotising enterocolitis—a serious infection of the intestine, with intestinal tissue death—a figure that increases to 30 times the risk after that time.

Even more serious diseases are also linked with bottle-feeding. Compared with infants who are fully breastfed even for only three to four months, a baby drinking artificial milk is twice as likely to develop juvenile-onset insulin-dependent (type 1) diabetes. There is also a five- to eightfold risk of developing lymphomas in children under 15 who were formulated, or breastfed for less than six months.

In later life, studies have shown that bottlefed babies have a greater tendency towards developing conditions such as childhood inflammatory bowel disease, multiple sclerosis, dental malocclusion, coronary heart disease, diabetes, hyperactivity, autoimmune thyroid disease and coeliac disease.

For all of these reasons, formula cannot be considered even 'second best' compared with breastmilk. Officially, the World Health Organization (WHO) designates formula milk as the last choice in infant-feeding: Its first choice is breastmilk from the mother; second choice is the mother's own milk given via cup or bottle; third choice is breastmilk from a milk bank or wet nurse and, finally, in fourth place, formula milk.

And yet, breastfed babies are becoming an endangered species. In the UK, rates are catastrophically low and have been that way for decades. Current figures suggest that only 62 per cent of women in Britain even attempt to breastfeed (usually while in hospital). At six weeks, just 42 per cent are breastfeeding. By four months, only 29 per cent are still breastfeeding and, by six months, this figure drops to 22 per cent.

These figures could come from almost any developed country in the world and, it should be noted, do not necessarily reflect the ideal of 'exclusive' breastfeeding. Instead, many modern mothers practice mixed feeding—combining breastfeeding with artificial baby milks and infant foods. Worldwide, the WHO estimates that only 35 per cent of infants are getting any breastmilk at all by age four months and, although no one can say for sure because research into exclusive breastfeeding is both scarce and incomplete, it is estimated that only 1 per cent are exclusively breastfed at six months.

Younger women in particular are the least likely to breastfeed, with over 40 per cent of mothers under 24 never even trying. The biggest gap, however, is a socioeconomic one. Women who live in low-income households or who are poorly educated are many times less likely to breastfeed, even though it can make an enormous difference to a child's health.

In children from socially disadvantaged families, exclusive breastfeeding in the first six months of life can go a long way towards cancelling out the health inequalities between being born into poverty and being born into affluence. In essence, breastfeeding takes the infant out of poverty for those first crucial months and gives it a decent start in life.

So Why Aren't Women Breastfeeding?

Before bottles became the norm, breastfeeding was an activity of daily living based on mimicry, and learning within the family and community. Women became their own experts through the trial and error of the experience itself. But today, what should come more or less naturally has become extraordinarily complicated—the focus of global marketing strategies and politics, lawmaking, lobbying support groups, activists and the interference of a well-intentioned, but occasionally ineffective, cult of experts.

According to Mary Smale, it's confidence and the expectation of support that make the difference, particularly for socially disadvantaged women.

'The concept of 'self efficacy'—in other words, whether you think you can do something—is quite important. You can say to a woman that breastfeeding is really a good idea, but she's got to believe various things in order for it to work. First of all, she has to think it's a good idea—that it will be good for her and her baby. Second, she has to think: 'I'm the sort of person who can do that'; third—and maybe the most important thing—is the belief that if she does have problems, she's the sort of person who, with help, will be able to sort them out.

'Studies show, for example, that women on low incomes often believe that breastfeeding hurts, and they also tend to believe that formula is just as good. So from the start, the motivation to breastfeed simply isn't there. But really, it's the thought that if there were any problems, you couldn't do anything about them; that, for instance, if it hurts, it's just the luck of the draw. This mindset is very different from that of a middle-class mother who is used to asking for help to solve things, who isn't frightened of picking up the phone, or saying to her midwife or health visitor, 'I want you to help me with this'.'

Nearly all women—around 99 per cent—can breastfeed successfully and make enough milk for their babies to not simply grow, but to thrive. With encouragement, support and help, almost all women are willing to initiate breastfeeding, but the drop-off rates are alarming: 90 per cent of women who give up in the first six weeks say that they would like to have continued. And it seems likely that long-term exclusive breastfeeding rates could be improved if consistent support were available, and if approval within the family and the wider community for breastfeeding, both at home and in public, were more obvious and widespread.

Clearly, this social support isn't there, and the bigger picture of breastfeeding vs bottlefeeding suggests that there is, in addition, a confluence of complex factors—medical, socioeconomic, cultural and political—that regularly undermine women's confidence, while reinforcing the notion that feeding their children artificially is about lifestyle rather than health, and that the modern woman's body is simply not up to the task of producing enough milk for its offspring.

'Breastfeeding is a natural negotiation between mother and baby and you interfere with it at your peril,' says Professor Mary Renfrew, Director of the Mother and Infant Research Unit, University of York. "But, in the early years of the last century, people were very busy interfering with it. In terms of the ecology of breastfeeding, what you have is a natural habitat that has been disturbed. But it's not just the presence of one big predator—the invention of artificial milk—that is important. It is the fact that the habitat was already weakened by other forces that made it so vulnerable to disaster.

Are infant formula manufacturers simply clever entrepreneurs doing their jobs or human-rights violators of the worst kind?

'If you look at medical textbooks from the early part of the 20th century, you'll find many quotes about making breast-feeding scientific and exact, and it's out of these that you can see things beginning to fall apart.' This falling apart, says Renfrew, is largely due to the fear and mistrust that science had of the natural process of breastfeeding. In particular, the fact that a mother can put a baby on the breast and do something else while breastfeeding, and have the baby naturally come off the breast when it's had enough, was seen as disorderly and inexact. The medical/scientific model replaced this natural situation with precise measurements—for instance, how many millilitres of milk a baby should ideally have at each sitting—which skewed the natural balance between mother and baby, and established bottlefeeding as a biological norm.

Breastfeeding rates also began to decline as a consequence of women's changed circumstances after World War I, as more women left their children behind to go into the workplace as a consequence of women's emancipation—and the loss of men in the 'killing fields'—and to an even larger extent with the advent of World War II, when even more women entered into employment outside of the home.

'There was also the first wave of feminism,' says Renfrew, 'which stamped into everyone's consciousness in the 60s, and encouraged women get away from their babies and start living their lives. So the one thing that might have helped—women supporting each other—actually created a situation where even the intellectual, engaged, consciously aware women who might have questioned this got lost for a while. As a consequence, we ended up with a widespread and declining confidence in breastfeeding, a declining understanding of its importance and a declining ability of health professionals to support it. And, of course, all this ran along the same timeline as the technological development of artificial milk and the free availability of formula.'

Medicalised Birth

Before World War II, pregnancy and birth—and, by extension, breastfeeding—were part of the continuum of normal life. Women gave birth at home with the assistance and support of trained midwives, who were themselves part of the community, and afterwards they breastfed with the encouragement of family and friends.

Taking birth out of the community and relocating it into hospitals gave rise to the medicalisation of women's reproductive lives. Life events were transformed into medical problems, and traditional knowledge was replaced with scientific and technological solutions. This medicalisation resulted in a cascade of interventions that deeply undermined women's confidence in their abilities to conceive and grow a healthy baby, give birth to it and then feed it.

The cascade falls something like this: Hospitals are institutions; they are impersonal and, of necessity, must run on schedules and routines. For a hospital to run smoothly,

patients must ideally be sedate and immobile. For the woman giving birth, this meant lying on her back in a bed, an unnatural position that made labour slow, unproductive and very much more painful.

To 'fix' these iatrogenically dysfunctional labours, doctors developed a range of drugs (usually synthetic hormones such as prostaglandins or syntocinon), technologies (such as forceps and vacuum extraction) and procedures (such as episiotomies) to speed the process up. Speeding up labour artificially made it even more painful and this, in turn, led to the development of an array of pain-relieving drugs. Many of these were so powerful that the mother was often unconscious or deeply sedated at the moment of delivery and, thus, unable to offer her breast to her newborn infant.

All pain-relieving drugs cross the placenta, so even if the mother were conscious, her baby may not have been, or may have been so heavily drugged that its natural rooting instincts (which help it find the nipple) and muscle coordination (necessary to latch properly onto the breast) were severely impaired.

While both mother and baby were recovering from the ordeal of a medicalised birth, they were, until the 1970s and 1980s, routinely separated. Often, the baby wasn't 'allowed' to breastfeed until it had a bottle first, in case there was something wrong with its gastrointestinal tract. Breastfeeding, when it took place at all, took place according to strict schedules. These feeding schedules—usually on a three- or four-hourly basis—were totally unnatural for human newborns, who need to feed 12 or more times in any 24-hour period. Babies who were inevitably hungry between feeds were routinely given supplements of water and/or formula.

'There was lots of topping up,' says Professor Renfrew. 'The way this 'scientific' breastfeeding happened in hospital was that the baby would be given two minutes on each breast on day one, then four minutes on each breast on day two, seven minutes on each on day three, and so on. This created enormous anxiety since the mother would then be watching the clock instead of the baby. The babies would then get topped-up after every feed, then topped-up again throughout the night rather than brought to their mothers to feed. So you had a situation where the babies were crying in the nursery, and the mothers were crying in the postnatal ward. That's what we called 'normal' all throughout the 60s and 70s.'

Breastmilk is produced on a supply-and-demand basis, and these topping-up routines, which assuaged infant hunger and lessened demand, also reduced the mother's milk supply. As a result, women at the mercy of institutionalised birth experienced breastfeeding as a frustrating struggle that was often painful and just as often unsuccessful.

When, under these impossible circumstances, breastfeeding 'failed', formula was offered as a 'nutritionally complete solution' that was also more 'modern', 'cleaner' and more 'socially acceptable'.

At least two generations of women have been subjected to these kinds of damaging routines and, as a result, many of today's mothers find the concept of breastfeeding strange and unfamiliar, and very often framed as something that can and frequently does not 'take', something they might 'have a go' at but, equally, something that they shouldn't feel too badly about if it doesn't work out.

Professional Failures

The same young doctors, nurses and midwives who were pioneering this medical model of reproduction are now running today's health services. So, perhaps not surprisingly, modern hospitals are, at heart, little different from their predecessors. They may have TVs and CD players, and prettier wallpaper, and the drugs may be more sophisticated, but the basic goals and principles of medicalised birth have changed very little in the last 40 years—and the effect on breastfeeding is still as devastating.

In many cases, the healthcare providers' views on infant-feeding are based on their own, highly personal experiences. Surveys show, for instance, that the most important factor influencing the effectiveness and accuracy of a doctor's breastfeeding advice is whether the doctor herself, or the doctor's wife, had breastfed her children. Likewise, a midwife, nurse or health visitor formulated her own children is unlikely to be an effective advocate for breastfeeding.

Women do not fail to breastfeed. Health professionals, health agencies and governments fail to educate and support women who want to breastfeed.

More worrying, these professionals can end up perpetuating damaging myths about breastfeeding that facilitate its failure. In some hospitals, women are still advised to limit the amount of time, at first, that a baby sucks on each breast, to 'toughen up' their nipples. Or they are told their babies get all the milk they 'need' in the first 10 minutes and sucking after this time is unnecessary. Some are still told to stick to four-hour feeding schedules. Figures from the UK's Office of National Statistics show that we are still topping babies up. In 2002, nearly 30 per cent of babies in UK hospitals were given supplemental bottles by hospital staff, and nearly 20 per cent of all babies were separated from their mothers at some point while in hospital.

Continued inappropriate advice from medical professionals is one reason why, in 1991, UNICEF started the Baby Friendly Hospital Initiative (BFHI)—a certification system for hospitals meeting certain criteria known to promote successful breastfeeding. These criteria include: training all healthcare staff on how to facilitate breastfeeding; helping mothers start breastfeeding within one hour of birth; giving newborn infants no food or drink other than breastmilk, unless medically indicated; and the hospital not accepting free or heavily discounted formula and supplies. In principle, it is an important step in the promotion of breastfeeding, and studies show that women who give birth in Baby Friendly hospitals do breastfeed for longer.

In Scotland, for example, where around 50 per cent of hospitals are rated Baby Friendly, breastfeeding initiation rates have increased dramatically in recent years. In Cuba, where 49 of the country's 56 hospitals and maternity facilities are Baby Friendly, the rate of exclusive breastfeeding at four months almost tripled in six years—from 25 per cent in 1990 to 72 per cent in 1996. Similar increases have been found in Bangladesh, Brazil and China.

Unfortunately, interest in obtaining BFHI status is not universal. In the UK, only 43 hospitals (representing just 16 per cent of all UK hospitals) have achieved full accreditation—and none are in London. Out of the approximately 16,000 hospitals worldwide that have qualified for the Baby Friendly designation, only 32 are in the US. What's more, while Baby Friendly hospitals achieve a high initiation rate, they cannot guarantee continuation of breastfeeding once the woman is back in the community. Even among women who give birth in Baby Friendly hospitals, the number who exclusively breastfeed for six months is unacceptably low.

The Influence of Advertising

Baby Friendly hospitals face a daunting task in combatting the laissez-faire and general ignorance of health professionals, mothers and the public at large. They are also fighting a difficult battle with an acquiescent media which, through politically correct editorialising aimed at assuaging mothers' guilt if they bottlefeed and, more influentially, through advertising, has helped redefine formula as an acceptable choice.

Although there are now stricter limitations on the advertising of infant formula, for years, manufacturers were able, through advertising and promotion, to define the issue of infant-feeding in both the scientific world (for instance, by providing doctors with growth charts that established the growth patterns of bottlefed babies as the norm) and in its wider social context, reframing perceptions of what is appropriate and what is not.

As a result, in the absence of communities of women talking to each other about pregnancy, birthing and mothering, women's choices today are more directly influenced by commercial leaflets, booklets and advertising than almost anything else.

Baby-milk manufacturers spend countless millions devising marketing strategies that keep their products at the forefront of public consciousness. In the UK, formula companies spend at least £12 million per year on booklets, leaflets and other promotions, often in the guise of 'educational materials'. This works out at approximately £20 per baby born. In contrast, the UK government spends about 14 pence per newborn each year to promote breastfeeding.

It's a pattern of inequity that is repeated throughout the world—and not just in the arena of infant-feeding. The food-industry's global advertising budget is $40 billion, a figure greater than the gross domestic product (GDP) of 70 per cent of the world's nations. For every $1 spent by the WHO on preventing the diseases caused by Western diets, more than $500 is spent by the food industry to promote such diets.

Since they can no longer advertise infant formulas directly to women (for instance, in mother and baby magazines or through direct leafleting), or hand out free samples in hospitals or clinics, manufacturers have started to exploit other outlets, such as mother and baby clubs, and Internet sites that purport to help busy mothers get all the information they need about infant-feeding. They also occasionally rely on subterfuge. Manufacturers are allowed to advertise follow-on milks, suitable for babies over six months, to parents. But, sometimes, these ads feature a picture of a much younger baby, implying the product's suitability for infants.

The impact of these types of promotions should not be underestimated. A 2005 NCT/UNICEF study in the UK determined that one third of British mothers who admitted to seeing formula advertisements in the previous six months believed that infant formula was as good or better than breastmilk. This revelation is all the more surprising since advertising of infant formula to mothers has been banned for many years in several countries, including the UK.

To get around restrictions that prevent direct advertising to parents, manufacturers use a number of psychological strategies that focus on the natural worries that new parents have about the health of their babies. Many of today's formulas, for instance, are conceived and sold as solutions to the 'medical' problems of infants such as lactose intolerance, incomplete digestion and being 'too hungry'—even though many of these problems can be caused by inappropriately giving cow's milk formula in the first place.

Helmut Maucher, a powerful corporate lobbyist and honorary chairman of Nestlé—the company that claims 40 percent of the global baby-food market—has gone on record as saying: 'Ethical decisions that injure a firm's ability to compete are actually immoral'.

The socioeconomic divide among breastfeeding mothers is also exploited by formula manufacturers, as targeting low-income women (with advertising as well as through welfare schemes) has proven very profitable.

When presented with the opportunity to provide their children with the best that science has to offer, many low-income mothers are naturally tempted by formula. This is especially true if they receive free samples, as is still the case in many developing countries.

But the supply-and-demand nature of breastmilk is such that, once a mother accepts these free samples and starts her baby on formula, her own milk supply will quickly dry up. Sadly, after these mothers run out of formula samples and money-off coupons, they will find themselves unable to produce breastmilk and have no option but to spend large sums of money on continuing to feed their child with formula.

Even when manufacturers 'promote' breastfeeding, they plant what Mary Smale calls 'seeds of 'conditionality' that can lead to failure. 'Several years ago, manufacturers used to produce these amazing leaflets for women, encouraging women to breastfeed and reassuring them that they only need a few extra calories a day. You couldn't fault them on the words, but the pictures which were of things like Marks & Spencer yoghurt and whole fish with their heads on, and wholemeal bread—but not the sort of wholemeal bread that you buy in the corner shop, the sort of wholemeal bread you buy in specialist shops.

The underlying message was clear: a healthy pregnancy and a good supply of breastmilk are the preserve of the middle classes, and that any women who doesn't belong to that group will have to rely on other resources to provide for her baby.

A quick skim through any pregnancy magazine or the 'Bounty' pack—the glossy information booklet with free product samples given to new mothers in the UK—shows that these subtle visual messages, which include luxurious photos of whole grains and pulses, artistically arranged bowls of muesli, artisan loaves of bread and wedges of deli-style cheeses, exotic mangoes, grapes and kiwis, and fresh vegetables artistically arranged as crudités, are still prevalent.

Funding Research

Manufacturers also ply their influence through contact with health professionals (to whom they can provide free samples for research and 'educational purposes') as middlemen. Free gifts, educational trips to exotic locations and funding for research are just some of the ways in which the medical profession becomes 'educated' about the benefits of formula.

According to Patti Rundall, OBE, policy director for the UK's Baby Milk Action group, which has been lobbying for responsible marketing of baby food for over 20 years, 'Throughout the last two decades, the baby feeding companies have tried to establish a strong role for themselves with the medical profession, knowing that health and education services represent a key marketing opportunity. Companies are, for instance, keen to fund the infant-feeding research on which health policies are based, and to pay for midwives, teachers, education materials and community projects.'

They are also keen to fund 'critical' NGOs—that is, lay groups whose mandate is to inform and support women. But this sort of funding is not allowed by the International Code of Marketing of Breastmilk Substitutes (see below) because it prejudices the ability of these organisations to provide mothers with independent information about infant feeding. Nevertheless, such practices remain prevalent—if somewhat more discreet than in the past—and continue to weaken health professionals' advocacy for breastfeeding.

Fighting Back

When it became clear that declining breastfeeding rates were affecting infant health and that the advertising of infant formula had a direct effect on a woman's decision not to breastfeed, the International Code of Marketing of Breastmilk Substitutes was drafted and eventually adopted by the World Health Assembly (WHA) in 1981. The vote was near-unanimous, with 118 member nations voting in favour, three abstaining and one—the US—voting against. (In 1994, after years of opposition, the US eventually joined every other developed nation in the world as a signatory to the Code.)

The Code is a unique instrument that promotes safe and adequate nutrition for infants on a global scale by trying to protect breastfeeding and ensuring the appropriate marketing of breastmilk substitutes. It applies to all products marketed as partial or total replacements for breastmilk, including infant formula, follow-on formula, special formulas, cereals, juices, vegetable mixes and baby teas, and also applies to feeding bottles and teats. In addition, it maintains that no infant food may be marketed in ways that undermine breastfeeding. Specifically, the Code:

- Bans all advertising or promotion of these products to the general public
- Bans samples and gifts to mothers and health workers
- Requires information materials to advocate for breastfeeding, to warn against bottlefeeding and to not contain pictures of babies or text that idealises the use of breastmilk substitutes
- Bans the use of the healthcare system to promote breastmilk substitutes
- Bans free or low-cost supplies of breastmilk substitutes
- Allows health professionals to receive samples, but only for research purposes
- Demands that product information be factual and scientific
- Bans sales incentives for breastmilk substitutes and direct contact with mothers
- Requires that labels inform fully on the correct use of infant formula and the risks of misuse
- Requires labels not to discourage breastfeeding.

This document probably couldn't have been created today. Since the founding of the World Trade Organization (WTO) and its 'free trade' ethos in 1995, the increasing sophistication of corporate power strategies and aggressive lobbying of health organisations has increased to the extent that the Code would have been binned long before it reached the voting stage.

However, in 1981, member states, corporations and NGOs were on a somewhat more equal footing. By preventing industry from advertising infant formula, giving out free samples, promoting their products in healthcare facilities or by way of mother-and-baby 'goody bags', and insisting on better labelling, the Code acts to regulate an industry that would otherwise be given a free hand to pedal an inferior food product to babies and infants.

Unfortunately . . .

Being a signatory to the Code does not mean that member countries are obliged to adopt its recommendations wholesale. Many countries, the UK included, have adopted only parts of it—for instance, the basic principle that breastfeeding is a good thing—while ignoring the nuts-and-bolts strategies that limit advertising and corporate contact with mothers. So, in the UK, infant formula for 'healthy babies' can be advertised to mothers through hospitals and clinics, though not via the media.

'Breastfeeding is a natural negotiation between mother and baby and you interfere with it at your peril'.

Professor Mary Renfrew,
University of York

What's more, formula manufacturers for their part continue to argue that the Code is too restrictive and that it stops them from fully exploiting their target markets. Indeed, Helmut Maucher, a powerful corporate lobbyist and honorary chairman of Nestlé—the company that claims 40 per cent of the global baby-food market—has gone on record as saying: 'Ethical decisions that injure a firm's ability to compete are actually immoral'.

And make no mistake, these markets are big. The UK baby milk market is worth £150 million per year and the US market around $2 billion. The worldwide market for baby milks and foods is a staggering $17 billion and growing by 12 per cent each year. From formula manufacturers' point of view, the more women breastfeed, the more profit is lost. It is estimated that, for every child exclusively breastfed for six months, an average of $450 worth of infant food will not be bought. On a global scale, that amounts to billions of dollars in lost profits.

What particularly worries manufacturers is that, if they accept the Code without a fight, it could set a dangerous precedent for other areas of international trade—for instance, the pharmaceutical, tobacco, food and agriculture industries, and oil companies. This is why the focus on infant-feeding has been diverted away from children's health and instead become a symbolic struggle for a free market.

While most manufacturers publicly agree to adhere to the Code, privately, they deploy enormous resources in constructing ways to reinterpret or get round it. In this endeavour, Nestlé has shown a defiance and tenacity that beggars belief.

In India, for example, Nestlé lobbied against the Code being entered into law and when, after the law was passed, it faced criminal charges over its labelling, it issued a writ petition against the Indian government rather than accept the charges.

Years of aggressive actions like this, combined with unethical advertising and marketing practices, has led to an ongoing campaign to boycott the company's products that stretches back to 1977.

The Achilles' heel of the Code is that it does not provide for a monitoring office. This concept was in the original draft, but was removed from subsequent drafts. Instead, monitoring of the Code has been left to 'governments acting individually and collectively through the World Health Organization'.

But, over the last 25 years, corporate accountability has slipped lower down on the UN agenda, far behind free trade, self-regulation and partnerships. Lack of government monitoring means that small and comparatively poorly funded groups like the International Baby Food Action Network (IBFAN), which has 200 member groups working in over 100 countries, have taken on the job of monitoring Code violations almost by default. But while these watchdog groups can monitor and report Code violations to the health authorities, they cannot stop them.

In 2004, IBFAN's bi-annual report *Breaking the Rules, Stretching the Rules,* analysed the promotional practices of 16 international baby-food companies, and 14 bottle and teat companies, between January 2002 and April 2004. The researchers found some 2,000 violations of the Code in 69 countries.

On a global scale, reinterpreting the Code to suit marketing strategies is rife, and Nestlé continues to be the leader of the pack. According to IBFAN, Nestlé believes that only one of its products—infant formula—comes within the scope of the Code. The company also denies the universality of the Code, insisting that it only applies to developing nations. Where Nestlé, and the Infant Food Manufacturers Association that it dominates, leads, other companies have followed, and when companies like Nestlé are caught breaking the Code, the strategy is simple, but effective—initiate complex and boring discussions with organisations at WHO or WHA level about how best to interpret the Code in the hopes that these will offset any bad publicity and divert attention from the harm caused by these continual infractions.

According to Patti Rundall, it's important not to let such distractions divert attention from the bottom line: 'There can be no food more locally produced, more sustainable or more environmentally friendly than a mother's breastmilk, the only food required by an infant for the first six months of life. It is a naturally renewable resource, which requires no packaging or transport, results in no wastage and is free. Breastfeeding can also help reduce family poverty, which is a major cause of malnutrition.'

So perhaps we should be further simplifying the debate by asking: Are the companies who promote infant formula as the norm simply clever entrepreneurs doing their jobs or human-rights violators of the worst kind?

Not Good Enough

After more than two decades, it is clear that a half-hearted advocacy of breastfeeding benefits multinational formula manufacturers, not mothers and babies, and that the baby-food industry has no intention of complying with UN recommendations on infant-feeding or with the principles of the International Code for Marketing of Breastmilk Substitutes—unless they are forced to do so by law or consumer pressure or, more effectively, both.

Women do not fail to breastfeed. Health professionals, health agencies and governments fail to educate and support women who want to breastfeed.

Without support, many women will give up when they encounter even small difficulties. And yet, according to Mary Renfrew, 'Giving up breastfeeding is not something that women do lightly. They don't just stop breastfeeding and walk away from it. Many of them fight very hard to continue it and they fight with no support. These women are fighting society—a society that is not just bottle-friendly, but is deeply breastfeeding-unfriendly.'

To reverse this trend, governments all over the world must begin to take seriously the responsibility of ensuring the good health of future generations. To do this requires deep and profound social change. We must stop harassing mothers with simplistic 'breast is best' messages and put time, energy and money into reeducating health professionals and society at large.

We must also stop making compromises. Government health policies such as, say, in the UK and US, which aim for 75 per cent of women to be breastfeeding on hospital discharge, are little more than paying lip service to the importance of breastfeeding.

Most of these women will stop breastfeeding within a few weeks, and such policies benefit no one except the formula manufacturers, who will start making money the moment breastfeeding stops.

To get all mothers breastfeeding, we must be prepared to:

- Ban all advertising of formula including follow-on milks
- Ban all free samples of formula, even those given for educational or study purposes
- Require truthful and prominent health warnings on all tins and cartons of infant formula
- Put substantial funding into promoting breastfeeding in every community, especially among the socially disadvantaged, with a view to achieving 100-per-cent exclusive breastfeeding for the first six months of life
- Fund advertising and education campaigns that target fathers, mothers-in-law, schoolchildren, doctors, midwives and the general public
- Give women who wish to breastfeed in public the necessary encouragement and approval
- Make provisions for all women who are in employment to take at least six months paid leave after birth, without fear of losing their jobs.

Such strategies have already proven their worth elsewhere. In 1970, breastfeeding rates in Scandinavia were as low as those in Britain. Then, one by one, the Scandinavian countries banned all advertising of artificial formula milk, offered a year's maternity leave with 80 per cent of pay and, on the mother's return to work, an hour's breastfeeding break every day. Today, 98 per cent of Scandinavian women initiate breastfeeding, and 94 per cent are still breastfeeding at one month, 81 per cent at two months, 69 per cent at four months and 42 per cent at six months. These rates, albeit still not optimal, are nevertheless the highest in the world, and the result of a concerted, multifaceted approach to promoting breastfeeding.

Given all that we know of the benefits of breastfeeding and the dangers of formula milk, it is simply not acceptable that we have allowed breastfeeding rates in the UK and elsewhere in the world to decline so disastrously.

The goal is clear—100 per cent of mothers should be exclusively breastfeeding for at least the first six months of their babies' lives.

Food News Blues

Fat is bad, but good fat is good. What about fish? Wine? Nuts? A new appetite for answers has put science on a collision course with the media.

BARBARA KANTROWITZ AND CLAUDIA KALB

You couldn't miss the headlines. The New York Times: LOW-FAT DIET DOES NOT CUT HEALTH RISKS, STUDY FINDS. The Atlanta Journal-Constitution: REDUCING FAT MAY NOT CURB DISEASE. The Boston Globe: STUDY FINDS NO MAJOR BENEFIT OF A LOW-FAT DIET. The Los Angeles Times: EATING LEAN DOESN'T CUT RISK. When the results of a massive, federally funded study were released last month, TV, newspapers and, yes, magazines around the country trumpeted what seemed to confound conventional wisdom and standard medical advice. Fat, these articles seemed to say, wasn't so bad for you after all. In fact, the results of the study, the Women's Health Initiative (WHI), were actually more complex—as all these articles explained to readers who got beyond the headlines.

'America, step away from the french fries . . . Despite new reports, less is still best'

—USA Today, Feb. 28, 2006

It wasn't (as many of us might have hoped) a signal to rush out and gorge on cheeseburgers—especially if you're a man of any age or a woman under 50. That's because the study involved only older women—from 50 to 79. And the primary goal was far narrower than those headlines implied: to test whether cutting fat would reduce the risk, specifically, of breast cancer. After an average of eight years, researchers found no statistically significant difference in breast-cancer risk between women on a low-fat diet and women who had made no changes in what they ate. But that is not the bottom line. The results showed what researchers call a "trend" toward a low-fat diet reducing breast-cancer risk; this effect was actually significant in those who started with the highest levels of fat. Scientists will observe the women until 2010, when we could hear a whole new message. "I wouldn't worry about the headlines of today as far as low fat

and breast cancer are concerned," says Dr. Jacques Rossouw, the WHI project officer. "They may be wrong."

To those of us without an M.D., it sometimes seems as if scientists are deliberately trying to mess with our heads—especially when it comes to nutrition research. The WHI study is the latest in what appears to be a series of dietary flip-flops. All fat was bad; now some fat is good. Eggs were bad; now they're OK in moderation. Nuts were *verboten;* now their fats are beneficial. Coffee has been up and down more often than hemlines. We've even been reading that chocolate could be a health food. (We've got some bad news on that. Read on.) Meanwhile, Americans are getting fatter and fatter. Two thirds are overweight or obese, and we're shelling out millions annually in a futile effort to shed those excess pounds.

Why all the mixed messages? Three words: too much information. Not so long ago patients got all their medical knowledge from their doctors. But now a media explosion has transformed that intimate relationship into an orgy of Web sites, cable- and network-TV medical reports, and magazine and newspaper stories heralding one breakthrough after another. Americans are more likely to hear first reports of the latest cancer treatment from CNN's Sanjay Gupta or ABC's Tim Johnson (both doctors) than from their own oncologist. From 1977 to 2004, the number of newspaper front-page stories on science tripled, from 1 to 3 percent, while foreign-affairs coverage plummeted from 27 to 14 percent, according to the Project for Excellence in Journalism, a group that monitors media coverage. In news magazines, the number of pages devoted to health and medical science has quadrupled since 1980. Last year, 10 out of 50 NEWSWEEK cover stories were on such health issues as lung cancer, autism and heart disease. The WHI fat story led TIP SHEET section in our Feb. 20 edition.

The pharmaceutical industry, wise to this proliferation of outlets and heightened consumer interest, spent $1.3 billion in magazine advertising last year, according to TNS Media Intelligence, a media-tracking service. An additional $2.4 billion went to network and cable TV.

Scientists themselves have become part of the media machine. In the old days, researchers who went public with their petri dishes were scorned by colleagues. Some still are. But the pressure to talk to reporters is enormous. Hospitals and universities send out press releases and publish glossy magazines about scientific advances within their ranks to generate buzz and maybe even research dollars. Drug companies hire physicians as consultants, then tout them as experts, setting up interviews with reporters about developments in a disease when the real motive is to promote a drug. And then there are the truly aggressive doctors—many of them in fields like dermatology and plastic surgery, where they are vying for patients—who hire their own public-relations reps who then mail press kits to reporters, complete with 8-by-10 photos. Even the most guarded scientists know that it's hard to hide, especially if their research is being paid for by the taxpaying public. They may seem like geeks in lab coats, but scientific research is hugely competitive—for attention, recognition and funding. The most egregious example: the South Korean stem-cell debacle. A supposed milestone in the controversial science—cloning human embryos to create stem cells—turned out to be a fraud. "Science is a contact sport," says Dr. Jeffrey Drazen, editor of the prestigious New England Journal of Medicine. "People think about it being genteel, but it's a tough game."

'Hold on to your olive oil. This study . . . did not differentiate between "good" and "bad" fats.'

—Knight Ridder, Feb. 28, 2006

All this coverage would be fine, perhaps even beneficial, if medical progress were as straightforward as it's often reported. Unfortunately, it's not. Headlines and sound bites can't capture the complexity of research. Science works in small steps, and failure and mistakes are an integral part of the process. Experiments flame out; hypotheses crash and burn. "Most science isn't a breakthrough," says Dr. Judah Folkman, the famed cancer researcher at Children's Hospital Boston who was involuntarily thrust into the spotlight by a 1998 New York Times story about his research. "It's incremental, brick by brick." But the public has big expectations. "Science and medicine have promised a lot," says Dr. Jerome Groopman of Harvard Medical School and a writer for The New Yorker. "We have all this technology, this information and resources, and we're making promises to people. In many cases, we still don't have the answers."

Published studies on the same topic can vary enormously in terms of sample size (small, medium, big), demographics (age, gender), data (self-reported versus objectively measured information) and length (weeks, months, years). Then there's the design of the study, a critical factor. The gold standard, a randomized, double-blind, placebo-controlled trial, is considered the most reliable because neither researchers nor participants know who is taking the medication being tested and who is taking the placebo (essentially a sugar pill).

Some studies, like the WHI, are prospective, which means a group of patients is watched from the beginning of a treatment, procedure or intervention. Others are retrospective: they look back at patient records to uncover hints about disease onset or patterns. Still others are "meta-analyses," overviews of existing studies on a similar theme. Even bad studies can get published in journals with less rigorous standards. "The media reports all studies as if they have the same degree of certainty," says Dr. Elias Zerhouni, director of the National Institutes of Health. "There's no real label of quality."

To really understand what's going on, you also have to follow the money. The government pays for much of basic science, but industries with a stake in the outcome often fund food and drug studies. An industry connection doesn't necessarily mean a study is wrong. Scientists have to rely on different sources of support in the increasingly ferocious battle for dollars. But, says Dr. Richard Deyo, professor of medicine at the University of Washington in Seattle, "when corporate sponsors fund research, it's more likely to show beneficial effects." For example, industry-funded studies have consistently concluded that soda can be part of a healthy diet. But non-industry studies find that sugary beverages contribute to obesity. The National Dairy Council pays for research on the link between dairy food and weight loss. The California Raisin Marketing Board underwrote a study showing that raisins fight oral bacteria. If raisins hadn't done the job, the public might never have known. Industry-funded studies with negative results are often not published.

The stars in this vast medical-research universe were perfectly aligned in the early 1990s, when the WHI began. Women's health advocates had been pushing for more research. The NIH had its first female director, Dr. Bernadine Healy. And there were serious questions about older women's health that needed answers. Observational studies, which follow people over time without intervening in their behavior, had suggested that estrogen might prevent heart disease; millions of women were urged to take it. Scientists also decided to study the role of a low-fat diet and the use of calcium and vitamin D supplements to protect against fractures from osteoporosis. Together, heart disease, breast cancer and osteoporosis represent major causes of death and disability in older women. Preventing these diseases could affect millions.

The WHI was a massive undertaking—the largest federally funded study of women's health, ultimately costing $725 million over 15 years. In the early to mid-1990s, WHI researchers recruited 161,808 women age 50 to 79 from all over the country. This in itself was a major achievement because joining the study was a serious commitment. The women had to agree to be tested regularly, fill in lots of forms, take medication without knowing whether it would help them or hurt them, and, in the case of the dietary study, learn to cook and eat in a completely different way.

From the beginning, the WHI was controversial. Scientists especially questioned the diet trial, which enrolled 48,835 women. Psychologist Kelly Brownell, director of Yale's Rudd Center for Food Policy and Obesity, was on a committee convened at the request of Congress in 1993 to review the WHI. He says committee members were concerned about the design.

Cancer and heart disease can take decades to develop. Would an eight-year trial be long enough? Would the women in the test group fully report their eating habits? Self-reports of dietary intake are notoriously inaccurate. On average, the participants weighed 170 pounds at the outset and reported that they ate 1,700 calories a day. By the end, they reported eating 1,400 to 1,500 calories daily. "They should have lost loads of weight," says Brownell. "Yet the women in the test group only lost three or four pounds. The control group actually gained about a pound. A scale is a scale. It won't lie. That screams out to me that the dietary records were inaccurate." It could mean that the difference in fat intake between the test and control groups wasn't large enough to show a distinct effect.

Docs may seem like geeks in lab coats, but scientific research is hugely competitive—for attention, recognition and funding.

The calcium and vitamin D study also had its critics. When it was designed, calcium was considered so important that researchers thought it would be unethical to tell women in the control group to stop taking supplements. In the end, the test subjects and the placebo group were both taking in roughly the same amount of calcium. So when the final results showed little difference in the fracture rate between the two groups, some scientists blamed the study design. And there was a second problem. The amount of vitamin D they were given is considered inadequate today. Most doctors still recommend calcium supplements if women can't get enough in their diets. "It was a disappointment that it was not better designed," says Joan Lappe, professor of medicine at the Osteoporosis Research Center at Creighton University. She and her colleagues are worried that the public is getting the message that calcium and vitamin D don't matter.

WHI investigators fired off their first bombshell in 2002, when they stopped the hormone study early after a safety-monitoring board concluded that the risks outweighed the benefits. Gynecologists' phones rang off the hook as millions of patients demanded to know if they'd been duped. That study continues to be a source of fierce debate. Although the results showed an increased risk of breast cancer, stroke, blood clots and heart disease in women who took estrogen and progestin, some scientists say the reaction was too strong. Many doctors believe younger women who take hormones for a short time to relieve menopausal symptoms like hot flashes are generally at low risk. There's also some evidence that estrogen might protect younger women against heart disease. Researchers are only beginning to study that issue.

Years ago this debate would have been confined to scientific circles. Medical journals would have filtered new research and doctors would have read the journals, discussed studies with colleagues and then figured out how to translate data into clinical practice. All this was hidden to patients. Now even the most respected journals have had to adapt to the growing demand for health information. When The Journal of the American Medical Association (JAMA) and The New England

Journal of Medicine were launched in the 19th century, they would have had no conception of a "publicity" department. But today, JAMA, which has published several WHI studies, spends $1 million annually on its media and communications program, says Dr. Catherine DeAngelis, the editor. Half goes to packaging video interviews, which TV reporters use in their stories. DeAngelis says the JAMA footage hits an average of 20 million viewers a week through local, national and international outlets. The other half of the money is used to run the communications office, hold press conferences and prepare press releases about upcoming studies, which reporters receive before the studies are published—if they tacitly agree not to print anything before the journal's publication date. If they agree to these "embargo" terms, they can question the scientists involved in the study and others who might have a more objective view of the research.

'Didn't the study find there's no value in taking calcium supplements?'
—The Washington Post, Feb. 28, 2006

All that was in place last month when the WHI released its diet study. The headline in the main JAMA article, published on Feb. 8, gave no hint that some readers might be tempted to head for Krispy Kreme: LOW-FAT DIETARY PATTERN AND RISK OF INVASIVE BREAST CANCER. Two other articles in the same issue discussed the impact of the diet on heart disease and colorectal cancer. Like any journal report, all three were laden with details, including the number of women in the trial (48,835) and the goals (to reduce fat to 20 percent of calories and to increase consumption of vegetables, fruit and grains). The conclusion of the breast-cancer study—that a low-fat diet did not lower risk—was fairly nuanced. It suggested that if the women were observed for a longer time, there might be more of an effect. At a conference last week at the National Institutes of Health, which sponsors the WHI, researchers were even more direct, saying that they hoped women would not start eating fat because of this study, but that message got lost in the headlines.

The diet study was a victim of its time. Fifteen years later, we know a lot more and understand that some fatty foods, like olive oil and avocados, may actually be beneficial. And some food labeled fat-free is full of calories, which might have accounted for some of the participants' weight issues. "These studies are more complicated than a simple headline or sound bite can convey, and that's an important lesson for all of us," says Dr. Elizabeth Nabel, director of the National Heart, Lung, and Blood Institute, which administers the WHI.

But to the average American, the WHI study just seemed like one more example of scientists unable to make up their minds. Dr. Mary Altz-Smith, a rheumatologist in Birmingham, Ala., is worried about the message it sent to her patients, many of whom are already overweight. "This information is all too likely to encourage patients to slide," she says. And who could blame them? Every day, the "truth" about diet seems ever more elusive even while scientists insist the picture is becoming clearer.

Coffee

- Experts used to believe that coffee could cause hypertension and heart disease.
- But in the 1990s studies refuted the link with heart attacks; a 2002 Johns Hopkins study found that, while male drinkers had higher blood pressure than nondrinkers, coffee was not a major factor.
- Although recent studies suggest that java may help ward off Parkinson's and diabetes, pregnant women may want to limit their intake.

Red Wine

- In the early '90s, red wine, which contains compounds like resveratrol, was thought to be especially good for heart health.
- But a 1996 Harvard study of beer, wine and spirits showed that drinking any alcoholic beverage in moderation—not just red wine— can be linked to lower rates of heart disease.
- Now experts say that 1–2 glasses a day may lower the risk of heart attack—but caution against starting to drink for health benefits alone.

Milk

- Nutritionists have long hyped calcium-rich milk for its strengthening effect on bones and teeth
- But recently some leading experts have questioned the need to drink milk in the government-recommended quantities. A 1997 Harvard study found that older women who drank more milk didn't suffer fewer fractures.
- The USDA still recommends 3 cups a day of low- or non-fat dairy, but also suggests leafy green veggies for calcium.

Nuts

- Thanks to the "carbs are good, fat is bad" trend of the '80s and '90s, dieters avoided nuts, which are high in fat.

- But most fat in nuts is "good," unsaturated fat that—when combined with nuts' fiber and antioxidants—could lower risk of heart disease. Recent studies—including 1998 Harvard research on women eating 5 oz. of nuts a week—have solidified the connection.
- Cut bad fats; sub in several ounces of nuts each week.

Eggs

- For decades, doctors believed that cholesterol-laden eggs were a major contributor to heart disease; in the '80s, Americans started to limit their intake.
- A '99 analysis by Harvard scientists found that eating up to one egg a day didn't increase the risk of heart disease or stroke in healthy people. Other studies have suggested that eggs don't raise cholesterol levels appreciably.
- Experts say eggs are fine in moderation.

Tuna

- Fish, including tuna, has traditionally been lauded as a good source of protein and other nutrients (most recently omega-3 fatty acids).
- But in 2001, growing concerns over mercury levels led the FDA to issue warnings directing children and pregnant women to limit consumption of certain fish. Tuna was added to the list in 2004.
- Those at risk should cut fish intake to 12 oz. a week; choose canned light tuna over albacore.

Olive Oil

- The USDA's 1992 food pyramid placed fats and oils at the very tip, telling Americans to consume these foods "sparingly."
- In 1999, a major clinical trial by French researchers showed that a diet high in olive and canola oils helped prevent heart attacks; other scientists have since singled out olive oil as a source of heart-healthy mono-unsaturated fat.
- Experts now recommend olive oil as an alternative to butter or margarine.

A classic case is margarine. Early on, it was touted to be better than butter, which contains saturated fat. But that was before scientists realized that margarine had an even more noxious ingredient: trans fat. Margarine became poison. Now the pendulum has shifted back a bit as manufacturers removed the bad fat and put in non-hydrogenated oils. "Those are better," says Dr. Walter Willett, chair of nutrition at the Harvard School of Public Health. "But it's still better to use liquid vegetable oils, like olive oil." And as for butter, the fact that margarine was worse doesn't make butter good. "It's not health food," Willett says.

'Diet fads and their alleged benefits have us eating in circles.'

—San Francisco Chronicle editorial, Feb. 20, 2006

More recently, chocolate appeared to be heading for that coveted health-food status, and the public was more than ready to gobble it up. It began when a 2001 study (funded by the American Cocoa Research Institute) found that cocoa powder and dark chocolate boosted good cholesterol by 4 percent. What most people didn't realize is that there were only 23 participants in this study, hardly enough to produce any serious conclusion. Nonetheless, it made headlines and was followed by additional chocolate studies that seemed to find even more benefits. But most of that research focused on a group of compounds in chocolate called flavanols—which unfortunately tend to get processed out of the chocolate you buy at the grocery store. And chocolate still has lots of fat, sugar and calories.

Just last week a study from the Netherlands published in the Archives of Internal Medicine found that participants who ate the most food containing chocolate (candy bars, spreads, pudding) had slightly lower blood pressure and were half as likely to have died from heart disease at the end of the 15-year follow-up. However, it's not clear that the results were strictly from chocolate. The biggest challenge in dietary research is that nobody eats only one thing. In this case, the chocolate lovers also ate less meat and more nuts. "This study is another piece of the puzzle," says Harold Schmitz, chief science officer of Mars Inc., the candy manufacturer. "As much as I'd love to say it puts the capstone on the research, it doesn't." And it could be years before there's a definitive answer.

Everyone's looking for an immediate solution, but science takes time. It took Judah Folkman decades to confirm his pioneering theory that cancerous tumors rely on a blood supply to grow. When The New York Times heralded his research on the front page with a headline that proclaimed HOPE IN THE LAB, TV, newspapers and magazines (including NEWSWEEK) picked up the story. Desperate patients flooded Folkman's lab with phone calls seeking help. But at the time, his research was only in mice, not men—a detail that many readers overlooked. It was years before Folkman's theory—called angiogenesis—translated into drugs that can actually help people. More than

anybody, Folkman understands how difficult it is to balance enthusiasm for scientific progress with the danger of hyping new developments. "That's the fundamental problem," he says. "We scientists don't always know how to share our excitement with the public without making our research sound overdone."

It's even more complicated with a study like the WHI, which is paid for by taxpayers and is of enormous interest to a wide range of people. What may have seemed like flip-flopping is actually an evolutionary process, says Stanford's Marcia Stefanick, chair of the WHI steering committee. "As we acquire new scientific information, we need to modify public-health recommendations." If the diet results were misinterpreted, there's probably blame all around. Journalists wanted juicy headlines and the public wanted a quick fix for fat. Scientists were trying to report their findings in the most digestible form while acknowledging that reality was more complex. It would be nice to think that everybody is a little bit wiser. For all their differences, scientists and journalists are on the same path. They should keep asking questions, not be discouraged by dead ends and be open-minded to surprising truths.

UNIT 4

Exercise and Weight Management

Unit Selections

Key Points to Consider

- How can exercise affect mental health and mental abilities?

- How important is exercise to achieving optimal health? Explain.

- Why should exercise be included in any weight control program?

- How do you feel about people who are overweight? Has your weight ever been a problem for you? If so, what have you done about it?

- Do you exercise on a regular basis? If not, why not? What would it take to get you exercising on a regular basis?

- For young athletes, is there such a thing as too much exercise?

- Should obesity be classified as a disease rather than a lack of willpower?

Student Web Site

www.mhcls.com/online

Internet References

Further information regarding these Web sites may be found in this book's preface or online.

American Society of Exercise Physiologists (ASEP)
   http://www.asep.org
Eating Disorders Awareness and Prevention, Inc.
   http://www.edap.org
Cyberdiet
   http://www.cyberdiet.com/reg/index.html
Shape Up America!
   http://www.shapeup.org

Recently, a new set of guidelines, dubbed "Exercise Lite," has been issued by the U.S. Centers for Disease Control and Prevention in conjunction with the American College of Sports Medicine. These guidelines call for 30 minutes of exercise, 5 days a week, which can be spread over the course of a day. The primary focus of this approach to exercise is improving health, not athletic performance. Examples of activities that qualify under the new guidelines are walking your dog, playing tag with your kids, scrubbing floors, washing your car, mowing the lawn, weeding your garden, and having sex. From a practical standpoint, this approach to fitness will likely motivate many more people to become active and stay active. Remember, since the benefits of exercise can take weeks or even months before they become apparent, it is very important to choose an exercise program that you enjoy so that you will stick with it. While a good diet cannot overcome lack of exercise, exercise can overcome a less than optimal diet. Exercise not lonely makes people physically healthier, it may also keep their brains healthy. While the connection hasn't been proven, there is evidence that regular workouts may cause the brain to better process and store information which results in a smarter brain.

While exercise and a nutritious diet can keep people fit and healthy, may Americans are not heeding this advice. For the first time in our history, the average American is now overweight when judged according to standard height/weight tables. In addition, more than 25 percent of Americans are clinically obese, and the numbers appear to be growing. Why is this happening, given the prevailing attitude that Americans have toward fat? One theory that is currently gaining support suggests that while Americans have cut back on their consumption of fatty snacks and deserts, they have actually increased their total caloric intake by failing to limit their consumption of carbohydrates. The underlying philosophy goes something like this: fat calories make you fat, but you can eat as many carbohydrates as you want and not gain weight. The truth is that all calories count when it comes to weight gain, and if cutting back on fat calories prevents you from feeling satiated you will naturally eat more to achieve that feeling. While this position seems reasonable enough, some groups, most notably supporters of the Atkins diet, have suggested that eating a high-fat diet will actually help people lose weight because of fat's high satiety value in conjunction with the formation of ketones (which suppress appetite). Whether people limit fat or carbohydrates, they will not lose weight unless their total caloric intake is less than their energy expenditure.

America's preoccupation with body weight has given rise to a billion-dollar industry. When asked why people go on diets, the predominant answer is for social reasons such as appearance and group acceptance, rather than concerns regarding health. Why do diets and diet aids fail? One of the major reasons lies in the mind-set of the dieter. Many dieters do not fully understand the biological and behavioral aspects of weight loss, and

Stockbyte/Punchstock

consequently they have unrealistic expectations regarding the process.

Being overweight not only causes health problems; it also carries with it a social stigma. Overweight people are often thought of as weak willed individuals with little or no self-respect. The notion that weight control problems are the result of personality defects is being challenged by new research findings. Evidence is mounting that suggests that physiological and hereditary factors may play as great a role in obesity as do behavioral and environmental factors. Researchers now believe that genetics dictate the base number of fat cells an individual will have, as well as the location and distribution of these cells within the body. The study of fat metabolism has provided additional clues as to why weight control is so difficult. These metabolic studies have found that the body seems to have a "setpoint," or desired weight, and it will defend this weight through alterations in basal metabolic rate and fat-cell activity. While this process is thought to be an adaptive throwback to primitive times when food supplies were uncertain, today, with our abundant food supply, this mechanism only contributes to the problem of weight control.

It should be apparent by now that weight control is both an attitudinal and a lifestyle issue. Fortunately, a new, more rational approach to the problem of weight control is emerging. This approach is based on the premise that you can be perfectly healthy and look good without being pencil-thin. The primary focus of this approach to weight management is the attainment of your body's "natural ideal weight" and not some idealized, fanciful notion of what you would like to weigh. The concept of achieving your natural ideal body weight suggests that we need to take a more realistic approach to both fitness and weight control and serves to remind us that a healthy lifestyle is based on the concepts of balance and moderation. That sentiment is echoed in "Exercise Abuse: Too Much of a Good Thing". Author Kate Jackson addresses individuals who abuse exercise by overdoing it to the point of physical injury, and other negative side effects.

Exercise Abuse
Too Much of a Good Thing

Know when your client has tipped the scales from healthy fitness to obsession.

Kate Jackson

Imagine a client who's diligent about exercise and walks every day for one hour. Sounds healthy, right? What if she never misses a day and exercises rain or shine, even after spraining an ankle or when she has the flu? As the picture becomes more complex, the client's behavior begins to sound less healthy and more obsessive and compulsive.

Excessive exercise—sometimes called *exercise abuse* or *addiction*—is defined as activity that has a deleterious effect on physical and psychological well-being, says Kelly Pedrotty, MA, exercise coordinator and program coordinator at the Renfrew Center of Philadelphia, a residential treatment center for individuals with eating disorders. "People who have a healthy view of exercise," she explains, "exercise because they enjoy it."

Those who exercise excessively have negative feelings about their workouts and may consider it painful. It's often difficult to discern, say experts, but the key difference between moderate and pathological exercise is that the latter is compulsive. The individuals have to do it all the time—every day—or they become anxious. "This need to engage in a behavior, such as exercise every day or repeatedly, is a sign of compulsion," says Elizabeth Carll, PhD, a psychologist and eating disorders specialist in private practice in Long Island, N.Y.

Rigorous activity by all means isn't always pathological. "Goals such as training for an athletic event or weight loss that is medically necessary are appropriate, and once those goals are reached, people cut back on the level of exercise intensity," explains Carll. "Exercise is compulsive and considered a disorder, however, when it is in response to free-floating anxiety, an obsessive need to improve the way one looks, or chronic dissatisfaction with one's appearance. The key difference is that those who have an addiction or compulsion can't stop."

Although men, women, and children can abuse exercise, it appears to be more common in women and is often linked with other psychological disorders such as depression or obsessive compulsive disorder. Compulsive patterns of exercise often go hand in hand with eating disorders, particularly anorexia nervosa.

Don't Go Gung-Ho

Juliet Zuercher, RD, director of nutrition at Remuda Ranch, cautions dietitians that gung-ho attitudes about healthful eating and regular exercise can be misinterpreted by individuals with exercise addiction or eating disorders. "Dietitians tend to be health-conscious and knowledgeable about exercise," she says, "and sometimes those who are not as adept or really experienced with eating disordered clients can almost feed into what might be a brewing exercise addiction."

All in the name of health, she says, dietitians not experienced in eating disorders may affirm, support, and unknowingly encourage what may sound like a healthy exercise pattern, not recognizing the extreme nature of the client's thinking. A dietitian, she warns, can unwittingly feed into distorted thought patterns by emphasizing low-fat foods, fewer calories, or extremely healthy foods—all good ideas for normal clients, but easily misconstrued by those with compulsive tendencies.

— KJ

"Many girls with anorexia also exercise compulsively in addition to restricting their intake of food in order to lose weight," says Carll. For these individuals, she explains, exercise and eating are linked, so that every time they eat, they feel they must exercise. They engage in activity, says Pedrotty, solely to compensate for eating.

Excessive exercise is also frequently associated with bulimia nervosa, says Christian Lemmon, PhD, department of psychiatry and health behavior, MCG Health Systems in Atlanta, a psychologist who specializes in treating people with eating disorders. In patients with bulimia, excessive exercise is another form of compensation for eating, such as inducing vomiting or taking laxatives or diuretics. It exists independently of eating disorders as well, most commonly in men, but appears to be more common in individuals who struggle with food-related issues.

Typically viewed as merely exercising too much, exercise abuse can be manifested in other behaviors, explains Pedrotty, especially when eating disorders are involved. Bulimic women in particular may exhibit what she calls all-or-nothing patterns of exercise: "They'll engage in a period of intense exercise, and then they'll avoid it. Perhaps they'll train hard for a month and then back off for three months because they feel burned out. Or their approach may vary from day to day. They may wake up one day and feel like they ate too much the day before and therefore they exercise like crazy and then take a week off." Another associated behavior is obsessing about exercise but never actually working out, says Pedrotty.

At the Root

Exercise abuse may have a gradual or quick onset and typically begins as a healthy pattern that goes wrong, often in people with propensity for compulsivity. Molly Kimball, sports and lifestyle nutritionist at Ochsner Clinic's Elmwood Fitness Center in New Orleans, notes that it can arise easily among perfectionists. "Usually it occurs in very driven people—those who are overachievers and people who get great grades in school, excel at work, are well liked, and tend to do things for the approval of others."

Individuals who have eating disorders and who abuse exercise often do so out of a lack of self-esteem and in an effort to punish themselves. "A lot of our patients use it as a form of self-harm, believing that they can't stop until they've experienced pain, until their heart rate reaches the maximum, until they're dripping with sweat, or until their bodies burn," says Pedrotty. They may feel they're not worthy of eating and that they must abuse their body. Many people derive a lot of self-esteem from their ability to maintain a certain kind of exercise regimen, agrees Lemmon, and it's difficult for them to see other reasons to feel good about themselves.

It's also highly likely to arise in people who by nature or circumstance have a need to control. Observes Kimball, "When other things feel out of control, exercise may become a control issue because it's one thing they can master. No one makes them do it and they don't let anyone or anything interfere." A person might have been a recreational exerciser for years, she says, but something happens to trigger the obsession, such as a divorce or death of a parent. It might even be a less drastic milestone—a move, a new job, or the start of college—that erodes control and causes exercise to become an excessive focus.

Carll suggests that the root of overzealous exercise is an obsession—along the lines of an anxiety disorder—with one's appearance, used as a way of reducing weight and changing shape. "Frequently, individuals are both anxious and depressed and display behaviors similar to those seen in people with obsessive compulsive disorder, which is an anxiety disorder." Exercise, she explains, is a way of coping with the anxious feelings and taking control of one's body, much like anorexia. Most clients she sees with anorexia started out by dieting, but the diets got out of control. These girls and women kept losing weight,

Telltale Signs: Spying the Hidden Problem

Since exercise abusers, like those with eating disorders, are typically skillful dissemblers, simple and straightforward questions may not always cut through their disguises. Nutrition and exercise professionals offer the following telltale signs of excessive exercise:

- using exercise merely as a way to lose weight, especially by an individual with an eating disorder;
- a strong emotional commitment to exercise;
- a sense of duty or obligation about exercise manifested by an inability to take a day off or anxiety when exercise is not possible;
- a strong relationship between intake and output— having to exercise after eating;
- talking about exercise in a regimented way, not having a relaxed attitude about exercise, and not expressing enjoyment about activity;
- exercising through illness or injury, in inclement weather, or in severe times of stress;
- using exercise as the only means of stress control or mental health;
- exercising at the expense of one's social life or responsibilities;
- expressing guilt about not exercising;
- spot training—picking a particular part of the body and focusing excessively on it (eg, doing 1,500 crunches per day);
- being inflexible about exercise schedules or having rigid patterns (eg, having to use the same equipment at the same time in the same amount);
- always talking about exercise;
- exercising secretively—hiding or lying about exercise;
- visiting the gym more than once per day;
- having all-or-nothing exercise patterns—going from extremes of no exercise to constant exercise; and
- having a preoccupation with health food, weight loss, or performance supplements and products.

—KJ

thinking that eventually they'd reach their ideal weights and goals. "They never do," she says. "It's always 5 pounds more. The same thing happens with exercise addiction."

Exercise abuse may also develop out of a habit that's widely promoted and generally considered healthy: working out to ward off stress. But once again, in vulnerable individuals, there's a tendency to turn a plus into a minus. According to Juliet Zuercher, RD, director of nutrition at Remuda Ranch, a treatment center for women and girls with eating disorders and related issues such as exercise addiction, "A client may dabble with exercise as a means of stress release, and it feels good, so they think more will be better." Then they get into higher intensity exercise, she explains, and are essentially self-medicating with endorphins. "If they were depressed or stressed, they exercise and they feel better. That's positive reinforcement that goes to the extreme and until the activity becomes compulsive and the person thinks he or she will be depressed if they don't run 10 miles every day."

Physicians and psychotherapists often recommend exercise as a means to keep depression and stress at bay, but it must be both moderate and balanced by proper nutrition. "I feel great when I exercise," says Lemmon, "but too much of anything isn't good for you." Exercise abusers, he says, also use negative reinforcement for their behaviors. "They engage in excessive exercise to avoid a noxious set of stimuli—the anxiety that comes from not exercising," he explains.

Lemmon observes that many teens' parents worry that their kids may sneak out of the house at night and engage in sexual or drug-related behaviors. Young people with exercise disorders, however, may tiptoe out to engage in exercise surreptitiously. He recalls one patient who waited until her parents were asleep to go out and run five miles each night and another who got up every day at 5 am to ride on a stationary bike for 25 minutes, run on a treadmill for 45 minutes, and then do hundreds of crunches.

In all these cases, a good thing has gone too far. "It's an extremist way of thinking. If a certain amount is good, then a lot more is better," explains Carll. "These individuals think that if it's great to exercise three or four times a week, imagine how much better shape they could be in and how much healthier they'd be if they exercised all the time."

"Healthy" Symptoms

Regular exercise is healthy, but compulsive exercise becomes pathological. It's more often than not a hidden problem, and the line that divides healthy from obsessive activity is seldom clear. One of the reasons the problem goes unnoticed and and that many eating disorders programs don't have exercise abuse components, says Pedrotty, is that exercise is the only symptom of an eating disorder that's actually healthy. "It's never healthy to binge-purge or use laxatives, but exercise is healthy when used in moderation and when there's a healthy mind set motivating it, so it's challenging to find the balance."

It's important that healthcare professionals know how to assess for excessive exercise, says Lemmon, who acknowledges that it's a hard set of behaviors to define. "If someone says he or she exercises seven days a week, that's almost culturally sanctioned. We would all envy a person who can work out seven days a week, not only because they'd be in good health but because we'd wish we had the time to do the same. So problems such as exercise addiction are actually reinforced by our society."

For these reasons, professionals in the field suggest that dietitians ask all clients—men or women, young or mature, thin or obese—about exercise. By asking about it routinely, RDs can begin to see beyond the camouflage exercise abusers wear. Even in the ordinary course of practice with all clients, dietitians need to know about daily input and output of energy since they can't determine recommended dietary allowances without knowing how much energy a person is burning, says Lemmon. It's an opportunity to expand the conversation, he suggests, and dig a bit deeper.

The Toll of Exercise Abuse

In addition to the psychological toll of excessive exercise, a host of physical complaints may arise, including the following:

- bone and muscle injuries
- inflamed joints, tendons, and ligaments
- decreased bone density
- disruption of the menstrual cycle
- infertility
- overuse injuries
- stress fracture
- plantar fasciatis

—KJ

Zuercher says that since excessive exercise is a problem that can easily be missed, it makes sense for RDs to question all clients about their feelings about exercise in the initial intake or interview. It's not necessary to go into great depth with all clients, but when responses to simple questions about activity levels and exercise patterns suggest a problem, further probing is warranted.

"Clients who exercise a lot may appear to have a healthy attitude. It's only after you ask specific questions to assess the degree of exercise that it may become apparent that it's no longer healthy," explains Carll. In our very health-oriented culture, exercise is seen as positive, so most people might not pursue an avenue of questions about it. Dietitians, she adds, should ask specific questions to determine what kind of exercise their clients engage in and how much time they spend exercising.

It's especially important, adds Pedrotty, to probe clients with eating disorders about their activity. "Their exercise patterns may seem to be healthy and normal, but you really have to get in there and figure out their mind-sets." The crux of the program she codesigned with Rachel Calogero, MA, at the Renfrew Center, she says, is geared toward getting at the thoughts and feelings clients have about exercise.

Lemmon says he'd begin simply by asking clients to tell him about their physical activity. "If she tells me that she does aerobics six days a week, would I worry about that? Not necessarily, but I'll begin to ask more questions. I'll want to know if she has a tendency to exercise more on or after days when she feels as if she's eaten too much, or if she eats less on a day when she didn't get a chance to work out. If she says yes to those kinds of questions, warning signals go off in my head and I'm going to ask more questions." He'll then want to explore whether clients' exercise regimens get in the way of their ability to function otherwise—if the behaviors disrupt their ability to function occupationally, academically, interpersonally, or socially. Many exercises abusers, especially those with eating disorders, he notes, make exercise their top priority. "They start limiting themselves socially because their social obligations can't fit into the structure to which their eating disorder symptoms bind them."

How to Help

Dietitians can help by discussing with clients the basics of energy balance, says Lemmon, explaining the need for a proper diet to compensate for exercise rather than the need for exercise to compensate for diet. They can also make a difference by educating clients to recognize unhealthy patterns and attitudes and understand the limits of healthy exercise.

For people in healthy body weight range, says Zuercher, "we suggest exercising for an hour at a time, three to five times a week—an amount based upon recommendations to the American College of Sports Medicine." She stresses the importance of taking one or two days off per week and advises people with weight issues to increase the cardio segment of each day's hour of exercise or increase exercise to six days per week rather than attempting to do more exercise each day. Anywhere from 30 to 60 minutes per day from three to six times per week—mostly cardiovascular exercise—is in the range of normal, suggests Kimball.

Ultimately, the healthy amount is different from person to person, says Pedrotty. Olympic athletes may exercise six days per week for eight hours per day, but that's not necessarily unhealthy because they fuel themselves appropriately, they enjoy what they're doing, and they take care of their bodies. "It's not the amount of exercise, it's the mind-set."

The simplest way dietitians can transform their clients' unhealthy attitudes about exercise is by being good role models, says Pedrotty. "They should have healthy views about exercise, know how much is enough and how much is too much, and understand and communicate that the sole purpose of exercise is not weight loss but rather that there are many purposes: to rejuvenate the body, to create a connection between the mind and body, to have fun, and to relieve stress." In the end, she says, make sure to promote the idea that we eat to exercise. We don't exercise to eat." Then follow up by providing healthy eating and exercising strategies.

Referring Clients

That said, more often than not, clients with exercise issues will need more help than you alone can provide. It's important to keep in mind that an eating or exercise disorder is a psychological illness, says Carll, so it's necessary to refer patients to mental health professionals who specialize in treating people with compulsive behaviors. These types of issues, she adds, have typically existed for some time and are not likely to change without therapeutic intervention. And the consequences of continuing these behaviors can be extremely serious. "Exercise by anorexic individuals with low body weight and low blood pressure can result in cardiac problems, including heart failure," says Carll.

In most cases, she says, people who exercise compulsively may not recognize that they have a problem because their behaviors give them a false sense of control. Your clients may not be receptive to the recommendation that they seek the care of a mental health professional, says Carll, who advises that it's still helpful to make the suggestion.

"If you see someone who has a very low body fat percentage and you discover that their intake isn't appropriate or their amount of exercise seems far in excess of what it needs to be, ask questions," says Lemmon, who stresses above all the need to be sensitive. "Communicate concern but also understanding, and recognize that if your clients are truly addicted to exercise, they're probably going to be a little bit skittish about seeking treatment and may even get downright angry or upset with you."

In a very loving, kind, empathic way, he urges, tell them your concerns and offer to help them find someone with whom they can talk about their issues. Then, ideally, he says, dietitians would continue to be part of an interdisciplinary team that includes physicians and psychotherapists working together to help clients with exercise addiction.

KATE JACKSON is a staff writer for *Today's Dietitian.*

The Female Triad

Lola Ramos and Gregory L. Welch, MS

In the past 30 years the opportunities for adolescent girls and young adult women to participate in all levels of sports competition have increased tremendously. This is certainly a positive direction for women because with increased physical activity comes associated wellness benefits. Chronic physiological adaptation to exercise training is well documented in regard to improved cardiovascular efficiency, muscular strength, self-esteem and overall body image (Wilmore and Costill 1999).

In addition to women who train at a competitive level, many noncompetitive women exercise vigorously as well. It is not just that they train at high intensities but that their ambition to train surpasses that of individuals who are more moderate in their exercise programs. This mindset is such that training becomes a lifestyle philosophy as well as a passion. While this is generally an admirable trait, it is not without significant risk. For example, "over training" injuries in the form of muscular strain, tendonitis and stress fractures will likely occur to many individuals who overprioritize their workouts at the expense of sufficient recovery and nutrition. Specifically for young women, there is an even greater health concern that far outweighs typical "overuse syndrome"—the female triad. If not dealt with appropriately, the female triad can damage women's wellness throughout their lives.

Defining the Female Triad

The female triad is a combination of three coexistent conditions associated with exercise training: disordered eating, amenorrhea and osteoporosis (Hobart and Smucker 2000). Originally termed "female athlete triad," the name was derived at a meeting led by members of the American College of Sports Medicine in the early 1990s (Yeager et al. 1993). Papanek (2003) reports that the meeting was called in response to the alarming increase in stress fracture rates, documented decreases in bone mineral density and menstrual dysfunction in otherwise healthy female athletes. Furthermore, the depiction of the triad as a triangle was developed to demonstrate the interrelationship between the three disorders normally considered independent medical conditions.

Over the last decade, the triad's definition has evolved to be more precise about the involvement of related clinical conditions. Anorexia nervosa (AN) and bulimia nervosa (BN) are the most common clinical disorders. A third category for eating disorders not otherwise specified (EDNOS) was created in an effort to expand treatment access for patients at high risk for an eating disorder (Papanek 2003). In other words, an athlete who falls short in meeting the criteria for AN or BN could still be recognized as needing treatment by being placed in the EDNOS category. *See Table 1.*

However, not all restrictive eating behaviors necessarily reach the clinical level (Beals and Manore 2000). Even with the addition of the EDNOS category, female athletes with the triad display a wide range of food-related pathologies. Therefore, the term "eating disorder" was found to be too restrictive and replaced by "disordered eating" to include the various forms of aberrant eating behaviors that disrupt caloric balance (Papanek 2003). Common disordered eating patterns exhibited by female athletes include food restriction, prolonged fasting as well as abuse of diet pills, diuretics and laxatives (Donaldson 2003).

Eumenorrheic or regular menstrual cycles are defined as regular flow occurring every 21 to 45 days, with 10 to 13 cycles per year, and oligomenorrhea refers to three to six cycles occurring per year (Rome 2003). Marshal (1994) classifies amenorrhea as primary or secondary and defines them as follows: primary amenorrhea or delayed menarche is defined as not having experienced a single menstrual cycle by the age of 16 and secondary amenorrhea is the absence of menses for six months or a length of time equivalent to at least three of the woman's previous menstrual cycle lengths. The main difference is that in secondary amenorrhea, at least one menstrual period has occurred. Physiologically, this means all parts of the reproductive axis (i.e., hypothalamus, pituitary, ovaries and uterus) worked together once, but for some reason, this integrative function has changed (Papanek 2003).

Osteoporosis is a systemic, skeletal disease characterized by low bone density and microarchitectural deterioration of bone tissue, with a consequent increase in bone fragility and fracture susceptibility (O'brien 2001). To clarify, the term osteoporosis, as referred to in this writing, is actually secondary osteoporosis because it is caused or exacerbated by other disorders (Stein and Shane 2003). Additionally, osteopenia, which is abnormally low bone density and believed to be an osteoporosis precursor (Nelson 2000), has also been included when identifying the female triad syndrome. Amenorrheic adolescent athletes do not acquire proper bone mass and, thus, will be osteopenic in their early adult years (Elford and Spence 2002).

Disordered Eating

Society has done a great disservice to adolescent females by perpetuating the "ideal" body image. For young women, this can intensify the pursuit of a thin physique at a time when nutrition plays a key role in proper growth and development. According to a 1997 Youth Risk Behavior Surveillance Survey, 34 percent of adolescent females were likely to consider themselves "too fat" and, therefore, limited their dietary intake (Kann et al. 1998). Hobart and Smucker (2000) add that many factors may create poor self-image and pathogenic weight-control behaviors in female athletes. Likewise, frequent weigh-ins, punitive consequences for weight gain, pressure to "win at all costs," an overly controlling parent or coach and social isolation caused by intensive sports involvement may increase a female athlete's risk of disordered eating behavior.

Disordered eating occurs in 5 percent of the general population (Donaldson 2003), but affects as many as two thirds of young female athletes (Nativ et al. 1994). According to Gidwani and Rome (1997),

Table 1 Diagnostic Criteria and Warning Signs for Eating Disorders

	Diagnostic Criteria	Warning Signs and Symptoms
Anorexia Nervosa (AN)	1. Refusal to maintain body weight at or above 85 percent of normal weight for age and height 2. Intense fear of gaining weight or becoming fat, even though underweight 3. Disturbance in the way in which one's body weight or shape is experienced, undue influence of body weight or shape on self-evaluation or denial of the seriousness of current low body weight 4. Amenorrhea	1. Fat and muscle atrophy 2. Dry hair and skin 3. Cold, discolored hands and feet 4. Decreased body temperature 5. Lightheadedness 6. Decreased ability to concentrate 7. Bradycardia (i.e., slowness of the heartbeat, so that the pulse rate is less than 60 per minute) 8. Past history of physical or sexual abuse

	Diagnostic Criteria	Warning Signs and Symptoms
Bulimia Nervosa (BN)	1. Recurrent episodes of binge eating 2. Sense of lack of control over eating during the episode (e.g., feeling that one cannot stop eating or control what or how much one is eating) 3. Recurrent inappropriate compensatory behavior to prevent weight gain (e.g., diuretics, enemas, self-induced vomiting, misuse of laxatives or other medications, fasting or excessive exercise) 4. The binge eating and inappropriate compensatory behaviors occur, on average, at least twice a week for three months 5. Self-evaluation is unduly influenced by body shape and weight 6. The disturbance does not occur exclusively during episodes of anorexia nervosa	1. Swollen parotid glands 2. Chest pain, sore throat 3. Fatigue, abdominal pain 4. Diarrhea or constipation 5. Menstrual irregularities 6. Callous formation or scars on knuckles

	Diagnostic Criteria	
Eating Disorder Not Otherwise Specified (EDNOS)	1. For females, all of the criteria for AN are met except the individual has regular menses 2. All criteria for AN are met except that, despite significant weight loss, the person's current weight is in the normal range 3. All the criteria for BN are met except that the binge eating and inappropriate compensatory mechanisms occur at a frequency of less than two per week for a duration of less than three months	4. Regular use of inappropriate compensatory behavior by an individual of normal body weight after eating small amounts of food (e.g., self-induced vomiting after consumption of two cookies) 5. Repeatedly chewing, but not swallowing, and spitting out large amounts of food 6. Binge-eating disorder: recurrent episodes of binge eating in the absence of the regular use of inappropriate compensatory behaviors characteristic of BN

32 percent of female athletes, at all levels of competition, practice pathogenic behavior for weight control. Rosen and Hough (1988) reported disordered eating behavior in 15 to 62 percent of female college athletes. Even before the triad was officially recognized as a distinct syndrome, Calabrese (1985) performed a study with collegiate gymnasts and discovered 62 percent displayed some type of disordered eating—26 percent vomited on a daily basis, 24 percent used diet pills, 12 percent fasted and 75 percent had been told by their coaches that they weighed too much. Disordered eating behavior is believed to con-

tribute to a disruption in the hypothalamic-gonadal axis, resulting in amenorrhea (Donaldson 2003).

The Interrelationship of the Triad

The three components of the female triad—disordered eating, amenorrhea and osteoporosis—pose serious health concerns for young athletic women. Shafer and Irwin (1991) state that the adolescent growth spurt accounts for approximately 25 percent of adult height and 50 percent of adult weight. Additionally, girls develop reproductive capacity during this time and dieting behaviors and nutrition can have an enormous impact on their gynecologic health (Seidenfeld and Rickert 2001).

While they can all occur independently, the interrelationship between the three parts of the triad is such that one component will affect another. In order to understand the physiological beginning of this syndrome, one must first realize that, in addition to the calories required for basal metabolic rate and physical activity, calories are required for menstruation, building and repairing muscle, healing and, in younger athletes, growth (Papanek 2003). The pathophysiology of the triad can be explained by a caloric deficit which disrupts the release of gonadotropin-releasing hormone, resulting in low levels of gonadotropins and secondarily reduced levels of estrogen and progesterone, leading to amenorrhea and osteopenia (Elford and Spence 2002).

Disordered eating behavior affects the number of calories available for normal life function. Manore (1999) states that any athlete, regardless of size, who consumes less than 1,800 calories per day is unable to meet caloric and nutrient requirements. Furthermore, a female athlete exercising 10 to 20 hours per week requires at least 2,200 to 2,500 calories per day to maintain body weight.

Negative Caloric Balance and Amenorrhea

Dueck, et al., (1996) reported that the average difference between amenorrheic and eumenorrheic athletes was only a caloric balance deficit of 250 calories per day. Many athletes do not realize the nutritional demands of their sports and, thus, it is this disordered eating that causes a negative caloric balance leading to amenorrhea (Papanek 2003). Even as early as 1981, Frisch, et al., found that amenorrheic competitive runners had an average intake of 1,700 calories per day, whereas eumenorrheic runners consumed 2,200 calories per day.

In addition to a caloric deficit due to disordered eating, physical training intensity plays an important role in the triad syndrome. Even if caloric deprivation does not occur through disordered eating, negative caloric imbalance can result from failing to support the training regimen with adequate recovery. Primary and secondary amenorrhea can occur in the context of eating disorders or intense athletics (Rome 2003). DiPietro and Stachenfeld support this by adding that a chronic negative energy balance, being underweight and exercise stress are important elements in the pathway to amenorrhea (1997). Cobb, et al., (2003) write that female athletes with disordered eating may limit their calorie and/or fat intakes but maintain high training levels, often resulting in a state of chronic energy deficit. Athletic amenorrhea occurs more frequently in activities such as running, ballet and gymnastics, in which intense physical training is combined with the desire to maintain a lean build (Warren 1980).

Osteoporosis and Negative Caloric Balance

Bones require a normal level of systemic hormones, adequate caloric intake (including protein, calcium and vitamin D, in particular) and regular, weight-bearing exercise throughout life (O'brien 2001). Exercise's effects on the growing skeleton are complex and influenced by many factors, including the nature and intensity of the activity, skeleton area primarily involved, body weight and dietary calcium intake (Stein and Shane 2003). Although moderate exercise protects against osteoporosis, too little or excessive exercise may actually cause it (O'brien 2001).

"In general, women struggle with the perception of the 'perfect body image' society has unfairly placed upon them. Regardless of the circumstances, we as health care providers, coaches and parents are ultimately responsible for protecting the wellness of the young women in our care. Therefore, we must provide a proper wellness environment by nurturing sound physical training and nutritional habits."

The minimum daily calcium requirement is 1,300 milligrams for people ages 11 to 23. Unfortunately, 85 percent of adolescent females do not consume this amount (National Institutes of Health and Child Development Publication 2001). Attitudes about their bodies during puberty can contribute to the dietary changes adolescent females make. This can lead to possible chronic dieting disorders, resulting in low bone mass and a risk for osteoporotic fractures later in life (Ali and Siktberg 1996).

Osteoporosis is a prevalent AN complication. In fact, the duration of AN is a predictor of low bone mineral density because the longer the illness lasts, the greater bone mineral density is reduced (Mehler 2003). For example, more than 50 percent of female patients with AN develop osteoporosis (Treasure and Surpell 2001). Miller and Klibanski (1999) add that the lack of nutrition is so severe in anorexics that an increased osteoporosis risk may exist due to associated endocrine abnormalities, including estrogen deficiency.

Amenorrhea and Osteoporosis

Continuing the triad syndrome's assault on the female athlete's wellness is the relationship between the absence of menses and bone deterioration. Some athletes see amenorrhea as a sign of appropriate training levels, while others regard it as a great solution to a monthly inconvenience (National Institutes of Health 2003). There is a prevailing myth in women's athletics that equates a disrupted menstrual cycle with the appropriate level of elite training (Papanek 2003). Mickelsfield, et al., (1995) state that amenorrheic/oligomenorrheic athletes on average have lower bone mineral density than eumenorrheic controls. Stein and Shane (2003) agree that low bone mineral density is a consequence of exercise-induced amenorrhea. Osteopenia or significantly reduced bone mass occurring with prolonged loss of menses has been associated with an increased risk of stress fractures (Mansfield and Emans 1993).

Summary

The female triad is a unique phenomenon that does not occur overnight but rather appears to gradually infiltrate female adolescents' lifestyle. Under intense pressure from parents, coaches teammates and often themselves, many young women begin to fall into patterns of disordered eating and/or overintense caloric expenditure without the support of adequate rest and nutrition. The triad is especially troubling due to the fact that, while each affliction can occur independently, they often are interrelated by a chain reaction. Amenorrhea/oligomenorrhea is likely to follow the caloric imbalance, which leads to osteopenia and ultimately osteoporosis. This downward spiral can result in termination of an athletic career as well as a chronically unhealthy adult life.

Identification of the triad can be difficult. When confronted by family, friends, coaches and physicians about their eating behavior, athletes can be anywhere from elusive in their explanation to perfectly convincing that nothing is wrong. Although it is more common to find this syndrome affecting athletic women, it is certainly not exclusive to this population. In general, women struggle with the perception of the "perfect body image" society has unfairly placed upon them. Regardless of the circumstances, we as health care providers, coaches and parents are ultimately responsible for protecting the wellness of the young women in our care. Therefore, we must provide a proper wellness environment by nurturing sound physical training and nutritional habits.

References

Ali, N. and Siktberg, L. "Osteoporosis prevention in female adolescents: Calcium intake and exercise participation," *Pediatr. Nurs.* 1996, 27 (2), 132–9.

Beals, K.A. and Manore, M.M. "Behavioral, psychological and physical characteristics of female athletes with subclinical eating disorders." *Int. J. Sports Nutr. Exerc. Metab.,* 2000, 10, 128–43.

Calabrese, L.H. "Nutritional and medical aspects of gymnastics." *Clin. Sports Med.,* 1985, 4, 23–37.

Cobb, K.L., et al. "Disordered eating, menstrual irregularity, and bone mineral density in female runners." *Med. Sci. Sports Exerc.,* 2003, 35 (5), 711–9.

DiPietro, L. and Stachenfeld, N.S. "The female athletic triad: American College of Sports Medicine position." *Med. Sci. Sports Exerc.,* 1997, 29, I–IX.

Donaldson, M.C. "The female athlete triad: A growing health concern." *Orthop. Nurs.,* 2003, 22 (5), 322–3.

Dueck, C.A., Manore, M.M. and Matt, K.S. "Role of energy balance in athletic menstrual dysfunction." *Int. J. Sports Nutr.,* 1996, 6, 165–190.

Elford, K.J. and Spence, J.E.H. "The forgotten female: Pediatric and adolescent gynecological concerns and their reproductive consequences." *J. Pediatr. Adolesc. Gynecol.,* 2002, 15 (2), 83–105.

Frisch, R.E., Gotz-Welbergen, A.V. and McArthur, J.W. "Delayed menarche and amenorrhea of college athletes in relation to age of onset of training." *JAMA,* 1981, 246, 1559.

Gidwani, G. and Rome, E. "Eating Disorders." *Clin. Obstet. Gynaecol.,* 1997, 40 (3), 601.

Hobart, J. and Smucker, D. "The female triad." *Am. Fam. Physician,* 2000, 61, 3357–64, 3367.

Kann, L., et al. "Youth risk behavior surveillance—United States, 1997." *MMWR,* 1998, 47 (SS-3), 1–89.

Manore, M.M. "Nutritional needs of the female athlete." *Clin. Sports Med.,* 1999, 18, 549–63.

Mansfield, M.J. and Emans, S.J. "Growth in female gymnasts: Should training decrease puberty?" *J. Pediatr.,* 1993, 122, 237–40.

Marshal, L.A. "Clinical evaluation of amenorrhea in active and athletic women." *Clin. Sports Med.,* 1994, 13, 371–87.

Mehler, P.S. "Osteoporosis in anorexia nervosa: Prevention and treatment." *Int. J. Eat. Disord.,* 2003, 33 (2), 113–26.

Mickelsfield, L.K., et al. "Bone mineral density in mature, premenopausal ultramarathon runners." *Med. Sci. Sports Exerc.,* 1995, 27, 688–96.

Miller, K.K. and Klibanski, A. "Amenorrheic bone loss." *J. Clin. Endocrinol. Metab.,* 1999, 84, 1775–83.

National Institutes of Health. "Fitness and Bone Health: The skeletal risk of overtraining." *National Resource Center,* 2003, Bethesda, Maryland.

National Institutes of Health and Child Development Publication. "Why milk matters now for children and teens under childhood adolescent nutrition." January 2001, no. 00-4864.

Nativ, A., et al. "The female athlete triad." *Clin. Sports Med.,* 1994, 13, 405–18.

Nelson, M. *Strong Women, Strong Bones.* New York: G.P Putnam's and Sons, 2000.

O'brien, M. "Exercise and osteoporosis." *Ir. J. Med. Sci.,* 2001, 170 (1), 58–62.

Papanek, P.E. "The female athlete triad: An emerging role for physical therapy." *J. Orthop. Sports Phys. Ther.,* 2003, 33 (10), 594–614.

Rome, E.S. "Eating disorders." *Obs. Gyn. Clin.,* 2003, 30 (2), 353–77.

Rosen, L.W. and Hough, D.O. "Pathogenic weight-control behaviors of female college gymnasts." *Phys. Sports Med.,* 1988, 16, 140–3.

Seidenfeld, M.D. and Rickert, V.I. "Impact of anorexia, bulimia and obesity on the gynecologic health of adolescents." *Am. Fam. Physician,* 2001, 64 (3), 445–50.

Shafer, M.B. and Irwin, C.E. "The adolescent patient." In Rudolf A. M., ed. *Rudolf's Pediatrics.* 19th ed. Norwalk: Appleton & Lange, 1991: 39.

Stein, E. and Shane, E. "Secondary osteoporosis." *Endocrinol. Metab. Clin.,* 2003, 32 (1) 889–92.

Treasure, J. and Serpell, L. "Osteoporosis in young people. Research and treatment in eating disorders." *Psychiatr. Clin. North Am.,* 2001, 24 (2), 359–70.

Warren, M.P. "The effects of exercise on pubertal progression and reproductive function in girls." *J. Clin. Endocrinol. Metab.,* 1980, 51, 1150.

Wilmore, J.H. and Costill, D.L. *Physiology of Sport and Exercise.* Champaign: Human Kinetics, 1999.

Yeager, K.K., et al. "The female athlete triad: disordered eating, amenorrhea, osteoporosis." *Med. Sci. Sports and Exerc.,* 1999, 25: 775–7.

LOLA RAMOS is pursuing her bachelor's degree in kinesiology and health promotion at California State University, Fullerton. She has recently completed an academic internship through the SpeciFit Foundation. **GREGORY L. WELCH, MS,** is an exercise physiologist and president of SpeciFit, An Agency of Wellness and Competitive Performance Enhancement, located in Seal Beach, California. He is also founder and CEO of the SpeciFit Foundation, a non-profit entity providing wellness concepts for adolescent women. Welch has published several articles regarding wellness of older adults and through his foundation has added adolescent women to the category of special populations. He can be reached at (562) 431-5206 and www.specifit.com.

From *American Fitness,* May/June 2004, pp. 57–62. Copyright © 2004 by Lola Ramos and Gregory L. Welch. Reprinted by permission of the authors.

How Sleep Affects Your Weight

DAVID SCHARDT

Are the sleepless counting doughnuts and pies instead of sheep? "Americans sleep less than they used to, and this could be part of the reason why more of us are now overweight," says David Dinges, Chief of the Division of Sleep and Chronobiology at the University of Pennsylvania School of Medicine.

Over the past 40 years, Americans have cut their snooze time by one to two hours a night. We now sleep less than people in any other industrialized country. And researchers are discovering that sleep affects hormones that regulate satiety, hunger, and how efficiently you burn calories.

Too little sleep may make you hungry, especially for calorie-dense foods, and may prime your body to try to hold on to the calories you eat. It may also boost your insulin levels, which increases the risk of heart disease and diabetes.

The Sleep-Weight Link

"Obesity is obviously a very complex issue, and no one is suggesting that lack of sleep is the cause of the obesity epidemic," says Carl Hunt, director of the National Center on Sleep Disorders Research at the National Institutes of Health in Bethesda, Maryland.

"But new research certainly supports the idea that sleeping less may be a previously unknown but important contributor to the obesity epidemic in the U.S."

The link between sleep and weight was first noticed in the 1990s, when European researchers were puzzling over why so many children were getting heavier.

"They were surprised to discover that it wasn't how much TV a child watched, but how much sleep the child got, that best predicted whether he or she was overweight," says Dinges. "The less children slept, the heavier they were."

Researchers in the U.S. are finding the same link in adults.

In the Wisconsin Sleep Cohort Study, which tracks the sleep habits of nearly 3,000 middle-aged state government employees, those who reported that they typically slept less than eight hours a night were more likely to be overweight.[1]

And researchers at Columbia University in New York City found that people who slept six hours a night were 23 percent more likely to be obese than people who slept between seven and nine hours. Those who slept five hours were 50 percent more likely—while those who slept four hours or less were 73 percent more likely—to be obese.

The connection between hours slept and weight wasn't significant for people 60 and older, says James Gangwisch, a psychiatric epidemiologist at Columbia, "probably because the sleep problems that are so common in older people obscure the link." (The analysis hasn't yet been published.)

Leapin' Leptin

Why would people who sleep less weigh more?

"The results are somewhat counterintuitive," says Gangwisch, since people burn more calories when they're awake. "We think it has more to do with what happens to your body when you deprive it of sleep, as opposed to the amount of physical activity you get."

What happens involves two hormones: Leptin, which is released by fat cells, signals the brain to *stop* eating. Ghrelin (pronounced GRELL-lin), which is made in the stomach, is a signal to *keep* eating. The two influence whether you go for a second helping or push yourself away from the table.

"Studies have shown that leptin levels are lower and ghrelin levels are higher in people who sleep fewer hours," says Gangwisch.

In the Wisconsin Sleep Cohort Study, those who slept for five hours had 15 percent lower leptin levels and 15 percent higher ghrelin levels than those who slept for eight hours.[1]

While the study wasn't designed to prove whether sleep deprivation causes changes in leptin and ghrelin levels, new research at the University of Chicago suggests that it does.

When Eve Van Cauter and co-workers limited 12 healthy young men to just four hours of sleep for two consecutive nights, their leptin levels were 18 percent lower and their ghrelin levels were 28 percent higher than after two nights of sleeping for ten hours.[2]

"The combination of low leptin and high ghrelin is likely to increase appetite," says Wisconsin Sleep Cohort Study researcher Emmanuel Mignot of Stanford University (though "short sleepers may also have more time to overeat," he points out).

In fact, the men in Van Cauter's study said that they were more hungry—and that they'd be more likely to eat salty foods like chips and nuts; sweets like cake, candy, and ice cream; and starchy foods like bread, cereal, and potatoes—after four hours of sleep than after ten hours.

Compounding the problem: the brain interprets a drop in leptin as a sign of starvation. So it responds not only by boosting hunger, but by burning fewer calories. That means you put on more weight even if you don't eat any more food.

Sweet Dreams

Sleep deprivation may stimulate more than your appetite.

"It also affects insulin resistance and blood glucose levels, which are two important components of the metabolic syndrome," says Carl Hunt of the National Center on Sleep Disorders Research.

The metabolic syndrome, also called insulin resistance syndrome, is a cluster of symptoms that increases the risk of heart attack, stroke, and diabetes. Signs of the syndrome are abdominal obesity, low HDL ("good") cholesterol, and elevated (though not necessarily high) triglycerides, blood pressure, and blood sugar.

When the University of Chicago's Eve Van Cauter and her colleagues limited 11 healthy men in their 20s to four hours of sleep for six straight nights, "it brought them to a nearly prediabetic state."

Their bodies were 40 percent less able to clear glucose from their blood and 30 percent slower in releasing insulin than when they were allowed to sleep for twelve hours.[3] In fact, four hours of sleep for six consecutive nights gave the young men the insulin sensitivity of 70- or 80-year-olds.

"We didn't expect to see a change of that magnitude," says Van Cauter.

(Insulin is a hormone that lets glucose, or blood sugar, enter the body's cells, where the sugar is burned for energy. When people are insulin insensitive, or insulin resistant, their insulin doesn't work efficiently.)

"The consensus that prevailed until recently was that sleep is for the brain, not for the rest of the body," says Van Cauter. "But sleep really affects everything. We are not wired biologically for sleep deprivation. We're the only animal that intentionally sleeps less than we need to."

Notes

1. *PLoS Med. 1:e62* 2004 (Epub.).
2. *Ann. Intern. Med. 141:* 846, 2004.
3. *Lancet 354:* 1435, 1999.

"Fat Chance"

Doesn't "everyone know" that serving supersize meals to a young couch potato with plus-size parents is a sure recipe for an obese child? So why is the current epidemic of childhood obesity such a mystery to science?

SUSAN OKIE

Rudolph L. Leibel's genes may have predisposed him to become a scientist, but his decision to spend his life trying to discover the causes of obesity was environmental happenstance, the result of a chance encounter. In the spring of 1977, Randall, a severely overweight child, and Randall's mother showed up at the pediatric clinic of Cambridge Hospital in Massachusetts, where Leibel was a specialist in hormone disorders. Leibel could find no evidence that hormone deficiency or, indeed, any other known medical condition, was the cause of Randall's obesity. But what struck the young doctor was the response of Randall's mother when Leibel told her there was little he or anyone else could do for her son: "Let's get out of here, Randall," she snapped. "This doctor doesn't know s--t."

Chastened by her words, Leibel soon traded his hospital post for the low-paying toil of a rookie laboratory scientist. At the Rockefeller University laboratory of Jules Hirsch, a leading figure in research on obesity, Leibel and Hirsch conducted extensive studies of weight homeostasis: how the body responds both to weight gain and weight loss by fighting to restore the status quo ante.

In one of the studies, volunteers were induced to overeat to gain weight—a task that proved remarkably difficult. Whether they were fat or lean at the outset, the volunteers' bodies responded by turning up the metabolic rate, boosting the levels of certain hormones, reducing hunger, and burning up more calories as heat—all in a coordinated effort by the autonomic nervous system to restore the body's original weight. By contrast, when volunteers' food intake was restricted in order to promote weight loss, their bodies fought back even more fiercely: metabolisms slowed; the volunteers moved around less often and, even when they were exercising, their muscles burned fewer calories; and everyone felt constantly and uncomfortably hungry. A host of physiological defense mechanisms had swung into play, all aimed at regaining the lost pounds.

Such tight physiological regulation of body weight persuaded Leibel that a chemical signal from the body's stores of fat was being sent to the brain. Leibel's hypothesis led to the discovery of a gene that coded for the hormone leptin, which is produced by fat cells. Animal studies soon proved that leptin does indeed pass through the circulatory system to the brain. Could leptin be the key player in the signaling system Leibel had envisioned? If the brain

detected enough leptin, would it decide that enough fat cells were storing energy, and so conclude that it was safe to stop eating? Sure enough, mice that could not produce leptin ate nonstop and grew enormously obese. Treating such mice with leptin normalized their body weight.

The gene for leptin was identified and sequenced as the result of an intensive collaborative effort between Leibel and his Rockefeller colleague Jeffrey M. Friedman. When the announcement was made in 1994, it was greeted with much fanfare. Many people (along with some drug companies) predicted that the newly identified gene would enable the hormone to become a miracle cure for obesity. It has not turned out that way.

Some evidence suggests body weight reaches a "set point" during puberty. So untreated childhood obesity can lead to the medical risks of adult obesity.

Today, instead, the United States and many other countries are faced with an epidemic. Most people tend to think of an epidemic as an outbreak of a contagious illness. But to public health officials, obesity rates since the mid 1980s have exploded dramatically and unexpectedly, just as if they reflected the outbreak of a new infectious disease. Noting that obesity and physical inactivity, along with tobacco smoking, are the major causes of "noncommunicable diseases," the World Health Organization estimated that 60 percent of the 56 million deaths worldwide in 2001 were caused by such obesity-related illnesses as heart disease and type 2 diabetes. Among children, obesity can have adverse effects that persist for life, just as surely as a virus can. For example, there is evidence suggesting that a person's general body weight reaches a "set point" sometime during puberty, and so extreme obesity in childhood, left untreated, carries with it all the health risks of obesity for the rest of one's life: substantial increases in the risks of diabetes, heart disease, and other adverse medical consequences. Some officials have even begun to respond with the kind of alarm that might greet the global resurgence of polio. As David L. Katz of the Yale School of Public Health puts it:

Children growing up in the United States today will suffer more chronic disease and premature death because of the way they eat and [because of] their lack of physical activity than [they will] from exposure to tobacco, drugs, and alcohol combined.

Even though the discovery of leptin has not led to a cure for childhood obesity, it has helped to show that the condition is largely biological, and not simply the result of faulty parenting or lack of willpower. And the years since the discovery have been hailed as a golden age for obesity research. In little more than a decade, investigators have sketched, in broad outlines, the biological system that regulates body weight. They have also learned a great deal about genetic vulnerability to obesity.

The control centers for tracking energy balance and regulating body weight are situated primarily in the hypothalamus, a small part of the brain that specializes in integrating messages from many parts of the body and orchestrating the organism's response to its environment [see illustration on opposite page]. The hypothalamus communicates via nerve pathways and chemical signals with many other areas of the brain, as well as with the organs of the cardiovascular, digestive, reproductive, and endocrine systems (the latter encompasses the glands that secrete the hormones circulating in the blood).

The output of the hypothalamus can fine-tune a number of unconscious processes that affect a person's weight, such as the rate at which the body burns calories in carrying out certain cellular processes or through spontaneous muscle activity, such as fidgeting. Conceptually, at least, understanding how the body controls such unconscious processes is fairly straightforward. What is surprising for some people is that signals from the hypothalamus also affect the cerebral cortex, the "thinking" part of the brain. The hypothalamus can modify such conscious, purposeful behaviors as food-seeking, simply by increasing or decreasing the appetite. As Leibel puts it, those unconscious signals contribute to such conscious actions as ordering a pizza or having a second piece of pie. Just because a behavior is conscious, he adds, doesn't mean that all aspects of it are voluntary.

To exert its control, the hypothalamus needs reliable, relevant information about the body's current need for food. But where does that information come from? Leptin and, to a lesser extent, insulin carry information about long-term energy depots. The level of leptin in the blood reflects how much fat is stored in the body. Its chief function seems to be to protect energy stores and prevent starvation. When a human or other mammal's food intake is severely restricted, leptin levels drop within twenty-four hours—well before fat stores have been materially depleted by being burned for energy. The fall in leptin immediately prompts the hypothalamus to lower the metabolic rate, increase the appetite, and, to some extent, suppress the reproductive and immune systems so as to focus the body's resources on gaining food.

Insulin, the hormone produced by the beta cells of the pancreas, is released into the bloodstream in response to glucose from food. It helps the body maintain a balance between storing glucose and fat and burning them. Insulin also serves as another signal to certain nerve cells in the brain, informing them about the body's overall nutritional status. The brain also receives messages from the digestive tract. Constant updates about food availability and the timing of meals are relayed to the hypothalamus by various messenger molecules released by cells in the stomach and intestinal tract.

What about the genetics? If Randall were Leibel's young patient today, the boy might undergo testing for a genetic cause of his obesity. A few unlucky people are born with a single genetic mutation that stacks the deck against them so overwhelmingly that they become severely overweight almost no matter what the environment. At least five distinct "obesity genes" have been identified so far. Each of them is so critical to the regulation of appetite and food intake that certain mutations in any of them can lead to extreme obesity.

The mutations that cause such "monogenic," or single-gene, obesity are quite rare. Moreover, even if a physician can diagnose such a condition, there is still no guarantee that it can be treated successfully. Nevertheless, monogenic cases of severe obesity have helped investigators understand how the body regulates food intake and fat stores in people without such debilitating mutations. And even though monogenic obesity is rare, Leibel notes, it does reinforce the idea that specific molecules are highly potent in determining energy balance and body weight in humans.

What about the vast majority of overweight children and adults, whose obesity is not the result of a single defective gene? The scientific consensus is that such people may have multiple genes whose net effect predisposes them to eat a few extra calories, burn up a bit less energy than they take in, or store the excess as fat. Like the members of a band, the genes in each person's personal collection play together, along with various factors in the environment, to determine the person's specific vulnerability to becoming overweight.

How many genes might be at play? Investigators don't yet know. At first, just after leptin was discovered, many people thought there must be a single obesity gene, and some believed it had been found. Now at least sixty genes are being investigated, and some workers fear that as many as a hundred genes could be contributing to the obesity risk.

Leibel's own suspicion, after examining patterns of obesity inheritance in families drawn from various populations and ethnic groups, is that the number of important players is much smaller. He suggests that each person may have as many as a dozen genes that combine to determine the individual risk of obesity. Some genes—perhaps six or seven of them—are probably major players that help determine the likelihood of obesity in people all over the planet. The rest of the dozen or so genes may have arisen from gene variants more common in one ethnic population than in another. That, says Leibel, is what makes the genetics so complicated. No one knows which genes are major players, and which genes are minor ones. And so the geneticists have no way of knowing how to apportion their efforts.

Most people, of course, do not become severely obese, even in today's calorie-rich environment. The average person consumes between 7.5 million and 10 million calories per decade, yet Americans and people in other developed countries typically gain only half a pound to a pound a year throughout their adult lives. To gain any weight at all, they must eat more calories than they burn—but the amount needed to account for the typical weight gain is only about ten to twenty calories a day. That's about the equivalent of one Ritz cracker, or less than 1 percent of the average adult's daily intake.

A calorie imbalance that small can't be reliably measured by studying people in their normal habitat. To study how weight gain and loss quantitatively affect people's appetite and metabolism, Leibel and his associates had to confine volunteers to hospital research wards and measure every mouthful. They found, surprisingly, that obese people do not eat more than lean people in proportion to their body size. Nor do obese people have slower metabolisms than lean ones, as long as they remain at what is their own "normal" weight. They still balance their calorie intake and output very precisely to maintain a constant weight, just as lean people do. It's just that the weight they maintain is higher.

To gain half a pound to a pound a year, an adult needs to eat just ten to twenty calories a day more than she burns. That's about the equivalent of one Ritz cracker.

Yet the laws of thermodynamics dictate that people who are overweight must, at some point, have taken in more energy than they spent in order to gain the extra pounds. "There's no way around it," Leibel says. "You cannot eat like a canary and become the size of a pterodactyl." But in most cases, once obese people have reached a personal set point determined by their own physiology, their weight stabilizes. Their food intake and their metabolic rates, when adjusted for their body size, are similar to those of lean people.

When a person loses weight, however, the circumstances shift dramatically. Whether people start out lean or obese, when they lose 10 to 20 percent of their body weight, their bodies respond by becoming more efficient and using less energy, in an effort to conserve calories and replenish lost reserves of fat. The reduction in energy expenditure is about 15 percent larger than would be expected for the amount of weight lost. That almost certainly accounts for some of the tremendous recidivism among dieters, Leibel says. Studies suggest that some 95 percent of people who lose weight by dieting gain it back within five years.

So though genes determine individual vulnerability to weight gain, environmental factors help dictate the outcome—the weight that a person reaches during childhood or adulthood. Imagine, Leibel says, that you can rank a hundred people, on the basis of their genetic endowment, from 1 to 100 according to their tendency to store excess calories as body fat. Then that same genetic ranking will tell you how they'll line up relative to one another in most environments. What it won't tell you, though, is what those hundred

people will look like in any particular environment. For example, if a hundred people were exposed to famine and had to subsist on a starvation diet, they would all become thin—but some would lose less weight than others, according to their genetic endowments.

In spite of the scientific progress made in disentangling the body's complex systems for regulating food intake, energy use, and energy storage, no one really knows how to treat most cases of obesity. Meanwhile, most of the developed world is facing an expanding public health crisis that clearly has not arisen because of newly mutated genes. Obesity is increasing at an unprecedented rate in the United States, and in many other countries as well. For example: in a study conducted in Europe between 1983 and 1986, more than half of the adults between the ages of thirty-five and sixty-five were either overweight or obese; and even in Japan and China, and throughout Southeast Asia, obesity rates have risen sharply during the past two decades. Recent shifts in the modern environment are undoubtedly at the root of the epidemic. People eat more and move around less. Most of us in the developed world enjoy an abundance of cheap, tasty, high-calorie foods, rely on cars, elevators, and other forms of motorized transportation, and lead sedentary lifestyles, in part because of the difficulty of incorporating walking and other kinds of activity into our daily routines.

Such a "toxic environment," in the words of Kelly D. Brownell, a health psychologist at Yale University, is playing on individual genetic vulnerability, thereby causing unhealthy weight gain in increasing numbers of people. And if environmental factors are at fault, then by changing the environment—or by learning ways whereby we can consciously change our responses to it—it may be possible to slow down or even reverse the trend. Nevertheless, one must sound a cautionary note on what may be too sanguine an assessment: obesity experts who are studying the epidemic think that a comprehensive solution to the rise in obesity will require broad environmental and social changes—a daunting task.

Leibel is proud that his genetic research has helped put a stop to "blaming the victim," shifting the blame for fatness away from the people who suffer from it. The continuing discovery of obesity genes is proof that biological variation in vulnerability to weight gain is the main reason some people are fat and others are lean. That's why Leibel views much of the current national debate about measures to prevent obesity with some concern. He points out that no one yet knows precisely what actions will be most effective. "On some level this is a disease that everybody thinks they understand, and yet in fact nobody understands," he says. "We really don't know what has happened, other than on a very macro, thermodynamic level. Food intake is greater than energy expenditure. Period."

This article was adapted from **Susan Okie's** forthcoming book, *Fed Up! Winning the War against Childhood Obesity,* which is being published by Joseph Henry Press (http://www.jhpress.org) in September 2006.

UNIT 5

Drugs and Health

Unit Selections

Key Points to Consider

- What are the risks associated with college students' drinking?

- How should athletes who abuse enhancement drugs be punished? How should professional sports teams prevent the use of these drugs among athletes?

- Do you think America has a drug problem? Defend your answer.

- Why do teenagers use drugs despite the messages they've heard from DARE and "Just Say No"?

- What are the risks of taking over the counter pain medications?

- Why have certain over the counter medicines been moved behind the counter of drugstores?

Student Web Site
www.mhcls.com/online

Internet References
Further information regarding these Web sites may be found in this book's preface or online.

Food and Drug Administration (FDA)
   http://www.fda.gov/
National Institute on Drug Abuse (NIDA)
   http://www.nida.nih.gov/
Prescription Drugs: The Issue
   http://www.opensecrets.org/news/drug/

As a culture, Americans have come to rely on drugs not only as a treatment for disease but also as an aid for living normal, productive lives. This view of drugs has fostered both a casual attitude regarding their use and a tremendous drug abuse problem. Drug use and abuse has become so widespread that there is no way to describe the typical drug abuser.

There is no simple explanation for why America has become a drug-taking culture, but there is certainly evidence to suggest some of the factors that have contributed to this development. From the time that we are children, we are constantly bombarded by advertisements about how certain drugs can make us feel and look better. While most of these ads deal with proprietary drugs, the belief is created that drugs are a legitimate and effective way to help us cope with everyday problems. Certainly drugs can have a profound effect on how we feel and act, but research has also demonstrated that our mind plays a major role in the healing process.

Growing up, most of us probably had a medicine cabinet full of over-the-counter (OTC) drugs, freely dispensed to family members to treat a variety of ailments. This familiarity with OTC drugs, coupled with rising health care costs, has prompted many people to diagnose and medicate themselves with OTC medications without sufficient knowledge of their possible side effects. While most of these preparations have little potential for abuse, that does not mean that they are innocuous. Generally speaking, OTC drugs are relatively safe if taken at the recommended dosage by healthy people, but the risk of dangerous side effects rises sharply when people exceed the recommended dosage. Another potential danger associated with the use of OTC drugs is the drug interactions that can occur when they are taken in conjunction with prescription medications. The gravest danger associated with the use of OTC drugs is that an individual may use them to control symptoms of an underlying disease and thus prevent its early diagnosis and treatment. In "Some Cold Medicines Move Behind the Counter", Linda Bren discusses why certain OTC cold and allergy medicines are being taken off the shelves and stored behind the counter. Many of these nonprescription drugs are ingredients in illegally produced methamphetamine.

Another category of over the counter medications, herbal preparations, has become extremely popular. They include approximately 750 substances such as herbal teas and other products of botanical origin that are believed to have medicinal properties. Many have been used for centuries with no ill effects, but others have questionable safety records. One drug with a checkered history is the herb ephedra, used in over the counter weight control products sold in pharmacies, mall kiosks, and via the Internet. The death of 23 year old Baltimore Orioles pitcher Steve Bechler in February 2003, attributed to the use of ephedra, brought attention to the risks of the herb. Soon after

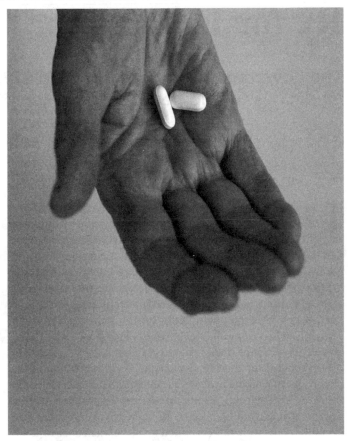

CORBIS Images/Jupiter Images

Bechler's death, minor league baseball banned the herb, joining other sports organization that had already banned its use. Health officials caution consumers against the use of the drug, especially if it's combined with other stimulants such as caffeine, or if strenuous exercise is involved.

As a culture, we have grown up believing that there is, or should be, a drug to treat any malady or discomfort that befalls us. Would we have a drug problem if there were no demand for drugs? One drug which is used widely in the US is alcohol especially on college campuses. Every year over 1,000 students die from alcohol-related causes, mostly drinking and driving. In "Drinking Too Much: Too Young", author Garry Boulard, discusses other risks associated with student drinking including missed classes, falling behind in school work, damage to property, and injuries which occur while under the influence of alcohol. In addition to alcohol, teenagers are also abusing drugs such as prescription pain relievers. In "The Changing Face of Teenage Drug Abuse: The Trend toward Prescription Drugs", Richard Friedman addresses the careless monitoring and regulation of addictive narcotics.

Rx for Fraud

The government is about to spend $720 billion over the next decade on medicines for old people. How much of this is going to be wasted or stolen?

NATHAN VARDI

It won't be long before bad guys start helping themselves to the giant honeypot created by the new Medicare drug benefit, beginning next January. How do we know? Because they're already busy going after the much smaller drug program—a warm-up to the big act—in place today.

The 2003 Medicare law included, for the first time in the 40-year-old program's history, broad prescription coverage. To start, people over 65 could apply for discount cards good for 25% off and for some other subsidies. This was a warm-up to the deeper coverage that kicks in next year.

No sooner was the ink dry on the 25% benefit than complaints started coming in about hucksters and providers violating the rules. The first calls came from Atlanta, where door-to-door salesmen were pitching phony $30 cards. (Even legitimate issuers of the cards were not permitted to hustle them door-to-door.) Then callers weighed in from other states, reporting cases of insurers and pharmacy benefit managers (PBMs) enrolling Medicare beneficiaries without their consent and billing them the $30 enrollment fee—or trying to lure them into other services and products, like medical devices, that Medicare reimbursed. One operator tried to pay pharmacies a fee for directing patients to its card, also verboten. Then there was the alleged scheme by Eileen and Leonardo de Oliveira, involving Canadian and U.S. telemarketers, who bilked 103 people in Illinois of $90,000 by offering them bogus cards, then forwarded their checking account numbers to the De Oliveiras' Florida company, which debited the accounts, according to Illinois Attorney General Lisa Madigan. She charged them civilly with consumer fraud; the De Oliveiras deny any wrongdoing.

Peanuts, compared with what's coming. In November an expected 29 million people 65 and older will start enrolling in Medicare's fully launched prescription drug insurance plan, costing an estimated $720 billion over the first decade. "This is the largest new social benefit program in the history of the country, and it is going to take effect not in pieces but all at once," says James Sheehan, the associate U.S. Attorney in Philadelphia, who has overseen 500 health care fraud cases, including the $330 million settlement by the former SmithKline Beecham for fraudulent billings, and the government's current

case against Medco Health Solutions, alleging kickbacks and false claims. "There are vulnerabilities, and there is going to be fraud in the first year or two."

Or, more likely, starting on Jan. 2. Why? Because the work of guarding the henhouse has been subcontracted, in large measure, to foxes. This vast and complex plan will be run by private middlemen—chiefly HMOs and PBMs, with assists from pharmaceutical companies—some of whom have been offenders in the past. Uncle Sam is relying on their honest accounting to determine how to dispense massive subsidies to them. To make matters worse, the three-phase benefit—each with its own set of rules—creates powerful incentives for old people, with the connivance or even the active participation of doctors and druggists, to pad their pill expenses.

Medicare has long been easy prey. The program has lured such small-time crooks as Mark Little, an Orange County, Calif. podiatrist sentenced to 51 months in April for billing Medicare $800,000 for phantom procedures, and big players like Tenet Healthcare, which, while it denied any wrongdoing, paid $51 million to settle charges that one of its hospitals tried to collect on unnecessary cardiac surgeries. Kickbacks are rife. Dialysis provider Gambro Healthcare agreed to pay $350 million in criminal and civil fines last December to settle charges it paid for doctor referrals; psychiatrist Lewis Gottlieb was convicted last year of taking $200 from wheelchair sellers for each of the hundreds of fraudulent certificates of medical necessity he signed for Medicare beneficiaries (*see box*).

HHS has repeatedly "missed opportunities to use claims data to target areas vulnerable to fraud."

How widespread is the abuse? In the Sept. 30 fiscal year, ending just before the big drug benefit starts up, Medicare will disburse $295 billion. The division of the Health & Human Services Department that runs the program estimates that last year

$20 billion in improper claims were paid out in fee-for-service care, the bulk of Medicare payments. How much of that was deliberate? Don't look to the feds for answers. HHS, says the Government Accountability Office, has repeatedly "missed opportunities to use claims data to target areas vulnerable to fraud."

Safeguarding the new benefit, which applies only to pills, may be even tougher. As Daniel Levinson, acting HHS inspector general, put it to the Senate in February: "Prescription drugs are especially vulnerable to fraud, waste and abuse."

Start with how complicated the three-part plan is. In part one most enrollees will pay $450 or so in annual premiums and a $250 deductible for coverage of 75% of their prescription drug costs up to $2,250—from Lipitor to Viagra. Then comes the controversial "doughnut hole" (*see box*), which leaves participants in financial limbo, paying all drug costs out of their own pockets until they've spent $3,600. (Couples are treated as individuals for insurance purposes.) At that point, phase three, catastrophic coverage kicks in, with Medicare paying 95% of expenses.

For its part the government is trying to identify and anticipate certain types of cheating. In March law enforcement officials and bureaucrats gathered in Omaha to discuss scenarios in which bad guys piggybacked on the new benefit to commit identity theft, or signed up without being qualified. The cops worried about how to prevent legitimate beneficiaries from being used to funnel lucrative and potentially dangerous drugs like OxyContin to black markets. They contemplated how easy it would be for older people qualifying for 95% coverage to buy more drugs than they intend to take, passing along the pills to relatives who aren't covered. Or simply giving, say, their Tamiflu to a sick neighbor or their Enbrel to a 59-year-old friend with arthritis. For that matter, what's to stop physicians from bulking up their prescription pads? After several decades of private insurance, doctors have come to rationalize a little fudging of diagnoses if that helps the patient with his insurance. No reason to expect the ethical dilemma to come out any differently when the victim is Uncle Sam rather than United Healthcare.

In April HHS identified 33 different areas of potential flimflammery. Among them:

Shifty Discounting

A bone of contention for the medicaid program, which shells out some $37 billion a year for poor patients' drugs, is whether the government is paying a fair price. The drug companies are forbidden to charge any more than they charge private-sector insurers. But sometimes they do. They give secret rebates to the private sector but bill Medicaid for the list price. "Inadequate oversight" and "limited checks" by the government mean complete rebates often do not get reported, leading to overpaying by the federal government, said the Government Accountability Office in February.

Schering-Plough settled a Medicaid case for $345 million last year that shows how tough it can be to track rebates. The feds claimed the maker of Claritin, in a price war with the producer of the competing drug Allegra, gave concealed discounts to Cigna and PacifiCare Health Systems in the form of "data processing fees," interest free loans and "risk share" rebates tied to growth in an insurer's outlays for antihistamine-like drugs.

The Black Hole

There are those on Capitol Hill who still remember what happened 16 years ago to Dan Rostenkowski, the former Democratic head of the House Ways & Means Committee. After he backed an $800 per capita surtax to pay for Medicare's catastrophic illness insurance, Medicarees in Chicago jumped on the hood of his car and chased him down the street. The surtax was repealed within months.

Nearly 7 million people will end up in the doughnut hole next year, says the Kaiser Family Foundation. This is the bracket (from $2,250 to $3,600 in drug outlays) in which Medicare recipients are supposed to cover 100% of their costs. Moreover, 7.4 million people will spend more on drugs than they currently do. Of those, according to the foundation, 2.4 million are retirees who will see a significant surge in their costs because they will be shifted from more generous employer plans to the new Medicare benefit.

They are prey for the unscrupulous—from those peddling nonexistent coverage to pharmaceutical firms that offer cash or in-kind drug assistance specifically to lure old people to a particular plan or help push them out of the doughnut hole and into catastrophic coverage, so that Medicare picks up almost the whole tab. The government offers no guidance to patients or corporations about how to fill the gap.

Political pressures will be hard to resist. Especially since the number of doughnut-hole denizens will peak right around election time next year. Plugging the hole could be "astronomically expensive," says Edmund F. Haislmaier, a research fellow at the Heritage Foundation, probably costing the government hundreds of billions of extra dollars.

—N.V.

The temptations will be all the larger in Medicare's new drug program. Suppose a manufacturer has a high-priced, branded drug for asthma, used mostly by younger patients, and a high-priced drug for arthritis, used mostly by the old. Both drugs face competition from equivalent remedies sold by other pharma companies. To win slots on the drug formulary of a middleman (PBM or HMO), the pharma outfit has to offer some discounts. Would it be 10% across the board? There's little to stop the negotiators from coming up with a package deal in which the asthma medication gets a 20% discount but the arthritis medication gets no discount. In other words, a disproportionate share of the nation's pharmacy bill gets shifted onto the taxpayer. "We're going to have a whole new creative urge, and such bundling is plausible," says Keith Korenchuk, a Washington, D.C. lawyer who advises drugmakers.

Drug Switching

HHS is already on record that this is a potential trouble spot. In this scenario a doctor prescribes Lipitor ($2.30 a pill), but the pharmacy benefit manager pushes the physician to use a more expensive drug, say, Zocor ($4). What the doctor and patient don't know, in an improper switch, is that the PBM gets some benefit from the manufacturer of the more expensive pill.

Associate U.S. Attorney Sheehan sued Medco in 2003, accusing the nation's largest PBM of, among other things, improper drug switching "to enhance its revenue regardless of health plan costs, or of any potential adverse or life-threatening clinical outcomes to patients." The government claimed Medco received "substantial sums" from Merck and other pillmakers to advocate switches to their drugs even when the disfavored drugs were cheaper or more effective. It also alleged the switches "resulted in increased costs to health plans and patients, primarily in follow-up doctor visits and tests." Medco got $440 million in 2001 from Merck, its then-parent, that was not disclosed to its clients, to favor Merck's products, the suit said. Reaping a financial benefit in return for health care referrals can qualify as an illegal kickback under federal law. Medco settled the drug-switching allegations last year without admitting wrongdoing, agreeing to pay $29 million to 20 states. It also agreed to disclose financial incentives for drug switches and not substitute more expensive drugs for cheaper ones.

Prescription Shorting

It's the oldest trick in the medicine cabinet and still has authorities worried. A pharmacy distributes high doses of AstraZeneca's Nexium, for example, billing the Medicare drug plan and the beneficiary for $380 for 90 tablets, but dispensing only 88.

In a recent case the Eckerd pharmacy chain paid $9 million in 2002 to the feds and 18 states to settle claims that it dispensed partial prescriptions but billed Medicaid and other programs for full quantities. Its Eckerd ECK MD affiliate also paid a $1.7 million fine to deal with a related criminal investigation in 2001. In both these cases inventories at drugstores were low, and customers did not return to stores to pick up the outstanding pills owed to them. Eckerd blamed the problem on processing limitations, adding that new systems were installed to deal with what was an "industrywide issue." Indeed, Walgreen Co., the nation's biggest pharmacy chain, settled governmental short-filling claims for $7.6 million in 1999.

Palm Greasing

Why would a doctor prescribe a $6 antibiotic instead of one that costs 12 cents? The pill industry is rife with incentives. "You can bet pharmaceutical companies do what they can to seduce doctors," says Jerome Kassirer, a kidney specialist and former editor-in-chief of the *New England Journal of Medicine*. "They entertain them at expensive restaurants, engage them as consultants and put them on their speakers' bureaus."

Pfizer paid $430 million last year to settle government charges that its Warner-Lambert unit dangled money and trips to persuade doctors to use its epilepsy drug, Neurontin, to treat other conditions for which it was not approved, like migraines, attention deficit disorder and alcohol withdrawal. The feds claimed Warner paid physicians consulting fees to attend dinners and trips to Florida, Hawaii and the Olympics, even though

Scam on Wheels

Government spending on power wheelchairs climbed 450% between 1999 and 2003, to $1.2 billion. A report released last year by Health & Human Services' inspector general found that only 13% of those it surveyed who got the most popular wheelchair met the Medicare coverage requirements. This is what happens when someone is spending other people's money.

The four contractors that process Medicare's wheelchair claims—Palmetto GBA, Cigna HealthCare, AdminaStar Federal and HealthNow New York—saw a spurt in spending as early as 1997, but the office that runs Medicare and Medicaid did not lead a coordinated response until 2003, says the Government Accountability Office.

In one egregious case last year the U.S. Attorney in Houston charged two physicians, Charles Skripka Jr. and Jayshree Patel, for conspiring to defraud Medicare of $40 million between February 2002 and June 2003. The duo allegedly approved wheelchairs for up to 50 Medicare beneficiaries per day, in return for kickbacks from the suppliers. The doctors have pleaded not guilty; the owner of their clinic, Lewis Gottlieb, has put in a guilty plea and is helping the government.

The feds in April sued the Scooter Store of New Braunfels, Tex., which billed Medicare for $400 million or so since 1997. In ads, the Scooter Store suggested to old folks that the government would pay for scooters. But, the government alleges, when customers called the company to inquire about reimbursement, the Scooter Store pushed motorized wheelchairs on them, with the result that Medicare ended up paying for expensive and unnecessary equipment. The government is supposed to pay for a motor-driven chair only if the patient would be confined to bed without one. The Scooter Store says it has done nothing wrong and that the government is trying to get out of repaying legitimate claims.

—N.V.

"there was little or no significant consulting provided by the physicians."

HHS is thinking about all manner of other kinds of skullduggery that haven't yet surfaced but surely will. Among them: A pharmacy submits bills for pills not provided and alters prescriptions to secure fatter payments, or bills for branded drugs but dispenses generics; an insurer gooses enrollment counts in order to increase subsidies.

Perhaps the biggest invitation to shenanigans is the doughnut hole—where old people pay for their own drugs. The incentive to produce fake receipts to inflate a patient's out-of-pocket spending and push him into 95% coverage is all too obvious. "If pharmacies or pharmaceutical companies are working to milk the system, they will all have an interest in getting them through the coverage gap by producing paperwork to show inflated volumes," says Malcolm Sparrow, a professor of public management at Harvard.

PBMs and HMOs that operate plans also have a financial interest in steering discounts they get from pill companies to the early part of the plan. That's because they receive a fixed, direct subsidy from Medicare unaffected by discounts from drugmakers during the first phase of 75% coverage. In the 95% bracket, by contrast, HMOs receive subsidies that vary, based on pill costs, and are reduced by discounts they receive from pharmas.

Watchdogging all this will be hellish. "We have some new electronic systems in place to help us stay on top of it," says Mark McClellan, M.D., Medicare's chief. Yet the HHS division that will do the work has lost one quarter of its executives in the last three years, and 46% of its workforce will be eligible for retirement in the next four years. Most oversight—auditing claims and reviewing Medicare payments—will be farmed out to private contractors.

The biggest invitation to abuse is the doughnut hole—where the elderly pay for their own drugs.

Palmetto GBA of Columbia, S.C., a BlueCross BlueShield unit of the state, was supposed to be minding the Medicare store in Florida. But according to a government suit against a Miami supplier, Palmetto okayed $144 million worth of claims for artificial limbs, many of which were not required by the recipients. A federal judge in Miami was recently quoted in the *Miami Herald* as saying, "It is unclear why Palmetto GBA is not a subject of the . . . investigation into criminal wrongdoing." Palmetto blames the overpayments on, among other things, a lack of government funding for its oversight, and notes that it denied $149 million of Medicare artificial-limb claims in the last two years.

The HHS Office of Inspector General is receiving a one-time $25 million boost to fight fraud associated with the prescription drug benefit. The FBI unit overseeing health care lost 121 agents between 2000 and 2003. As for the $114 million the FBI receives each year to fight health care fraud, the GAO says some of the funds may have been improperly used to fight other crimes, like terrorism. The government probably won't invest heavily in protecting its $720 billion investment until a fair amount of money has been lost.

From *Forbes* Magazine, June 20, 2005, pp. 124–130. Reprinted by permission of Forbes Magazine, © 2005 Forbes Media Inc.

Some Cold Medicines Move Behind Counter

Some over-the-counter (OTC) cold and allergy medicines are being moved behind the counter at pharmacies nationwide as part of the fight against illegal drug production.

LINDA BREN

Under the Patriot Act signed by President Bush on March 9, 2006, all drug products that contain the ingredient pseudoephedrine must be kept behind the pharmacy counter and must be sold in limited quantities to consumers after they show identification and sign a logbook.

Pseudoephedrine is a drug found in both OTC and prescription products used to relieve nasal or sinus congestion caused by the common cold, sinusitis, hay fever, and other respiratory allergies. The drug is also a key ingredient in making methamphetamine—a powerful, highly addictive stimulant often produced illegally by "meth cooks" in home laboratories.

The new legal provisions for selling and purchasing pseudoephedrine-containing products are part of the Combat Methamphetamine Epidemic Act of 2005, which was incorporated into the Patriot Act. These "anti-meth" provisions introduce safeguards to make certain ingredients used in methamphetamine manufacturing more difficult to obtain in bulk and easier for law enforcement to track.

According to the National Institute on Drug Abuse, methamphetamine use and abuse is associated with serious health conditions including memory loss, aggression, violence, paranoia, hallucinations, and potential heart and brain damage. The Drug Enforcement Administration says there is a direct relationship between methamphetamine abuse and increased incidents of domestic violence and child abuse.

Meth users ingest the substance by swallowing, inhaling, injecting, or smoking it. There are currently no safe and tested medications for treating methamphetamine addiction.

The new law affects several hundred OTC products for children and adults, such as Sudafed Nasal Decongestant Tablets, Advil Allergy Sinus Caplets, TheraFlu Daytime Severe Cold SoftGels, Tylenol Flu NightTime Gelcaps, and Children's Vicks NyQuil Cold/Cough Relief. "There are very few decongestants on the market that don't contain pseudoephedrine," says Charles Ganley, M.D., director of the Food and Drug Administration's Office of Nonprescription Products.

Ganley says that products containing pseudoephedrine are still available without a prescription and that they are packaged the same way as any OTC drug. "The only difference is that people will have to go to the pharmacist to buy them," he says. "They just need to ask for them and show ID, and know that there's a limit to the amount they can purchase."

Buyers must show a government-issued photo ID, such as a driver's license, and sign a logbook. Stores are required to keep a record about purchases, which includes the product name, quantity sold, name and address of purchaser, and date and time of the sale, for at least two years. Single-dose packages containing 60 milligrams or less of pseudoephedrine are excluded from the recordkeeping requirement, but must still be stored behind the counter.

The federal law limits the amount of pseudoephedrine an individual can purchase to 3.6 grams in a single day and 9 grams in a month at a retail store. For example, a person may buy Advil Allergy Sinus Caplets, which contain pseudoephedrine and other ingredients, in quantities of up to 146 tablets in one day and 366 tablets in one month. The number of pills or amount of liquid medicine allowable will vary depending on the type of product and its strength.

The limits on the amount an individual can purchase became effective April 8, 2006. The requirements to place products behind the counter and to keep a logbook take effect Sept. 30, 2006. Many drug stores are already complying voluntarily or because some state laws require similar controls.

Drug companies are reformulating some of their products to eliminate pseudoephedrine. Pfizer, for example, while still offering Sudafed nasal decongestants, which contain pseudoephedrine, also markets a line called Sudafed PE as an "on the shelf" alternative. Sudafed PE contains the active ingredient phenylephrine, which is not used to make methamphetamine, and so is not under the same restrictions as pseudoephedrine.

"Drugs that contain phenylephrine are also safe and effective," says Ganley. "The dosing is a little different—you have to take them a little more frequently than the pseudoephedrine-containing drugs because their effects are not as long-lasting."

The anti-meth provisions of the Patriot Act restrict the sale of two other drug ingredients, ephedrine and phenylpropanolamine, because of their potential to be used illegally to make methamphetamine. Like pseudoephedrine, drugs containing these ingredients must be placed behind the counter, and buyers must show identification to purchase a limited quantity.

Synthetic ephedrine is used in some topical drugs, such as nose drops, to temporarily relieve congestion due to colds, hay fever, sinusitis, or other upper respiratory allergies. It is also used orally for temporary relief of asthma symptoms.

Phenylpropanolamine was commonly used in OTC decongestants and weight-loss drugs. Today, it is unlikely that consumers will find phenylpropanolamine in their drug stores, says Ganley. In 2000, the FDA asked drug manufacturers to discontinue marketing products containing phenylpropanolamine because of an increased risk of bleeding in the brain (hemorrhagic stroke) associated with the ingredient. The FDA has taken regulatory actions to remove phenylpropanolamine from all drug products.

From *FDA Consumer*, July/August 2006, pp. 18–19. Published 2006 by U.S. Food and Drug Administration. www.fda.gov

Drinking Too Much, Too Young

Trying to find an answer to the persistent habit of binge drinking among young people vexes the nation's policymakers.

GARRY BOULARD

The stories have been shocking, abruptly reminding a nation of a problem that remains unsolved: in the last half of 2004, six college-age students in Colorado died as a result of binge drinking.

Although each fatality was different in its circumstance—Samantha Spady, 19, a sophomore at Colorado State University, died after drinking vanilla vodka and more than two dozen beers, while Benett Bertoli, 20, also a CSU student, was found dead on a couch at an off-campus party from a combination of alcohol, methadone and benzodiazepene—the events leading up to the deaths were maddeningly familiar.

In almost every case, the fatalities were the unexpected ending to a boisterous party almost always involving large gatherings of young people on weekend nights consuming prodigious amounts of alcohol, sometimes for two days straight.

The number of Colorado deaths from binge drinking in late 2004 was exceptionally large, but the state is not alone. It killed Thomas Ryan Hauser, 23, a student at Virginia Tech in September. Blake Hammontree, 19, died at his fraternity house at the University of Oklahoma, also in September. Bradley Kemp, 20, died in October at his home near the University of Arkansas, where he was a student. Steven Judd died celebrating his 21st birthday with fraternity friends at New Mexico State University in November.

Those deaths did not occur in a vacuum. According to statistics from the National Institute for Alcohol Abuse and Alcoholism, more than 1,400 college students die from alcohol-related deaths each year including motor vehicle crashes. Unfortunately, that number has remained constant even though both high school and college-age drinking has decreased.

"The numbers have been going in the right direction," says Peter Cressy, the president of the Distilled Spirits Council of the United States. "There is today less regular use of alcohol on college campuses than there was 20 years ago. There has been a drop in the number of college students both of age and not of age who drink at all during any given month. And the data for eighth, 10th, and 12th graders who consume alcohol has also shown a downward trend."

Bucking the Trend

But what hasn't changed, industry, health and alcohol experts all agree, is the stubborn number of young people who continue to engage in destructive behavior.

"The issue is not the 30,000 kids on the campus of the University of Colorado, or any other school, who drink legally or illegally, but somehow manage to do it without any great peril," says Ralph Blackman, the president of the Century Council, a not-for-profit organization dedicated to fighting drunk driving and underage drinking.

"The issue is binge drinking and the continuing large numbers of kids who insist on over consumption to a level that has a very decided risk for a dangerous result," continues Blackman. "That is a phenomenon that very much remains with us."

Trying to find a specific reason for the persistence of binge drinking among the young is a subject that both vexes and causes great debate among the nation's policymakers. Do younger people just naturally like to get drunk, or in some cases, very drunk? Is it a matter of upbringing or income? Is it a reflection of a troubled and anxious society?

"You could ask questions like that all day, and not really get any solid answers," says Paul Hanson, a professor emeritus of sociology at the State University of New York, Potsdam.

"The only thing you could be sure of is that no matter how many different ways we approach it with different solutions, binge drinking continues among the very young, generation after generation."

But some experts believe one thing that is different with those who are a part of what demographers call the Millennials—those born in 1980 or after—and their predecessors, is that binge drinking today is out of the closet and celebrated on almost a worldwide basis due to the Internet.

"There is a huge difference from when many of us went to school in the 1960s and '70s and today," says Stephen Bentley, a coordinator of substance abuse services at the Wardenberg Health Center at the University of Colorado.

"Back in our day we really did not want any attention of any kind, we did not want adults or the world to know that we were drinking and partying excessively," continues Bentley.

"But today young people who engage in this kind of behavior are actually very proud of what they are doing, they post their own Web sites about their parties so that everyone else can see what they did."

One of the Web sites, called shamings.com, features pictures of drunken young men, updated on a regular basis, sometimes sleeping in their own vomit, often half naked, and many times covered with magic marker salutations alluding to their drinking prowess or lack thereof.

One of the Web site creators, Ricky Van Veen, explained to the Washington Post the guidelines used by the Web site in determining whether or not to post a binge drinker's picture: "The standard rule is, if you fall asleep with your shoes on, you're fair game," he said.

Youth Targets

For Julia Sherman, field director with the Center on Alcohol Marketing and Youth, binge drinking self-promotion is almost a natural outgrowth of what she says is the alcohol industry's "preoccupation with the young."

"The ads that are being put out there today are not your Mom and Pop, 'Mabel, Black Label,' ads of another era, but ads that are very much geared toward an exceedingly young demographic," she says.

"The whole ad focus of the alcohol industry has changed both in tenor and in numbers," says Sherman. "Their Web site ads now feature computer games and premiums for downloading music. They run ads in what are called the 'laddie magazines,' that are edgier than anything adults are seeing in their magazines. It is all part of a non-stop, never-ending pitch for the youth market."

According to a study released by the Center on Alcohol Marketing and Youth last October, the number of alcohol ads on TV jumped by nearly 90,000 between 2001 and 2003, with some 23 percent of the ads "more likely to be seen by the average under-age person for every four seen by the average adult."

Cressey of the Distilled Spirits Council, among other industry leaders, disputes that there has been any concerted targeting of young people, and notes that his group will not permit any member to advertise where the media is not at least a 70/30, adult to minor, demographic.

"We also require through our code that all models in our ads be at least 25 years old," adds Cressey, a requirement that is also generally followed by members of the Beer Institute.

But even working within those parameters, the impact of drinking ads, usually showing young people at a beach party, rap concert, or skate boarding, remains a matter of contention.

"The problem is that how we view television has changed greatly in the last generation," says Sherman. "It used to be that there was

---

Binge Drinking—The Facts

- In 2001, 44% of U.S. college students engaged in binge drinking; this rate has not changed since 1993.
- 51% of the men drank five or more drinks in a row.
- 40% of the women drank four or more drinks in a row.
- Students more likely to binge drink are white, age 23 or younger, and are residents of a fraternity or sorority.
- 75.1% of fraternity residents and 62.4% of sorority residents report binge drinking.
- Binge drinkers in high school are three times more likely to binge in college.
- From 1993 to 2001, more students abstained from alcohol (16% to 19%), but more also frequently drank heavily (19.7% to 22.8%).
- Just as many freshman (those under 21) as seniors binge drink.
- Frequent binge drinkers are eight times more likely than others to miss a class, fall behind in schoolwork, get hurt or injured, and damage property.
- 91% of women and 78% of the men who are frequent binge drinkers consider themselves to be moderate or light drinkers.
- 1,400 college students every year die from alcohol-related causes; 1,100 of these deaths involve drinking and driving.

Sources: Harvard University's School of Public Health; Robert Wood Johnson Foundation

---

one TV and the entire family was watching it, which meant that there would probably be some sort of adult filtering or response to whatever the ad message was. But that is much harder today when over 30 percent of kids aged two to eight, and two-thirds over the age of eight, have their own TVs in their own rooms."

The end result may not only be a message received early on that drinking alcohol is attractive, but an actual inability at an age leading all the way up to college to discern alcohol's potential danger. "There is a lot of research out there showing that even up to the age of 21 and beyond a young body is not fully developed and it does not absorb alcohol as well as it might in an older person," says Blackman of the Century Council. "Just as important is the evidence that your brain is not fully developed at that point either, so that issues of risk-taking and behavior are assessed in a different way."

To make matters worse, State University of New York's Hanson says, zero tolerance alcohol programs or efforts to make campuses virtually alcohol-free have a funny way of backfiring. "Prohibition is a classic example of how the laws in these matters can end up being counterproductive by actually making the thing that is being prohibited more attractive. That remains especially true for young people who don't like to be told what not to do."

"And when that happens," says Hanson, "young people very often find themselves involved in these dangerous events centered around heavy episodic drinking, which is the very last thing we want to see happen."

Teaching Moderation

Hanson has also noticed in his own research that the percentage of students who drink tends to decrease as they go from being freshmen to seniors. He says policymakers would be wiser to focus on what he calls "harm reduction policies" that acknowledge young people are going to drink no matter what, but emphasize responsible drinking through education—even to minors.

Similarly Colorado University's Bentley has noticed the effectiveness of the restorative justice approach on many college campuses that require students who have engaged in binge drinking to face the people who suffered the consequences of their behavior when they were drunk.

"That means the neighbors who were trying to study when the party was blaring," says Bentley, "or friends who had to take care of them when they were throwing up all over themselves or were otherwise dead drunk."

Legislatively, some lawmakers are looking at keg-registration laws in order to keep better track of who buys what for whom, particularly when such kegs end up at parties heavily populated with minors. So far, 24 states and the District of Columbia have adopted keg registration laws of varying severity.

"It is only a tool that might possibly reduce binge drinking and underage drinking," says Arizona Representative Ted Downing, who has introduced legislation requiring the state to put tracking numbers on every keg of beer sold.

"The way my legislation reads is that if you want to buy a keg, you have to show identification, fill out a form, leave a deposit, and detail where the keg is going to go and for what purpose" says Downing.

Other lawmakers believe that by making underage consumption and distribution more legally challenging, they can, at the very least, chip away at the roughly 33 percent of the nation's college students who are below the age of 21.

"It's worth a try," says Colorado Representative Angie Paccione, who has introduced legislation making it a class one misdemeanor to distribute alcohol to someone under the age of 21, with jail time of up to 18 months and fines topping out at $5,000.

"We want to give the DAs a tool that they can use for prosecuting and that the police can use in order to effect behavior changes," Paccione says, adding that problem college drinking is very often proceeded by problem high school drinking.

"I was a dean in a high school and have seen more than my share of kids who have had liquid lunches," she says. "So I know that this is a problem that begins very early."

Education Works

And although a new look at both underage and binge drinking from the legislative perspective may be in order, Jeff Becker, president of the Beer Institute, says lawmakers should not lose sight of the progress that has already been made in reducing both high school and college drinking.

"The education and awareness programs have really worked, whether it is at the college or high school level; and I think lawmakers should take credit for any support they have given to those efforts and continue those programs," says Becker.

"Maybe these most recent deaths will serve as a wake-up call and get all of us to look once more at what works and what doesn't work," he adds. "But from the community, family and school level it is very clear that making kids aware of the dangers has also made them smarter. And I don't think we should stop doing that."

In Connecticut, Senator Biagio "Billy" Ciotto, a long-time advocate of programs that educate high school students on the harmful effects of both drinking and driving and binge drinking, says he remains convinced that lawmakers should concentrate on what he calls the "realistic goal of reduction" vs. the "impossible idea," of elimination.

"You are never going to get rid of this kind of drinking completely," Ciotto says. "But I have no doubt in my mind that you can reduce the abuse simply by staying with it, never giving up, always trying to let kids know, without lecturing them, about the harmful effects of alcohol abuse."

Ciotto's efforts have even won the support of the Connecticut Coalition to Stop Underage Drinking, which named him "Outstanding Legislator in Reducing Underage Drinking" in 2004.

"I think they and just about everyone else recognize that we have to work on the big majority of kids who will not abuse alcohol if they know the dangers, and just figure that there is always going to be a minority that will do what they want to do no matter what, he says."

Arizona's Downing agrees: "It would be very foolish for any state representative or senator to feel that you can propose a bill that will somehow magically get rid of the problems of binge drinking or underage drinking."

"You can't," says Downing. "And we have to admit that. All you can really do is nudge things in a certain direction, which is what so many of our laws do anyway. If people are going to behave in the wrong way no matter what, there is only so much we can do. But we can help those who want to do the right thing, or don't want to break any laws just to have a little fun. That is the group we need to appeal to."

Free-lancer **GARRY BOULARD** is a frequent contributor to State Legislatures.

The Changing Face of Teenage Drug Abuse—The Trend toward Prescription Drugs

Richard A. Friedman, MD

When Eric, an 18-year-old who lives in San Francisco, wants to get some Vicodin (hydrocodone–acetaminophen), it's a simple matter. "I can get prescription drugs from different places and don't ever have to see a doctor," he explained. "I have friends whose parents are pill addicts, and we 'borrow' from them. Other times I have friends who have ailments who get lots of pills and sell them for cheap. As long as prescription pills are taken right, they're much safer than street drugs."

Eric's habits reflect an emerging pattern in drug use by teenagers: illicit street drugs such as "ecstasy" (3,4-methylenedioxymethamphetamine) and cocaine are decreasing in popularity, whereas the nonmedical use of certain prescription drugs is on the rise. These findings were reported in the Monitoring the Future survey, which is sponsored by the National Institute on Drug Abuse and designed and conducted by researchers at the University of Michigan.[1] The study, which began in 1975, annually surveys a nationally representative sample of about 50,000 students in 400 public and private secondary schools in the United States.

"We're living in a time that seems decidedly more apocalyptic. . . . Maybe we need something to slow down."

Overall, the proportion of teens who reported having used any illicit drug during the previous year has dropped by more than a third among 8th graders and by about 10 percent among 12th graders since the peaks reported in the mid-to-late 1990s, according to the 2005 survey. Alcohol use and cigarette smoking among teens are now at historic lows. In contrast, the number of high-school students who are abusing prescription pain relievers such as oxycodone (OxyContin), a potent and highly addictive opiate, or sedatives is on the rise. A total of 7.2 percent of high-school seniors reported nonmedical use of sedatives in 2005, up from a low of 2.8 percent in 1992 (see graph). Reported use of oxycodone in this group increased from 4.0 percent in 2002 to 5.5 percent in 2005.

The survey did not ask teenagers how they obtained their prescription drugs, but there is little doubt that the medications are easy to get from a variety of sources. "Prescription drugs are a lot easier to get than street drugs," said John, a high-school sophomore in Austin, Texas. "Kids can get them on the street, from parents and friends, or on the Internet."

They can also get them all too easily from physicians, according to recent data from the National Center on Addiction and Substance Abuse at Columbia University.[2] A 2004 survey of physicians found that 43 percent did not ask about prescription-drug abuse when taking a patient's history, and one third did not regularly call or obtain records from the patient's previous physician before prescribing potentially addictive drugs. These alarming data suggest that physicians are much too lax in prescribing controlled drugs. Claire, an 18-year-old who lives in Maine, told me, "You can always find a doctor who you can convince that you have a sleeping problem to get Ambien [zolpidem] or that you have ADD [attention-deficit disorder] and get Adderall." And even if most teenagers do not seek controlled prescription drugs directly from doctors, physicians are surely the original source of much of the medication that teens use, which has been diverted from its intended recipients.

In explaining the increase in the recreational use of prescription drugs, many teenagers draw key distinctions between these drugs and illicit street drugs. Teenagers whom I interviewed said that whereas they used illicit drugs only for recreation, they often used prescription drugs for "practical" effects: hypnotic drugs for sleep, stimulants to enhance their school performance, and tranquilizers such as benzodiazepines to decrease stress. They often characterized their use of prescription drugs as "responsible," "controlled," or "safe." The growing popularity of prescription drugs also reflects the perception that these drugs are safer than street drugs. According to the Monitoring the Future survey, for example, the use of sedatives among

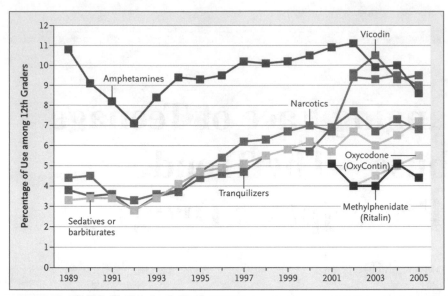

Figure 1 Prevalence of Use of Prescription Drugs without Medical Supervision among 12th Graders.

Data are from the Monitoring the Future survey. In 2001, the text of the question regarding tranquilizers was changed in half the questionnaire forms: Miltown (meprobamate) was replaced by Xanax (alprazolam) in the list of examples. This resulted in a slight increase in the reported prevalence. In 2002, the remaining questionnaire forms were changed. Also in 2002, the text of the question about narcotics other than heroin was changed in half the questionnaire forms: Talwin (pentazocine–naloxone), laudanum, and paregoric (which all reportedly had negligible rates of use by 2001) were replaced with Vicodin (hydrocodone–acetaminophen), OxyContin (oxycodone), and Percocet (oxycodone–acetaminophen). This resulted in an increase in reported prevalence, and in 2003, the remaining questionnaire forms were changed.

high-school seniors has increased in tandem with a decrease in the perceived risk and an increase in peer-group approval of the use of sedatives, whereas amphetamine use has steadily dropped as the perceived risk and societal disapproval have increased.

What might explain the growing confidence in the safety of prescription drugs? Negative media attention is frequently cited as a factor in the decreasing popularity of cocaine and stimulants among teenagers. The converse appears to be true regarding prescription medications. Nowadays, it is nearly impossible to open a newspaper, turn on the television, or search the Internet without encountering an advertisement for a prescription medication. Expenditures by the pharmaceutical industry for direct-to-consumer advertising increased from $1.8 billion in 1999 to $4.2 billion in 2004.[3,4] One effect has been to foster an image of prescription drugs as an integral and routine aspect of everyday life. Any adverse effects are relegated to the fine print of an advertisement or dispatched in a few seconds of rapid-fire speech.

Not all prescription drugs, however, have equal appeal among teenagers. According to the Monitoring the Future study, calming prescription drugs have become more popular, whereas the use of stimulants is decreasing. Whether this trend reflects the differential availability of sedative drugs, the selective effects of advertising, or other social factors is anyone's guess. Asked to speculate about it, teenagers said more or less what John, the teen from Austin, expressed in an e-mail message: "We're

living in a time that seems decidedly more apocalyptic, especially since 9/11 and all the recent natural disasters. Maybe we need something to slow down."

The perception that prescription drugs are largely safe seems to justify the attitude that occasional use poses little risk. And indeed, there is little doubt that many more people try drugs than become serious drug abusers. For example, in the 2004 National Household Survey on Drug Abuse, 19 percent of persons between 12 and 17 years of age reported ever having used marijuana, whereas 14.5 percent reported use during the previous year, and only 7.6 percent reported use during the previous month.[5]

Still, the fact that 50 percent of students have tried an illicit drug by the time they finish high school—another finding of the Monitoring the Future survey—is nothing to be happy about, not to mention the 5.5 percent of 12th graders who have tried the highly addictive oxycodone. For a substantial number of teenagers with risk factors, such as a psychiatric illness or a family history of drug abuse, crossing the line from abstinence to exposure will be the first step toward serious substance abuse.

Moreover, even in small doses, sedatives, hypnotics, and opiates have subtle effects on cognition and motor skills that may increase the risk of injury, particularly during sports activities or driving. From a longer-term perspective, the brains of teenagers are still developing, and the effects of drug abuse may be harmful in ways that are not yet understood. Do we really want teenagers to think nothing of popping a pill to relax, get through the tedium of a long homework assignment, or relieve normal anxieties?

Clearly, physicians play an important role in this problem, given their apparent laxness in prescribing controlled drugs. Physicians should routinely assess their patients for substance use and psychiatric illness before they put pen to a prescription pad. They should also discuss with their adult patients who have teenage children the risks associated with controlled drugs and the need to restrict the availability of such drugs at home.

In order to address these problems appropriately, physicians need adequate education in substance abuse. The survey by the National Center on Addiction and Substance Abuse reveals that physicians do not feel they are well trained to spot signs of substance abuse or addiction—a skill that should be taught in all medical schools and residency programs.

Finally, educators and parents must address the potential dangers of prescription-drug abuse with teenagers. As Claire put it, "In a way, prescription drugs are more dangerous than street drugs, because we don't recognize their dangers."

(The names of the teenagers who were interviewed have been changed to protect their privacy.)

Notes

1. Johnston LD, O'Malley PM, Bachman JG, Schulenberg JE. Monitoring the future: national results on adolescent drug use: overview of key findings, 2005. Bethesda, Md.: National Institute on Drug Abuse (in press).

2. Doe J. Under the counter: the diversion and abuse of controlled prescription drugs in the U.S. New York: National Center on Addiction and Substance Abuse of Columbia University, 2005.

3. R&D spending. In: PhRMA annual membership survey. Washington, D.C.: Pharmaceutical Research and Manufacturers of America, 2004.

4. Promotional data. In: Integrated Promotional Services and CMR. Fairfield, Conn.: IMS Health, June 2004.

5. Office of Applied Studies. Results from the 2004 National Survey on Drug Use & Health: national findings. NSDUH series H-28. Rockville, Md.: Substance Abuse and Mental Health Services Administration, 2005. (DHHS publication no. SMA 05-4062.)

Dr. Friedman is a psychiatrist and the director of the Psychopharmacology Clinic at Weill Cornell Medical College, New York.

The Price of Pain

You get relief. You also get some health risk. This is the deal you cut

AMANDA SPAKE AND JILL KONIECZKO

In the past few months, David Borenstein's life and his Washington, D.C., rheumatology practice have become something of a nightmare. Most of his patients suffer chronic pain and inflammation from arthritis, back pain, or muscular-skeletal diseases. "I see over 100 patients a week," says Borenstein. "My life is about trying to keep these people functional."

And that mission is becoming an increasingly difficult challenge every day. In the past few weeks, both Celebrex and Bextra—which belong to a popular class of pain relievers known as Cox-2 inhibitors—and the widely used over-the-counter pain reliever naproxen, sold as Aleve, have been linked to an increase in heart attacks and strokes. Two large government-funded trials of these drugs to prevent colon cancer and Alzheimer's disease have been stopped, though officials admit that the heart risk revealed in these studies is preliminary and conflicts with data from other studies. The drugmaker Pfizer agreed to stop direct-to-consumer advertising of Celebrex after patients taking the drug had a 2.5-fold increased risk of major cardiovascular events. The Food and Drug Administration issued an advisory recommending that doctors limit use of the Cox-2 inhibitors and that consumers adhere to the label directions for nonprescription pain pills, taking them no longer than 10 days without physician supervision.

Nation in pain. As a result, many doctors have been deluged with calls from frightened patients. "Everybody takes these drugs," says Elizabeth Tindall, president of the American College of Rheumatology and in private practice in Portland, Ore. Indeed, pain reliever sales are estimated by Kalorama Information at more than $18.8 billion in 2004, not surprising when over 30 million Americans take a nonsteroidal anti-inflammatory drug, or NSAID, every day.

Until recently, the NSAID naproxen was thought to be mildly protective of the heart. Available over the counter for the past decade, naproxen is recommended to treat everything from the muscle soreness suffered by weekend jocks to severe joint pain among rheumatoid arthritis sufferers. Yet, a $26 million, five-year Alzheimer's trial was suspended by the National Institutes of Health last month after naproxen was linked to a 50 percent increase in cardiovascular events.

"They stopped the trial for an unclear reason," says Eric Topol of the Cleveland Clinic. "This would be the only study of its kind to show harm with naproxen. A 50 percent increase in heart attacks and strokes? Fifty percent of what?" But no additional data have been forthcoming, and NIH refused to provide any scientist to answer questions about why the trial was stopped or what it might reveal.

Topol is one of many scientists skeptical of the unconfirmed results and critical of this type of medicine by press release. "It had already been a terrible situation for patients on Vioxx," says Topol, who believes the FDA should have insisted on warnings about the drug sooner, so patients could evaluate their heart risk with their doctors. Now, he says, stopping the Aleve study has "added to the fear and panic that already exists about pain relievers."

Danger for the heart. The panic over pain relievers has raged since Vioxx was withdrawn from the market in September. Patients taking the drug in a cancer prevention trial experienced a more than twofold increase in heart attacks and strokes. Like Vioxx, Celebrex and Bextra also block the Cox-2 enzymes, which trigger the body's pain and inflammatory responses.

Studies show that the pain relief from older NSAIDs like aspirin and ibuprofen is comparable to that from the Cox-2s. But researchers have also learned that blocking only the Cox-2 enzyme may protect the stomach but also endanger the heart. The Cox-2 inhibitors reduce production of a natural body fat that prevents blood platelets from clumping together. Reducing this lipid "is like removing a natural break to clotting," explains Garret FitzGerald, chairman of pharmacology at the University of Pennsylvania. FitzGerald was the first to identify the mechanism by which the Cox-2s enhance clotting and may hasten hardening of the arteries.

"The phase we're moving into now," says FitzGerald, "is that these drugs have value, and we need to conserve their value while managing the risk. The main question to answer is what exactly is the cardiovascular risk in people with conditions the drugs were designed to treat, namely arthritis." The problem, says Cleveland's Topol, is that we don't have the data to make that calculation: "We know from some surveys that about half of arthritis patients have heart disease. But we have never looked at this enormous population of patients."

Janet Woodcock, acting deputy commissioner for operations at the FDA, agrees that the lack of studies is a problem in evaluating all pain relievers. "Look at naproxen. It's always looked better against other NSAIDs, more like aspirin. But we don't know if that's because it is better, or the other NSAIDs are worse, in that they increase the risk of heart attack more than naproxen." And none of this uncertainty will be resolved until an FDA advisory committee meets next month on the safety of arthritis drugs.

So what are patients to do? "It's a good time to review family history of strokes, heart attacks and try to make the best possible decision with limited information," says Oregon's Tindall. Internist A. Mark Fendrick, at the University of Michigan Hospital, agrees. "If you are taking any chronic nonsteroidal anti-inflammatory drug—over the counter, prescription, Cox-2, or not—it's very important to talk to your doctor and evaluate whether you need an NSAID in light of these real gastrointestinal and possible cardiovascular risks." Fendrick worries about the large number of people taking Cox-2s plus aspirin for heart protection, because aspirin eliminates the gastrointestinal benefit of Cox-2s."My preference is not to use an NSAID at all."

David Borenstein thinks that's unrealistic for many of his patients. Diseases like arthritis have enormous impact on cardiovascular health, he says. "If you can't move, your heart gets flabby and it doesn't work well. So whether to take these drugs, or what drugs to take, has to be a balance."

UNIT 6

Sexuality and Relationships

Unit Selections

Key Points to Consider

- Do you feel at risk of contracting AIDS or other STDs? If not, why not? If you do, what are you doing to reduce your risk?

- Is the viewing of pornography by couples a harmless or harmful activity?

- What specific issues do non-traditional couples face?

- Should parents be permitted to choose the sex of their baby before birth?

Student Web Site

www.mhcls.com/online

Internet References

Further information regarding these Web sites may be found in this book's preface or online.

Planned Parenthood
  http://www.plannedparenthood.org/
Sexuality Information and Education Council of the United States (SIECUS)
  http://www.siecus.org/

Sexuality is an important part of both self awareness and intimate relationships.

How important is physical attraction in establishing and maintaining intimate relationships? Researchers in the area of evolutionary psychology have proposed numerous theories that attempt to explain the mutual attraction that occurs between the sexes. The most controversial of these theories postulates that our perception of beauty or physical attractiveness is not subjective but rather a biological component hardwired into our brains. It is generally assumed that perceptions of beauty vary from era to era and culture to culture, but evidence is mounting that suggests people everywhere share a common sense of beauty that is based on physical symmetry.

While physical attraction is clearly an important issue when it comes to dating, how important is it in long-term loving relationships? For many Americans the answer may be very important, because we tend to be a "Love Culture," a culture that places a premium on passion in the selection of our mates. Is passion an essential ingredient in love, and can passion serve to sustain a long-term meaningful relationship? Since most people can't imagine marrying someone that they don't love, we must assume that most marriages are based on this feeling we call love. That being the case, why is it that so few marriages survive the rigors of day-to-day living? Perhaps the answer has more to do with our limited definition of love than love itself. An interesting look at love can be found in "Love at the Margins" which discusses non-traditional couples and the demands they face. These relationships can mean a need for extreme commitments along with the coping of social disapproval. A related topic is that sex is good for health. Studies are showing that an active sex life may lead to a longer life, better ability to withstand pain, a healthy immune system, less heart disease and cancer, and lower rates of depression.

In "Girl or Boy? As Fertility Technology Advances, So Does an Ethical Debate, Denise Grady questions whether couples should have the option of choosing the gender of their baby. Currently, some doctors are willing to accommodate parents while others question the ethics of choosing the sex before birth.

Perhaps no topic in the area of human sexuality has garnered more publicity and public concern than the dangers associated with unprotected sex. Although the concept of "safe sex" is nothing new, the degree of open and public discussion regarding sexual behaviors is. With the emergence of AIDS as a disease of epidemic proportions and the rapid spreading of other sexually transmitted diseases (STDs), the surgeon general of the United States initiated an aggressive educational campaign based on the assumption that knowledge would change behavior. If STD rates among teens are any indication as to the effectiveness of this approach, then we must conclude that our educational efforts are failing. Conservatives believe that while education may play a role in curbing the spread of STDs, the root of the

Digital Vision/Getty Images

problem is promiscuity, and promiscuity rises when a society is undergoing a moral decline. The solution, according to conservatives, is a joint effort between parents and educators in which students are taught the importance of values such as respect, responsibility, and integrity. Liberals, on the other hand, think that preventing promiscuity is unrealistic, and instead the focus should be on establishing open and frank discussions between the sexes. Their premise is that we are all sexual beings, and the best way to combat STDs is to establish discussions between sexual partners so that condoms will be used correctly when couples engage in intercourse.

While education undoubtedly has had a positive impact on slowing the spread of STDs, perhaps it was unrealistic to think that education alone was the solution, given the magnitude and the nature of the problem. Most experts agree that for education to succeed in changing personal behaviors the following conditions must be met: (1) The recipients of the information must first perceive themselves as vulnerable and, thus, be motivated to explore replacement behaviors, and (2) the replacement behaviors must satisfy the needs that were the basis of the problem behaviors. To date most education programs have failed to meet these criteria. Given all the information that we now have on the dangers associated with AIDS and STDs, why is it that people do not perceive themselves at risk? It is not so much the denial of risks as it is the notion that when it comes to choosing sex partners, most people think that they use good judgment. Unfortunately, most decisions regarding sexual behavior are based on subjective criteria that bear little or no relationship to one's actual risk. Even when individuals do view themselves as vulnerable to AIDS and STDs, there are currently only two viable options for reducing the risk of contracting these diseases. The first is the use of a condom and the second is sexual abstinence, neither of which is an ideal solution to the problem.

You, Me, and Porn Make Three

Pornography can be a harmless pleasure—or a source of bitter resentment. How do you prevent the XXX explosion from undermining your relationship?

LIZA FEATHERSTONE

When her new boyfriend confessed that he looked at porn, Donna, 37, made her views clear to him. "I'm very anti-pornography," she says. "I think it's very degrading to women. I told him: This is something I can't have in a relationship." He assured her that he'd only been interested in porn because he was single and lonely. Then, last year, after the two had been married nine months, she found out he'd never stopped, at times spending as much as $120 a month on Internet raunch.

Donna, who lives in a small town in Connecticut, was stunned. "I blamed myself—I wasn't attractive enough. I have a weight problem—I blamed it on that." She also worried that she was overreacting: "Was I too strict? Too moral? Missing something?" Beyond her doubts about herself, she had a larger problem to deal with: "It broke my trust in the marriage."

Porn-gazing—whether chronic or casual—can become an explosive issue for a couple, corroding intimacy and demolishing the sexual connection. But reactions to pornography can be as varied as human desire itself, and fault is often in the eye of the beholder. For couples who already have sexual conflicts or difficulty trusting each other, porn can play a particularly destructive role. Yet in some situations, erotic material can be a healthy outlet for sexual fantasy, possibly bringing a couple closer together. Even a conflict over pornography, handled constructively, can improve a relationship.

Erotic images are more available—and more mainstream—than ever. According to comScore, which measures Internet traffic, 66 percent of Internet—using men between the ages of 18 and 34 look at online porn at least once a month. In the past, guys hid their liking for smut; now, they can openly embrace it, thanks to Jenna Jameson, *Stuff* magazine and a porn-friendly culture. As a result, pornography-related conflicts among couples are becoming more common, marriage counselors say. The argument often has a similar refrain: He looks at it, she hates it and each resents the other. In a 2003 study published in the *Journal of Sex and Marital Therapy,* Ana Bridges and her co-authors found that while most women weren't bothered by their partner's X-rated interest, a significant minority were extremely distressed by it. But are they right to be worried? Is the anguish misdirected—or is there something to fear about porn?

The Facts of Life

Many women feel betrayed by porn, even though their mates don't necessarily perceive it as a transgression. "It was infidelity," says Suzanne Vail, 43, of Nashua, New Hampshire, describing her ex-boyfriend's habit. "I felt cheated on." More than a quarter of the women in Bridges's study agreed. The feelings may arise from an unrealistic understanding of fantasy in adult sexuality, suggests marital therapist Michele Weiner-Davis, author of *The Sex-Starved Marriage* and founder of Divorce-Busting, a therapy and coaching service aimed at saving marriages. Partners, even long-term ones, may have never discussed fantasies. "On the conservative end of the spectrum, some wives are upset that the husband would think about any other images or other women," she says. "I'm just amazed at that—some of these couples have been together a long time!"

Weiner-Davis will often try to "do a little sexual education," explaining that fantasy is normal and that a lot of people enjoy sexually explicit images—especially men, who tend to be more visually oriented. If that "doesn't make a dent, if the wife is truly beside herself, it is a betrayal and I treat it as such." Weiner-Davis doesn't necessarily agree that a husband in this situation is cheating, but the emotional dynamics are much the same: The porn user needs to understand his partner's hurt feelings, and she needs to find a way to forgive him.

> **Looking at porn in terms of right or wrong isn't helpful. The question is: What can couples do about it?**

Many women feel that the guy who looks at porn must harbor some hostility toward women. Yet research hasn't established a link between pornography consumption and misogyny.

One 2004 study found that porn users actually had slightly more positive and egalitarian views of women than other men did, though porn users were also more likely to hold stereotypical beliefs—for example, that women are more moral.

It's a counterintuitive finding, likely to annoy both conservatives and antiporn feminists. But simultaneously liking porn and respecting women is consistent with a liberal outlook, which typically combines tolerance with an egalitarian perspective. If your boyfriend has an abortion-rights bumper sticker and a stash of hardcore smut on his computer, he may be Jerry Falwell's worst nightmare, but he's not all that unusual. Or perhaps the connection between porn watching and pro-female attitudes is more fundamental, suggests James Beggan, a University of Louisville sociologist who co-authored the study with psychologist colleagues at Texas Tech University. "If you spend your time looking at pictures of naked women," he observes, "that's not really consistent with not liking women. It's consistent with liking them."

Living Up to the Fantasy

Phil, a 46-year-old writer in New York City, doesn't enjoy porn that much. But when it first became readily available online, the novelty sucked him in. "In the early days of the Internet, I would sometimes surf through reams of online flesh," he recalls wryly, "but I found it numbingly repetitive, and the opposite of arousing." Partly out of boredom, Phil (not his real name) used some of the images to teach himself graphic design. When his wife found the files on his computer, "she freaked," he recalls. "I was just pasting women's heads on different naked bodies— you know, perfectly normal behavior," he jokes, "but it did not sit at all well with the real-life woman I was living with."

Phil's wife was the kind of gorgeous blonde that most men only fantasize about, yet he suspects that his looking at porn made her feel inadequate. He was bewildered. Any notion that he was looking at cheesy Internet images because she wasn't good enough, he says, "would have been wildly misguided." (The couple has since divorced for other reasons.)

That fear is very real for many women, who worry they can't compete with the airbrushed perfection of the porn star. And they are "absolutely right," says Barry McCarthy, author of *Rekindling Desire,* and a therapist in Washington—they can't. But not measuring up to an illusion shouldn't be cause for worry, he adds. What makes the woman in porn so erotic is not her red lips and her fake breasts, but the fact that she's "crazy," says McCarthy: she's ever ready, always willing to do anything to please a man. No real woman could or would want to be that way.

Psychologically healthy men don't have much trouble distinguishing between reality and the weird world of commercial raunch. The trouble emerges, McCarthy says, when a person "can't differentiate between fantasy and reality: 'Why isn't my girlfriend like that? Why isn't she into sex with animals? Why won't she let me ejaculate on her face?'" Suzanne Vail, who operates an online group for women who believe their partners are sex addicts, says women in her group have attempted to please porn-obsessed men through liposuction, breast surgery and crash dieting. If a man has a driving need to make his real-life partner into a porn star, he's got a problem. A woman who acquiesces in such an impossible pursuit may quickly find that she's got one, too.

When Porn Is Good for You

Porn can actually help foster emotional and sexual intimacy, says Colorado psychologist David Schnarch, author of *Resurrecting Sex,* who runs a couples therapy practice with his wife. He explains: "A significant portion of our work in helping couples develop a deeper sexual connection is through erotic images. Erotica, as well as couples' own masturbatory fantasies, can be useful tools for helping them develop as adults." How couples intensify their sexual relationship differs radically depending on the individuals and on the dynamic between them. But fantasy is certainly a part of a healthy sex life, and porn does contribute significantly to the archive of sexy scenarios in our heads. It can also inspire couples to experiment more.

Interestingly, in Ana Bridges's study, the women with the most positive views of porn's role in their relationship were engaged in a more creative activity: The couples were taking sexy pictures of one another, removing entirely the problem of competition with the busty and lascivious commercial sex bomb. "It's very validating," says Bridges. "It's me turning you on. Even in my absence, you want to look at me."

She's Looking, Too

While men do look at porn more than women do, the ease and privacy of the Internet allow many women who would never have dared in the past to explore this realm. Fully half of the women in Bridges's study said they looked at pornography themselves.

And women can become just as obsessed as men. Jennifer Schneider, an M.D. who has studied sex addicts, interviewed several women who became hooked on smut. One 35-year-old married woman said the pictures (especially those depicting S&M scenarios) "would haunt me day and night." The habit began to erode her marriage. "My husband could no longer satisfy me," she told Schneider. "I wanted what I saw in the videos and pictures and was too embarrassed to ask him for it." The woman said she was freed from her obsessions by God, but a good marital therapist might have viewed this as an opportunity for the couple to learn to talk to each other about their desires—and perhaps try something new.

There is little solid research on how men feel about their female partner's porn use—or, for that matter, on how porn figures into gay relationships, which could help illuminate how much a straight couple's porn conflict is really a matter of gender differences. Some men clearly find it sexy, perhaps seeing her porn interest as a sign of a woman's experimental nature or aggressive libido. But writer Pamela Paul argues in her new book, *Pornified: How Pornography Is Transforming Our Lives, Our Relationships and Our Families,* that while many men hope their partner approves of (or at least tolerates) their own porn interest, they may be critical of a girlfriend or wife who uses pornography herself. A 2004 *Elle*MSNBC.com poll found that six in ten men were concerned about their partner's interest in Internet smut.

Drawing the Line

Dose matters. According to research by the late Alvin Cooper of the Silicon Valley Psychotherapy Center, people engaged in any kind of online sexual activity for less than an hour a week said it had little impact on their lives; people using it for 11 or more hours a week said it affected both their self-image and their feelings about their partners. Anywhere between one and ten hours a week is ambiguous terrain. It may just be a way to release stress, but as Cooper has pointed out, "the Internet is . . . a very powerful force that people can quickly develop a problem with, like crack cocaine."

Because it's sexual, porn is a more loaded distancing strategy than golf or too much time at the office.

Donna's husband, Steve, was just such a person. "Before, the pain and embarrassment of buying a magazine or going into a sex shop would stop him," she says. "Once he got the computer, that was it." Some individuals are vulnerable to compulsive porn use because of their own psychological makeup. Steve is a diagnosed obsessive-compulsive, and in his case, the availability and anonymity of Internet porn lent itself to ritualistic, uncontrollable behavior. But online pornography can become an obsession even for people without psychological disorders, simply because it is so easily available and taps into such a powerful appetite.

Sometimes a Dirty Picture Isn't Just a Dirty Picture

Not everyone is going to embrace porn as a positive force. But it is usually possible to work through the conflicts posed by pornography use. Michele Weiner-Davis encourages couples to explore what it means in the dynamic of the relationship: Why does it bother her so much? Is there something he gets from it that he could be getting from the relationship? "Sometimes it is relational," she says. "For example, the wife may not understand the importance of a good sex life. Sometimes she's not experimental or passionate. If, in a long-term marriage, couples

don't have a common goal of keeping marriage passionate," she says, an X-rated habit can be a symptom of restlessness.

A heavy reliance on porn may be an outgrowth of other sexual discontents. Many men complain that their wives have gained weight and are no longer very attractive, says Weiner-Davis. Others prefer smut to real sex because while they're viewing porn, they're in control, McCarthy and Weiner-Davis agree. Says McCarthy, "Couple sex is much more complicated." Says Bridges, "People think it's just a way to masturbate, but in a relationship it can be a punishment: 'I don't want to be with you right now.'"

In the case of one couple Bridges saw, the husband had pulled away from his wife's constant criticism and retreated into fantasy. She had to learn not to be so mean, says Bridges. While there are countless ways to withdraw from a spouse, porn is both satisfying and readily available. And because it's sexual, it's a far more loaded distancing strategy than playing golf or spending too much time at the office.

One solution to the porn dilemma that clearly doesn't work: surveillance. It undermines trust and can foster its own obsessions. Suzanne Vail says partners may get compulsive about monitoring, just as those married to drug addicts or alcoholics can become overly involved in policing addictions.

Researchers and therapists concur that couples are better off treating the conflict as a practical matter rather than a moral issue. Faith may not be such an important consideration: Bridges found that nonreligious women were just as likely as religious women to be upset over a partner's porn use. "Looking at this in terms of right or wrong isn't helpful," says Weiner-Davis. "There's a great deal of variation in what turns people on, and the question is: What can we as a couple do about it?" As she points out, couples work hard to reach agreement on many issues—how they will spend money, where they will live, whether they will have children—but often neglect to achieve any sort of consensus on their sex life: how often, what sort of activities, how much extracurricular interest is acceptable.

A couple may never see eye-to-eye on porn; even if he's not compulsive, she may always feel that it's disgusting (or immoral). As David Schnarch has often pointed out, tolerating discomfort—and recognizing that a partner's desires may be different from yours—is critical to a fully adult, intimate sexual relationship. Then again, if porn is repellent to someone you love, it may be worthwhile to call it quits, like smoking or other cherished habits we give up for the sake of a relationship. As Weiner-Davis says of porn, "You won't get a disease, but it could cost you your marriage."

LIZA FEATHERSTONE is a Manhattan-based freelance writer.

It's Just Mechanics

Viagra is just the start: we'll soon have pills that make you feel deep love and video games that give vibrations. Ziauddin Sardar on the masturbatory society

ZIAUDDIN SARDAR

Is your sex life normal? The question was raised recently on the *Oprah Winfrey Show.* Tell us, the show asked its 20 million viewers, what turns you on, what turns you off, and what makes good sex.

The problem with such questions is that there are no "normal" answers. The normal is problematic because our ideas about sex have changed fundamentally. What constitutes normal is constantly refurbished. Its boundaries shift rapidly, and continue to shift. So what was abnormal yesterday—say, pornography—becomes normal today. And what is shunned today (say paedophilia) may just as easily become normal tomorrow.

One huge jump was provided by Viagra. In less than six years since the impotence pill came on the market, Viagra and its competitors, Levitra and Cialis, have transformed sexual norms and practices. As Meika Loe argues in *The Rise of Viagra* (New York University Press), it has redefined the concept of normal and changed the language of sex.

From the beginning, this was a treatment branded and marketed as normal. Impotence was called "erectile dysfunction", or simply ED—a common condition, as the football legend Pele assured us in TV ads, but not normal. Moreover, it did not arise from psychological causes or physical damage; rather, it was a simple medical condition rectified by a pill. Suddenly, drug company surveys discovered that more than half the US adult male population suffered from ED; figures for Europe were not far behind.

So if you can't get it up because you're pissed, stressed out, simply not in the mood or no longer find your partner attractive, you are actually suffering from a disease. And like all diseases, it must be cured. The cure is to swallow a pill and have sex no matter what, any where, any time, whenever. This has now become the norm.

Viagra is another step in stripping sex of all its complexity. Sex has been reduced to a simple question: for men, "how big?"; for women, "how long?". Combine these conundrums with other features of a market economy, such as availability on demand, choice, flexibility to mix'n'match, and we have new definitions not just of sex and love but of what it means to be human.

Today, to be normal, humans have sex right up to their last breath. It's the way to go. Sex is no longer the indulgence of the young. Nowadays, it is people over 50 who are having the most sex. With demographic shifts, high divorce rates and early retirement, the erstwhile golden generation of Sixties swingers who let it all hang out are now the "silver singles" (as they are called in America). The preoccupations of their youth have been sustained through their later years by medical enhancements. The wet dreams of 60-year-olds, who turned on to chemical enhancement in the Sixties, are a manifest example of future normality for us all.

What Viagra actually treats is loss of male power. In a confusing, depersonalising world busy reassigning status, regendering the social order, manipulating the ever-increasing demands of a commodified existence, sexual potency is the last bastion. Men, who have lost status and power almost everywhere, from workplace to home, must repair to the bedroom. Only there can they find the redemption of their true nature.

However, in an age of sexual equality, men cannot be left alone with their predicament. The other half of humanity, too, finds it is not exempt from malfunction. Just a few months ago, the disease "female sexual dysfunction" hit the headlines. But female sexuality being what it is, women probably need something more than a pill. Simple enhanced blood flow, as laboratory tests have shown, is not good enough. So a female Viagra won't do the job as well as a vibrator or a dildo—soon to be widely and cheaply available from a Boots near you. A vibrator outperforms even a man on Viagra.

More serious aids to female performance are in the pipeline. In the next few years, patches and drugs to enhance vaginal lubrication and sensitivity will become available. A US surgeon has already patented a pacemaker-sized device which, implanted under the skin, triggers an orgasm. Last month, clinical trials for the device were approved by the US Food and Drug Administration. Within a decade, it will be normal for every woman to have a perpetual orgasm whenever she wants it, wherever she needs it.

Love, too, will be available on demand. Recent research on love suggests that it consists of three basic biochemical elements. First, testosterone—which produces lust. Second, a group of amphetamine-like chemicals (dopamine, noradrenaline and phenylethylamine) produces feelings of euphoria that lead to infatuation. Third, if a relationship survives the first two rushes, a new biochemical response emerges, based on oxytocin, vasopressin and endorphins. This produces feelings of intimacy, trust and affection. Pharmaceutical companies are currently working on this third phase. So a "love pill" that modulates your subtler emotions and takes you straight to deep feelings of intimacy, trust and affection is just over the horizon. Science will fulfill the fairy tale. It will come up with a genuine love potion.

Science will fulfill the fairy tale. It will come up with a genuine love potion, modulating your subtler emotions

The sexual liberation of every woman and man approaches its apotheosis: availability on demand with peak performance, assured gratification and enduring emotion. But much more has been let out of the bottle. The physical and psychological barriers to sex, identified as the ultimate metaphor for all the ills of humanity, had to be overcome. The consequence is that most sexual taboos have evaporated. No matter how dark your thoughts, how unethical your desires, how absurd your fetish, everything is normal. Your desire to dress up as a stuffed toy, your dreams of having sex with obese or dead people, your obsession with plastic or rubber, your fixation with asphyxiation—all that is sexually driven is OK.

Pornography's status as a taboo is rapidly disappearing. It has become part of the mainstream of western culture. Ancient Egyptians, Greeks and Romans had their erotica as esoterica on scrolls, pottery and frescos. Hindus have their erotic sculptures on temples. But in western culture pornography in unparalleled quantities and forms is communicated in every mass medium. Never before in history has there been so much pornography to be had by so many in such numerous ways.

Everyone is now just a click away from explicit, hard-core material. It is impossible to miss pornography on the internet because it seeks you out persistently, unannounced, at every opportunity. It is there on Channels 4 and 5, Sky and innumerable digital channels every night.

On MTV's reality show *The Real World,* you can witness bisexual group sex. Explicit sex, including shots of erect penises, can be viewed on Sky's revisionist western drama *Deadwood.* Michael Winterbottom's *9 Songs,* which will go on general release shortly, offers a stream of close-ups of intercourse, fellatio, ejaculation and cunnilingus. The French art-house director Catherine Breillat has pioneered the transfer of porn stars into mainstream cinema. Her new film, *Anatomy of Hell,* is as graphic as it is bizarre. And if that doesn't satisfy you, you can go to a new breed of "pornaoke bars", just opened in Edinburgh, where you can groan and grind karaoke-style to porno tapes.

When pornography becomes normal, where will we go next?

There are only two taboos left: sex with children, and incest. Attempts to "normalise" paedophilia have begun. A thesis by Richard Yuill, awarded a PhD by Glasgow University in December 2004, suggests that sex between adults and minors is a good and positive thing. Yuill's research, based on interviews with paedophiles and their victims, "challenges the assumption" that paedophiles are inherently abusive. It is only a matter of time before other academics start arguing that incest, too, is decent and wholesome. Graphic art films and television documentaries will follow. The organisations campaigning for the rights of paedophiles will have their case for "normality" made for them.

They may then be able to take their place among the bewildering array of sexual orientations already being normalised. Once upon a time, there were heterosexuals and the love that dared not speak its name. Gay men and lesbians have long since lost their reticence. Then bisexuals, transsexuals and the "kinky" found their identity. Now we have intersexuals and the polyamorous. A few months ago, *New Scientist* announced the discovery, in breathless prose, of asexuals. These folk don't like to have sex—horror of horrors—with *anybody.* There are even orientations within orientations. So we have such self-definition as non-op transsexual, TG butch, femme queen, gender-queer, cross-dresser, third gender, drag king or queen and transboy. In one recent episode of Channel 5's *CSI: crime scene investigation,* a murder victim was said to be part of a community of "plushies", people who enjoy sex while dressed up as stuffed animals.

It is now normal to have your breasts removed or added to, have new genitals constructed, or sprinkle a dash of hormones for the appropriate, desired effect. Things are about to become even more complex. Within a decade or so, you will be able to modify your body almost totally, as you wish. You will be able to turn off all physical signs of gender, switch off the hormones and get rid of all secondary sexual characteristics. Then you can add on the bits you wish and "sculpt" your body in any shape you like. When gene therapy becomes common, things will be even easier. Already, there are people who are experimenting with this; and a "body-mod" subculture is thriving on the internet.

The shifting of the boundaries of what is normal and our obsession with sex have not improved our sex lives

What you can't do in reality will soon be available in simulation. The emerging technology of haptics, or the telecommunication of sensation using a computer interface, will enable you to live your most horrific dreams in virtual reality. Haptic technologies simulate physical sensation of real objects and feed them to the user. The first generation of haptic technology can be experienced in certain video games for the Sony PlayStation where the joystick is used to simulate vibrations. The next generation, on its way from Rutgers University, will simulate pressure, texture and heat. Combine this with state-of-the-art graphics and some innovative software and you have a complete pornographic universe. As Eric Garland points out in the December 2004 issue of the American magazine *The Futurist,* among its first uses could be "pornography involving children and featuring violence". But what's the harm, as it is only a digitised child?

Am I the only person to wonder if the constant shifting of the boundaries of the normal, while increasing our obsession with sex, has really improved our sex lives? On the contrary, I would argue, it has led to a decline in real sex. Genuine intimacy cannot be generated through a pill. Neither can sincere, unconditional love be simulated. When sex is reduced to mechanics and endurance, there is little to differentiate it from plumbing and maintenance. When gender becomes meaningless, sex becomes empty. When sexual choice becomes an end in itself, then the end is destined to be tragic.

Sex used to be intercourse because it was part of a context, a loving relationship. When sex is just sex, without any context, what good does it do you? That is the crux of the problem. It becomes the ultimate narcissism, the sole gratification of self-love.

Welcome to the masturbatory society.

Ziauddin Sardar is editor of *Futures,* the monthly journal of policy, planning and futures studies.

Love at the Margins

Extreme Relationships Demand Extreme Commitment

Nontraditional couples may be seen as weird, discomfiting or even sinful by others, but if they survive the crucible of social censure and self-doubt they can forge powerful bonds—and teach others about enduring love.

MARK TEICH

It's not easy being a lesbian couple in a suburban New Jersey community. "We're surrounded by married couples and families, and we stand out," says Allison. Madeleine adds, "By now I'm sure the neighbors can guess our situation. I feel comfortable with a few, but I'd rather keep things secret from the rest."

When they first dated, Allison, an artist, was in her element in Manhattan. Madeleine spent weekends at Allison's place. "In the city, no one noticed us," Allison says. "I never felt we were marginalized until I moved to New Jersey." Ultimately she'd felt she had to make the commitment to move in with Madeleine, because her girlfriend was the major breadwinner then, with a stable job as a computer software engineer 20 minutes from home.

"I love my work," notes Madeleine. "But there's a lot of prejudice in this field, so I don't mention Allison. I'd never bring her to an office party."

Sustaining a relationship is a challenge for anyone, but couples deemed inappropriate or abnormal by traditional social norms must forge their unions in the face of both internal and external pressures. Walking down the street or dining out, a gay or interracial couple or, say, a 50-year-old man embracing a 27-year-old woman (or vice versa) may be stared at, or viewed as suspect or even unnatural. More important, they may often face the wrath and rejection of their families, colleagues and friends. Couples considered marginal can encounter impediments from the law or organized religion—any institution built on traditional belief. No wonder they often hesitate to invest emotionally in one another, balking at moving in together or taking their partners to Christmas gatherings with their friends or families.

Nonetheless, many nontraditional couples end up thriving for decades. How do they move past the stigmas, ridicule and rejection to build some of the most enduring unions?

The answer lies in a kind of emotional trifecta. First, somewhere amid the prejudice, resentment and doubt they face, they find a support system that sustains them and confirms their relationship; second, like Romeo and Juliet, they discover an us-against-them inner strength that defies all naysayers; third, they simply stand the test of time, until both they and those who doubted them come to be believers.

The Glue That Binds

The question is: Why do it—especially with all the extra stress from such disapproval? Why begin a romance with so many strikes against you?

Certainly, physical attraction can override social concerns. Floridians Ken and Sara Benjamin were immediately drawn to one another at a computer conference 18 years ago, even though she had just turned 40 (a blond, young-looking 40) and he was only 24. "I thought she was an attractive female with great legs," he remembers. "But I also felt something deeper almost immediately. I wanted something much more than a one night stand."

For some nontraditional couples, friendship comes first. Steven and Joyce Boro, a Jewish-American married to a black emigrant from Dominica, were roommates and buddies at Brooklyn College in New York well before they became involved. "We knew one another a full year first," says Steven. "We hung out, hitchhiked around together and became good friends before anything romantic happened. I always felt good being with her."

While relatives usually react badly at first to these unions, in some cases family acceptance launches the relationship. Stephanie, a young Chinese-American from California, who planned a career in medicine, met Juan, a poor construction worker, in a little town in Honduras when she was serving as a Peace Corps health worker. His family was the initial glue; Stephanie actually met them first, when Juan was working out of town. His mother, a coworker, kept inviting her home. "He has a big family, with 10 brothers and sisters, and lots of cousins, and they

Steven and Joyce Boro, Portland, Oregon

Couples on the margins of society may discover that a relationship frowned on in one locale is encouraged elsewhere. For Steven and Joyce Boro, a white Jewish man and a black Caribbean woman, that meant moving their show west—far from the disapproving eyes of family and friends in New York—to a commune. "I'd mainly dated white guys, but I never brought them to meet my mother," says Joyce. "It was probably intentional, because I wanted to avoid the racial issue with her. And Steven's mother thought blacks were the scum of the earth." By moving to the commune, they simultaneously limited their contact with their parents and gained a network of supportive friends. Ultimately they moved to Portland, where they raised their two children and have remained happily married for more than 30 years. Of course, like all interracial couples, they have been subject to some negative scrutiny. "Just the other day, I got angry looks from a black guy when we were walking together in Seattle," says Steven. "We've had our share of looks from whites, too. But none of that means anything to me. I've never really seen Joyce's color. It looks good on her, though."

Steven Pearl and Gino Grenek, Brooklyn, New York

Steven, a 40-year-old editor, and Gino, a 33-year-old dancer, finish each other's sentences with an edgy intimacy. They met at a party six years ago, felt an instant simpatico and attraction, and soon became a pair. Today they share an apartment in Brooklyn and consider themselves official domestic partners even if New York rejects same-sex marriage. This barrier notwithstanding, Steven and Gino find New York City especially accepting ("It's not Brokeback Mountain out here," Gino says)—so much so that their greatest relationship challenges come not from their same-sex status but from religion and involvement with work. Steven is Jewish, while Gino is Russian Orthodox. Both come from observant families. "We have learned to celebrate these differences and participate in each other's rituals," Steven explains. Gino travels with his troupe, while Steven works regular hours as an editor. "I told him that dance comes first and he comes second, but I've softened a bit on that," Gino states. According to Steven, the one complexity that may rear its head in the future involves having a family. "A lot of gay men and women don't often think of themselves as having children," he comments, "and to some degree I've internalized that." Yet, growing their family is something they consider. Says Gino, "If we decide to have a family I think we'll both be fantastic fathers and role models for our kids."

interact every day. They were all so nice, and kind of adopted me."

By the time Juan arrived on the scene, she was already a fixture. "We never really dated, we just spent a lot of time together," she recalls.

Vive La Difference

Marginalized couples come together for many of the same reasons as other couples. But the very extremity of their differences may give their relationship an extra dimension. "The primary thing people look for in relationships is to expand themselves," asserts Arthur Aron, psychologist at the State University of New York at Stony Brook. "Those we grow close to become part of who we are, widening our social resources and our perspective. We want someone different from ourselves to increase our efficacy and range of influence. If you're black and they're white, if you're older and they're younger, if you're one nationality and they're another, you've expanded your knowledge and opportunities."

The more you and your partner differ, the better—until the stress exceeds the thrill.

As a same-sex couple fairly close in age, Allison and Madeleine clearly don't have these kinds of disparities. But their personalities couldn't be more different. Allison is a free-spirited artist, Madeleine a meticulous software expert. Allison is comfortable living hand to mouth, while Madeleine thrives on the security of a lucrative career; Allison is assertive and public about being gay, displaying her pictures online with other lesbian artists; Madeleine likes to keep her sexual orientation off the radar. "When I met Allison, she would blatantly flirt with me so that everyone knew she had a crush on me, and I was horrified," Madeleine says.

The more radical your choices in a partner, the better—until the stress exceeds the thrill. "The key to a successful relationship is the tension between similar and opposite," says Aron. "Difference increases excitement and resources, but similarity ups the chance of maintaining the relationship long-term."

Allison's free-spiritedness and openness (as well as a slinky black dress) helped win Madeleine over, while Madeleine's intelligence, seriousness and solidity did the trick for Allison. Ultimately they learned that despite major personality differences, they had lots in common.

Coming to the Crossroads

The tension between commonality and difference eventually brings most nontraditional couples to a crossroads. Families' and communities' initial reactions reflect age-old cultural fears of letting the invaders in, of polluting and depleting the race.

That's why, for example, Hasidic Jewish families traditionally hold funerals when a family member marries outside the faith.

Faced with such strong disapproval, even the happiest partners experience serious reservations early on, which can lead to moments of reckoning. Purdue University social psychologists Justin Lehmiller and Christopher Agnew have shown that at the start, nontraditional couples invest less of themselves in their relationships and are less committed than traditional couples, probably for this very reason.

Differences increase excitement, but similarity ups the chance of maintaining the relationship long-term.

Steven Boro, whose father (a Holocaust survivor) and mother were appalled that he was dating a black woman, simply set off without Joyce, hitching around the U.S. and Canada the moment he graduated from college, though Joyce and he had been involved for months. He had no plans of coming back. "I was committed not to her but to what I saw as my 'spiritual journey,'" Steven recalls. "Really I was floating like a leaf on a stream. On my 22nd birthday, I vowed that I wouldn't marry until I was 30 and that I'd never have kids.'"

It took Joyce to save the relationship. When she received a letter from Steven that he had settled on a commune in the Washington wilderness—and was involved with another woman there—she sought out his brother Fred to help her go after her boyfriend. "I hadn't been in this country that long, and I was still very naive. I didn't even know what a commune was, and I almost headed for Washington, D.C.,'" says Joyce. "Fred put me on the right bus. I was still in school, and I thought I was going for the weekend, but it took me four days just to cross the country."

"Halfway there, in Nebraska, she called to tell me she was coming," says Steven. "I was really happy. I told her the other relationship was over."

Neither of them ever came back. They settled, along with 30 other people, on 120 acres of rolling hills and forests. Within a few weeks, their commune friends began suggesting they get married. "'You look so good together. You're such a great couple,' they kept telling us," says Steven. "I thought about it, and I realized they were right. Joyce was wonderful. So I said sure." Two months later, they were married. Three decades later, their two grown children are now out on their own, and the couple no longer live on the commune.

"Despite investing less in their relationship at first, marginalized partners ultimately tend to be significantly more committed than nonmarginalized couples," Lehmiller notes.

Family Feuds

Often it takes every bit of that commitment for these couples to survive the extreme pressures their families impose on them; no other stressor is typically as great.

Ken and Sara Benjamin, Taverna, Florida

When Ken and Sara were dating 18 years ago, they faced problems: Ken wanted to marry, but Sara was twice divorced. Ken, then 24, was interested in having children, but Sara, then 40, already had two going off to college. "I liked marriage, but I was at the end of child-rearing and wanted to stretch my wings," Sara recalls. Adding insult to injury, people kept mistaking Sara for Ken's mother.

They found a unique way to solve their dilemmas: They backpacked around the world for two years. "I wouldn't say we went on the trip to escape the problems," says Sara. "We just needed to get into a neutral area to work things out." They went to India and Nepal, stayed in hostels and hiked mountains. "In these places, where people's life spans were very contracted, we would tell people we were a couple, and they would respond flat out: 'That's not possible; she's too old,'" remembers Ken.

There was no escaping the issues, but the longer they were together, the more they loved one another. So they compromised: On their return, Sara agreed to marry Ken and he passed up having children. "I didn't want children as a concept, I just wanted her children," says Ken. In fact, it all worked out. "Even though I'm only five years older than Sara's daughter, she needed support and I was glad to fill that role."

Like Steven and Joyce, Stephanie and Juan came to a crossroads relatively early in their relationship, in their case because of issues with *both* families. It started when Stephanie's Peace Corps stint was ending. She had to return home, and though she and Juan had been together a year and a half, he wasn't ready to go with her.

"Stephanie meant a lot to me, but I didn't want to leave my family," he says. They weren't dying to lose him either, even though they loved Stephanie. His parents were divorced. As the oldest brother, Juan was seen as "Papi" at home. So Stephanie headed back to the States thinking the relationship was over.

They kept communicating, though, and soon realized they missed each other too badly to stay apart. Juan applied for a fiance visa, and that's when the trouble with Stephanie's father began.

When he learned she was planning to marry Juan, he felt disrespected. He pointed to all the egregious differences between her and Juan: She was Chinese-American, he was Hispanic; she had been raised Buddhist, he was Catholic; she was a well-off medical school candidate, and he hadn't completed high school. What's more, Juan didn't speak English. "He's just using you to get a green card," her father said. When Stephanie married Juan and moved with him to the Bronx, New York, her father didn't talk to her for years.

Stephanie lived with a pang in her heart for her lost family. "I was with Juan for three and a half years before my family

Tracie and Leo Auguste, Miami, Florida

Tracie Auguste, 30, is Chinese, and her husband, Leo, 31, is Haitian—but cultural and racial differences have never stood in their way. One reason: At North Miami Senior High, where they met when she was a junior and he a senior, they were simply fellow minority students in the multicultural melting pot that was their school. "People might have noticed if Tracie were white," comments Leo, "but we were both minorities and no one batted an eye." Even their families were accepting. "Leo's family wouldn't have cared if I was purple, they loved me like a daughter," says Tracie. Though Tracie's parents were more standoffish, they have heartily embraced Leo since the arrival of the couple's two children, ages four and one. By living and working in Miami (he's a carpenter and she's an assistant policy director for the mayor of Miami Dade) Leo and Tracie have continued to escape stigma. Leo is mindful, however, of the judgments his children may face. "America still teaches us to view people based on appearance," he says. "The best thing we can do for our children is to teach them to be proud of who they are."

Stephanie and Juan Carlos Valderramos, Bronx, New York

Serving as a Peace Corps volunteer in Honduras in 1998, Stephanie, an educated Chinese-American, was "adopted" by the family of a friendly coworker who happened to have a son named Juan. "I didn't have a TV, so I'd go to their house after work and watch it there. I had most of my meals there, "Stephanie recalls. Meeting Juan in the bosom of his nurturing family showed her just what she was getting, and their relationship took off.

To outsiders, they seemed mismatched: Stephanie had already applied to medical school, while Juan, who needed to work to pay the bills, was still in high school. But the differences didn't bother them. "Juan is really smart. We talk about everything—at first in Spanish, now more in English—and he always has an opinion," says Stephanie, who notes that Juan served as her cultural guide during their time in Honduras. Juan concurs: "I'm proud of who I am, and I liked her the way she was. If she wanted to be with me, it made no difference that she had more money or education."

Stephanie now works as a physician and Juan is studying at Bronx Community College and plans to become an environmental engineer.

met him, and I'd never spoken to my father in all that time. I've always been close to my family, so it was awful," she says. "Juan is such a good, honest man, such a gentle soul, that I knew they would love him if they ever met him."

Marginalized partners ultimately tend to be significantly more committed than mainstream couples.

Finally, the couple was invited home one Christmas, and the response to Juan was everything Stephanie had hoped for: Her father was nice to him from the moment he met him. And after five years of marriage, Juan, now preparing to become an environmental engineer, has shown that he deserved the trust Stephanie always placed in him.

The advent of children typically brings a whole new level of familial turmoil to marginalized couples, as the in-laws are now involved. For the Boros, for instance, Steven's mother was a continual irritant whenever she visited, "as much because Joyce wasn't Jewish as because she was black," Steven explains. "She was concerned about what faith the children would be raised in." Joyce recalls, "She'd tell my friends how disappointed she was that Steven was married to me, and though she grew to love the kids very much she felt embarrassed to be seen with them because they were dark."

When the World Rushes In

While families cause the most havoc, the censure of the world contributes its own share of trouble. The mixed-race Boro children, for instance, received some of the same rejection in school that they got from their grandmother. Trying to give the kids an ethnic identity and please Steven's parents, Joyce had converted to Judaism and enrolled the children in Jewish schools, but the schools never fully accepted them. Feeling rejected by Jewish people, they've committed themselves to black culture and are exclusively dating African-Americans. "But the black community tends to see them as white and hasn't embraced them either," Joyce says.

Partners with wide age differences experience a subtler form of marginalization, but social pressures can still be great. While they're not discriminated against in housing or social services, and not barred from marrying as gays are, they may make their families, friends and neighbors uneasy, and are often the butt of insulting misunderstandings or jokes.

"It's so nice that you brought your mother with you" is a typical comment that Ken, now 42, hears about his 58-year-old wife Sara. In the early days of their relationship it bothered them, but they had larger hurdles to worry about: Sara was reluctant to marry for a third time, and Ken had to accept that they might never have a biological child. (Sara was already the mother of teenagers.) Three years ago, Sara had a stroke that left her weak on her left side, in need of a cane and prone to epilepsy-related

Advice for the Rest of Us

Nontraditional couples who make it have a lot to teach us. Here's what we can learn from their success.

- The more you trust your gut instinct and the more comfortable you feel in your own skin, the less outsiders will be able to interfere.
- When partners bring different skills to a relationship, they enhance each other's positions in the world.
- You may be attracted to your opposite, but if you want the relationship to last, you need lots in common as well.
- Don't let outside disapproval of your partner determine the way you feel about him or her.
- Extended family or a close circle of friends can nurture your relationship.
- Friends and family who initially disapprove may change their minds as your relationship stands the test of time. But accept the possibility that they may not. Be prepared to reduce contact and forge new ties with others.
- If in-laws interfere in your relationship or take a strong stance on how you must raise your children, it may be time to limit their role.
- If you can deal with it together as a team, adversity will strengthen the relationship.
- Traditional couples can enhance their bonds by introducing exciting challenges. Climbing a mountain or building a company together can spice up the love.

blackout seizures. "I can't imagine any physical infirmity that would test my commitment. The stroke is a life challenge, not a relationship challenge," says Ken.

Ever since, they have remained so secure in their relationship that rude comments roll off their backs. "We always understood we were abnormal in society's eyes," Sara says, "but what anybody else thinks about our relationship is far less important to us than the relationship itself."

"She's the love of my life," Ken says.

Staying the Course

In their research, Lehmiller and Agnew found that the key reason most marginal couples stayed together was not deep satisfaction in their relationships, but a sense of limited alternatives. In other words, they didn't think they could do better, so they settled for what they had.

But when told about these findings, the couples we interviewed couldn't have disagreed more.

"Joyce and I have been blessed to be as close as we are, and I can't imagine any couple being closer," asserts Steven Boro. "That sounds conceited," chides Joyce. "But we are extremely close."

"I liked and learned from my first two husbands, but neither was my soulmate," says Sara.

Having settled for less is the furthest thing from these couples' minds.

"Lehmiller and Agnew argue that people who stay in marginalized relationships feel they have worse options, but I'm not fully convinced," says Douglas T. Kenrick, Ph.D., professor of evolutionary psychology at Arizona State University. "We all make trade-offs. Maybe these couples just happened to land on partners who were well worth the trade-offs." You might not automatically put a poor construction worker from Honduras on your checklist of potential partners, but then you run into him and he has a wealth of other characteristics that are wonderful to you. If you have confidence in your feelings, you see that instinct through.

In fact, the chance to be true to yourself may be one of the greatest surprises—and rewards—of these relationships.

"You find a lot of freedom at the margins," says Joshua Gamson, a Jew married to a biracial man. "When you're at the center of society, you feel forced to obey the norms. Marginalized couples have a lot of disadvantages, but since they're already outcasts in a sense, they're far freer to do what they really want, to put on their own show and be purely themselves."

MARK TEICH, a freelance writer living in Connecticut, has written for *Sports Illustrated, Redbook* and other magazines.

Girl or Boy? As Fertility Technology Advances, So Does an Ethical Debate

Denise Grady

If people want to choose their baby's sex before pregnancy, should doctors help?

Some parents would love the chance to decide, while others wouldn't dream of meddling with nature. The medical world is also divided. Professional groups say sex selection is allowable in certain situations, but differ as to which ones. Meanwhile, it's not illegal, and some doctors are already cashing in on the demand.

There are several ways to pick a baby's sex before a woman becomes pregnant, or at least to shift the odds. Most of the procedures were originally developed to treat infertility or prevent genetic diseases.

The most reliable method is not easy or cheap. It requires in vitro fertilization, in which doctors prescribe drugs to stimulate the mother's ovaries, perform surgery to collect her eggs, fertilize them in the laboratory and then insert the embryos into her uterus.

Before the embryos are placed in the womb, some doctors will test for sex and, if there are enough embryos, let the parents decide whether to insert exclusively male or female ones. Pregnancy is not guaranteed, and the combined procedures can cost $20,000 or more, often not covered by insurance. Many doctors refuse to perform these invasive procedures just for sex selection, and some people are troubled by what eventually becomes of the embryos of the unwanted sex, which may be frozen or discarded.

Another method, used before the eggs are fertilized, involves sorting sperm, because it is the sperm and not the egg that determines a baby's sex. Semen normally has equal numbers of male- and female-producing sperm cells, but a technology called MicroSort can shift the ratio to either 88 percent female or 73 percent male. The "enriched" specimen can then be used for insemination or in vitro fertilization. It can cost $4,000 to $6,000, not including in vitro fertilization.

MicroSort is still experimental and available only as part of a study being done to apply for approval from the Food and Drug Administration. The technology was originally developed by the Agriculture Department for use in farm animals, and it was adapted for people by scientists at the Genetics and IVF Institute, a fertility clinic in Virginia. The technique has been used in more than 1,000 pregnancies, with more than 900 births

so far, a spokesman for the clinic said. As of January 2006 (the most recent figures released), the success rate among parents who wanted girls was 91 percent, and for those who wanted boys, it was 76 percent.

Regardless of the method, the American College of Obstetricians and Gynecologists opposes sex selection except in people who carry a genetic disease that primarily affects one sex. But allowing sex selection just because the parents want it, with no medical reason, may support "sexist practices," the college said in an opinion paper published this month in its journal, Obstetrics and Gynecology.

Some people say sex selection is ethical if parents already have one or more boys and now want a girl, or vice versa. In that case, it's "family balancing," not sex discrimination. The MicroSort study accepts only people who have genetic disorders or request family balancing (they are asked for birth records), and a company spokesman said that even if the technique was approved, it would not be used for first babies.

The obstetricians group doesn't buy the family-balance argument, noting that some parents will say whatever they think the doctor wants to hear. The group also says that even if people are sincere about family balance, the very act of choosing a baby's sex "may be interpreted as condoning sexist values."

Much of the worry about this issue derives from what has happened in China and India, where preferences for boys led to widespread aborting of female fetuses when ultrasound and other tests made it possible to identify them. China's one-child policy is thought to have made matters worse. Last month, Chinese officials said that 118 boys were born for every 100 girls in 2005, and some reports have projected an excess of 30 million males in less than 15 years. The United Nations opposes sex selection for nonmedical reasons, and a number of countries have outlawed it, including Australia, Canada and Britain, and other nations in Asia, South America and Europe. Left unanswered is the question of whether societies, and families, that favor boys should just be allowed to have them, since attitudes are hard to change, and girls born into such environments may be abused.

The American Society for Reproductive Medicine, a group for infertility doctors, takes a somewhat more relaxed view of sex selection than does the college of obstetricians. Instead of opposing sex selection outright, it says that in people who already need in vitro fertilization and want to test the embryos' sex without a medical reason, the testing should "not be encouraged." And those who don't need in vitro fertilization but want it just for sex selection "should be discouraged," the group says.

But sperm sorting is another matter, the society says. It is noninvasive and does not involve discarding embryos of the "wrong" sex. The society concludes that "sex selection aimed at increasing gender variety in families may not so greatly increase the risk of harm to children, women or society that its use should be prohibited or condemned as unethical in all cases." The group also says it may eventually be reasonable to use sperm sorting for a first or only child.

Dr. Jamie Grifo, the program director of New York University's Fertility Center, said that he opposed using embryo testing just for sex selection, but that it was reasonable to honor the request in patients who were already having embryos screened for medical reasons, had a child and wanted one of the opposite sex. In those cases, he said, the information is already available and doesn't require an extra procedure.

"It's the patient's information, their desire," he said. "Who are we to decide, to play God? I've got news for you, it's not going to change the gender balance in the world. We get a handful of requests per year, and we're doing it. It's always been a controversy, but I don't think it's a big problem. We should preserve the autonomy of patients to make these very personal decisions."

Dr. Jeffrey M. Steinberg, from Encino, Calif., who has three clinics that offer sex selection and plans to open a fourth, in Manhattan, said: "We prefer to do it for family balancing, but we've never turned away someone who came in and said, 'I want my first to be a boy or a girl.' If they all said a boy first, we'd probably shy away, but it's 50-50."

"Reproductive choice, as far as I'm concerned, is a very personal issue," Dr. Steinberg said. "If it's not going to hurt anyone, we go ahead and give them what they want."

Many patients come from other countries, he said. John A. Robertson, a professor of law and bioethics at the University of Texas, said: "The distinction between doing it for so-called family balancing or gender variety would be a useful line to draw at this stage of the debate, just as maybe a practice guideline, and let's just see how it works out."

In the long run, Mr. Robertson said, he doubted that enough Americans would use genetic tests to skew the sex balance in the population, and he pointed out that so far, sperm sorting was more successful at producing girls than boys.

He concluded, "I think this will slowly get clarified, and people will see it's not as big a deal as they think."

UNIT 7

Preventing and Fighting Disease

Unit Selections

Key Points to Consider

- What is the relationship between obesity and diabetes (Type 2)?

- What lifestyle changes could you make that would reduce your risk of developing cardiovascular disease, cancer, diabetes, and AIDS?

- What are some steps individuals can take to reduce their risk of contracting cancer? What life changes could *you* make to reduce your risk of cancer?

- Why do fewer Americans consider AIDS a national health priority in 2006 as opposed to 20 years ago?

- Should all young girls be vaccinated against HPV? What are the risks vs. benefits?

Student Web Site

www.mhcls.com/online

Internet References

Further information regarding these Web sites may be found in this book's preface or online.

American Cancer Society
http://www.cancer.org

American Heart Association
http://www.amhrt.org

National Institute of Allergy and Infectious Diseases (NIAID)
http://www3.niaid.nih.gov/

American Diabetes Association Home Page
http://www.diabetes.org

Cardiovascular disease and cancer are the leading killers in this country. This is not altogether surprising given that the American population is growing increasingly older and one's risk of developing both of these diseases is directly proportional to one's age. Another major risk factor, which has received considerable attention over the past 30 years, is one's genetic predisposition or family history. Historically the significance of this risk factor has been emphasized as a basis for encouraging at-risk individuals to make prudent lifestyle choices, but this may be about to change as recent advances in genetic research, including mapping the human genome, may significantly improve the efficacy of both diagnostic and therapeutic procedures.

Just as cutting-edge genetic research is transforming the practice of medicine, startling new research findings in the health profession are transforming our views concerning adult health. This new research suggests that the primary determinants of our health as adults are the environmental conditions we experienced during life in the womb. According to Dr. Peter Nathanielsz of Cornell University, conditions during gestation, ranging from hormones that flow from the mother to how well the placenta delivers nutrients to the tiny limbs and organs, program how our liver, heart, kidneys, and especially our brains function as adults. While it is too early to draw any firm conclusions regarding the significance of the "life in the womb factor," it appears that this avenue of research may yield important clues as to how we may best prevent or forestall chronic illness.

Of all the diseases in America, coronary heart disease is this nation's number one killer. Frequently, the first and only symptom of this disease is a sudden heart attack. Epidemiological studies have revealed a number of risk factors that increase one's likelihood of developing the disease. These include hypertension, a high serum cholesterol level, diabetes, cigarette smoking, obesity, a sedentary lifestyle, a family history of heart disease, age, sex, race, and stress. In addition to these well-established risk factors, scientists think they may have discovered several additional risk factors. These include the following: low birth weight, cytomegalovirus, *Chlamydia pneumoniae*, porphyromonasgingivalis, and c-reactive protein (CRP). CRP is a measure of inflammation somewhere in the body. In theory, a high CRP reading may be a good indicator of an impending heart attack.

One of the most startling and ominous health stories was the recent announcement by the Centers for Disease Control and Prevention (CDC) that the incidence of Type 2 adult onset diabetes increased significantly over the past 15 years. This sudden rise appears to cross all races and age groups, with the sharpest increase occurring among people aged 30 to 39 (about 70 percent). Health experts at the CDC believe that this startling rise in diabetes among 30- to 39-year-olds is linked to the rise in obesity observed among young adults (obesity rates rose from 12 to 20 percent nationally during this same time period). Experts at the CDC believe that there is a time lag of about 10–15 years between the deposition of body fat and the manifestation of Type 2 diabetes. This time lag could explain why individuals in their 30s are experiencing the greatest increase in developing Type 2 diabetes today. Current estimates suggest that 16 million Americans have diabetes; it kills approximately 180,000 Americans each year. Many experts now believe that our couch-potato culture is fueling the rising rates of both obesity and diabetes. Given what we know about the relationship between obesity and Type 2 diabetes, the only practical solution is for Americans to watch their total calories and exercise regularly. "Diabesity, a Crisis in an Expanding Country" examines the rapid rise in the incidence of Type 2 diabetes among our youth and young adults and suggests that the term "adult onset diabetes" may be a misnomer given the growing number of young adults and teens with this form of diabetes.

Cardiovascular disease is America's number one killer, but cancer takes top billing in terms of the "fear factor." This fear of cancer stems from an awareness of the degenerative and disfiguring nature of the disease. Today, cancer specialists are employing a variety of complex agents and technologies, such as monoclonal antibodies, interferon, and immunotherapy, in their attempt to fight the disease. Progress has been slow, however, and the results, while promising, suggest that a cure may be several years away. A very disturbing aspect of this country's battle against cancer is the fact that millions of dollars are spent each year trying to advance the treatment of cancer, while funding for the technologies used to detect cancer in its early stages is quite limited. A reallocation of funds would seem appropriate, given the medical community's position that early detection and treatment are the key elements in the successful management of cancer. Until such time that we have more effective methods for detecting cancer in the early stages, our best hope for managing cancer is to prevent it through our lifestyle choices. "Why We Are Still Losing the Winnable Cancer War" takes an extensive look at the major forms of cancer in the United States and provides useful suggestions on the steps one can take to lower one's risk. While many questions remain unanswered regarding both cardiovascular disease and cancer, scientists are closing in on important clues.

It has now been over 20 years since the CDC first became aware of HIV/AIDS, and over that period of time more than 58 million people worldwide have been infected with the HIV virus and 22 million have died of AIDS. Despite medical advances in the war against AIDS there is no cure in sight and a vaccination may be several years away. The complications associated with AIDS are not only medical, but include complex financial, political and social issues. With medical advances in the treatment of AIDS, complacency grew, and many people abandoned the philosophy of safe sex. Today many medical experts are worried that unless we remain vigilant in our fight against this disease we will find ourselves back where we were in the early days in terms of infection rates. "How AIDS Changed America" examines the disease, its origins, and its impact on America.

Two new articles address two interesting issues: fighting disease among prison inmates and the new vaccine to prevent cervical cancer. In the first, Susan Okie discusses the risky health behaviors that occur among inmates. These behaviors increase the risk of transmitting HIV. In the second article, Kate O'Beirne addresses the vaccine and the questions that remain over who should be immunized.

'Diabesity,' a Crisis in an Expanding Country

Jane E. Brody

I can't understand why we still don't have a national initiative to control what is fast emerging as the most serious and costly health problem in America: excess weight. Are our schools, our parents, our national leaders blind to what is happening—a health crisis that looms even larger than our former and current smoking habits?

Just look at the numbers, so graphically described in an eye-opening new book, "Diabesity: The Obesity-Diabetes Epidemic That Threatens America—and What We Must Do to Stop It" (Bantam), by Dr. Francine R. Kaufman, a pediatric endocrinologist, the director of the diabetes clinic at Children's Hospital Los Angeles and a past president of the American Diabetes Association.

In just over a decade, she noted, the prevalence of diabetes nearly doubled in the American adult population: to 8.7 percent in 2002, from 4.9 percent in 1990. Furthermore, an estimated one-third of Americans with Type 2 diabetes don't even know they have it because the disease is hard to spot until it causes a medical crisis.

An estimated 18.2 million Americans now have diabetes, 90 percent of them the environmentally influenced type that used to be called adult-onset diabetes. But adults are no longer the only victims—a trend that prompted an official change in name in 1997 to Type 2 diabetes.

More and more children are developing this health-robbing disease or its precursor, prediabetes. Counting children and adults together, some 41 million Americans have a higher-than-normal blood sugar level that typically precedes the development of full-blown diabetes.

'Then Everything Changed'

And what is the reason for this runaway epidemic? Being overweight or obese, especially with the accumulation of large amounts of body fat around the abdomen. In Dr. Kaufman's first 15 years as a pediatric endocrinologist, 1978 to 1993, she wrote, "I never saw a young patient with Type 2 diabetes. But then everything changed."

Teenagers now come into her clinic weighing 200, 300, even nearly 400 pounds with blood sugar levels that are off the charts.

But, she adds, we cannot simply blame this problem on gluttony and laziness and "assume that the sole solution is individual change."

The major causes, Dr. Kaufman says, are "an economic structure that makes it cheaper to eat fries than fruit" and a food industry and mass media that lure children to eat the wrong foods and too much of them. "We have defined progress in terms of the quantity rather than the quality of our food," she wrote.

Her views are supported by a 15-year study published in January in The Lancet. A team headed by Dr. Mark A. Pereira of the University of Minnesota analyzed the eating habits of 3,031 young adults and found that weight gain and the development of prediabetes were directly related to unhealthful fast food.

Taking other factors into consideration, consuming fast food two or more times a week resulted, on average, in an extra weight gain of 10 pounds and doubled the risk of prediabetes over the 15-year period.

Other important factors in the diabesity epidemic, Dr. Kaufman explained, are the failure of schools to set good examples by providing only healthful fare, a loss of required physical activity in schools and the inability of many children these days to walk or bike safely to school or to play outside later.

Genes play a role as well. Some people are more prone to developing Type 2 diabetes than others. The risk is 1.6 times as great for blacks as for whites of similar age. It is 1.5 times as great for Hispanic-Americans, and 2 times as great for Mexican-Americans and Native Americans.

Unless we change our eating and exercise habits and pay greater attention to this disease, more than one-third of whites, two-fifths of blacks and half of Hispanic people in this country will develop diabetes.

It is also obvious from the disastrous patient histories recounted in Dr. Kaufman's book that the nation's medical structure is a factor as well. Many people do not have readily accessible medical care, and still many others have no coverage for preventive medicine. As a result, millions fall between the cracks until they are felled by heart attacks or strokes.

A Devastating Disease

There is a tendency in some older people to think of diabetes as "just a little sugar," a common family problem. They fail to take it seriously and make the connection between it and the costly, crippling and often fatal diseases that can ensue.

Diabetes, with its consequences of heart attack, stroke, kidney failure, amputations and blindness, among others, already ranks No. 1 in direct health care costs, consuming $1 of every $7 spent on health care.

Nor is this epidemic confined to American borders. Internationally, "we are witnessing an epidemic that is the scourge of the 21st century," Dr. Kaufman wrote.

Unlike some other killer diseases, Type 2 diabetes issues an easily detected wake-up call: the accumulation of excess weight, especially around the abdomen. When the average fasting level of blood sugar (glucose) rises above 100 milligrams per deciliter, diabetes is looming.

Abdominal fat is highly active. The chemical output of its cells increases blood levels of hormones like estrogen, providing the link between obesity and breast cancer, and decreases androgens, which can cause a decline in libido. As the cells in abdominal fat expand, they also release chemicals that increase fat accumulation, ensuring their own existence.

The result is an increasing cellular resistance to the effects of the hormone insulin, which enables cells to burn blood sugar for energy. As blood sugar rises with increasing insulin resistance, the pancreas puts out more and more insulin (promoting further fat storage) until this gland is exhausted. Then when your fasting blood sugar level reaches 126 milligrams, you have diabetes.

Two recent clinical trials showed that Type 2 diabetes could be prevented by changes in diet and exercise. The Diabetes Prevention Program Research Group involving 3,234 overweight adults showed that "intensive lifestyle intervention" was more effective than a drug that increases insulin sensitivity in preventing diabetes over three years.

The intervention, lasting 24 weeks, trains people to choose low-calorie, low-fat diets; increase activity; and change their habits. Likewise, the randomized, controlled Finnish Diabetes Prevention Study of 522 obese patients showed that introducing a moderate exercise program of at least 150 minutes a week and weight loss of at least 5 percent reduced the incidence of diabetes by 58 percent.

Many changes are needed to combat this epidemic, starting with schools and parents. Perhaps the quickest changes can be made in the workplace, where people can be encouraged to use stairs instead of elevators; vending machines can be removed or dispense only healthful snacks; and cafeterias can offer attractive healthful fare. Lunchrooms equipped with refrigerators and microwaves will allow workers to bring healthful meals to work.

Dr. Kaufman tells of a challenge to get fit and lose weight by Caesars Entertainment in which 4,600 workers who completed the program lost a total of 45,000 pounds in 90 days. Others could follow this example.

Sex, Drugs, Prisons, and HIV

Susan Okie, MD

One recent morning at a medium-security compound at Rhode Island's state prison, Mr. M, a middle-aged black inmate, described some of the high-risk behavior he has witnessed while serving time. "I've seen it all," he said, smiling and rolling his eyes. "We have a lot of risky sexual activities. . . . Almost every second or minute, somebody's sneaking and doing something." Some participants are homosexual, he added; others are "curious, bisexual, bored, lonely, and . . . experimenting." As in all U.S. prisons, sex is illegal at the facility; as in nearly all, condoms are prohibited. Some inmates try to take precautions, fashioning makeshift condoms from latex gloves or sandwich bags. Most, however, "are so frustrated that they are not thinking of the consequences except for later," said Mr. M.

Drugs, and sometimes needles and syringes, find their way inside the walls. "I've seen the lifers that just don't care," Mr. M said. "They share needles and don't take a minute to rinse them." In the 1990s, he said, "needles were coming in by the handful," but prison officials have since stopped that traffic, and inmates who take illicit drugs usually snort or swallow them. Tattooing, although also prohibited, has been popular at times. "A lot of people I've known caught hepatitis from tattooing," Mr. M said. "They use staples, a nail . . . anything with a point."

Mr. M had just undergone a checkup performed by Dr. Josiah D. Rich, a professor of medicine at Brown University Medical School, who provides him with medical care as part of a long-standing arrangement between Brown and the Adult Correctional Institute in Cranston. Two years ago, Mr. M was hospitalized with pneumonia and meningitis. "I was scared and in denial," he said. Now, thanks to treatment with antiretroviral drugs, "I'm doing great, and I feel good," he reported. "I am HIV-positive and still healthy and still look fabulous."

U.S. public health experts consider the Rhode Island prison's human immunodeficiency virus (HIV) counseling and testing practices, medical care, and prerelease services to be among the best in the country. Yet according to international guidelines for reducing the risk of HIV transmission inside prisons, all U.S. prison systems fall short. Recognizing that sex occurs in prison despite prohibitions, the World Health Organization (WHO) and the Joint United Nations Program on HIV/AIDS (UNAIDS) have recommended for more than a decade that condoms be made available to prisoners. They also recommend that prisoners have access to bleach for cleaning injecting equipment,

that drug-dependence treatment and methadone maintenance programs be offered in prisons if they are provided in the community, and that needle-exchange programs be considered.

Prisons in several Western European countries and in Australia, Canada, Kyrgyzstan, Belarus, Moldova, Indonesia, and Iran have adopted some or all of these approaches to "harm reduction," with largely favorable results. For example, programs providing sterile needles and syringes have been established in some 50 prisons in eight countries; evaluations of such programs in Switzerland, Spain, and Germany found no increase in drug use, a dramatic decrease in needle sharing, no new cases of infection with HIV or hepatitis B or C, and no reported instances of needles being used as weapons.[1] Nevertheless, in the United States, condoms are currently provided on a limited basis in only two state prison systems (Vermont and Mississippi) and five county jail systems (New York, Philadelphia, San Francisco, Los Angeles, and Washington, DC). Methadone maintenance programs are rarer still, and no U.S. prison has piloted a needle-exchange program.

The U.S. prison population has reached record numbers—at the end of 2005, more than 2.2 million American adults were incarcerated, according to the Justice Department. And drug-related offenses are a major reason for the population growth, accounting for 49% of the increase between 1995 and 2003. Moreover, in 2005, more than half of all inmates had a mental health problem, and doctors who treat prisoners say that many have used illicit drugs as self-medication for untreated mental disorders.

In the United States in 2004 (see table), 1.8% of prison inmates were HIV-positive, more than four times the estimated rate in the general population; the rate of confirmed AIDS cases is also substantially higher (see graph).[2] Some behaviors that increase the risk of contracting HIV and other bloodborne or sexually transmitted infections can also lead to incarceration, and the burden of infectious diseases in prisons is high. It has been estimated that each year, about 25% of all HIV-infected persons in the United States spend time in a correctional facility, as do 33% of persons with hepatitis C virus (HCV) infection and 40% of those with active tuberculosis.[3]

Critics in the public health community have been urging U.S. prison officials to do more to prevent HIV transmission, to improve diagnosis and treatment in prisons, and to expand programs for reducing high-risk behavior after release. The

HIV–AIDS among Prison Inmates at the End of 2004.*

Jurisdictions with the Most Prisoners Living with HIV–AIDS	No. of Inmates Living with HIV–AIDS	Prevalence of HIV–AIDS %
New York	4500	7.0
Florida	3250	3.9
Texas	2405	1.7
Federal system	1680	1.1
California	1212	0.7
Georgia	1109	2.2

*Data are from Maruschak.[2]

debate over such preventive strategies as providing condoms and needles reflects philosophical differences, as well as uncertainty about the frequency of HIV transmission inside prisons. The UNAIDS and WHO recommendations assume that sexual activity and injection of drugs by inmates cannot be entirely eliminated and aim to protect both prisoners and the public from HIV, HCV, and other diseases.

But many U.S. prison officials contend that providing needles or condoms would send a mixed message. By distributing condoms, "you're saying sex, whether consensual or not, is OK," said Lieutenant Gerald Ducharme, a guard at the Rhode Island prison. "It's a detriment to what we're trying to enforce." U.S. prison populations have higher rates of mental illness and violence than their European counterparts, which, some researchers argue, might make providing needles more dangerous. And some believe that whereas European prison officials tend to be pragmatic, many U.S. officials adopt a "just deserts" philosophy, viewing infections as the consequences of breaking prison rules.

Studies involving state-prison inmates suggest that the frequency of HIV transmission is low but not negligible. For example, between 1988—when the Georgia Department of Corrections began mandatory HIV testing of all inmates on entry to prison and voluntary testing thereafter—and 2005, HIV seroconversion occurred in 88 male inmates in Georgia state prisons. HIV transmission in prison was associated with men having sex with other men or receiving a tattoo.[4] In another study in a southeastern state, Christopher Krebs of RTI International documented that 33 of 5265 male prison inmates (0.63%) contracted HIV while in prison.[5] But Krebs points out that "when you have a large prison population, as our country does . . . you do start thinking about large numbers of people contracting HIV."

Studies of high-risk behavior in prisons yield widely varying frequency estimates: for example, estimates of the proportion of male inmates who have sex with other men range from 2 to 65%, and estimates of the proportion who are sexually assaulted range from 0 to 40%.[5] Such variations may reflect differences in research methods, inmate populations, and prison conditions that affect privacy and opportunity. Researchers emphasize that classifying prison sex as either consensual or forced is often overly simplistic: an inmate may provide sexual favors to another in return for protection or for other reasons. Better information on sexual transmission of HIV in prisons may eventually become available as a result of the Prison Rape Elimination Act of 2003, which requires the Justice Department to collect statistics on prison rape and to provide funds for educating prison staff and inmates about the subject.

Theodore M. Hammett of the Domestic Health, Health Policy, and Clinical Research Division of Abt Associates, a Massachusetts-based policy research and consulting firm, acknowledged that for political reasons U.S. prisons are unlikely to accept needle-exchange programs, but he said adoption of other HIV-prevention measures is long overdue. "Condoms ought to be widely available in prisons," he said. "From a public health standpoint, I think there's little question that that should be done. Methadone, also—all kinds of drug [abuse] treatment should be much more widely available in correctional settings." Methadone maintenance programs for inmates have been established in a few jails and prisons, including those in New York City, Albuquerque, and San Juan, Puerto Rico. Brown University's Rich is currently conducting a randomized, controlled trial at the Rhode Island facility, sponsored by the National Institutes of Health, to determine whether starting methadone maintenance in heroin-addicted inmates a month before their release will lead to better health outcomes and reduced recidivism, as

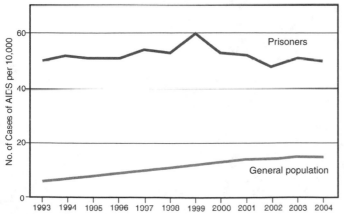

Rates of Confirmed AIDS Cases in the General Population and among State and Federal Prisoners, 1993–2004.

Data are from Maruschak.[2]

compared with providing either usual care or referral to community methadone programs at the time of release.

At the Rhode Island prison, the medical program focuses on identifying HIV-infected inmates, treating them, teaching them how to avoid transmitting the virus, addressing drug dependence, and when they're released, referring them to a program that arranges for HIV care and other assistance, including methadone maintenance treatment if needed. The prison offers routine HIV testing, and 90% of inmates accept it. One third of the state's HIV cases have been diagnosed at the prison. "These people are a target population and a captive one," noted Rich. "We should use this time" for health care and prevention. Nationally, 73% of state inmates and 77% of federal inmates surveyed in 2004 said they had been tested for HIV in prison. State policies vary, with 20 states reportedly testing all inmates and the rest offering tests for high-risk groups, at inmates' request, or in specific situations. Researchers said inmate acceptance rates also vary widely, depending on how the test is presented. Drugs for treating HIV-infected prisoners are not covered by federal programs, and prison budgets often contain inadequate funding for health services. "You can see how, in some cases, there could be a disincentive for really pushing testing," Hammett said.

Critics of U.S. penal policies contend that incarceration has exacerbated the HIV epidemic among blacks, who are disproportionately represented in the prison population, accounting for 40% of inmates. A new report by the National Minority AIDS Council calls for routine, voluntary HIV testing in prisons and on release, making condoms available, and expanding reentry programs that address HIV prevention, substance abuse, mental health, and housing needs as prisoners return to the community. "Any reservoir of infection that is as large as a prison would warrant, by simple public health logic, that we do our best . . . to reduce the risk of transmission" both inside and outside the walls, said Robert E. Fullilove of Columbia University's Mailman School of Public Health, who wrote the report. "The issue has never been, Do we understand what has to happen to reduce the risks? . . . It's always been, Do we have the political will necessary to put what we know is effective into operation?"

Notes

1. Dolan K, Rutter S, Wodak AD. Prison-based syringe exchange programmes: a review of international research and development. Addiction 2003;98:153–158.
2. Maruschak LM. HIV in prisons, 2004. Washington, DC: Bureau of Justice Statistics, November 2006.
3. Hammett TM, Harmon MP, Rhodes W. The burden of infectious disease among inmates of and releasees from US correctional facilities, 1997. Am J Public Health 2002;92:1789–1794.
4. HIV transmission among male inmates in a state prison system—Georgia, 1992–2005. MMWR Morb Mortal Wkly Rep 2006;55:421–6.
5. Krebs CP. Inmate factors associated with HIV transmission in prison. Criminology Public Policy 2006;5:113–36.

DR. OKIE is a contributing editor of the *Journal*.

The Battle Within
Our Anti-inflammation Diet

What do paper cuts, spicy foods, stubbed toes and intense workouts at the gym have to do with your odds of getting colon cancer, drifting into Alzheimer's or succumbing to a heart attack? A lot more than you might think.

The more scientists learn about these and other serious diseases, the more they are being linked with the long-term effects of inflammation on the body.

MICHAEL DOWNEY

The inflammation-disease connection has become a hot research topic. And it's about to explode.

Vital Nuisance

Inflammation is a vital immune response to infection, injury or irritation. It is the basis of humanity's earliest survival.

It's what causes the redness in that paper cut—the result of extra blood walling off the area and rushing macrophages, histamine and other bacteria-fighting immune factors to the wound.

The same inflammatory process is what makes your throat burn when you decide to impress your friends by chugging the extra-spicy suicide sauce—blood vessels leak fluid, proteins and cells to repair or remove damaged tissues. And fever is yet another form of that inflammatory burning.

Inflammation sparks the swelling in that stubbed toe—caused by fluid released into the banged-up cells to speed healing and cushion that toe against further injury.

It also causes that tenderness you feel after hours at the gym—because your immune system rushes fluids to the torn muscles to protect and repair them, compressing sensitive nerve endings in the process.

Inflammation isolates foreign invaders and rushes our strongest natural infection-fighters to the site deemed under attack. It cleans away debris from destroyed tissue; slows bleeding; starts clotting; and—if tissues cannot be restored—produces scar tissue. Without this sophisticated immune response, our species would have died out long ago.

But it's a double-edged sword. In addition to its telltale redness, heat, swelling or pain, inflammation can cause serious dysfunction.

Defensive Nutrition

- oily fish and fish oil supplements
- olive, walnut or flaxseed oil
- walnuts, flaxseeds and soy foods
- fruits and vegetables
- red wine
- antioxidant supplements
- garlic, ginger and turmeric (enreumin)
- sunflower seeds, eggs, herring, nuts or zinc tablets
- pineapple or bromelain supplements
- S-adenosyl-methionine (SAMe)

Problems begin when—for one reason or another—the inflammatory process becomes chronic, persisting long after it's needed.

Heart disease researchers were the first to notice that inflammation can play a role in cardiovascular disease.

Heart Mystery

Not long ago, doctors viewed heart disease as a plumbing problem. Cholesterol levels in the blood get too high, and, over the years, fatty deposits clog the pipes and cut off the blood supply.

There's just one problem with that explanation: Sometimes, it's dead wrong.

Half of all heart attacks occur in people with normal cholesterol levels and normal blood pressure. Something causes relatively minor deposits to burst, triggering massive clots that block the blood supply.

That something has turned out to be inflammation.

C-reactive protein (CRP)—a blood measure of inflammation—shoots up during an acute illness or infection. But CRP is also somewhat elevated among otherwise healthy people. And studies show that those with the highest CRP levels have three times the heart attack risk as those with the lowest levels. The inflammatory response, possibly reacting to cholesterol that has seeped into the lining of the artery, makes even normal fatty deposits unstable.

There are several causes of heart disease: smoking, high blood pressure and, yes, cholesterol. But we must now add inflammation to that list.

Runaway Reaction

Heart disease is just the tip of the inflammation iceberg. Studies over the past couple of years have suggested that higher CRP levels raise the risk of diabetes. It's too early to say whether lowering inflammation will keep diabetes from developing. But before insulin was isolated at the University of Toronto in the 1920s, doctors found that blood sugar levels could be decreased by using salicylates, a group of aspirin-like compounds known to reduce inflammation.

In the 1860s, German pathologist Rudolph Virchow speculated that cancerous tumors start at the site of chronic inflammation—basically, a wound that never heals. Then, in the middle of the 20th century, we came to understand the role of genetic mutations in cancerous tissue. Today, researchers are investigating the possibility that mutations and inflammation work together to turn normal cells into deadly tumors. Reducing chronic inflammation may yet become a prescription for keeping cancer at bay.

Researchers have found that people who take anti-inflammation medications—for arthritis, for example—succumb to Alzheimer's disease later in life than those who don't. Plaque and tangles accumulate in the brains of Alzheimer's patients. Perhaps the immune system mistakenly sees these abnormalities as damaged tissue that should be eliminated. Early information suggests that low-dose aspirin and fish oil capsules—both known to reduce inflammation—lower the risk of Alzheimer's.

The cause of asthma is still unknown, but some suspect the inflammatory attack. The treatments that help relieve asthma work by reducing the inflammation involved.

Sometimes, for reasons that are not clear, perfectly healthy cells trigger the body's immune system. The inflammatory response is launched against normal cells in the joints, nerves, connective tissue or any part of the body. These autoimmune disorders include rheumatoid arthritis, multiple sclerosis, lupus, vitiligo, psoriasis and other versions of a body at war with itself. Even Crohn's disease and cystic fibrosis are associated with inflammation.

Some level of inflammatory immune reaction is usually present in our bodies, whether we're aware of it or not. And if inflammation really is the biological engine that drives many of our most feared illnesses, it suggests a new and possibly much simpler way of warding off disease. Instead of different treatments for all of these disorders, simply turning down the degree of our inflammatory attack might be a partial prevention for all of them.

Dampening the Fires

Many attributes of a Western lifestyle—such as a diet high in sugars and saturated fats, accompanied by little or no exercise—make it much easier for the body to become inflamed.

Losing weight helps because fat cells produce cytokines, which crank up inflammation. Thirty minutes a day of moderate exercise dampens the fire as well. Flossing your teeth combats gum disease, another source of chronic inflammation. And, of course, you should avoid excess alcohol intake and smoking.

Despite the injury they can do to the stomach, anti-inflammatory drugs such as aspirin and ibuprofen are often prescribed for treatment of inflammatory diseases, but they're not appropriate for prevention. Fish oil capsules have been shown to produce the same reduction in inflammatory cytokines.

Inflammation-promoting prostaglandins are made from the trans fats found in partially hydrogenated oils. So avoid margarines and vegetable shortenings that are made with them.

Getting a good supply of omega-3 fatty acids—and a minimum of omega-6 fats—is key to an immune system that's not overreactive. Opt for oily fish such as salmon, sardines, herring and mackerel; and on days that you don't have fish, take a fish oil supplement, eat walnuts, freshly ground flaxseeds or flaxseed oil and soy foods. Steer away from safflower, sunflower, corn and sesame oils, as well as polyunsaturated vegetable oils. Use walnut, flaxseed or extra virgin olive oils instead.

Fruits and vegetables are full of antioxidants that disable free radicals and minimize inflammation. All are good, but you should focus your diet on those that produce the highest antioxidant activity: blueberries and kiwi. Consider antioxidant supplements such as resveratrol, grape seed extract, quercetin, pycnogenol or citrus bioflavonoids, as well as beta-carotene and vitamins, C and E. And drink red wine in small quantities.

Garlic, ginger and turmeric are natural anti-inflammatory agents. Include them in your diet.

Zinc controls inflammation while promoting healing. It is found in sunflower seeds, eggs, nuts, wheat germ, herring and zinc supplements.

S-adenosyl-methionine (SAMe), alpha lipoic acid and coenzyme Q10 act as inflammation fighters. Also, bromelain—found in pineapple and supplements—may reduce inflammation.

So if you want to stop inflammation, get off that couch and head out to pick up oily fish, fresh produce, garlic and supplements. And try not to stub your toe on the way.

Why We Are Still Losing the Winnable Cancer War

Samuel S. Epstein, MD

For more than thirty years we in the United States have been losing the war on cancer because we've used the wrong "generals" and the wrong strategies. The war has been and continues to be waged using screening, diagnosis, treatment, and related research with the primary goal of "damage control." By contrast, cancer *prevention* through the reduction of avoidable exposures to carcinogens in the totality of the environment remains a minimal priority.

Ever since President Richard Nixon declared the "War on Cancer" in 1971 the country's primary generals—the federal National Cancer Institute (NCI) and the worlds wealthiest non-profit organization, the American Cancer Society (ACS)—have misled the nation. At first they promised a cure in time for the United States' 1976 bicentennial. Then in 1984, and again in 1986, the NCI declared that cancer mortality would be halved by 2000. In 1998 the NCI and ACS trumpeted that the nation had "turned the corner" in the war on cancer. Most recently, in 2003, NCI Director Andrew C. von Eschenbach pledged unrealistically to "eliminate the suffering and death from cancer by 2015." This pledge was shortly followed by a joint NCI and ACS claim that "considerable progress has been made in reducing the burden of cancer."

On June 3, 2004, a joint NCI and ACS *Annual Report to the Nation on the Status of Cancer, 1975–2001* stated that "cancer incidence and death rates are on the decline from 1991–2001, due to progress in prevention, early detection, and treatment." This report prompted a flurry of positive headlines in national newspapers, such as "Cancer cases, death rates declining," supposedly by 7 to 8 percent from 1991 to 2001. But these decreases have largely resulted from the reduction of lung cancer cases and deaths due to decreased smoking by men and, to a lesser extent, women. Also, with few exceptions, the incidence rates of a wide range of nonsmoking related cancers continued to increase from 1991 to 2001. (These rates are based on statistics that are adjusted for the aging population.)

Confidence in the latest claim of the NCI and ACS of declining death rates was further shaken by the NCI's admission in a "Questions and Answers" release of "statistical uncertainties related to changes in data collection." These included discrepancies between the claim that death rates "are on the decline from 1991–2001" in contrast to their previous annual report

that "death rates were stabilizing." Even more to the point is the alarming fact that death rates have remained virtually unchanged since 1975.

Today cancer strikes about 1.3 million people annually. Nearly one in two men and more than one in three women develop cancer in their lifetimes. This translates into approximately 56 percent more cancer in men and 22 percent more cancer in women over the course of just one generation. Cancer has become a "disease of mass destruction."

These trends have developed over the last three decades during which the NCI's annual budget has skyrocketed by about thirtyfold, now approaching $5 billion. By one recent estimate, total public and private spending on cancer will have amounted to $14 billion for 2004.

Paradoxically, it seems that the more money spent fighting cancer the more cancer is discovered in patients. Certainly, major funding is essential for early detection, treatment, and related research. But much less money would be needed if more cancers were prevented, resulting in less to treat. Representative John Conyers (Democrat, Michigan), the ranking minority member of the House judiciary Committee, recently warned that "so much carnage is preventable. Preventable that is, if the NCI gets off the dime and does its job."

The Cancer Establishment

The NCI is a federal agency funded by taxpayers while the ACS is a private, nonprofit "charity." However, despite their institutional independence, the NCI and ACS are joined at the hip. They are well dubbed the "cancer establishment."

The ACS powerfully and seemingly independently reinforces the NCIs strategies through well-orchestrated and aggressive public relations directed toward the public, the media, and Congress. This PR is underwritten by the multibillion dollar cancer drug industry ("Big Pharma"), other industries that are major ACS donors, and public donations. In spite of its smaller size and budget, the ACS is the dominant partner in the cancer establishment—"the tail that wags the NCI dog."

The institutional relationship between the NCI and the ACS is reinforced nationally at the rank-and file level. About half of ACS board members are surgeons, radiologists, oncologists, and basic scientists. Most are interlocked with the NCI, particularly with regard to finding for treatment and related research. And with the February 2002 appointment of ACS President elect von Eschenback as NCI director, the relationship between ACS and the NCI became further consolidated.

The Wrong Strategies

The cancer establishments strategies are overwhelmingly imbalanced. They are fixated on damage control—screening, diagnosis, and treatment—and related research to the virtual exclusion of prevention. These current strategies reflect professional mindsets within the estahlishment's leadership—predominantly oncologists, surgeons, radiotherapists, and research scientists. Such biases are exacerbated by strong and pervasive conflicts of interest.

At the April 2004 annual meeting of the American Association of Cancer Research, Leland Hartwell, president of the Fred Hutchinson Cancer Research Center and 2001 Nobel laureate, admitted the facts plainly when he said, "Congress and the public are not paying [NCI] \$4.7 billion a year just to learn about cancer [through basic research]. They are paying to cure the disease." Hartwell further stressed that most resources for cancer research are spent on "promoting ineffective drugs" for terminal disease.

Hartwell wasn't the first establishment figure to admit these facts. As reported by the Associated Press on July 27, 2003, leading oncologists have questioned whether cancer "will ever be reliably and predictably cured." They also admitted that the biotech industry's new magic bullet, "targeted" drugs, have turned out to be "as powerless as old-line chemotherapy," increasing survival by a few months at best. In this connection, Memorial Sloan-Kettering's Leonard Saltz estimated that the price for new biotech drugs "has increased 500-fold in the last decade." Unchecked, these runaway costs could implode the entire health care system.

Hartwell also agreed with Clifton Leaf's March 22, 2004, *Fortune* article, "Why We're loosing the War on Cancer" which reports that cancer mortality rates have remained almost stable over the past five decades, during which time there have been major reductions in mortality from heart disease and stroke. Taken aback by Hartwell and Leaf's conclusions, von Eschenbach responded with an irrelevant stump speech; "You are transforming the world. You are saving lives. God bless you for it, and God continue to bless you in your work."

In this connection, it should be stressed that the standard criterion for the success of drug treatment is based on the shrinkage of tumor size by over 50 percent within six months, regardless of whether the patients life is prolonged. In fact, some "successful" treatments actually shorten survival due to drug toxicity while successes, particularly with the recent targeted drugs, are questionably based on brief increased survival in small trials.

When it comes to prevention, NCI and ACS strategies are fixated on faulty lifestyle, particularly smoking, to the virtual exclusion of a wide range of other avoidable causes of cancer. These include pervasive environmental contamination of air and water, hazardous waste sites, workplaces with carcinogenic industrial chemicals, contamination of food with carcinogenic pesticides, carcinogenic prescription drugs and high-dose

Incidence Rates of Non-Smoking Cancers

Cancer*	% Change, 1975–2001	% Change, 1991–2001
Melanoma	+137	+28
Liver	+100	+21
Kidney	+69	+13
Thyroid	+67	+48
Non-Hodgkin's Lymphoma (female)	+63	+8
Brain (childhood)	+61	+6
Testes	+46	+6
Breast (post-menopausal)	+37	+4
Acute Myeloid Leukemia	+15	+18
Multiple Myeloma	+8	−12
Colorectal	−13	−13

*Prostate cancer omitted because of diagnostic uncertainties relating to the PSA test

diagnostic radiation, and carcinogenic ingredients in cosmetics, toiletries, and household products.

Arthur Andersen's silence regarding Enron's misconduct pales in comparison to the cancer establishment's silence regarding reckless misconduct by the petrochemical and other industries. The former caused a financial meltdown while the latter has resulted in the cancer epidemic.

In sharp contrast to inflationary expenditures on treatment, the NCI's prevention budget has been and remains parsimonious. For instance, an unchallenged published analysis of its \$2 billion 1992 budget revealed that less than 2.5 percent—not the 20 percent the NCI had claimed—was earmarked for research on avoidable causes of cancer, furthermore, no funds were allocated toward making any such information available to the public.

In 1998 U.S. Representative David Obey (Democrat, Wisconsin) asked then–NCI Director Richard Klausner to back up the claim that 20 percent of NCI's \$2.5 billion budget was allocated toward research on environmental causes of cancer. Klausner simply increased his 20 percent figure to 40 percent without providing any supportive evidence. Another example of the NCI's frank misrepresentation of its prevention policies appears in the "Highlights" of its 2001 *Cancer Facts*. The opening sentence states, "Cancer prevention is a major component and current priority—to reduce suffering and death from cancer."

Sometimes NCI's false claims and indifference to avoidable causes of cancer extend to outright denial. For example, it holds that the causes of childhood cancer are largely unknown, in spite of substantial contrary evidence. The ACS takes a similar position. In the childhood cancer section of its 2003 *Cancer Facts & Figures,* no mention is made of any avoidable causes.

Indifference and denial can extend even to the outright suppression of information. At a 1996 San Francisco town hall meeting on breast cancer, chaired by U.S. Represenative Nancy

Avoidable Causes of Childhood Cancer

Environmental

- Proximity of residence to nuclear energy plants.
- Proximity of residence to petrochemical industries.
- Exposure to carcinogenic pesticides from agricultural and urban spraying and uses in schools, including wood playground sets treated with chromated copper arsenate.
- Maternal or paternal exposures (preconception, conception, and post-conception) to occupational carcinogens.

Domestic

- Drinking and cooking water contaminated with carcinogenic pesticides or other industrial pollutants.
- Exposure to carcinogenic pesticides from uses in the home and garden and pet flea collars.
- Contamination of infant and childhood food with carcinogenic pesticides.
- Nitrite preservatives in hot dogs (interacting with naturally occurring amines to form carcinogenic nitrosamines).
- Maternal or paternal carry home of occupational carcinogens.

Medical

- Maternal X-radiation during late pregnancy.
- Ionizing radiation for treatment of scalp ringworm or enlarged tonsils.
- High-dose diagnostic X radiation, particularly computerized tomography scans.
- Prescription drugs during pregnancy, such as DES and Dilantin.
- Pediatric prescription drugs, such as Lindane shampoos and Ritalin.

Pelosi (a California Democrat, now the House minority leader), Klausner insisted that "low-level diagnostic radiation does not demonstrate an increased risk." Actually, the NCI's long-term studies on patients with scoliosis (spinal curvature) showed that such radiation was responsible for 70 percent excess breast cancer mortality.

Perhaps the most egregious violation of the public's right to know concerns the belated release in 1997 of decade-old data predicting up to 210,000 thyroid cancers from exposure to radioactive fallout following the hydrogen bomb tests in Nevada during the 1950s. Had the public been warned in time, these cancers, whose incidence almost doubled since 1973, could have been readily prevented with thyroid medication. In a 1999 hearing, the Senate Committee on Governmental Affairs charged that the NCI investigation was "plagued by lack of public participation and openness" and that failure to "release this information (to the public) was a travesty."

As long as the NCI shirks its job of providing Congress and regulatory agencies with scientific evidence on avoidable causes of cancer, corrective legislative and regulatory action remains discouraging. Meanwhile, this silence also encourages petrochemical and other industries to continue manufacturing carcinogenic products and corporate polluters to continue contaminating the environment unchallenged.

Responding to growing criticism of its policies, the NCI now claims to allocate 12 percent of its budget toward "prevention and control" and to require its nationwide Comprehensive Cancer Centers to have a "prevention component." However, prevention continues to be narrowly defined in exclusionary terms of faulty lifestyle and screening, with no reference to environmental causes due to exposure to a wide range of industrial carcinogens.

The NCI goes even further by defining environmental causes of cancer as those other than genetic in origin. Commenting on the NCI's June 17, 2004, news release, "The Majority of Cancers Are Linked to Environment," Dr. Aaron Blair, NCI's leading epidemiologist, explained that "environmental" causes include all causes of cancer other than genetic. Blair thus claimed that environmental causes are predominantly smoking, diet, alcohol, and obesity and that industrial pollutants of air, water, and the workplace account for 5 percent or less of all causes of cancer.

The ACS indifference to prevention extends to hostility, as reflected in a decades-long history of pro-industry bias and even collusion. Examples are legion. In 1978 the ACS in effect protected auto industry interests by refusing to support the Clean Air Act. In 1992 the ACS supported the Chlorine Institutes defense of the continued use of chlorinated pesticides, despite clear evidence of their carcinogenicity, persistence, and pervasive environmental contamination. In 1993, just before PBS aired a *Frontline* program warning of contamination of infant and children's food with carcinogenic pesticides, the ACS blanketed its forty-eight regional divisions and 3,000 local offices with false reassurances of safety crafted by the agribusiness industry. Then in its 2003 *Cancer Facts & Figures,* the ACS offered reassurance that carcinogenic exposures from dietary pesticides, "toxic wastes in dump sites," and radiation from "closely controlled" nuclear energy plants are all "at such low levels that risks are negligible."

The ACS pro-industry agenda is further exemplified by its lack of research on prevention. In spite of bloated contrary claims, less than 0.1 percent of its approximately $800 million budget has been assigned to address "environmental carcinogenesis."

Conflicts of Interest

The cancer establishment generals have longstanding conflicts of interest. A current case in point is the highly touted "anti-cancer" nutritional supplement, PC–SPES.

PC–SPES (*PC* for prostate cancer, and the Latin *spes* for hope) has been widely sold by International Medical Research (IMR) to prostate cancer patients, as well as to healthy men, to maintain "good prostate health without any adverse reaction." However, PC–SPES is laced with prescription drugs, including the potent carcinogen DES (diethylstilbestrol, a synthetic estrogen). Aside from the lack of any evidence of benefits, symptoms and prostate-specific antigen (PSA) levels in cancer patients are likely to have been dangerously masked by DBS in the supplement.

In February 2004 more than twenty personal injury suits filed in Los Angeles County Superior Court alleged that IMR directors Richard Klausner and Michael Milken (the latter a securities felon turned philanthropist and founder and chair of the Prostate Cancer Foundation) systematically promoted PC–SPES. Other IMR directors include leading oncologists and scientists in the NCI's twenty-plus nationwide Comprehensive Cancer Centers.

Conflicts of interest of the PC–SPES type aren't just matters of personal wrongdoing. The conflicts are deeply rooted in the NCI's institutional structure. Founded in 1937 and incorporated into the National Institutes of Health in 1941, the NCI was divorced from the NIH by the 1971 National Cancer Act. Far beyond a mere reshuffling of bureaucratic boxes, this action in effect politicized the NCI and effectively insulated it from the scientific and public health communities. The NCI director reports to the U.S. president through the Office of Management and Budget, bypassing the NIH and the Department of Health and Human Services.

Nixon created a three-member NCI executive President's Cancer Panel, naming as its first chair Benno C. Schmidt, an investment banker and senior drug company executive with close ties to the oil, steel, and chemical industries. Schmidt's successor in the 1980s was Armand Hammer, the late chair of Occidental Petroleum, one of the nation's largest manufacturers of industrial chemicals and infamous for its involvement in the Love Canal disaster. Not surprisingly, Schmidt and Hammer showed no interest in cancer prevention, Instead, they focused on the highly profitable development and marketing of cancer drugs.

The NCI's prototype Comprehensive Cancer Center, Memorial Sloan Kettering, jointly funded by the ACS, represents another example of entrenched conflicts of interest. An analysis of the center's board reveals the predominant representation of cancer drug industries and close affiliations with oil and petrochemical industries. Dr. Samuel Broder, NCI director from 1989 to 1995, admitted the obvious in a 1988 *Washington Post* interview: "The NCI has become what amounts to a government pharmaceutical company" Broder left the NCI to take executive posts at IVAX and Celera Genomics, two major manufacturers of cancer drugs.

This revolving door between the NCI and industry— particularly industries indifferent or hostile to cancer prevention— has been and remains commonplace. The late Dr. Frank Rauscher, appointed NCI director by Nixon to spearhead his cancer war, resigned in 1976 to become the ACS senior vice president for research. He then moved on to become executive director of the Thermal Insulation Manufacturers Association, which promoted the unregulated use of carcinogenic fiberglass. Dr. Richard Adamson, the NCI's former director of research and policy on cancer causation, left the NCI in 1994 to head the National Soft Drinks Association, which vigorously promoted the use of artificial sweeteners, particularly the carcinogenic saccharin.

In a June 30, 2003, CNBC program, "Titans of Cancer" hosted by Maria Bartiromo, four cancer "titans" enthused about alleged breakthroughs in treatment with targeted biotech drugs while at the same time they ignored cancer prevention. Included on the program was Dr. Harold Varmus, president of Memorial Sloan-Kettering Cancer Center and a past recipient of major NCI research grants. In 1995 Varmus, then NIH director, struck down the "reasonable pricing clause" that protected against gross industry profiteering from cancer and other drugs developed with taxpayer dollars. Varmus" action also gave senior NCI and NIH staff free rein to consult with the drug industry. Another titan on the program—Dr. John Mendelsohn, president of NCI's University of Texas M. D. Anderson Comprehensive Cancer Center has been embroiled in conflicts of interest over ImClone's targeted drug Erbitux.

Following the *Los Angeles Times* series of revelations on extensive private consulting by senior NCI scientists, some of whom have earned as much as $300,000 or more per year since 1995, the House Energy and Commerce Committee and the Senate Appropriations Subcommittee convened hearings in December 2003 and January 2004. An illustrative case was that of Dr. Jeffrey Schlom, head of NCI's Laboratory of Tumor Immunology and Biology since 1982. Schlom built himself another substantial career as consultant on Taxol to Cytoclonal Pharmaceuticals and on colorectal and prostate cancer vaccines to Jenner Biotherapie.

Meanwhile, further conflicts of interest hearings and a General Accounting Office investigation are pending. Klausner, now director of global health programs for the Bill and Melinda Gates Foundation, remains under congressional investigation for violating ethics rules. He allegedly accepted "lecture awards" from NCI's Comprehensive Cancer Centers while serving as NCI director more than two years ago. Congress is also investigating Klausners questionable travel arrangements and business connections.

For all that, the NCI's conflicts of interest are dwarfed by those of the American Cancer Society. The ACS openly trumpets its financial ties to Big Pharma and polluting industries. Designated as "Excalibur" donors for their annual contributions of $100,000 or more, these benefactors include such drug and biotech companies as Bristol-Myers Squibb, Pfizer, AstraZeneca, Eli Lilly, Amgen, Genentech, and Johnson and Johnson. Among polluting industries on the donor ledgers are more than ten major petrochemical and oil companies, including DuPont, Akzo Nobel, Pennzoil, British Petroleum, and Concho Oil.

A total of some 300 other industries and companies make similar contributions to the total annual ACS budget of about $800 million, not counting government grants or income from about $1 billion in reserves. The ACS honors these contributions with more than a wink and a nod. Such collusion between agency and industry is normally unthinkable. For example, one would never find the American Heart Association advocating low tar cigarettes. But the ACS continually crosses the line. Not surprisingly, a January 28, 1992, report in the *Chronicle of Philanthropy,* the nation's leading charity watchdog, has charged: "The ACS is more interested in accumulating wealth than saving lives."

Privatizing the War

The most disturbing development in the cancer war has been its privatization by ACS and NCI generals. In 1998 the ACS created and funded the National Dialogue on Cancer (NDC), co-chaired by former President George H. W. Bush and Barbara Bush. Members included cancer survivor groups, some 100 representatives of the cancer drug industry, and Shandwick International Public Relations. Dr. John Durant, executive president of the American Cancer Society for Clinical Oncology, charged that the hidden purpose of ACS was "protecting their own fund raising capacity . . . from competition from survivor groups. It has always seemed to me that this was an issue of control by the ACS over the cancer agenda."

Without informing the NDC, the ACS then spun off a small legislative committee, the explicit aim of which was to increase NCI's autonomy and budget and to shift major control of cancer policy to the ACS—in other words, from the public purse to private hands. Shandwick International played a key role in managing the NDC and drafting the proposed legislation.

When news surfaced that R. J. Reynolds Tobacco Holdings was one of Shandwicks major clients, the ACS claimed prior ignorance and fired Shandwick. Astoundingly, the ACS next hired Edelman Public Relations Worldwide, another well-known tobacco public relations firm, to conduct a voter cancer education campaign for the 2000 presidential election.

Ever since von Eschenbach was appointed NCI director, the National Cancer Program has been effectively privatized. Von Eschenbach obtained George W. Bush's agreement to continue as vice chair of NDC, of which he was a main founder. The NDC since has been spun off as a nonprofit organization and renamed C-Change. The group then again hired Edelman as its PR firm, following Edelmans signed pledge that it would sever its relations with the tobacco industry. Edelman represents the Brown and Williamson Tobacco Company and the Altria Group, the parent company of Philip Morris, the largest cigarette maker in the United States. Edelman's clients also include Kraft and fast food and beverage companies now targeted by anti-obesity litigation.

In July 2003 it was discovered that Edelman, in violation of its pledge, was continuing to fight tobacco control programs from its Malaysian offices. Edelman executives apologized for this "oversight" and agreed once more to terminate its support of the tobacco industry. It further promised to donate this income to charity. Commenting on the ACS and NDC relationship with Edelman, Dr. Stanton Glantz, a prominent anti-smoking activist, commented, "It's like . . . Bush hiring alQaeda to do PR, because they have good connections to al Jazeera."

Equally disturbing is the growing and secretive collaboration between the NCI and the C-Change organization. The latest example is the joint planning of a massive national tumor tissue bank for cancer drug and genetic research. According to the Washington insider *Cancer Letter,* this project would cost up to $1.2 billion to operate in addition to construction costs in the billions. This initiative would be privatized, ripe with conflicts of interest, and exempt from the public scrutiny required by the Federal Advisory Committee and Freedom of information acts.

Behind the scenes, strong support for privatization of the cancer war comes from Michael Milken. As noted in the *Cancer Letter,* "Milken is the single most influential player in cancer politics within the last decade."

How to Win the War

After all this time we don't need another thirty years of research on cellular mechanisms of cancer and treatment or more billions of dollars spent on illusory wonder drugs to start winning the war. The war must be fought with the right generals implementing the right strategies. This goal should be supported by an array of interlocking initiatives.

The National Cancer Institute: For over three decades, NCI generals have violated the mandates of the 1971 National Cancer Act and its amendments to "disseminate cancer information to the public" and to call for "an expanded and intensified research program for the prevention of cancer caused by occupational and environmental exposures to carcinogens." The highest priority should be directed toward drastically changing the NCI high command. Those responsible for prevention should be given at least the same authority as those responsible for damage control. Responsibility for prevention should also be extended to the twenty-member National Cancer Advisory Board, as the Cancer Act requires, and to presidents of NCI's Comprehensive Cancer Centers. NCI's generals, senior staff, and Cancer Center presidents involved in illegal activities or in flagrant conflicts of interest with the cancer drug industries should resign or face dismissal.

The American Cancer Society: The public and media should be fully informed of the ACS's hostile record on cancer prevention, beyond identifying the dangers of an unhealthy lifestyle. They should also be explicitly informed of flagrant conflicts of interest between the ACS and the cancer drug, petrochemical, and other industries as well as its close ties to the tobacco industry. Armed with this information, the public would then be in a position to decide whether to continue giving funds to this charity or to donate instead to individuals, groups, and organizations with strong scientific and public health policy concerns on cancer prevention.

Developing Grass-Roots National Support: Cancer affects virtually every family in the nation. Still, the epidemic is likely to be met with passivity or even denial unless citizens are provided with practical information on how to reduce their own risks. The most realistic strategy for developing broad public support for cancer prevention will stress self-interest rather than abstractions or ideology. Preventing smoking, particularly prior to addiction in adolescence, is obviously important. Much less recognized, though, is the critical need for user-friendly information on avoidable causes of a wide spectrum of non-smoking cancers, incidence of which has escalated dramatically over recent decades.

The public's right to know about avoidable causes of cancer is the fundamental basis for building a national grass-roots coalition. The continuing failure of the NCI and the ACS to provide the public. Congress, and regulatory agencies with such information is a flagrant denial of this right. The right can be restored by empowering consumers, citizens, workers, and patients in a number of areas:

Instituting explicit label warnings on carcinogenic ingredients and contaminants in food, cosmetics and toiletries, and household products. Consumers then would be empowered to boycott mainstream companies selling unsafe products and reward smaller, "green" companies marketing safe alternatives. With increasing demand for the latter, economies of scale would reduce their higher prices.

Utilizing the "Environmental Defense Scorecard." Citizens have increasing opportunities for empowerment on an individual and community basis by plugging in their zip code on the scorecards website, www.scorecard.org, in order to obtain basic information on toxic and carcinogenic pollutants to which they are exposed locally by local chemical industries and power plants. They can then organize, alert the media, and join with environmental groups to express their concerns to local and state health authorities, including state governors. Regardless of their politics, governors are generally sensitive to citizen lobbies in their states.

Informing workers of potential high risks of cancers because of exposures to a wide range of occupational carcinogens can enable them to act to reduce such exposures both individually and through their unions and health and safety committees.

Advising patients to exercise their right to know by requesting full information on cancer and other risks of prescription drugs, as detailed in the "Precautions" section of the *Physicians Desk Reference,* empowers them to take charge of their own health. Thus, for the wide range of common prescription drugs carrying cancer risks, safe alternatives may be requested In accordance with legal as well as ethical requirements for informed consent. Made aware of the carcinogenic risks of high-dose X-ray procedures, particularly pediatric CT scans and fluoroscopy, patients can request dosage records for each examination, make informed decisions, and seek those (still few) informed radiologists and clinics practicing dose-reduction techniques.

Publicizing the Failure of the Cancer War:
An aggressive critique of the cancer generals and their unwinnable strategies is well overdue. For decades the mainstream media have mostly ignored the failed cancer policies and conflicts of interest of the cancer establishment. Activist citizen groups could generate a mounting series of reports, initially in smaller independent newspapers and radio stations nationwide, focusing on hot button topics—local or regional exposures to environmental carcinogens, "cancer clusters" in the vicinity of petrochemical and nuclear power plants, and escalating rates of cancers in children and retirees, together with the known or suspect causes of such cancers.

Key to such media activities should be emphasis on the escalating rates of nonsmoking cancers, along with the cancer establishment's refusal to prioritize the overdue need to reduce exposures to environmental carcinogens and to recognize the public's right to know about these avoidable exposures. It might be argued that regulatory agencies, or industry itself, should be primary targets for media attention. However, considering the multibillion-dollar cancer establishment's responsibility for and control of basic information about cancer prevention, primary emphasis should be directed at exposing the establishments noninformation or, worse, willful misinformation.

Legislative Initiatives: In view of the NCI's exaggerated and inconsistent claims for its prevention budget, U.S. Representative Jan Schakowsky (Democrat, Illinois) recently asked the General Accounting Office to investigate the NCI's "fight against cancer." Specifically, she requested information on the dollar amounts spent on "funding for research on prevention" and "funding for outreach" to disseminate this information. Meanwhile, Congress is investigating conflicts of interest by NCI generals and scientists with particular reference to consulting with drug industries. This investigation should be extended by an order of magnitude to the NCI's institutional conflicts with the multi-billion dollar Big Pharma.

In response to congressional concerns about NCI policies, the National Academy of Sciences recently examined NCI's relationship with the NIH. In July 2003 the NAS reported that NCI's "special status" of independence from twenty-six other NIH bodies was problematic. It created "an unnecessary rift" between "the goals, mission and leadership of the NIH and those of NCI." In a startling statement that drew minimal media attention, the NAS emphasized, "Perhaps more important is the fact that the National Cancer Act has had little discernible effect on scientific and clinical progress for the diagnosis, treatment, or prevention of cancer."

The NAS report makes it clear that the NCI should be folded back into the NIH and integrated with the scientific community once again. But that is only the beginning of drastically needed reforms. Funding for cancer prevention should equal that of all other programs combined. Congress should direct the NCI to provide the public with all available information on avoidable and unknowing exposures to carcinogens in consumer products, prescription drugs, the workplace, and the environment.

Legislative initiatives should also be developed at the state and local levels. Since the 2002 midterm elections Congress has remained divided and grid-locked. Accordingly, leadership and innovative policies on domestic agendas is likely to shift further from the national to state, county, and city levels.

The Bottom Line: Citizens, the media, and Congress must belatedly recognize that, after spending thirty years and some $50 billion, we are now further from winning the war on cancer than when it was first declared. Furthermore, we all must recognize, albeit belatedly, that the cancer epidemic can still be arrested and reversed. But this goal will never be achieved until we recruit new generals and develop new strategies making prevention at least as urgent as damage control.

SAMUEL S. EPSTEIN, MD, is professor emeritus of environmental and occupational medicine at the University of Illinois Chicago School of Public Health.

How AIDS Changed America

The plague years: It brought out the worst in us at first, but ultimately it brought out the best, and transformed the nation. The story of a disease that left an indelible mark on our history, our culture and our souls.

DAVID JEFFERSON

Jeanne White-Ginder sits at home, assembling a scrapbook about her son, Ryan. She pastes in newspaper stories about his fight to return to the Indiana middle school that barred him in 1985 for having AIDS. She sorts through photos of Ryan with Elton John, Greg Louganis and others who championed his cause. She organizes mementos from his PBS special, "I Have AIDS: A Teenager's Story." "I just got done with his funeral. Eight pages. That was very hard," says White-Ginder, who buried her 18-year-old son in 1991, seven years after he was diagnosed with the disease, which he contracted through a blood product used to treat hemophiliacs. The scrapbook, along with Ryan's bedroom, the way his mother left it when he died, will be part of an exhibit at the Children's Museum of Indianapolis on three children who changed history: Anne Frank. Ruby Bridges. And Ryan White. "He put a face to the epidemic, so people could care about people with AIDS," his mother says.

At a time when the mere threat of avian flu or SARS can set off a coast-to-coast panic—and prompt the federal government to draw up contingency plans and stockpile medicines—it's hard to imagine that the national response to the emergence of AIDS ranged from indifference to hostility. But that's exactly what happened when gay men in 1981 began dying of a strange array of opportunistic infections. President Ronald Reagan didn't discuss AIDS in a public forum until a press conference four years into the epidemic, by which time more than 12,000 Americans had already died. (He didn't publicly utter the term "AIDS" until 1987.) People with the disease were routinely evicted from their homes, fired from jobs and denied health insurance. Gays were demonized by the extreme right wing: Reagan adviser Pat Buchanan editorialized in 1983, "The poor homosexuals—they have declared war against nature, and now nature is exacting an awful retribution." In much of the rest of the culture, AIDS was simply treated as the punch line to a tasteless joke: "I just heard the Statue of Liberty has AIDS," Bob Hope quipped during the rededication ceremony of the statue in 1986. "Nobody knows if she got it from the mouth of the Hudson or the Staten Island Fairy." Across the river in Manhattan, a generation of young adults was attending more funerals than weddings.

In 1995, Americans regarded HIV/AIDS as the nation's most urgent health problem. Today, only 17% rank it as the top concern.

All poll results are from the Kaiser family foundation's 2006 "Survey of Americans on HIV/AIDS," conducted among 2,517 Americans nationwide.

As AIDS made its death march across the nation, killing more Americans than every conflict from World War II through Iraq, it left an indelible mark on our history and culture. It changed so many things in so many ways, from how the media portray homosexuality to how cancer patients deal with their disease. At the same time, AIDS itself changed, from a disease that killed gay men and drug addicts to a global scourge that has decimated the African continent, cut a large swath through black America and infected almost as many women as men worldwide. The death toll to date: 25 million and counting. Through the crucible of AIDS, America was forced to face its fears and prejudices—fears that denied Ryan White a seat in school for a year and a half, prejudices that had customers boycotting restaurants with gay chefs. "At first, a ton of people said that whoever gets AIDS deserves to have AIDS, deserves to literally suffer all the physical pain that the virus carries with it," says Tom Hanks, who won an Oscar for playing a gay lawyer dying of the disease in 1993's "Philadelphia." "But that didn't hold." Watching a generation of gay men wither and die, the nation came to acknowledge the humanity of a community it had mostly ignored and reviled. "AIDS was the great unifier," says Craig Thompson, executive director of AIDS Project Los Angeles and HIV-positive for 25 years.

Without AIDS, and the activism and consciousness-raising that accompanied it, would gay marriage even be up for debate today? Would we be welcoming "Will & Grace" into our living rooms or weeping over "Brokeback Mountain"? Without red ribbons, first worn in 1991 to promote AIDS awareness, would we be donning rubber yellow bracelets to show our support for cancer research? And without the experience of battling AIDS, would scientists have the strategies and technologies to develop the antiviral drugs we'll need to battle microbial killers yet to emerge?

AIDS, of course, did happen. "Don't you dare tell me there's any good news in this," says Larry Kramer, who has been raging against the disease—and those who let it spread unchecked—since it was first identified in 1981. "We should be having a national day of mourning!" True. But as we try to comprehend the carnage, it's impossible not to acknowledge the displays of strength, compassion and, yes, love, that were a direct result of all that pain and loss. Without AIDS, we wouldn't have the degree of patient activism we see today among people with breast cancer, lymphoma, ALS and other life-threatening diseases. It was Kramer, after all, who organized 10,000 frustrated AIDS patients into ACT UP, a street army chanting "Silence equals death" that marched on the White House and shut down Wall Street, demanding more government funding for research and quicker access to drugs that might save lives. "The only thing that makes people fight is fear. That's what we discovered about AIDS activism," Kramer says.

Fear can mobilize, but it can also paralyze—which is what AIDS did when it first appeared. And no one—not the government, not the media, not the gay community itself—reacted fast enough to head off disaster. In the fiscally and socially conservative climate of Reagan's America, politicians were loath to fund research into a new pathogen that was killing mostly gay men and intravenous drug users. "In the first years of AIDS, I imagine we felt like the folks on the rooftops during Katrina, waiting for help," says Dr. Michael Gottlieb, the Los Angeles immunologist credited as the first doctor to recognize the looming epidemic. When epidemiologist Donald Francis of the federal Centers for Disease Control in Atlanta tried to get $30 million in funding for an AIDS-prevention campaign, "it went up to Washington and they said f---off," says Francis, who quit the CDC soon after, defeated.

"Gay Cancer," as it was referred to at the time, wasn't a story the press wanted to cover—especially since it required a discussion of gay sex. While the media had a field day with Legionnaire's disease, toxic shock syndrome and the Tylenol scare, few outlets paid much attention to the new syndrome, even after scores of people had died. The New York Times ran fewer than a dozen stories about the new killer in 1981 and 1982, almost all of them buried inside the paper. (NEWSWEEK, for that matter, didn't run its first cover story on what "may be the public-health threat of the century" until April 1983.) The Wall Street Journal first reported on the disease only after it had spread to heterosexuals: NEW, OFTEN-FATAL ILLNESS IN HOMOSEXUALS TURNS UP IN WOMEN, HETEROSEXUAL MALES, read the February 1982 headline. Even the gay press missed the story at first: afraid of alarming the community and inflaming antigay forces, editors at the New York Native slapped the headline DISEASE RUMORS LARGELY UNFOUNDED atop the very first press report about the syndrome, which ran May 18, 1981. There were a few notable exceptions, particularly the work of the late Randy Shilts, an openly gay journalist who convinced his editors at the San Francisco Chronicle to let him cover AIDS as a full-time beat: that reporting led to the landmark 1987 book "And the Band Played On," a detailed account of how the nation's failure to take AIDS seriously allowed the disease to spread exponentially in the early '80s.

Many gay men were slow to recognize the time bomb in their midst, even as people around them were being hospitalized with strange, purplish skin cancers and life-threatening pneumonia. Kramer and his friends tried to raise money for research during the 1981 Labor Day weekend in The Pines, a popular gay vacation spot on New York's Fire Island. "When we opened the collection boxes, we could not believe how truly awful the results were," says Kramer. The total? $769.55. "People thought we were a bunch of creeps with our GIVE TO GAY CANCER signs, raining on the parade of Pines' holiday festivities." The denial in some corners of the gay community would continue for years. Many were reluctant to give up the sexual liberation they believed they'd earned: as late as 1984, the community was bitterly debating whether to close San Francisco's gay bathhouses, where men were having unprotected sex with any number of partners in a single night.

With death a constant companion, the gay community sobered up from the party that was the '70s and rose to meet the unprecedented challenge of AIDS. There was no other choice, really: they had been abandoned by the nation, left to fend for themselves. "It's important to remember that there was a time when people did not want to use the same bathroom as a person with AIDS, when cabdrivers didn't want to pick up patients who had the disease, when hospitals put signs on patients' doors that said WARNING. DO NOT ENTER," recalls Marjorie Hill, executive director of Gay Men's Health Crisis in New York. Organizations like GMHC sprang up around the country to provide HIV patients with everything from medical care to counseling to food and housing. "Out of whole cloth, and without experience, we built a healthcare system that was affordable, effective and humane," says Darrel Cummings, chief of staff of the Los Angeles Gay & Lesbian Center. "I can't believe our community did what it did while so many people were dying." Patients took a hands-on approach to managing their disease, learning the intricacies of T-cell counts and grilling their doctors about treatment options. And they shared what they learned with one another. "There's something that a person with a disease can only get from another person with that disease. It's support and information and inspiration," says Sean Strub, who founded the magazine Poz for HIV-positive readers.

It took a movie star to get the rest of the nation's attention. In the summer of 1985, the world learned that Rock Hudson—the romantic leading man who'd been a symbol of American virility—was not only gay, but had full-blown AIDS. "It was a bombshell event," says Gottlieb, who remembers standing on the helipad at UCLA Medical Center, waiting for his celebrity patient to arrive, as news helicopters circled overhead. "For many Americans, it was their first awareness at all of AIDS. This prominent man had been diagnosed, and the image of him looking as sick as he did really stuck." Six years later, basketball legend Magic Johnson announced he was HIV-positive, and the shock waves were even bigger. A straight, healthy-looking superstar athlete had contracted the "gay" disease. "It can happen to anybody, even me, Magic Johnson," the 32-year-old announced to a stunned nation, as he urged Americans to practice safe sex.

Given the tremendous stigma, most well-known public figures with AIDS tried to keep their condition a secret. Actor Brad Davis, the star of "Midnight Express," kept his diagnosis hidden for six years, until he died in 1991. "He assumed, and I think rightly so, that he wouldn't be able to find work," says his widow, Susan Bluestein, a Hollywood casting director. After Davis died, rumors flew that he must have been secretly gay. "That part of the gossip mill was the most hurtful to me and my daughter," says Bluestein, who acknowledges in her book "After Midnight" that her husband was a drug addict and unfaithful—but not gay.

With the disease afflicting so many of their own, celebrities were quick to lend support and raise money. Elizabeth Taylor was among the first, taking her friend Rock Hudson's hand in public, before the TV cameras and the world, to dispel the notion that AIDS was something you could catch through casual contact. Her gesture seems quaint today, but in 1985—when the tabloids were awash with speculation that Hudson could have infected actress Linda Evans by simply kissing her during a love scene in "Dynasty"—Taylor's gesture was revolutionary. She became the celebrity face of the American Foundation for AIDS Research. "I've lost so many friends," Taylor says. "I have so many friends who are HIV-positive and you just wonder how long it's going to be. And it breaks your heart."

Behind the scenes, Hollywood wasn't nearly as progressive as it likes to appear. John Erman recalls the uphill battle getting the 1985 AIDS drama, "An Early Frost," on TV. "The meetings we had with NBC's Standards and Practices [the network's censors] were absolutely medieval," says Erman. One of the censors' demands: that the boyfriend of the main character be portrayed as "a bad guy" for infecting him: "They did not want to show a positive gay relationship," Erman recalls. Ultimately, with the support of the late NBC Entertainment president Brandon Tartikoff, Erman got to make the picture he wanted—though major advertisers refused to buy commercial time during the broadcast. Within a decade, AIDS had changed the face of television. In 1991, "thirtysomething" featured a gay character who'd contracted the disease. And in 1994, on MTV's "The Real World," 23-year-old Pedro Zamora, who died later that same year, taught a generation of young people what it meant to be HIV-positive.

If TV was slow to deal with AIDS, cinema was downright glacial. "Longtime Companion," the first feature film about the disease, didn't make it to the screen until 1990, nine years into the epidemic. "There was a lot of talk before the movie came out about how this was going to hurt my career, the same way there was talk about Heath Ledger in 'Brokeback Mountain'," says Bruce Davison, who received an Oscar nomination for his

role. As for "Philadelphia," Hanks is the first to admit " it was late to the game."

Broadway was the major exception when it came to taking on AIDS as subject matter—in part because so many early casualties came from the world of theater. "I remember in 1982 sitting in a restaurant with seven friends of mine. All were gay men either working or looking to work in the theater, and we were talking about AIDS," recalls Tom Viola, executive director of Broadway Cares/Equity Fights AIDS. "Of those eight guys, four are dead, and two, including myself, are HIV-positive." By the time Tony Kushner's Pulitzer Prize-winning "Angels in America" made its Broadway debut in 1993, some 60 plays about the disease had opened in New York. Producer Jeffrey Seller remembers how he was told he "could never do a show on Broadway that's about, quote unquote, AIDS, homosexuality and drug addiction." He's talking about "Rent," which a decade later still draws capacity crowds.

The world of "Rent" is something of an artifact now. Just before it hit Broadway in 1996, scientists introduced the anti-retroviral drug cocktails that have gone on to extend the lives of millions of patients with HIV. Since then, the urgency that once surrounded the AIDS fight in the United States has ebbed, as HIV has come to be seen as a chronic, rather than fatal, condition. But the drugs aren't a panacea—despite the fact that many people too young to remember the funerals of the '80s think the new medications have made it safe to be unsafe. "Everywhere I go, I'm meeting young people who've just found out they've been infected, many with drug-resistant strains of the virus," says Cleve Jones, who two decades ago decided to start stitching a quilt to honor a friend who had died of AIDS. That quilt grew to become an iconic patchwork of more than 40,000 panels, each one the size of a grave, handmade by loved ones to honor their dead. Ever-expanding, it was displayed several times in Washington, transforming the National Mall into what Jones had always intended: a colorful cemetery that would force the country to acknowledge the toll of AIDS. "If I'd have known 20 years ago that in 2006 I'd be watching a whole new generation facing this tragedy, I don't think I would have had the strength to continue," says Jones, whose own HIV infection has grown resistant to treatment.

Inner strength is what has allowed people living with HIV to persevere. "They think I'm gonna die. You know what, they better not hold their breath," Ryan White once told his mother. Though given six months to live when he was diagnosed with HIV, Ryan lived five and a half years, long enough to prod a nation into joining the fight against AIDS. When he died in 1990 at the age of 18, Congress named a new comprehensive AIDS funding act after him. But the real tribute to Ryan has been the ongoing efforts of his mother. "I think the hostility around the epidemic is still there. And because of religious and moral issues, it's been really hard to educate people about this disease and be explicit," says White-Ginder, who continues to give speeches about watching her son live and die of AIDS. "We should not still be facing this disease." Sadly, we are.

A Mandate in Texas

The story of a compulsory vaccination and what it means

KATE O'BEIRNE

On February 2, Texas became the first state to require that young girls be vaccinated against some sexually transmitted viruses. This happened when Gov. Rick Perry issued an executive order requiring that students receive a new vaccine before entering the sixth grade. Perry's order has met with criticism from state legislators who object to his unilateral action, medical groups that welcome the breakthrough vaccine but oppose a mandate, and parents who believe that such coercion usurps their authority. The vaccine's manufacturer is aggressively lobbying other state legislatures to back mandates, and legislation to require the new vaccine is pending in over a dozen states.

Last June, the Food and Drug Administration approved Merck & Co.'s Gardasil vaccine for females aged 9 to 26. When administered to girls before they become sexually active, the vaccine can protect against two of the strains of the human papillomavirus (HPV) that cause about 70 percent of cervical cancers. Within a few weeks of the approval, the vaccine was added to the federal list of recommended routine immunizations for eleven- and twelve-year-old girls. The duration of immunity for the three-dose vaccine series, at a cost of about $360, is not yet known. The federal, means-tested Vaccines for Children program will now include the HPV vaccine, and insurance companies are expected to begin covering its costs.

There is little controversy over the recommendation that the vaccine be broadly used. HPV is the most common sexually transmitted infection, with about half of those who are sexually active carrying it at some point in their lives and about 6.2 million infected annually. The number of sexual partners is the most important risk factor for genital HPV infection. There are no treatments to cure HPV infections, but most are cleared by the immune system, with 90 percent disappearing within two years. Some infections do persist, causing genital warts, cancers of the cervix, and other types of cancer. Each year, over 9,000 new cases of cervical cancer are diagnosed, and the disease kills 3,700 women. Routine Pap tests have dramatically reduced the incidence of cervical cancers over the past 50 years, and it is recommended that even those immunized with the new vaccine continue to be tested, as the vaccine doesn't guard against eleven other high-risk strains of HPV that cause cancer.

Governor Perry recognized that "the newly approved HPV vaccine is a great advance in the protection of women's health" in a "whereas" clause on the way to his "therefore" order that rules be adopted to "mandate the age appropriate vaccination of all female children for HPV prior to admission to the sixth grade." In turning a federal recommendation into a state mandate, Perry has thrilled the vaccine manufacturer, while acting against the balance of medical opinion. And critics object to an opt-out provision that puts the onus on parents to file an affidavit seeking approval of their objection.

The American College of Pediatricians opposes requiring the vaccination for school attendance, saying that such a mandate would represent a "serious, precedent-setting action that trespasses on the rights of parents to make medical decisions for their children as well as on the rights of the children to attend school." The chairman of the American Academy of Pediatrics Committee on Infectious Diseases, Dr. Joseph A. Bocchini, believes a vaccine mandate is premature. "I think it's too early," he said. "This is a new vaccine. It would be wise to wait until we have additional information about the safety of the vaccine." The Texas Medical Association also opposes the mandate, expressing concerns over liability and costs.

Mandatory-education laws create a responsibility to make sure that children are vaccinated against contagious diseases they might be exposed to at school. Now states are considering compelling vaccination in the name of a broad public good, even though the disease in question would not be spread at schools.

Dr. Jon Abramson, the chairman of the Advisory Committee on Immunization Practices of the Centers for Disease Control, explains that protecting children against a virus that is spread by sexual activity is different from preventing the spread of measles. Abramson believes that mandating the HPV vaccine "is a much harder case to make, because you're not going to spread it in a school unless you're doing something you're not supposed to be doing in school." Non-vaccinated students would pose no risk to others while at school.

Texas state senator Glenn Hegar has introduced legislation to reverse Governor Perry's order on the grounds that research trials are still underway and "such mandates take away parents' rights to make medical decisions for their children and usurp parental authority." Twenty-six of 31 state senators believe the governor has usurped legislative authority too, and are calling on him to rescind the executive order. Perry stands by the order, but the rising controversy has discouraged other supporters of mandates.

The *Washington Post* recently reported that Virginia and 17 other states are considering the vaccine requirement "at the urging of New Jersey—based pharmaceutical giant Merck & Co. . . . [which] stands to earn hundreds of millions of dollars annually on Gardasil, according to Wall Street estimates." Public-health organizations have joined Merck in urging that the vaccine be made available in public clinics and encouraging its coverage by private insurers, but they don't support Merck's push for a school requirement.

There were 210 cases of cervical cancer in Maryland last year. Democratic state senator Delores Kelley introduced a bill to require the HPV vaccine for sixth-grade girls. Following complaints from parents and recent non-compliance problems with current mandated vaccinations, Kelley has withdrawn her bill (though she has spoken openly of reintroducing it next session). She explains that she was unaware of Merck & Co.'s lobbying efforts, and that she learned about the new HPV vaccine through a nonpartisan group of female legislators called Women in Government. More than half of its listed supporters are pharmaceutical manufacturers or other health-related companies. Women in Government is spearheading the campaign to mandate the HPV vaccine through school requirements, and some watchdog groups question the support it receives from Merck & Co. "It's not the vaccine community pushing for this," explains the director of the National Network for Immunization Information. Governor Perry's critics point to his own connection with Gardasil's manufacturer: His former chief of staff is a lobbyist for Merck & Co. in Texas.

The profit motive of a company can coincide with public-health interests, but the case for an HPV-vaccine mandate has not been made. The new vaccine does not prevent cervical cancer, but is a welcome protection against some strains of HPV. It is already available to parents who can decide whether it is appropriate for their young daughters. In substituting his judgment for theirs, Governor Perry has attempted to intrude upon their prerogatives and responsibilities. He has also substituted his own judgment for expert medical opinion. State officials who follow his lead won't enjoy immunity from the firestorm of criticism they will rightly earn.

UNIT 8

Health Care and the Health Care System

Unit Selections

Key Points to Consider

- Is health care just another commodity? Should it be treated differently from other consumer services?

- Is quality health care a right or a privilege? Defend your answer.

- What can you as an individual do to help reduce health care costs? Give specific actions that can be taken.

- What steps can you take to reduce your risk of injury during hospitalization?

- What can be done to reduce unnecessary medical treatment?

- Should pharmacists be permitted to refuse to fill certain prescriptions?

- How does illiteracy effect health status?

Student Web Site

www.mhcls.com/online

Internet References

Further information regarding these Web sites may be found in this book's preface or online.

American Medical Association (AMA)
   http://www.ama-assn.org

MedScape: The Online Resource for Better Patient Care
   http://www.medscape.com

Americans are healthier today than at any time in this nation's history. Americans suffer more illness today than at any time in this nation's history. Which statement is true? They both are, depending on the statistics you quote. According to longevity statistics, Americans are living longer today and, therefore, must be healthier. Still other statistics indicate that Americans today report twice as many acute illnesses as did our ancestors 60 years ago. They also report that their pain lasts longer. Unfortunately, this combination of living longer and feeling sicker places additional demands on a health care system that, according to experts, is already in a state of crisis.

Despite the clamor regarding the problems with our health care system, if you can afford health care, the American system is one of the best in the world. However, being the best does not mean that it is without its problems. Each year more than half a million Americans are injured or die due to preventable mistakes made by medical care professionals. In addition, countless unnecessary tests are preformed that not only add to the expense of health care but may actually place the patient at risk. Reports such as these fuel the fire of public skepticism regarding the quality of health care that Americans receive.

While these aspects of our health care system indicate a system in need of repair, they represent just the tip of the iceberg. In "A System in Crisis", Steve Riczo claims that one of our most pressing issues should be health care reform since the US lags behind other industrialized nations in expenditures and lack of universal health coverage. We also trail other advanced countries in both infant mortality and overall life expectancy. The health care system also must deal with adults without reading skills. In "The Silent Epidemic: The Health Effects of Illiteracy", the authors indicate that illiterate patients may avoid seeing doctors because they are unable to fill out the necessary paperwork. These patients also tend to have overall poor health and health practices. In "Medicine's Turf Wars", Christopher J. Gearon reports on the number of non-physician specialists such as psychologists, chiropractors, and pharmacists who are moving into areas once managed solely by physicians. While some pharmacists seeking greater medical autonomy, others are refusing to fill prescriptions for certain medications which violate their personal beliefs. These typically include oral contraceptives and morning after pills which some pharmacists believe cause abortions.

While choices in health care providers are increasing, paying for services continues to be a challenge as medical costs continue to rise. Why have health care costs risen so high? The answer to this question is multifaceted and includes such factors as physicians' fees, hospital costs, insurance costs, phar-

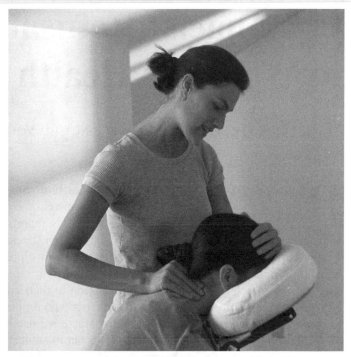

maceutical costs, and health fraud. It could be argued that while these factors operate within any health care system, the lack of a meaningful form of outcomes assessment has permitted and encouraged waste and inefficiency within our system. Ironically, one of the major factors driving up the cost of health care is our rapidly expanding aging population—tangible evidence of an improving health care delivery system. This is obviously one factor that we hope will continue to rise. Another significant factor that is often overlooked is the constantly expanding boundaries of health care. It is somewhat ironic that as our success in treating various disorders has expanded, so has the domain of health care, and often into areas where health care previously had little or no involvement.

Traditionally, Americans have felt that the state of their health was largely determined by the quality of the health care available to them. This attitude has fostered an unhealthy dependence upon the health care system and contributed to the skyrocketing costs. It should be obvious by now that while there is no simple solution to our health care problems, we would all be a lot better off if we accepted more personal responsibility for our health. While this shift would help ease the financial burden of health care, it might necessitate more responsible coverage of medical news to educate and enlighten the public on personal health issues.

Pharmacist Refusals: A Threat to Women's Health

MARCIA D. GREENBERGER AND RACHEL VOGELSTEIN

Pharmacist refusals to fill prescriptions for birth control based on personal beliefs have been increasingly reported around the world. In the United States, reports of pharmacist refusals have surfaced in over a dozen states. These refusals have occurred at major drugstore chains like CVS and Walgreens and have affected everyone from rape survivors in search of emergency contraception to married mothers needing birth control pills. Pharmacists who refuse to dispense also often have refused to transfer a woman's prescription to another pharmacist or to refer her to another pharmacy. Other pharmacists have confiscated prescriptions, misled women about availability of drugs, lectured women about morality, or delayed access to drugs until they are no longer effective.

Pharmacist refusal incidents have also been reported in other countries. For example, a pharmacist at a popular London pharmacy chain recently refused to fill a woman's prescription for emergency contraception (EC), or the "morning-after pill," due to religious beliefs; two pharmacists refused to fill contraceptive prescriptions for women at a pharmacy in Salleboeuf, France; and in the small country town of Merriwa, Australia, the local pharmacist refuses to stock EC altogether.[1–3] Pharmacists for Life International, a group refusing to fill prescriptions for contraception, currently claims to have over 1600 members worldwide and represents members in 23 countries.[4]

Pharmacist refusals can have devastating consequences for women's health. Access to contraception is critical to preventing unwanted pregnancies and to enabling women to control the timing and spacing of their pregnancies. Without contraception, the average woman would bear between 12 and 15 children in her lifetime. For some women, pregnancy can entail great health risks and even life-endangerment. Also, women rely on prescription contraceptives for a range of medical reasons in addition to birth control, such as amenorrhea, dysmenorrhea, and endometriosis. Refusals to fill prescriptions for EC (a form of contraception approved by the U.S. Food and Drug Administration and relied on worldwide) are particularly burdensome, as EC is an extremely time-sensitive drug. EC is most effective if used within the first 12 to 24 hours after contraceptive failure, unprotected sex, or sexual assault. If not secured in a timely manner, this drug is useless. Rural and low-income women, as well as survivors of sexual assault, are at particular risk of harm.

In the United States, most states have an implied duty to dispense. Personal beliefs are omitted from the enumerated instances where pharmacists are authorized to refuse; such as where the pharmacist has concerns about therapeutic duplications, drug-disease contraindications, drug interactions, incorrect dosage, or drug abuse. In New Hampshire, the pharmacy regulations' Code of Ethics states that a pharmacist shall "[h]old the health and safety of patients to be of first consideration and render to each patient the full measure of his/her ability as an essential health practitioner."[5] Pharmacists who refuse to fill valid prescriptions based on personal beliefs do not hold patient health and safety as their first consideration.

Illinois explicitly charges pharmacies with a duty to ensure that women's prescriptions for birth control are filled without delay or interference.[6] Massachusetts and North Carolina have interpreted their laws to ensure that women's access to medication is not impeded by pharmacists' personal beliefs.[7,8] However, Arkansas, Georgia, Mississippi, and South Dakota explicitly grant pharmacists the right to refuse to dispense prescriptions for birth control based on personal beliefs.[9]

In addition, a small number of administrative and judicial bodies have considered challenges to pharmacist refusals. In the United States, the Wisconsin pharmacy board found that a pharmacist's failure to transfer a birth control prescription fell below the expected standard of care and constituted a danger to the health and welfare of the patient. The board formally reprimanded the pharmacist for his actions, charged him with the $20,000 cost of adjudication, and conditioned his license on provision of proper notification to his employer about anticipated refusals and his assurances about steps he will take to protect patient access to medication.[10]

Outside of the United States, the European Court of Human Rights rejected an appeal of a conviction of pharmacists under the French consumer code for a refusal to sell contraceptive pills. The Court held that the right to freedom of religion does not allow pharmacists to impose their beliefs on others, so long as the sale of contraceptives is legal.[2]

Some have questioned how such rules comport with the treatment of other medical professionals. In general, medical professionals have a duty to treat patients, with only limited exceptions. The majority of refusal laws apply to doctors and nurses and are limited to abortion services. Allowing pharmacists to refuse to dispense prescriptions for contraception would dramatically expand the universe of permissible refusals. Moreover, unlike doctors and nurses, pharmacists do not select or administer treatments or perform procedures. Therefore, pharmacists' involvement is not as direct, nor would patients' safety be potentially compromised in the same way as would be the case if a doctor or nurse were forced to perform a procedure that they personally oppose.

Since 1997, 28 states have introduced legislation that would permit pharmacists to refuse to dispense, and sometimes to refer or transfer, drugs on the basis of moral or religious grounds. Fifteen states have introduced such bills in the 2005 legislative session alone; while some are specific to contraception, others apply to all medication. These bills have implications for future refusals to fill prescriptions, such as in HIV regimens or treatments derived from embryonic stem cell research. On the other hand, bills have been introduced in four state legislatures and the U.S. Congress that would require pharmacists or pharmacies either to fill prescriptions for contraception or ensure that women have timely access to prescription medication in their pharmacies.

Some professional and medical associations have issued guidelines that protect women against pharmacist refusals. Value VIII of the *Code of Ethics* of the College of Pharmacists of British Columbia requires pharmacists to ensure "continuity of care in the event of . . . conflict with moral beliefs."[11] It permits pharmacists to refuse to dispense prescriptions based on moral beliefs, but only if there is another pharmacist "within a reasonable distance or available within a reasonable time willing to provide the service."

In the United States, several associations have issued similar, although not legally binding, policies. The American Public Health Association states that "[h]ealth systems are urged to establish protocols to ensure that a patient is not denied timely access to EC based on moral or religious objections of a health care provider."[12] The American Medical Women's Association has stated that "pharmacies should guarantee seamless delivery, without delay (within the standard practice for ordering), judgment, or other interference, of all contraceptive drugs and devices lawfully prescribed by a physician."[13]

The American Pharmacists Association (APhA) articulates a standard of professionalism in its *Code of Ethics* that is not legally binding. It mandates that pharmacists place "concern for the well-being of the patient at the center of professional practice"[14]. The code also emphasizes that pharmacists are "dedicated to protecting the dignity of the patient" and must "respect personal and cultural differences . . ."[14] This language precludes refusals, lectures, and other barriers erected by pharmacists who disagree with a woman's decision, made in consultation with her health-care provider, to use birth control. Some state pharmacy associations have similar codes.

However, the APhA has another policy that conflicts with these principles. It allows for refusals based on personal beliefs, as long as pharmacists refer prescriptions to another pharmacist or pharmacy.[15] The APhA has not formally explained how to square this policy with its ethical principles of patient-protective care, let alone with state laws and regulations.

Recommendations

Women must be provided timely access to prescription medication. One solution is to require pharmacists to dispense all drugs despite their personal beliefs, in line with their professional duties and ethical obligations. Another solution is to shift the duty to fill from pharmacists onto pharmacies. Under this approach, pharmacies would be charged with ensuring that prescriptions for all drugs are filled without delay or other interference. Such a requirement would allow pharmacies to make arrangements to accommodate the personal beliefs of individual pharmacists. However, active obstruction by pharmacists of women's access to prescription medication—such as withholding or delaying prescriptions or providing misinformation—should be deemed unethical or unprofessional conduct subject to legal sanction.

References and Notes

1. "I Won't Sell Pill, It's Against My Religion," *Sunday Mirror* (27 February 2005).
2. Pichon and Sajous v. France, App. No. 49853/99, Eur. Court H.R. (2001).
3. "U.S. Firm Ships Free Contraceptives to Condom-Deprived Australian Town," *Financial Times,* 31 March 2005 [source: Agence France-Presse].
4. See www.pfli.org/main.php?pfli=locations.
5. N.H. Code Admin. R. Ph. 501.01(b)(1) (2005).
6. Illinois Pharmacy Practice Act, § 1330.91 (j)(1) (2005).
7. Massachusetts Board of Pharmacy, letter on file with the National Women's Law Center, 6 May 2004.
8. Conscience concerns in pharmacist decisions, *North Carolina Board Pharm. Newsl.* **26** (3), 1 (2005), 1; available as item 2061 at www.ncbop.org/Newsletters/NC012005.pdf.
9. Ark. Code. Ann. § 20-16-304 (1973); Ga. Comp. R. & Regs. r. 480-5-.03(n) (2001); Miss. Code. Ann. § 41-107-1 (2004); S.D. Codified Laws § 36-11-70 (1998).
10. See www.naralwi.org/assets/files/noesendecision &finalorder.pdf
11. See www.bcpharmacists.org/standards/ethicslong/

12. American Public Health Association (APHA), Policy statement 2003-15 (APHA, Washington, DC, 2003).

13. American Medical Women's Association (AMWA), Statement of AMWA supporting pharmacies' obligation to dispense birth control (Alexandria, VA, 2005) (on file with the National Women's Law Center).

14. See www.aphanet.org/AM/Template.cfm ?Section=Pharmacy_ Practice&CONTENTID=2903&TEMPLATE=/CM/ HTMLDisplay.cfm.

15. S. C. Winckler, American Pharmacists Association (1 July 2004) (letter to the editor, unpublished); available at www.aphanet.org/AM/Template.cfm? Section=Public_ Relations&Template=/CM/HTML Display .cfm&ContentID=2689.

The authors are with the National Women's Law Center, Washington, DC 20036, USA. For correspondence, e-mail: rlaser@nwlc.org.

A System in Crisis

"Health care reform should be elevated to the same level as our other most pressing issues, such as the revamping of Social Security, energy conservation and development, and terrorism prevention."

STEVE RICZO

Health care concerns consistently rank near the top of surveys of Americans pertaining to issues that are important to them. There is good reason for concern. Compared to other industrialized nations, health care in the U.S. is much more expensive.

The average spending of the 30-member nations of the Organization for Economic Cooperation and Development (OECD)—other than the U.S.—as a percentage of gross domestic product is 10.6% vs. 15% in the U.S. Our per capita health care costs are close to $5,635, approximately twice the average of other OECD nations, including Canada ($3,003), Germany ($2,996), France ($2,903), Australia ($2,699), the United Kingdom ($2,231), and Japan ($2,139). As a nation, we spend more than $5,000,000,000 per day on health care; that is a staggering two trillion dollars per year. The Center for Medicare and Medicaid Services projects health care spending to exceed four trillion dollars annually—20% of GDP—by 2015. Moreover, the U.S. lags behind other advanced economies in a number of outcome measures, such as infant mortality and life expectancy.

Not only do other industrialized nations spend less, they manage to do so while providing health care coverage to all of their citizens. Canada, for example, has a publicly financed delivery system that utilizes a national insurance plan that covers basic and supplemental benefits coordinated by provinces and territories. Great Britain's system is based almost entirely on tax revenues provided primarily by its National Health Service. Japan's national health insurance requires some personal contribution determined by employment and age. Germany's compulsory health insurance was established more than 100 years ago, and shares administration among governmental and nongovernmental bodies. Israel's Ministry of Health coordinates compulsory membership for its citizens in one of four plans that offers a mandated package of basic medical services. In the U.S., however, more them 40,000,000 individuals remain uninsured.

Spending on health care is not the only determining factor of good health. For instance, this country has an ever-widening disparity in its distribution of income between the rich and poor, and studies have demonstrated lower health status in states with the largest disparities. It has been shown that there is a direct correlation between poverty and certain health risk factors, including drug and tobacco use, teen pregnancy, victimization from violence, sexually transmitted diseases, and alcoholism. Money spent on health care does not solve societal issues that contribute to poor health. As far as universal health coverage is concerned, a number of proposals have been put before Congress, but none have passed.

One of the most significant contributors to high health care costs is our current system of insurance and reimbursement, which distorts the fundamental economic principles of price, supply, and demand. When a consumer purchases a house or an automobile, he or she usually will shop carefully in order to get the best value. Not so with health care, as a majority of insurance plans pay most of the expenses, making price less relevant.

An aging population and more advanced technology are contributing factors to rising health care costs as well. As people get older, they simply have more need for medical care. Remember, too, that even though high-technology care is expensive, it is exacerbated by the fact that medical innovations are not evaluated consistently by health insurers using scientifically based formulas that include cost-benefit analysis. Effective use of technology—such as computerized axial tomography or magnetic resonance imaging—actually has reduced costs by precluding expensive procedures such as exploratory surgeries. If used wisely, technology has the potential to act as a countervailing force to an aging population.

While factors relating to aging and technology must be taken into account, they serve to obscure a much more important factor: the vast majority of health care expenditures are related to payrolls in health care organizations, not for high-tech medical equipment. Health care is a labor-intensive industry that continues to employ a system riddled with inefficiencies and subject to political manipulation—namely lobbyists who represent clients with insatiable appetites for government funding, which ultimately drives up the cost of insurance.

Our system of insurance coverage is highly variable and consists of a mix of plans that can be broken down into several major categories. The first is employer-based, which covers the majority of Americans. Most of these employers select from a small number of health insurance plans offered by the largest carriers. These include Blue Cross/Blue Shield (coveting 92,000,000 individuals) as well as Aetna, CIGNA, United Healthcare Group, Wellpoint, and from HMOs such as Kaiser Permanente. HMOs collectively cover an additional 80,000,000 Americans. In most of these plans, the employer covers the majority of the cost of the premium and the employee generally pays a lesser amount in addition to co-payments and deductibles.

The government, meanwhile, pays approximately 60% of the nation's health care bill through large programs such as Medicare, which covers approximately 41,000,000 primarily elderly individuals. Other government programs include Medicaid and State Children's Insurance programs, which cover more than 52,000,000 low-income individuals. The number of enrollees in Medicaid has increased dramatically in recent years, severely stressing state budgets. The Veterans Administration and Department of Defense provide care for about 7,000,000 veterans and active military personnel. There also are relatively small government programs such as Community Health Centers that give primary care in urban and rural areas, as well as the Indian Health Service for Native Americans. While some individuals purchase health insurance directly, these numbers are small, at least in part because health insurance is so expensive.

Given the myriad of health insurance plans available, why are there more than 40,000,000 uninsured Americans? According to Health Services Research, the rolls of the uninsured go up by 164,000 for every one percent increase in premiums. There is a common misconception that those without health insurance are unemployed or not contributing members of society. The reality is that close to half of all companies with fewer than 50 employees do not offer health insurance to their workers. In fact, the percentage of employers offering health coverage has fallen from 69% to 60% in the last five years. Approximately 65% of uninsured families have at least one member who works full time for a small business or is self-employed. This creates a double-jeopardy situation for those uninsured Americans who are working at low-wage jobs; they face financial devastation if they or a member of their family is struck with a significant illness or accident.

What to Do

Any reforms must focus on high costs and the uninsured. Due to the enormity of the situation, consideration should be given to establishing a Federal commission consisting of leading experts from health care and academia who would be provided with a very clear mandate of establishing a national spending target for health care that would take into account the performance of other industrialized nations. Germany and France have taken this approach. To be successful, however, spending targets must be combined with reforms that create incentives for efficiency and the restoration of sound economic principles to the health care system. Credit card and home-equity debt are at an all-time high, and Americans filing for bankruptcy frequently cite medical bills as a major factor.

High health care costs also have been a primary cause of the well-documented stagnation of wages of middle-income Americans. Employers correctly view their contributions to their employees'

health insurance as part of a total compensation package. The more funding that goes to health care premiums, the less is available for wage increases. Establishing spending targets would be an important first step in help guide public policy regarding reimbursement rates for Medicare and Medicaid, as commercial insurance companies often peg their rates to these two programs. This commission should provide guidance to Congress pertaining to potential benefit reform for Medicare and Medicaid as well as technology evaluation.

Here are various strategies to help control health care costs:

- Become more aggressive in tackling fraud and abuse. Many hospitals have engaged in "up-coding" of diagnostic related groups—which does not reflect accurately the diagnosis of the patient—in order to increase Medicare payment to those hospitals. In one recent five-year period, the 10 largest health care fraud settlements averaged $540,000,000. "There isn't an aspect of medical care that isn't scammed," opines *Modern Healthcare*. Increasing government audits of insurance coding would be a step in the right direction.

- Provide health insurance only for diagnostic tests and treatments that meet the criteria of evidence-based medicine. We are saddled with an inconsistent system of coverage determination for diagnostic tests and therapeutic treatments, with many of these made at local levels. Congress should support having the Center for Medicare and Medicaid Services adopt a formula—such as that proposed in 1980—that would require economic, safety, ethical, and other considerations in order to determine if a diagnostic test or treatment will be covered. For instance, chiropractic care has been questioned by some in the scientific community and yet it is reimbursed widely by insurance companies. The Academy of Science, National Institutes of Health, and other well-respected organizations should participate in the evaluation process. Formulas must take into account whether the test or treatment offers patients clinically meaningful benefits as it relates to cost, quality of life, and life expectancy.

"We would be better served by converting what rural hospitals there are to Community Health Centers that provide cost-effective primary and urgent care to residents."

- Eliminate all remaining cost-based reimbursement formulas that are used to pay health care providers. Review government reimbursement schemes to providers that subsidize inefficiency, such as those made to rural hospitals through the relatively new "critical access designation" program. The truth is, most rural communities do not have their own hospitals. We would be better served by converting what rural hospitals there are to Community Health Centers that provide cost-effective primary and urgent care to residents.

- Pursue aggressive antitrust action against health care providers and insurers that reduce competition below a given standard (*i.e.*, no hospital should have more than a 25% share of the market in its primary service area). *Health Affairs* has reported that there is evidence that consolidation of hospitals allows them to negotiate higher rates with health insurance companies, confirming the findings of the Federal Trade Commission. Another report funded by the Robert Wood Johnson Foundation concludes that hospital mergers have raised prices and likely compromised quality.

- Encourage global competition. Many Americans now travel overseas to undergo procedures that are too expensive at home. Many physicians train here in the U.S. before returning to their native country to practice medicine. Nations that offer high-quality medical services coupled with low labor costs will find Americans visiting their shores in increasing numbers.

- Streamline cumbersome regulations and accelerate the shift to electronic medical recordkeeping for providers as a requirement to participate in government insurance programs. This will reduce or eliminate the expensive paper processing system used by many providers and improve care to patients through effective presentation of key information to practitioners. Tax breaks or other incentives would help small group practices make this expensive, but vital, shift.

- Mandate the use of managed care for all Medicare recipients, just as many states have done for Medicaid. Most Americans in private insurance plans are in managed care programs such as HMOs (health maintenance organizations) and PPOs (preferred provider organizations). The *Journal of Health Services Research* contends that HMOs reduce unnecessary hospitalizations, utilize more comprehensive preventative services, and provide roughly comparable quality of care to other types of health plans. Every request to hospitalize a Medicare or Medicaid patient should undergo a careful utilization management review to assure that the admission meets published hospital practice standards. While the current Diagnostic Related Groups (DRG) payment system to hospitals for inpatient care creates an incentive to reduce lengths of stay, it does not prevent unnecessary admissions, which become all the more riskier when considering the fact that approximately 100,000 people die each year due to errors and hospital-induced infections.

- A Federal Patients Bill of Rights should be passed by Congress to augment those states that do not have one. As HMO enrollment increased rapidly in the 1980s, patient protection legislation failed to keep up, resulting in HMOs getting paid on a capitated basis, whereby necessary care was withheld to increase profits. When capitation is used as a payment method, consumers are best served in nonprofit health plans.

- Create an environment that promotes the use of generic drugs. Pharmaceuticals have been the fastest growing component of health care costs in recent years. Americans now spend $250,000,000,000 a year on prescription drugs. An estimated 2,000,000 individuals purchase their prescription drugs from Canada because of cost considerations. A review should be made pertaining to the use of prescription drugs for nursing home residents, as it is not unusual for a patient to be on several prescription drugs—some that are prescribed for the sole purpose of mitigating the negative side effects of other drugs. It also would be prudent for Congress to reevaluate the length of time granted for patent protection for new drugs that are immune from competition through the development of generic substitutes. While it is true that research and development costs need to be recouped, the 13 largest U.S. pharmaceutical companies spend more than twice as much of their revenue on marketing and administrative functions (32.8%) than on R&D (14%) while still maintaining a very healthy profit margin (20.6% of sales).

- To help offset the economic distortions of price, supply and demand caused by health insurance, copayments, and deductibles should be used with a built-in sliding scale for the poor. Providing free health care through government programs for low-income Americans through Medicaid creates a disincentive for some older (potential) workers from seeking gainful employment in low-wage jobs that provide no health insurance. Similar to welfare reform efforts, programs can be developed that require work in return for benefits. Establishing time limits that families would be permitted to remain on Medicaid could prove effective if combined with a system of employer-mandated health insurance. As a nation, we will pay the costs either way. Isn't it better to do so in a manner that incentivizes gainful employment?

- Implement medical malpractice reform that provides guidelines for juries for punitive damages—while not eliminating them in cases where grossly negligent health care providers have devastated the lives of individuals and their families. Nobel Laureate Gary Becker correctly has pointed out that punitive damages often are valuable because they deter dangerous behavior. Supreme Court Justice Antonin Scalia noted in *State Farm v. Campbell* that the determination of punitive damages should be left to individual judges and juries, which vary based on the circumstances. (Recent studies claim that medical malpractice is not a major contributing factor to runaway health care costs.)

- Establish demonstration projects that employ capitation strategies with organized networks of nonprofit health care providers that discourage excessive use of hospitalization and encourage the employment of good managed-care techniques. An ideal system would feature large organized medical groups (not hospital based) that compete against other such groups on the basis of cost-effectiveness, quality, and service while preserving competition by not permitting any one group to control more than 25% of the local market. Capitation creates a fixed budget for the care of a patient or population of patients while discouraging the provision of excessive services.

- Through appropriate financial incentives, strongly encourage the use of assisted-living and home health care for the elderly, with nursing homes only being used as a last resort. Nursing homes not only are more expensive, but frequently demeaning places for seniors to spend their final years. There are some elderly Americans in nursing homes today because their stays are reimbursed by Medicare and Medicaid, combined with the fact we have not yet developed enough affordable home care and assisted-living models.

- Require individuals to pay a larger percentage of their health-care expenses if they have made personal decisions to abuse their bodies from the use of tobacco, drugs, excessive alcohol, etc. Personal responsibility should be an important feature of any health system reform plan.

- Rigorous use of Health Savings Accounts should be encouraged. The employee uses his or her own money for the purchase of services while simultaneously accruing any savings that result from efficient utilization of resources, which ultimately can be put toward retirement or other personal use by the individual. However, much greater transparency concerning pricing and quality from health plans and providers is needed. For instance, California requires hospitals to publish their pricing information, and some health insurers are posting such data on their websites.

"There are some . . . Americans who feel that the country should have a single-payer health care system with the Federal government replacing the multiple commercial providers."

- Large employers should utilize a vertical integration strategy of providing basic health care services directly to employees whenever possible in order to avoid paying the costs of fraud, inefficiencies, anticompetitive practices, etc. that are built into today's system. Wal-Mart, for example, has begun hiring physicians to provide medical care in stores for employees as well as the general public.

There are some well-intentioned Americans who feel that the country should have a single-payer health care system with the Federal government replacing the multiple commercial providers. This proposal has two major flaws. It would eliminate the competition that results from plans vying for an employer's business. The success of our economic system is based upon free-enterprise principles, especially competition. The second flaw is that the government's track record of running anything efficiently and

effectively is quite suspect. The list of failures, as we all know, is endless. Let's not add health care to the pile. Government can work in conjunction with the private sector to oversee Medicaid, the VA system, Children's Health Insurance Programs, Medicare, etc. Its role, though, should be to complement, assist, and regulate the private sector—not replace it.

Government, for instance, could restructure Medicaid and other subsidized programs for the uninsured in a cost-effective manner and provide some level of care to any American who does not have health insurance. One vehicle would be to expand the number of Community Health Centers, which should be located not only in low-income communities, but the suburbs. The focus of Community Health Centers is not on expensive high-tech care, but cost-effective primary care and routine diagnostic testing such as blood work and X-rays. Rather than a government handout, the care provided would be on a means-tested basis and tees could be paid on a sliding scale. This would encourage a better use of resources where individual consumers would use cost-benefit analysis in their decisionmaking, as they do with all other purchases. The more complex care, when needed, can be provided by existing public hospitals that already receive government funding for such purposes. Once these Community Health Centers are in operation, patients must use them for all nonemergency conditions and preserve the use of emergency rooms for true emergencies.

Catastrophic Coverage

Another way in which a Federal commission can play an important role is to develop a proposal for a system of catastrophic coverage that makes cost-effective plans available for uninsured Americans. Employer mandates for health insurance coverage should be considered as well. This is analogous to the concept of a minimum wage. Today, if a small business opts to provide coverage for its employees, it may be put at a competitive disadvantage with its competition. This would not be the case if both employers provide comparable health benefits. Sen. Ted Kennedy (D.-Mass.) long has advocated for employer mandated health insurance.

As a nation, we should not feel helpless concerning high health care costs and the uninsured. The two trillion dollars spent should be sufficient to provide quality care for all Americans if we develop the fight system. Health care reform should be elevated to the same level as our other most pressing issues, such as the revamping of Social Security, energy conservation and development, and terrorism prevention. Like the fight against terrorism, this is a long-term battle requiring that we be ever-vigilant, but it is a battle that can be won.

STEVE RICZO, author of *Ten Steps to American Greatness,* is director of Specialty Services for health insurer Kaiser Permanente, Ohio region, and professor of business management at the University of Akron.

Medicine's Turf Wars

**Specialists without MD's are pushing for more medical power.
Are they ready—and are you?**

CHRISTOPHER J. GEARON

You've probably noticed it at your own doctor's office, the subtle yet revolutionary changes in the way Americans receive their healthcare. The tipoff may have come when a physician assistant wrote your child a prescription instead of the pediatrician. If you've recently switched doctors, chances are you saw a nurse practitioner and not the primary-care physician listed on your health insurance card. Perhaps you live in a place where you can bypass the doctor and go directly to the pharmacist for immunizations. Or maybe you're one of the millions of patients directly spurring these changes, deliberately asking for these providers because you're fed up with your doctor, had to wait too long to see him, or simply couldn't afford it.

Nonphysician clinicians—nurse practitioners, nurse anesthetists, dentists, optometrists, chiropractors, and others—have become prominent health providers. Often working alongside doctors, well-trained, nonphysician clinicians provide front-line medical care to patients increasingly needing preventive care or monitoring for diabetes, congestive heart failure, and other chronic diseases. These new faces of American medicine are more willing to go to rural or inner-city areas and to work beyond the limited office hours typically kept by physicians. Minneapolis nurse practitioner May Hang, for instance, sees a wide variety of patients early mornings and nights at a Target store that houses her mini medical office, MinuteClinic. The clinic is designed to treat a limited set of common acute ailments, including ear, bladder, and sinus infections and strep throat. No appointments are necessary, and visits take only 15 minutes.

Yet as health professionals such as Hang have advanced into territory once held solely by doctors, a larger medical turf war has begun. The battles take place away from patients and are fought before state legislatures, the courts, and other venues as non-M.D. professions try to broaden their responsibilities even further. Oklahoma recently allowed optometrists to do limited surgery, podiatrists in California can perform partial foot amputations, and Idaho last year removed requirements of physician supervision over nurse practitioners and certified nurse midwives, giving them more freedom to practice. Nurse anesthetists in New Jersey have been lobbying for the same type of autonomy. And right now, psychologists in Tennessee are fighting for the right to write prescriptions—a battle the non-M.D.'s have already won in New Mexico and Louisiana.

Their primary weapons are the issues of access and patient safety. In Tennessee, for example, psychologists argue that patients must typically wait six weeks for an initial psychiatrist's appointment; low-income patients wait several months. The result is that many people don't get proper treatment, the psychologists contend. Roughly three quarters of the people in Tennessee who seek help for depression are treated by physicians with only limited training in mental disorders. Psychologists, who tout Ph.D.'s and many years of training, say they're better equipped than an internist or OB-GYN to prescribe drugs for emotional conditions.

Psychiatrists, not surprisingly, don't agree. "The cure to the access problem being proposed is worse than the disease," says Steven Sharfstein, president-elect of the American Psychiatric Association, adding that psychologists' proposed medical education equals a few weeks of what physicians get in medical school. "We need more psychiatrists, but I don't think the solution is to entitle or enable poorly trained physicians to provide a level of medical care that is potentially unsafe."

Behind the claims about safety for patients, however, lurks the specter of self-interest on both sides. "It's a political and economic issue," says physician Richard Cooper, professor of medicine and health policy at the Medical College of Wisconsin. Physicians want to maintain control of care and the financial rewards that come with it. They don't want to be undercut in the market by less costly providers.

Indeed, rising healthcare costs are a huge factor for consumers, health insurers, states, and employers all looking for less costly alternatives. "Nonphysician providers continue to achieve enhanced stature," notes Andrew McKinley, an analyst for Health Policy Tracking Service in Falls Church, Va. "There is growing support for the concept that the public health is best served by the broadest access to primary care, along with the safe use of pharmaceuticals." And for many, that concept is best supported by clinicians who don't have medical degrees.

Playing It Safe

The safety issue isn't just a "he said, she said" debate. Research has shown that many nonphysician providers perform safely, or at least as safely as physicians do, in their expanded roles. But that doesn't mean there's nothing to worry about. "In the main, it's been very safe," notes Cooper, "because roles have expanded commensurate with training and supervision." Cooper, who studies the enlarging roles of nonphysician clinicians and writes on quality and patient safety, adds that research, however, has not been done on leading-edge practices now being undertaken by some of these providers. "There are no outcomes on podiatrists doing amputations," and that's just one example, Cooper notes.

What research has established most notably is that an assortment of nurses with advanced training, including nurse practitioners and certified nurse midwives and other registered nurses with master's- or Ph.D.-level education, are safe. They relieve our pain during surgery, deliver our babies, treat our kids' asthma, care for our aging parents, and help alleviate the suffering of those with AIDS/HIV and other devastating conditions. More than 100 studies have examined, for example, the care delivered by nurse practitioners. "To my knowledge, there is not a single study showing negative impact of [nurse practitioner] practice on health," says Linda Aiken, director of the University of Pennsylvania's Center for Health Outcomes and Policy Research and a nursing professor. She adds that numerous studies of advanced practice nurses show the care they deliver is equal to or better than that delivered by physicians.

Robert Wise, vice president for standards and survey methods at the Joint Commission on Accreditation of Healthcare Organizations, the oversight group that inspects the nation's hospitals and healthcare facilities on quality and safety, says that "the critical issue here is not what they are allowed to do, but do they know what they can't do?" A wide scope of practice doesn't mean that a provider, physician or not, knows it all. They should refer patients to other clinicians when appropriate. "If they know what they can do and what they can't do, they are [most likely to be] a pretty safe practitioner."

Safety studies have played a major role in the mother of all turf battles, which has been waged between those two professions, anesthesiologists and nurse anesthetists, who ensure that, every year, more than 26 million Americans feel no pain when they go under the knife. In general, anesthesia is extremely safe (only one death occurs for every 250,000 times it's administered, a dramatic improvement since the early 1980s, when two deaths occurred per 10,000 anesthetics administered). And 65 percent of all anesthesia care is delivered by certified registered nurse anesthetists, critical-care nurses with a graduate degree in anesthesia, who train for several years in order to sit for certification. Medicare has long recognized their qualifications and reimbursed them for their services. The two professions are extremely courteous to one another when individuals meet in an operating room.

The federal government concluded that the psychologists were indeed trained to provide patients safe pharmacological care.

But that courtesy masks a fierce dispute raging between the American Society of Anesthesiologists and the American Academy of Nurse Anesthetists. One part of this row involved nurse anesthetists' wanting to be paid for services rendered in hospitals and surgical centers without physician supervision. It has been left up to each state to allow—or disallow—that care without physician oversight.

To date, 12 mostly rural states have said there's no need for docs. The states have been swayed by safety data on anesthesia providers. "If there is a difference, the studies to date have not shown that," says Cooper.

Now the battle has shifted to doctors' offices. Florida has been the flashpoint. During the late 1990s, the number of office-based surgeries—largely lucrative cosmetic surgery operations—in the state skyrocketed. The practice wasn't well regulated, office facilities often lacked emergency care, and there were a number of highly publicized deaths.

"Office surgery is like the Wild West; it's the last frontier," says Rebecca Welch, president of the Florida Society of Anesthesiologists. While there are no data showing that CRNAs have trouble providing safe anesthesia in office settings, Welch says, "we feel like we are the experts" with a medical school background. Florida's state medical board apparently agreed and created standards for office-based surgeries that insisted anesthesiologists had to supervise CRNAs.

Nurse anesthetists felt the impact immediately. Victor Ortiz, a CRNA from Davie, Fla., says that right after the supervision rule took effect in 2002, "70 percent of my income got swept away." Why? Most surgeons concluded it wasn't economical or necessary to have both an anesthesiologist and a CRNA in their office. "[The medical board] was saying you're unsafe . . . but you read unbiased studies, and they show that you are safe. This was about control and turf," Ortiz says. So Ortiz sued the state medical board. Last summer, a Florida appellate court ruled the board overstepped its bounds with the anesthesiologist supervision rule, a decision affirmed last month by the Florida Supreme Court. "I'm elated," Ortiz says.

Now, another anesthesia battle is shaping up in New Jersey. The Garden State has passed an office-based-supervision rule similar to the one recently knocked down in Florida. It goes into effect in February. Local nurse anesthetists are gearing up for a court challenge, and they hope the outcome will be similar to Florida's as well.

Power of the Pad

The right to write prescriptions is the subject of another skirmish. The psychologists pushing for prescribing privileges in Tennessee and five other states will point to the gains they've made in New Mexico in 2002 and Louisiana last year, perhaps their best evidence and best way to assure doubters that they know what they are doing. In New Mexico, for example, psychologists have to take 450 hours of classes in psychopharmacology and other sciences, as well as log years of supervision and collaboration with physicians in order to prescribe. Advocates will also be holding up a Department of Defense experiment that followed the patients of 10 psychologists trained to prescribe medications, a demonstration that ran from 1991 to 1997 with program graduates going on to prescribe medications in conjunction with other kinds of therapy to active and retired members of the military and their families. The federal government and outside evaluators concluded the psychologists were indeed trained to provide safe pharmacological care. But psychiatrists argue about the results anyway. They say that the DOD training was more comprehensive than the training specified in legislation pushed in the states.

But Elaine LeVine, a Las Cruces psychologist, who helped persuade New Mexico's Legislature to give her colleagues prescribing privileges, says far from endangering her patients by writing them prescriptions, her patients will do better when she can choose their meds. She has no problems with psychiatrists—when enough of them are available for patients. It's physicians without mental health training but with a prescription pad who give her pause. While a patient may see his primary care provider for only very short visits, she notes, psychologists' patients may spend an hour a week in therapy.

As the two professions debate the finer points, Carmen Catizone, who has seen a lot of prescription pads, chuckles. Catizone, executive director of the National Association of Boards of Pharmacy, has seen many professionals duke it out over nonphysician prescribing privilege, including his own group. Pharmacists used to only make and hand out medications but today have authority to vaccinate patients in 37 states and can prescribe "morning after" emergency contraception in California, New Mexico, Alaska, and a handful of other places. Pharmacist prescribing generally is authorized under collaborative agreements with physicians but also allows pharmacists to monitor patients' ongoing conditions.

In the late 1960s and 1970s, the prescription battle was waged between M.D.'s and doctors of osteopathy. Today, like M.D.'s, D.O.'s have unlimited, independent prescribing authority in every state. In the early 1980s, optometrists battled ophthalmologists for the privilege. Now, optometrists can prescribe at least some eye-related medications in every state. Physician assistants, a profession devised by physicians to work under their supervision, had a much easier time in the early 1990s obtaining the ability to write prescriptions under the auspices of M.D.'s. Nurse practitioners have gotten some level of prescribing privileges in most states. Such battles cool as few significant problems are found and as more states grant a particular profession prescribing privileges. Instead, organized medicine focuses on preventing professions just starting to seek prescribing authority from getting it.

Knife Fights

Even mightier than the prescription pen, when it comes to medical practice, is the sword—actually, the scalpel. And fights are breaking out around the nation over whether non-physicians can wield one. Such fights, often fought in the absence of quality data, are among the feistiest around—and some of the most difficult for patients who need to choose which hand will do their surgery.

One such hand could belong to Richard Joseph. He finished his residency in 1977. He started out in trauma surgery, rebuilding faces mangled by car accidents and violence in Jacksonville, Fla. Eventually, he got permission from Jacksonville's Baptist Medical Center to perform face lifts as well. Now, his private practice includes face-lifts, eyelid surgery, Botox injections, and the occasional impacted wisdom tooth. Joseph is an oral surgeon, or, more properly, an oral and maxillofacial surgeon, a dental school graduate, and he's never been to medical school.

Oral surgeons are increasingly getting involved in doing cosmetic surgery. In a world of unhappy doctors and insurance hassles, cosmetic surgery looks like a good place to be. Oral surgeons are, technically, dentists. But they do at least four more years of training after dental school, when they learn to cut open, sew up, and improve the appearance of faces and necks, and they say they are just as qualified as plastic surgeons to do cosmetic surgery. Much of the facial trauma in the nation is handled by oral and maxillofacial surgeons; hospitals designated as Level I and Level II trauma centers are required to have one around to deal with facial injuries. And oral surgeons don't do the things you usually associate with dentists. Oral and maxillofacial surgeon Mark Steinberg, who teaches at Loyola University Medical Center in Chicago, says he hasn't filled a cavity in 25 years.

Plastic surgeons, for their part, go through medical school and several years of training in general surgery and plastic surgery. Oral surgeon training just doesn't match up, says Scott Spear, a plastic surgeon at Georgetown University Hospital and the president of the American Society of Plastic Surgeons. He and his colleagues insist that their concern is only for patient safety and good surgical results; predictably, oral surgeons shoot back that plastic surgeons just want to keep others off their lucrative turf.

State regulations that define dentistry have been the arena for the plastic surgeons' and oral surgeons' dust-ups. At issue is the American Dental Association's 1997 definition, which states that dentistry includes work on "the oral cavity, maxillofacial area and/or the adjacent and associated structures."

That is so ambiguous as to be useless, scoffs Bill Seward of the American Society of Plastic Surgeons. "The jaw is connected to the neck, which is connected to the torso. You can drive a Mack truck through that hole." He claims the "adjacent and associated structure" language gives oral surgeons the right to do breast augmentations, abdominal liposuction, or anything else they want, but oral surgeons point out that the definition also says they're only supposed to do work within the scope of their training.

Yet despite the plastic surgeons' objections, 16 states have adopted the ADA's definition, and several others also give permission for oral surgeons to do any procedures they have the training and credentials to do—which could include cosmetic surgery.

A patient who wants cosmetic surgery by a qualified surgeon—oral or any other—is bound to be a little confused. But there are some common-sense checks to make. Check to see if the surgeon is board certified, for example, and how many of the procedures the doctor does in a year. If the surgeon has hospital privileges to do your procedure, that's an indication that his or her peers think he or she is qualified.

These battles, without good information for patients to make good decisions, have made many people quite concerned.

In another cutting-edge battle, organized medicine has gone on the warpath in Oklahoma, the only state that allows optometrists to do laser and nonlaser eye surgeries. The state was apparently swayed by the access argument, specifically Oklahoma's greater supply of optometrists than ophthalmologists. Last year, ophthalmologists tried to overturn the law authorizing the scope of optometry practice, charging that it gave optometrists too much surgical authority. The challenge didn't quite work out. Instead, Oklahoma's Legislature and governor clarified optometrists' practice boundaries, allowing these nonphysicians to continue scalpel surgery around the eyelids and lashes and other eye-related surgeries. "It was politically motivated, and they picked a fight and it backfired on them," says Stillwater, Okla., optometrist David Cockrell, who is president of the Oklahoma Board of Examiners in Optometry.

These battles, without good information with which patients can make good choices, have many people concerned. "Unless we drastically change course, patients will see a much more fragmented system, and it will be more difficult to know whom to see and the quality of care they deliver," says Robert Phillips Jr., director of the Robert Graham Center, a policy center sponsored by family physicians looking at primary-care and quality issues. The course change that Phillips recommends is more collaboration and less conflict. He notes that the widening responsibilities allied health professionals are getting shouldn't leave them isolated from physicians. Most nurse practitioners, physician assistants, and others gaining more practice authority still work collaboratively and harmoniously with physicians. In fact, one thing physicians and allied health clinicians agree on is that a team approach to care is best for patients.

This spring, the Federation of State Medical Boards—a group that monitors physicians' licenses and practices—plans to release a document designed to help healthcare regulatory bodies and legislatures to make better-informed decisions on scope of practice changes. One would expect the FSMB document to boost the physician side in the turf battles, but FSMB President and CEO James Thompson, M.D., won't show his hand. Thompson does say that he believes calls from the Institute of Medicine to forge more collaborative relationships are getting the attention of physicians, and he expects to see that trend continue over the next five to 10 years.

Calls for collaboration are all very well, but many observers think that stronger intervention is needed. Market forces—in other words, money or the lack of it—are going to continue to draw primary-care physicians away from patients and draw allied health professionals in to take their places. "The system of medicine is pushing people to the edges of their competence," says the Medical College of Wisconsin's Cooper. "Is this a crisis? No, it's not a crisis. But is the system pushing nonphysicians to the limit of their capability? I think so."

The Silent Epidemic—The Health Effects of Illiteracy

ERIN N. MARCUS, MD, MPH

He came in for a "tune-up." He was 64 years old, with a "history of noncompliance," according to the resident, and he hadn't taken his diabetes or cardiac medications for weeks. We weren't quite sure why. He was alert, he appeared to be intelligent and interested in getting well, and he was able to get his prescriptions filled at a reduced cost. Before he went home, we explained why he needed to take his medicines and reviewed the frequency and doses with him several times. He told us he would follow up with his doctor (though he couldn't remember the doctor's name or telephone number) and left the hospital with a hand-written discharge summary.

Five months later, he appeared at the community clinic. He said he was taking his medications, but he wasn't sure of their names or how often he took them. A medical student and I reviewed the regimen again. The student typed up simple instructions in big letters for him to follow, as well as a list of dates and times at which he should record his blood sugar levels. We asked him to come back in two weeks.

When he returned, the student saw him first—and made a diagnosis that no one else had considered: illiteracy. The clue lay in the jumbled mess of his glucose log. Many of the sugar values were written next to future dates. We quietly asked him to read his list of medications aloud. Haltingly, he told us he couldn't do it. Born in the rural South, he had left school in the second grade. He lived alone. He had been able to support himself as a gas-station attendant and handyman, but he had never learned to read.

We were stunned. We had tried to avoid jargon and to use simple language in explaining our instructions, and he had seemed to understand everything we had told him. He had seen scores of doctors, nurses, and social workers over the years without anyone's guessing he had a reading problem.

Although we had been blind to his illiteracy, our patient's problem is not uncommon. The National Assessment of Adult Literacy (NAAL), a large survey conducted by the National Center for Education Statistics, recently estimated that 14 percent of adults in the United States have a "below basic" level of "prose literacy"—defined as the ability to use "printed and written information to function in society, to achieve one's goals, and to develop one's knowledge and potential."[1] The NAAL describes "below basic" skills as "no more than the most simple and concrete literacy skills," specifying that adults with this level of prose literacy range from being nonliterate in English to being able to locate easily identifiable information in short, commonplace prose text—able to find out, for example, "what a patient is allowed to drink before a medical test." They generally cannot, say, find "in a pamphlet for prospective jurors an explanation of how people were selected for the jury pool." Like my patient, 55 percent of those in the lowest prose-literacy group had not finished high school.

On the basis of the NAAL results, 12 percent of U.S. adults are estimated to have below basic "document literacy," the ability to read and understand documents such as transportation schedules and drug or food labels—they may be able to sign a form, but they cannot use "a television guide to find out what programs are on at a specific time." In addition, 22 percent of adults are estimated to have below basic "quantitative literacy," the ability to perform fundamental quantitative tasks—they may be able to sum the numbers on a bank deposit slip, but they cannot compare the ticket prices for two events. Older adults fared poorest on the NAAL: 23 percent of those more than 64 years of age had below basic prose literacy, 27 percent below basic document literacy, and 34 percent below basic quantitative skills.

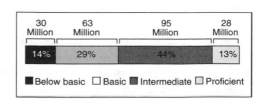

Prose Literacy Levels among U.S. Adults in 2003. Percentages are based on a sample of 18,102 household respondents and 1156 prison inmates. Data are from the National Assessment of Adult Literacy.

There is also a growing body of research on health literacy, the ability to comprehend and use medical information. Survey results indicate that more than a third of English-speaking patients and more than half of primarily Spanish-speaking patients at U.S. public hospitals have low health literacy. One analysis found that Medicare enrollees with low health literacy were more likely than enrollees with adequate health literacy to use the emergency room and to be admitted as inpatients.[2]

Patients with reading problems may avoid outpatient doctors' offices and clinics because they are intimidated by paperwork, according to Joanne Schwartzberg, director of aging and community health at the American Medical Association and editor of a textbook on health literacy. "Emergency rooms are user-friendly if you don't read," she pointed out, "because somebody else asks the questions and somebody else fills out the form."

The exact relation between literacy and health is still unclear, but people with low literacy are more likely to report having poor health, and are more likely to have diabetes and heart failure, than those with adequate literacy.[3,4] Some studies have found correlations between literacy and measures of disease such as glycated hemoglobin levels in people with diabetes.[3] Of course, factors other than literacy (such as educational level, income, primary language, sex, and age) affect the management of many conditions, and whereas "some studies have attempted to control for income and social circumstances . . . many didn't," according to Darren DeWalt, an internist at the University of North Carolina who has reviewed the evidence for the Agency for Healthcare Research and Quality.

Many researchers describe low literacy as a silent epidemic: despite its high prevalence, many physicians and other health care workers remain unaware that their patients may have reading problems. "I think most doctors are blind to the problem," said Barry D. Weiss, a professor of family and community medicine at the University of Arizona. "It's hard for them to believe."

Patients with poor literacy skills often are ashamed of their problem and are adept at hiding it. In one study, more than two thirds of patients with low literacy in public hospitals said they had never told their spouses about it. Nearly a fifth said they had never told anyone. Forty percent of the patients with low literacy said they felt shame about it.[5] "A clinical psychologist once told me that the shame experienced by people with literacy problems is comparable to the shame experienced by incest victims," said Ruth Parker, a professor of medicine at Emory University, who coauthored the study. "In our society, it is very embarrassing not to know. Nobody wants to look dumb, especially not in front of their doctor."

Weiss advocates routine screening for literacy as a new "vital sign." He has created a brief, bilingual literacy-screening test that entails asking patients six questions about a nutrition label. He recommends that physicians screen some of their patients to assess literacy levels and then tailor the way they talk with patients accordingly. "The average doctor who's thinking he or she is talking in simple, plain language probably isn't," he said. "It may be more practical to screen a sample of patients to see what's needed."

But routine screening is controversial. Some worry that it takes too long, embarrasses patients, and could stigmatize those with low literacy. Moreover, in an era of "pay for performance," physicians might avoid low-literacy patients, viewing them as time-consuming and difficult to treat. Many literacy experts say that physicians often perceive inquiring about reading ability as opening Pandora's box, releasing a sprawling, unwieldy problem that they haven't been trained to handle and that is beyond the scope of a 15-minute office visit. "Physicians are not prepared to know what [their] immediate response should be," said Dean Schillinger, an internist at San Francisco General Hospital who has conducted several studies of physicians and health literacy. He added that the health care system does not help physicians who treat low-literacy patients.

Some experts advocate an approach to communication similar to universal precautions for preventing HIV infection. Health care workers, they say, should assume that all patients have a limited understanding of medical words and concepts, whether or not they have passable general-reading skills. Schwartzberg advocates that physicians organize their discussions with patients around three key points per visit and use a teach-back approach, asking patients to explain what they have been told.

Parker, a general internist, routinely carries an empty pill bottle in her pocket when she works in the clinic. "I tell patients, 'This is not your medication, but if it were, tell me how you would take it,'" she said. "It's never been validated [as a screening test], but I pick up a lot of people who can't do it, and it's an immediate way for me to know, does this patient need help?"

Other interventions such as educational videotapes, simplified brochures, and color-coded medication schedules have had mixed results in improving the health of patients with low literacy, according to Michael Pignone, an internist and associate professor at the University of North Carolina. Pignone and other researchers have shown that disease-management programs specifically designed for low-literacy patients with diabetes and congestive heart failure—approaches involving simply written educational materials or reminders, individualized educational sessions, and teach-back methods—can be effective in reducing symptoms and improving disease markers such as glycohemoglobin levels. A variety of professional groups have launched initiatives to improve patients' health literacy—as well as physicians' skills in communicating with low-literacy patients.

With the help of a social worker, our patient enrolled in an adult reading program, which he attends regularly. Three years later, it's not clear that he always takes his medications as prescribed. But he feels that the literacy program has been useful in helping him to decipher his pill labels and to function in the world. And these days, I think twice whenever I explain anything to a patient—or jot down instructions on a pad of paper.

Notes

1. Kutner M, Greenberg E, Baer J. A first look at the literacy of America's adults in the 21st century. Washington, D.C.: National Center for Education Statistics, Department of Education, December 2005. (Accessed July 6, 2006, at *http://nces.ed.gov/naal/.*)

2. Howard DH, Gazmararian J, Parker RM. The impact of low health literacy on the medical costs of Medicare managed care enrollees. Am J Med 2005;118:371–7. [Erratum, Am J Med 2005;118:933.]

3. Dewalt DA, Berkman ND, Sheridan S, Lohr KN, Pignone MP. Literacy and health outcomes: a systematic review of the literature. J Gen Intern Med 2004;19:1228–39.

4. Wolf MS, Gazmararian JA, Baker DW. Health literacy and functional health status among older adults. Arch Intern Med 2005;165:1946–52.

5. Parikh NS, Parker RM, Nurss JR, Baker DW, Williams MV. Shame and health literacy: the unspoken connection. Patient Educ Couns 1996;27:33–9.

DR. MARCUS is an assistant professor of clinical medicine in the Division of General Internal Medicine at the University of Miami Miller School of Medicine, Miami.

UNIT 9

Consumer Health

Unit Selections

Key Points to Consider

- What are some concrete examples of actions you can take to ensure that you get what you want from your doctor's visit?

- How can consumers determine which health care products are fraudulent?

- What are the risks of daily use of tooth whiteners?

- Why are humans getting less and less sleep and what are the health implications?

Student Web Site

www.mhcls.com/online

Internet References

Further information regarding these Web sites may be found in this book's preface or online.

FDA Consumer Magazine
   http://www.fda.gov/fdac
Global Vaccine Awareness League
   http://www.gval.com

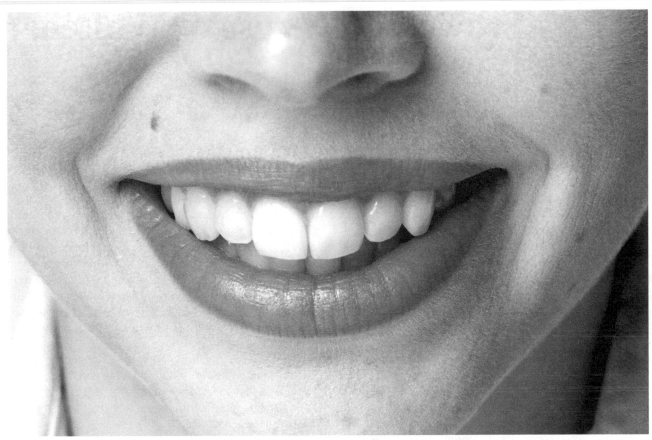

For many people the term "consumer health" conjures up images of selecting health care services and paying medical bills. While these two aspects of health care are indeed consumer health issues, the term consumer health encompasses all consumer products and services that influence the health and welfare of people. A definition this broad suggests that almost everything we see or do may be construed to be a consumer health issue whether it's related to products or recommendations such as getting enough sleep. In many ways consumer health is an outward expression of our health behavior and decision-making processes and as such is based on both our desire to make healthy choices, be assertive, and to be in possession of accurate information on which to base our decisions. These decisions are particularly important when it comes to pain management. Many people have fortunately turned to their doctors following the withdrawal of the pain medication Vioxx from the market. This, and other pain treatments, were found to increase the risk of cardiovascular disease. In "How to Ease Your Pain", consumers are offered advice on managing acute and chronic pain.

A health-related issue that is heavily promoted is the alleged safety of teeth whitening. In "Dentists Frown at Overuse of Whiteners", Natasha Singer discusses how many patients are overexposing themselves to bleach-base teeth whiteners. While dentists generally consider whiteners to be safe, they are concerned over the overuse of these products. There is also concern that continually whitening teeth will make them more sensitive and may permanently damage teeth and gums.

The health-conscious consumer seeks to be as informed as possible when making dietary and medical decisions—but the best intentions come to no avail when consumers base their decisions on inaccurate information, old beliefs, or media hype that lacks a scientific basis. Knowledge (based on accurate information) and critical thinking skills are the key elements required to become proactive in managing your daily health concerns.

Dentists Frown at Overuse of Whiteners

Natasha Singer

Kevin Ross, a psychologist in Queens, is a serial tooth whitener. He started out seven years ago with custom-fitted bleaching trays, the kind dentists sell. When his teeth became sensitive, he switched to over-the-counter whitening strips, which use less bleach. These were gentler, but not as effective. So earlier this year Mr. Ross upgraded to professional-strength whitening strips dispensed by his dentist.

"I insist on having my teeth as white as possible," he said. "I guess it's like skinny people who always think they could be a little skinnier. I'd like to get another whitening treatment tomorrow."

But when Mr. Ross recently asked for a new set of whitening strips, his dentist said no. "I had to cut him off temporarily," said Dr. Marc M. Liechtung, who practices in New York City, "because his teeth are as white as they are going to get. It's our job not to indulge them when they want touch-ups they don't need."

Mr. Ross is not even the most avid whitener among Dr. Liechtung's patients. Some, Dr. Liechtung said, come back "like drug addicts pleading, 'Doc, sell me more just this once.' "Meanwhile, on their own, they use every type of drugstore whitening product: not only the strips but also whitening toothpaste, floss, rinse and chewing gum.

More and more, dentists like Dr. Liechtung are putting their foot down for fear that these patients may be overexposing themselves to bleach. "In the long run," Dr. Liechtung said, "chronic whiteners could end up causing themselves tooth damage."

Dentists generally consider whitening to be a safe treatment when patients, following a proper dental exam, choose a bleaching product from a reputable brand, adhere to package instructions and don't overdo it. But tooth bleaching was never intended to become a daily grooming habit like shampooing or shaving. And some dentists suspect that uninterrupted whitening, using a hodgepodge of high-strength products, not only will make teeth more sensitive, but may also cause permanent damage to tooth enamel and gum tissue.

Until more studies have been done to assess the potential side effects of constant bleaching, these dentists say, consumers should take care to avoid going overboard.

"We see younger and younger patients wanting whiter and whiter teeth," said Dr. Bruce A. Matis, the director of the Clinical Research Section at Indiana School of Dentistry in Indianapolis. "We'll know in 10 years if they've damaged their teeth."

A fondness for pearly white teeth is ancient. In the Bible, Jacob hopes that his son Judah will have "teeth white with milk." But never in history have paper-white teeth been as popular or easy to obtain as they are now. The market for dentist-dispensed tooth whitening products and in-office treatments is expected to reach more than $2 billion this year, up from $435 million in 2000, according to a report from Mintel International Group, a market research firm. Mintel expects sales of over-the-counter whitening kits to reach $351 million in 2005, up from $38 million five years ago.

All this bleaching has made teeth so white that manufacturers of dental materials used for bonding and filling have had to create ever-lighter shades to match them. The very whitest are an unnatural color that did not exist before bleaching, a shade dentists have nicknamed "Regis white."

Given that even short-term whitening can cause temporary tooth sensitivity and gum irritation, some dentists speculate that continuous bleaching could erode tooth enamel or cause gum inflammation. Some people's teeth have even taken on a translucent blue or gray color around the edges, dentists say.

Many clinical studies have indicated it is safe for teeth to be bleached—either professionally or with name-brand do-it-yourself kits—once or twice a year. Procter & Gamble, maker of Crest Whitestrips, has also done research on the safety of uninterrupted bleaching using the company's products; one of its clinical trials, conducted with researchers at Tufts University in Boston, found it was safe to use Whitestrips twice a day for six months.

Today's 'Regis white' may be tomorrow's gray, or worse.

Still, some dentist say that when people routinely use high-strength bleaches, or use whitening products in every step of their oral-care routine, it may add up to a level of exposure to bleaching agents that goes beyond what has been studied.

"We don't know how the body handles regular use of high concentrations of peroxide," said Dr. Van B. Haywood, a professor at the School of Dentistry at the Medical College of Georgia in Augusta, who in 1989 was an author of the first paper published on the effectiveness and safety of overnight bleaching trays.

The peroxides used in tooth bleach, hydrogen peroxide and carbamide peroxide (which contains hydrogen peroxide) produce free radicals that can damage cells of the gums or pulp inside teeth, said Dr. Yiming Li, the director of the Center for Dental Research at Loma Linda University School of Dentistry in California. "The lower your overall exposure," Dr. Li said, "the lower your risk."

Because of the unknown risks of high peroxide exposure, some dentists advise pregnant women as well as cancer patients and smokers (who are at risk of developing cancer) to avoid tooth whitening altogether.

Some dentists say certain over-the-counter bleaching products are riskier than professional whitening treatments because the bleach more easily strays from the teeth to the rest of the mouth. Ill-fitting one-size-fits-all trays easily leak bleaching material onto the gums and down the throat, Dr. Matis said.

Dentists say they prevent such leaks. "We protect the gums by painting on a semiplastic barrier, so no bleaching material touches the soft tissue," said Dr. Laurence R. Rifkin, a dentist in Beverly Hills, Calif. "We also make custom-fitted trays for home use that keep the whitening gel in close contact with your teeth."

In Europe only whitening products that are no more than one-tenth of a percent peroxide may be sold over the counter. Earlier this year, after examining the potential risks, the European Union's Scientific Committee on Consumer Products concluded that higher-strength bleaching is safe only when it is supervised by a dentist.

American products are much more powerful and getting stronger all the time, raising the risk of overexposure to bleach, dentists say. Fifteen years ago the first trays dispensed by dentists used gels that were 10 percent carbamide peroxide, equivalent to about 3 1/3 percent hydrogen peroxide. Today, Discus Dental Nite White ACP Deluxe Kit, dispensed by dentists, contains 22 percent carbamide peroxide gel (about 7 percent hydrogen peroxide).

The Minute White Laser Speed Tooth Whitening System, sold on the QVC shopping channel, includes a 22 percent carbamide peroxide whitener. And the strongest bleaching strips sold by dentists now contain 14 percent hydrogen peroxide gels.

"Once you get above 15 percent carbamide, you are pushing the envelope," Dr. Haywood said.

Manufacturers counter that it is the amount of gel used, rather than the strength of its bleaching agent, that determines whether a product is safe. The gel in Crest Whitestrips Premium, for example, is 10 percent hydrogen peroxide, but the overall amount is small, the company said.

"The gel on each strip is as thin as two or three pieces of paper," said Dr. Robert W. Gerlach, a principal scientist at Procter & Gamble. "A tray-based system uses 4 to 10 times as much peroxide. And a whitening mouthwash could contain up to 20 times as much peroxide." Consumers often do not know how much bleach over-the-counter whiteners contain, however, because manufacturers are not required to quantify it on the label. Some dentists say that practice endangers consumers.

"The consumer cannot make an informed decision without concentrations listed on the labels," Dr. Matis said.

Dentists do not agree on how often their patients should use today's powerful whiteners. After his patients have completed their initial 10- to 14-day tray bleaching treatment, Dr. Rifkin permits them to wear the trays again once or twice a year for one- or two-day touch-ups. Dr. Matis advises patients to wait one to three years. And Dr. Haywood says that once a decade may be enough for some people.

Try telling that to Dale Michele Asti, a boutique owner in Beverly Hills who uses her 22 percent carbamide peroxide bleaching tray several times a week.

"I admit I'm obsessed," said Ms. Asti, a patient of Dr. Rifkin. "Whitening has become part of my routine when I'm getting ready for a date. I'll do it to make my smile sparkle while I'm shaving my legs or putting on makeup."

When told of Ms. Asti's habit, Dr. Rifkin said: "She shouldn't be doing that."

"It's not going to make her teeth any whiter," he added, "and it's potentially irritating. I may have to limit her number of whitening kits."

Cracking Down on Health Fraud

MICHELLE MEADOWS

On April 19, 2006, the Federal Trade Commission (FTC) led a massive "Hispanic Multimedia Surf" to identify potentially fraudulent advertising aimed at Spanish-speaking consumers. More than 160 participants from government agencies and Hispanic consumer and student groups "surfed" the Internet, Spanish radio and television broadcasts, and print media for deceptive advertising in the areas of credit, work opportunities, and health.

"The FDA's role in the surf was to focus on unapproved products with claims to cure, treat, or prevent serious diseases such as diabetes, cancer, HIV/AIDS, and heart disease," says Gary Coody, national health fraud coordinator in the Food and Drug Administration's Office of Enforcement. More than 30 Spanish-speaking employees from the FDA's headquarters in Rockville, Md., and 14 FDA district offices nationwide and in Puerto Rico participated.

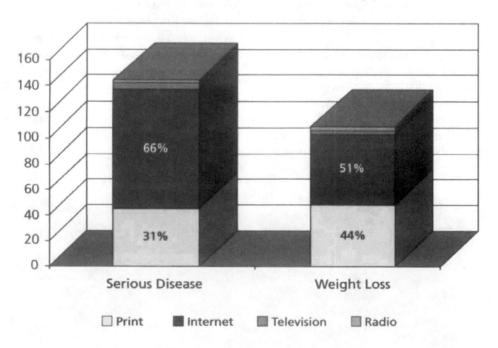

Hispanic Multimedia Surf

Possibly Deceptive Health-Related Ads by Category and Media Type

Federal Trade Commission

The FTC's Hispanic Multimedia Surf revealed that about half of the potentially deceptive ads identified were health-related, such as ads promoting products for weight loss and serious diseases.

The FTC released results of the project in September 2006, reinforcing the need for consumers to recognize the signs of health fraud and to communicate with their doctors before using new medical products.

"Diabetes-related ads were prevalent," according to Laura Koss, an FTC senior attorney who coordinates the agency's Hispanic Law Enforcement and Outreach Initiative. "We also observed that many of the advertisements were for 'natural' or 'herbal' alternatives to traditional medicine. And many ads promoted cure-alls, products that promise to cure a wide variety of ailments including diabetes, asthma, and depression."

Whether an ad runs in English or Spanish, the characteristics of health fraud are the same, Coody says. A product is promoted as offering some type of health benefit, but the claims have not been scientifically proven. The product may be ineffective or even harmful.

Promoters of fraudulent products employ a wide range of tactics—aggressive advertising, reliance on personal testimonials, pseudomedical jargon, dubious science and so-called "experts," and claims of revolutionary or exotic ingredients.

"The same ad that clearly looks like a scam to one consumer may attract someone else who is vulnerable," Coody says. "Some companies go after people with serious conditions who are desperate for a cure, or they go after people who want a quick fix."

The FDA sent a Warning Letter to one foreign-owned Web site touting an unapproved product, "The Antidote." Purportedly derived from the blood of crocodiles, the Antidote was promoted as a drug, with claims that it can treat cancer, AIDS, and other life-threatening diseases. "The miracle healing powers of the Antidote can now be used to fight all known human viruses and bacteria . . . ," the Web site claimed. This product violated the Federal Food, Drug, and Cosmetic Act because it failed to comply with applicable licensing and pre-approval requirements. The FDA issued an Import Alert intended to prevent all shipments of the Antidote from entering U.S. borders.

The FDA also warned another firm that marketed a product "Viralsol." The firm's Web site claimed the product could treat herpes and HIV/AIDS. Patients were instructed to take varying amounts of Viralsol based on their viral load. "The FDA considers Viralsol to be an unapproved new drug," Coody says. "Before a new drug may be legally marketed, it must be approved by the FDA." Drug sponsors must submit scientific data to demonstrate that a drug is safe and effective.

In 2005, the FDA sent Warning Letters to 29 businesses making unproven health-related claims about fruit products on their Web sites and on product labels. The companies marketed dried fruit, fruit juice, and juice concentrate for treating and preventing cancer, heart disease, arthritis, and other diseases.

"Warning letters are one of the primary tools for the FDA to achieve voluntary compliance," Coody says. "When companies fail to heed warning letters or if their actions pose serious health risks, the agency can take more formal measures." Such measures could include criminal prosecution, seizure of goods, and injunction against a firm or individual responsible for marketing violative products. An injunction is a civil action taken to stop production or distribution of a product that violates the law.

For example, the FDA issued Warning Letters to Lane Labs-USA Inc. of Allendale, N.J., for selling three products: BeneFin, produced from shark cartilage, promoted as a treatment for cancer; SkinAnswer, a glycoalkaloid skin cream, marketed as a treatment for skin cancer; and MGN-3, a rice bran extract, promoted as a treatment for cancer and HIV, the virus that causes AIDS.

Despite the Warning Letters, Lane Labs continued promoting the products through mailings and on the Web. The FDA requested a permanent injunction based on the company's unwillingness to comply with the law. In 2004, a judge permanently barred Lane Labs from distributing the three products unless they either received FDA approval to market their products or held an acceptable Investigational New Drug Application for each of their products for purposes of conducting a clinical trial.

In August 2006, the FDA announced that a federal District Court in Newark, N.J., ordered Lane Labs to pay refunds to people who bought BeneFin, MGN-3, and SkinAnswer between Sept. 22, 1999, and July 12, 2004.

In another health fraud case, the FDA seized unapproved devices because they posed serious health risks. Stephen B. Edelson, working at the Edelson Center for Environmental and Preventive Medicine in Atlanta, promoted an ozone generator device and other alternative therapies as cures for autism. Some marketers of ozone generators claim that inhaling ozone can "detoxify" the body or stimulate the immune system. According to the FDA, ozone is an unapproved drug. This toxic gas can cause lung damage and other health problems.

The parents of an autistic child, who was 4 years old at the time, paid Edelson $40,000 to $50,000 for a bogus treatment that included ozone therapy. According to court documents, the treatments were painful for the child. He also endured multiple sessions of sauna "sweat" therapy, intense exercise, and nutritional supplements of 50 pills and capsules a day.

FDA investigators recovered ozone generator machines from Edelson's center in 2004, and Edelson's medical license was revoked by the Georgia Medical Board. This case was jointly investigated by the FDA's Atlanta District Office, the FDA's Office of Criminal Investigations, the Georgia Medical Board, and the Georgia Drugs and Narcotics Agency.

Coody says, "Because of the sheer volume of fraudulent health products and their accessibility from foreign locations, FDA has forged partnerships with many federal, state, and international enforcement agencies." These agencies include the FTC, the U.S. Department of Justice, the Drug Enforcement Agency, the Federal Bureau of Investigation, the U.S. Postal Service, the U.S. Customs Service, and State Attorney General Offices.

The FDA also helps fund a network of State Health Fraud Task Forces in 10 states, Puerto Rico, and the U.S. Virgin Islands. Members of these task forces include volunteers from community-based organizations, health care practitioners, educators, federal and state government officials, and local health care departments. They develop workshops and educational materials to prevent health fraud through consumer education.

Here is an overview of more regulatory actions against fraudulent health products.

Weight Loss Fraud

False and misleading claims in weight loss ads are widespread. Since 2003, the member organizations of the Mexico, United States, Canada Health Fraud Working Group (MUCH) have taken more than 700 compliance actions against companies pushing bogus and misleading weight loss schemes. The FDA and the FTC are MUCH members under a Trilateral Cooperation charter agreement between the three countries. The agreement increases communication and collaboration among the three countries in the areas of drugs, biologics, medical devices, food safety, and nutrition.

As part of the MUCH weight loss initiative, the FDA sent Warning Letters to 25 firms that were promoting products with false weight loss claims. The FDA has also sent letters to more than 1,000 manufacturers and distributors of dietary supplements, including major retail chains, reminding them of the legal requirements tot dietary supplement claims.

The FTC's efforts against weight loss fraud included Operation Big Fat Lie, a law enforcement sweep against companies making false weight loss claims for diet powders, patches, and pills. The FTC also established a Red Flag initiative that encourages the media to screen out fraudulent weight loss ads, and a FatFoe "teaser" Web site in English, French, and Spanish. A teaser Web site is designed to look like a real Web site. It uses buzzwords and makes exaggerated diet claims. But when consumers try to order a product, they find out the site is an FTC consumer education tool to warn them about diet rip-offs.

"Weight loss ads often promise miraculous results that make losing weight look easy and fast," says Richard Cleland, assistant director of the FTC's Division of Advertising Practices. "They use teasers like: 'Lose 30 pounds in 30 days without dieting or exercising.' They also ignore the true ways to lose weight—calorie reduction and exercise."

In 2004, the FDA banned dietary supplements that contain ephedrine alkaloids after concerns over their cardiovascular effects, including increased blood pressure and irregular heart rhythm. Products with ephedrine alkaloids have a history of being promoted for weight loss and increased energy, in August 2006, the U.S. Court of Appeals for the Tenth Circuit in Denver upheld the FDA's final rule declaring all dietary supplements containing ephedrine alkaloids illegal for marketing in the United States. This ruling reversed a decision by the District Court of Utah.

The FDA recently warned consumers not to use Emagrece Sim Dietary Supplement, also known as the Brazilian Diet Pill, and Herbathin Dietary Supplement. Both products are made in Brazil by Fitoterapicos and Phytotherm Sim. These products may contain prescription drug ingredients that could lead to serious side effects or injury. FDA analysis found that samples of Emagrece Sim and Herbathin contained chlordiazepoxide, the active ingredient in Librium, and fluoxetine, the active ingredient in Prozac. Chlordiazepoxide is used to relieve anxiety and to control the symptoms of alcohol withdrawal. It may be habit-forming, and can cause drowsiness and dizziness and impair the ability to drive.

Fluoxetine is an antidepressant medication used to treat obsessive-compulsive disorder, panic disorder, and bulimia. It has been linked to several serious drug interactions and adverse events, including suicidal thinking and behaviors in pediatric patients, anxiety and insomnia, and abnormal bleeding. These drugs should be taken only by patients who are under the supervision of a health care provider.

Emagrece Sim and Herbathin were also found to contain Fenproporex, a stimulant converted in the body to amphetamine and not approved for marketing in the United States. The FDA has increased efforts to prevent importation of the products.

Consumers are advised not to use Emagrece Sim and Herbathin and to return them to suppliers.

Sexual Enhancement Supplements

In July 2006, the FDA warned consumers not to buy several drugs that were promoted and sold on Web sites as dietary supplements for treating erectile dysfunction (ED) and for enhancing sexual performance. The products are Zimaxx, Libidus, Neophase, Nasutra, Vigor-25, Actra-Rx, and 4EVERON. Marketed as dietary supplements, they are really illegal drugs that contain ingredients not mentioned in the labeling.

"These products threaten the public health because they contain undeclared chemicals that are similar or identical to the active ingredients used in several FDA-approved prescription drug products," says Steven Galson, M.D., director of the FDA's Center for Drug Evaluation and Research. "This risk is even more serious because consumers may not know that these ingredients can interact with medications and dangerously lower their blood pressure."

Chemical analysis by the FDA revealed that Zimaxx contains sildenafil, the active ingredient in the prescription drug Viagra, which is approved to treat ED. The other products contain chemical ingredients that are similar to either sildenafil or vardenafil. Vardenafil is the active ingredient in Levitra, another drug approved by the FDA to treat ED.

These ingredients could interact with nitrates in some prescription drugs such as nitroglycerin and could lower blood pressure to dangerous levels. Consumers with diabetes, high blood pressure, high cholesterol, or heart disease often take nitrates.

The enforcement actions taken against manufacturers and distributors of these drugs followed an FDA survey that analyzed 17 dietary supplements marketed on the Internet to treat ED and to enhance sexual performance in men. The survey found that some of these products contain non-dietary chemicals, including chemicals used as active ingredients in FDA-approved drugs.

The FDA has also warned the public not to purchase certain dietary supplements sold by Hi-Tech Pharmaceuticals Inc., and a related corporation, National Urological Group Inc. FDA test results found the supplements, which were marketed for ED, contained taldalafil, the active ingredient in the approved ED drug Cialis. The FDA encourages consumers with ED to seek guidance from a health professional before buying any products to treat it.

Diabetes Health Fraud

November is American Diabetes Month, a time of heightened awareness for a disease that affects nearly 21 million Americans. An estimated 14.6 million people have been diagnosed with diabetes, and more than 6 million don't know that they have it. Diabetes is a disease in which the body does not make or properly use insulin, the hormone needed to convert sugar, starches, and other food into energy.

Over the past year, the Mexico, United States, Canada Health Fraud Working Group (MUCH) has focused enforcement and consumer education efforts on fraudulent products to treat diabetes. The MUCH group works closely with the International Consumer Protection and Enforcement Network.

"Fighting bogus products to treat diabetes is a key priority for all three countries because diabetes is a major and growing public health problem," says Gary Coody, national health fraud coordinator in the FDA's Office of Enforcement.

In October 2006, MUCH member agencies announced that they had taken nearly 200 compliance actions against companies promoting bogus products that provide false hope to people with diabetes. The compliance actions include Advisory Letters, Warning Letters, and import refusals. Many of the actions are still pending, but some firms have voluntarily removed false claims and discontinued sales of the bogus products.

Examples of unproven claims to treat diabetes:

- Drop your blood sugar 50 points in 30 days, or it's free . . .
- Eliminate insulin resistance.
- Prevent the development of type 2 diabetes.
- Reduce or eliminate the need for diabetes drugs and/or insulin.
- Prevent diabetes-related eye disease, damage to cells caused by poor blood sugar control.
- Take the natural alternative to . . . the diabetes drug metformin.

In this cooperative enforcement action, the FTC sent letters to 91 domestic Web sites making questionable diabetes treatment or cure claims. Some sites changed false claims or closed their sites, and others continue to work with the FTC to modify their Web sites. The FTC referred 21 Web sites to foreign law enforcement agencies. In October 2006, the FDA sent more than 20 Warning Letters to firms that continued to make fraudulent diabetes claims after being advised by the FTC.

These compliance actions were also accompanied by a new FTC educational "teaser" Web site, which is designed to appear when consumers search the Web for diabetes information. Teaser sites are designed to look like real sites. But when consumers try to place an order, they find out the site is an FTC consumer education tool about health fraud.

Regulatory authorities in Canada and Mexico also released educational materials for consumers and announced the compliance actions they took against bogus diabetes treatments.

For more information on MUCH actions, visit www.hc-sc.gc.ca/fn-an/intactivit/trilateral-coop/coop_health_fraud_e.html

For more information on diabetes, visit www.fda.gov/diabetes/

'Natural Healer' Convicted

In August 2006, a federal judge sentenced John E. Curran to 12.5 years in prison for fraud and money laundering. Promoting himself as a natural healer and posing as a medical doctor, Curran operated the Northeastern Institute for Advanced Natural Healing in Providence, R.I. He made false claims about his qualifications, educational background, and training. For instance, he bought three backdated degrees from Chatworth College of Health Sciences for $2,650.

Curran sold bogus products called "E-water" and "Green Drink." He asserted that E-water was "uniquely charged water wherein molecules spin in reverse direction and emit electrical energy." He claimed to have formulated Green Water, a powdered vegetable drink, though he really bought it from a dietary supplement distributor. He also treated patients with machines that use heat and oxygen.

In promotional materials, Curran claimed to have cured people of cancer. One 17-year-old girl with ovarian cancer reportedly drank only Green Drink in the last weeks of her life.

In other instances, Curran used scare diagnosis tactics so that he could prescribe the phony cures to healthy people. Curran sold about 1.4 million dollars' worth of treatment and products after making his false diagnoses. He told patients they had "live parasites" in their blood, reduced blood cell counts, and ruined immune systems. He led people to believe they either had or would develop a life-threatening disease. The investigation of Curran's practices also uncovered that he commonly drew blood samples from patients and conducted unnecessary and incorrect tests.

"This defendant eagerly victimized unsuspecting people by falsely telling them that he had diagnosed life-threatening diseases, and then he bilked them out of their money by selling them 'cures' that were worthless," says Terry Vermillion, director of the FDA's Office of Criminal Investigations. "He placed hunger for money over the well-being of his fellow man."

In 2005, the Rhode Island Department of Health suspended Curran's health care practice. The FDA and the U.S. Attorney's Office confiscated equipment from Curran's office for misuse of medical devices and other offenses. This case was jointly investigated by the FDA's Office of Criminal Investigation, the Internal Revenue Service, the U.S. Postal Inspection Service, and the Rhode Island Department of Health.

Home Genetic Tests

In July 2006, the FDA, the Federal Trade Commission, and the Centers for Disease Control and Prevention (CDC) alerted consumers about the facts surrounding direct-to-consumer marketing of genetic tests. Genetic tests examine genes and DNA to see whether they indicate particular diseases and disorders.

Some companies claim their tests can screen for diseases, evaluate health risks, or suggest treatments. But genetic tests should be performed in a specialized laboratory, and the results should be interpreted by a trained health care professional or a genetic counselor.

Genetic testing provides only one piece of information about a person's susceptibility to disease. Other factors, like family background, medical history, and environment also contribute to the likelihood of getting a particular disease.

According to the FDA, which regulates genetic test manufacturers, and the CDC, which promotes health and quality of life, some of these tests lack scientific validity. Others provide medical results that are meaningful only in the context of a full medical evaluation. Home genetic tests are not a suitable substitute for a medical checkup.

To access "At-Home Genetic Tests: A Healthy Dose of Skepticism May Be the Best Prescription," visit www.ftc.gov/bcp/edu/pubs/consumer/health/hea02.htm

To find out whether an over-the-counter genetic test is FDA approved/cleared, search the FDA's Over the Counter tests database at: www.accessdata.fda.gov/scripts/cdrh/cfdocs/cfIVD/Search.cfm

Influenza Treatment Scams

Consumers should be aware that there have been cases involving contaminated, counterfeit, and subpotent influenza products. The FDA, with the U.S. Customs and Border Protection Service, has intercepted products claiming to be a generic version of the influenza drug Tamiflu (oseltamivir). But the products really contained vitamin C and other substances not shown to be effective in treating or preventing influenza.

In January 2006, a licensed practical nurse named Michelle Torgerson was sentenced to nine months in prison for running unauthorized influenza vaccine clinics at Augsburg College in Minneapolis. She also was ordered to pay $4,598 in restitution to the victims.

The director of security at the school reported to Minneapolis Police that a woman was administering influenza shots to students and faculty members for $20 per shot without authorization by the college. Torgerson admitted to giving shots to 46 students and faculty at the college.

Police seized vials of Fluzone Influenza Vaccine from Torgerson. Fluzone is an approved vaccine manufactured by Sanofi Pasteur Inc. The FDA's Office of Criminal Investigations analyzed the seized vials and found that the labeling and packaging were consistent with authentic Fluzone, but two of the vials were diluted with saline solution, which lowers the quality and effectiveness of the vaccine.

Other cases involve marketers who prey on consumers' fears about avian (bird) influenza. Bird influenza is caused by influenza A avian viruses that occur naturally among birds. While there are vaccines to protect against seasonal influenza, there are no vaccines for preventing or treating avian influenza in people. There are also no drugs approved for treating the specific symptoms of bird influenza.

In 2005 and 2006, the FDA issued Warning Letters to marketers of bogus influenza products claiming to prevent the avian influenza and other forms of influenza. These sites claimed to sell products that "kill the virus," among other claims. In 2006, the FDA's Center for Devices and Radiological Health issued eight Warning letters to firms that were selling masks on the Internet that claimed to prevent or cure avian influenza.

"The use of unproven flu cures and treatments increases the risk of catching and spreading the flu rather than lessening it because people assume they are protected and safe and they aren't," says Acting FDA Commissioner Andrew C. von Eschenbach. "I consider it a public health hazard when people are lured into using bogus treatments based on deceptive or fraudulent medical claims."

Health Fraud Red Flags

Consumers should be wary of . . .

- Statements that the product is a quick and effective cure-all or a diagnostic tool for a wide variety of ailments. "Beneficial in treating cancer, ulcer, prostate problems, heart trouble, and more . . ."
- Statements that suggest the product can treat or cure diseases. "Shrinks tumors, cures impotency . . ."
- Promotions that use words like "scientific breakthrough," "miraculous cure," "secret ingredient," and "ancient remedy."
- Text that uses impressive-sounding terms like these: "hunger stimulation point" and "thermogenesis" for a weight loss product.
- Undocumented case histories or personal testimonials by consumers or doctors claiming amazing results. "After eating a teaspoon of this product each day, my pain is completely gone . . ."
- Limited availability and advance payment requirements. "Hurry! This offer will not last."
- Promises of no-risk money-back guarantees. "If after 30 days you have not lost at least 4 pounds each week, your uncashed check will be returned to you."
- Promises of an "easy" fix.

Sources: The Federal Trade Commission, the U.S. Food and Drug Administration

What Consumers Can Do

To avoid becoming a victim of health fraud, consumers should learn how to evaluate health-related claims. "I advise consumers to avoid web sites that offer quick and dramatic cures for serious diseases," says David Elder, director of the FDA's Office of Enforcement. "Recognize the red flags and always consult a health professional before using any product or treatment."

Some products may interact with prescribed medicines or keep them from working the way they should. Reliance on fraudulent products may also prevent consumers from getting treatments that are proven to be safe and effective.

Promotion of fraudulent health products on the Internet is common. And despite enforcement efforts, many products maintain their hold in the marketplace. Internet sites can be easily installed, moved, and removed, and foreign-based Web sites can be difficult or impossible to investigate.

When buying prescription drugs over the Internet, consumers should look for the National Association of Boards of Pharmacy Verified Internet Pharmacy Practice Sites (VIPPS) seal. The FDA recommends that consumers buy medicines only from U.S. state-licensed pharmacies and only take medicine that has been prescribed by their doctor.

Elder adds, "There are bogus treatments and sophisticated scares out there for every ailment and problem. You can protect yourself by learning how to spot health fraud and by seeking out reliable sources of information to make better-informed choices about your health."

From *FDA Consumer,* November/December 2006, pp. 17–23. Published 2006 by U.S. Food and Drug Administration. www.fda.gov

How to Ease Your Pain

Here's what you need to know to get safe relief.

The withdrawal in late September 2004 of the painkilling drug rofecoxib (*Vioxx*) because of increased heart-attack risk—plus subsequent concerns raised about celecoxib (*Celebrex*), naproxen (*Aleve, Naprosyn*), and valdecoxib (*Bextra*)—left millions of Americans scrambling for a safe and effective way to control their pain. But it's not just users of those drugs who face that predicament.

Virtually all prescription and nonprescription pain relievers pose some risks, even when used properly. Many people multiply the risks by overusing such drugs. And even high doses may not quell the pain if the doctor or patient chooses the wrong drug. Indeed, studies suggest that roughly half of people with chronic or recurrent pain fail to get adequate relief despite drug therapy.

"Over-the-counter acetaminophen is often a good first choice for relieving chronic pain."

That's a huge amount of needless suffering. "Even when pain can't be completely eliminated, we now have numerous ways to rein it in so it doesn't interfere with your daily life," says Morris Levin, M.D., a pain-control expert at the Dartmouth-Hitchcock Medical Center in Hanover, N.H.

The key is knowing when and how to use nonprescription drugs, such as acetaminophen (*Tylenol*) or ibuprofen (*Advil, Motrin IB*), and, when prescription drugs are needed, being aware of the choices your doctor should consider. While the withdrawal of rofecoxib and concerns about its cousins celecoxib (*Celebrex*) and valdecoxib (*Bextra*) have made picking prescription drugs more difficult, there are several other good options, provided you and your doctor can overcome certain misconceptions.

For example, too many people refuse to consider opioids, such as codeine, because of excessive concerns about addiction. Others fail to consider drugs not normally considered painkillers, such as certain antidepressants and anticonvulsants, despite growing evidence that they're effective against some types of pain. Equally important, proper pain management means knowing which nondrug measures can sometimes relieve pain and even treat the underlying cause.

The accompanying table, "Targeted Pain Relief," describes proven or possible treatments for several common kinds of pain. Below we describe the proper use of over-the-counter (OTC) pain relievers and advise when to see a doctor for prescription drugs or other options.

Acute Pain: Rate It and Treat It

For occasional or sudden pain (from common headaches, menstrual cramps, or injuries, for example), appropriate treatment starts with assessing the pain's severity. The best way is to grade your pain along a scale from 0 (no pain) to 10 (the worst pain you've ever had).

For mild-to-moderate pain, rated 5 or less, nonprescription drugs usually suffice. Though some evidence suggests that nonsteroidal anti-inflammatory drugs (NSAIDs), such as ibuprofen and, to a lesser extent, ketoprofen (*Orudis KT*) and naproxen (*Aleve*), may provide slightly faster and greater relief than aspirin or acetaminophen, all are often adequate. But certain individuals may want to choose or avoid specific pain relievers:

- Avoid aspirin if you're breast-feeding, since aspirin might cause bleeding or other problems in the baby.
- Avoid acetaminophen if you're a heavy drinker or have liver disease; even modest doses can harm the liver in such cases.
- Choose acetaminophen if you have hypertension, heart failure, ulcers, or kidney disease, which may be worsened by the other drugs. Also stick with acetaminophen if you take a daily aspirin to protect your heart. Additional aspirin might cause bleeding, while ibuprofen and possibly other NSAIDs have been shown to undermine aspirin's coronary benefits. And pick acetaminophen if you're pregnant, since the other drugs may harm the fetus and prolong labor.

If your pain is relatively severe (rated 6 or more) or persists despite the recommended doses of nonprescription medication, it's important to see your doctor for several reasons. Treating yourself by boosting the doses increases the risks, particularly with acetaminophen, since more than 4 grams a day—the daily maximum for adults—can damage the liver. And the drug you've chosen may not work against your type of pain, regardless of the

Targeted pain relief

Most people should treat each kind of pain listed below by trying lifestyle changes and the first treatment option. If those don't help, talk with your doctor about other options. You could also consider alternative therapies, though the evidence is usually weaker and the possible benefits smaller.

Condition	Lifestyle measures	First choice	Second choice	Alternative therapies	Cautions
Osteo-arthritis	• Lose excess weight and do low-impact exercise.	• Acetaminophen (*Tylenol*). • Capsaicin cream (*Capsin, Zostrix*).	• Ibuprofen (*Advil*). Combine with stomach-protecting drugs such as misoprostol (*Cytotec*) or omeprazole (*Prilosec, Prilosec OTC*) if you've had ulcers or gastrointestinal bleeding or have signs of GI reactions to ibuprofen.	• Glucosamine and chondroitin supplements. • Relaxation techniques, such as biofeedback, guided imagery, progressive muscle relaxation, or massage.	• Acetaminophen can harm liver when used in high doses or by heavy drinkers or liver patients. • Ibuprofen and related drugs in high doses or with extended use can cause ulcers and stomach bleeding, increase blood pressure, trigger asthma attacks, and worsen kidney problems and heart failure.
Rheumatoid arthritis	• Low-impact exercise. • Avoid triggers, such as stress, infection, and insufficient sleep.	• Ibuprofen. Combine with stomach-protecting drug such as misoprostol or omeprazole if you've had ulcers or gastrointestinal bleeding. • Capsaicin cream.	• Corticosteroids, such as prednisone (*Deltasone*), for short-term relief of acute pain. • New immunosuppressants, such as adalimumab (*Humira*), etanercept (*Enbrel*), or infliximab (*Remicade*). • Older drugs, such as gold (*Solganal*) or methotrexate (*Rheumatrex*).	• Fish oil or gamma-linolenic acid, though risks (including upset stomach, diarrhea, and increased risk of bleeding) may outweigh slight benefit.	• Steroids can cause weight gain, bruising, thin bones, cataracts, and diabetes. • Immunosuppressants can increase chance of infection. • Older drugs cost less but are riskier and less effective.
Headache	• Identify possible triggers (such as red wine, chocolate, or stress) or underlying causes (such as sleep apnea, sinus infection, or caffeine withdrawal) and try to avoid or control them.	• Acetaminophen, aspirin, or ibuprofen.	• One or more first-choice drugs combined with caffeine (*Anacin, Excedrin Migraine*). • Triptans, such as sumatriptan (*Imitrex*) or zolmitriptan (*Zomig*), for migraines. Nasal sumatriptan works fastest but is more expensive. • Ergot alkaloids, such as dihydroergotamine (*Migranal Nasal Spray*) or ergotamine (*Ergomar*).	• Relaxation techniques. • The herb feverfew (products contain variable amounts of possible active ingredient). • Botulinum toxin (*Botox*) (requires up to 30 injections, must be repeated every few months, and isn't reimbursible).	• Triptans and caffeine drugs more likely to cause "rebound" headaches as drug wears off. • Triptans can cause flushing, dizziness, tightness in chest; can't be used if you have heart disease. • Ergot alkaloids cost less but are less effective. Can cause nausea, vomiting, diarrhea, and muscle cramps.
Back pain	• Apply cold pack for first day or two, then heating pad; resume gentle exercise as soon as possible. • Strengthen muscles in the abdomen and back to prevent pain.	• Aspirin. • Ibuprofen. Combine with stomach-protecting drugs such as misoprostol or omeprazole, or take acetaminophen, if you've had ulcers or gastrointestinal bleeding. • Capsaicin cream.	• For acute, severe pain, possibly opioids, such as oxycodone (*Oxycontin*) or fentanyl (*Duragesic*); muscle relaxants, such as cyclobenzaprine (*Flexeril*) or methocarbamol (*Carbacot, Robaxin*); or, for pinched nerve, steroid injections. • For chronic pain, tricyclic antidepressants, such as amitriptyline, or possibly surgery.	• Hands-on care, including chiropracty, massage, or physical therapy. • Botulinum (*Botox*) injections.	• Opioids, muscle relaxants, and tricyclic antidepressants can cause sedation, dizziness, confusion, urinary retention, and other problems, especially in older people.
Muscle or joint injury	• Rest, ice, compression, and elevation for first 24-48 hours or until inflammation subsides, then heat. • Resume gentle activity as soon as possible.	• Acetaminophen, aspirin, or ibuprofen.	• Physical therapy for chronic muscle pain and possibly surgery.	• Massage • Acupuncture.	• Acetaminophen can harm liver when used in high doses or by heavy drinkers or liver patients. • Ibuprofen and related drugs in high doses or with extended use can cause ulcers and stomach bleeding, increase blood pressure, trigger asthma attacks, and worsen kidney problems and heart failure.
Irritable bowel syndrome (IBS)	• Drink more fluids, limit triggering foods, and eat more high-fiber foods (except beans and cabbage, which can cause gas). • Regular physical activity.	• For IBS with constipation, high-fiber supplements or, for short-term use, nonprescription laxatives such as docusate (*Colace, Sof-lax*). • For IBS with diarrhea, OTC loperamide (*Imodium A-D*).	• For IBS with constipation, tegaserod (*Zelnorm*). • For IBS with diarrhea, diphenoxylate (*Lomotil*); cholestyramine (*Questran*); antispasmodics, such as hyoscyamine (*Levsin*); combination products, such as *Donnatal*; or tricyclic antidepressants.	• Relaxation techniques, especially stress management.	• Tegaserod for short-term use only; can cause severe diarrhea and intestinal problems. See doctor immediately if rectal bleeding, bloody diarrhea, or new or worse abdominal pain develops. • Frequent laxative use can worsen constipation.
Neuropathy (from diabetes, shingles, fibromyalgia, other causes)	• Treat underlying condition, such as diabetes.	• Tricyclic antidepressants; anticonvulsants, such as gabapentin (*Neurontin*); lidocaine patch (*Lidoderm*); or capsaicin cream.	• Nerve-block injections or surgery, especially for face and head pain caused by nerve damage. • Psychotherapy to develop pain-management strategies.	• Relaxation techniques. • Acupuncture.	• Consider seeking referral to pain clinic if pain persists.

dosage. Moreover, it's essential to stop acute, severe pain early because it becomes harder to control as it worsens.

Prescription NSAIDs, some of them stronger versions of the corresponding OTC drug, may yield additional relief. However, the risks generally increase along with the benefits as the dosage rises. A better approach to severe, acute pain is often a prescription opioid, such as codeine or hydrocodone. With proper dosing, you can remain reasonably alert, and short-term treatment carries little risk of addiction.

Drugs that pair an opioid with acetaminophen, aspirin, or ibuprofen may be an even better choice: They provide greater relief, since the two ingredients work in different ways, and they reduce the risk of side effects because the combination permits smaller doses of each one.

Chronic Pain: Limit the Risks

You should also see your physician if you've taken a nonprescription analgesic regularly for more than about 10 days, regardless of the pain's severity. Drug risks rise with prolonged use, and your doctor may be able to recommend a better treatment. Tell him or her how severe the pain is and what it feels like—a steady ache, a sharp pain, or a burning or shooting sensation, for example—because different types respond to different drugs.

People with osteoarthritis or other chronic pain should first try the nondrug measures described in the accompanying table that may reduce or even eliminate the need for medication. If those steps don't help, their physician may first recommend a nonprescription drug. Acetaminophen is a good initial choice because even frequent, prolonged use is reasonably safe if you stick with the recommended doses and have no increased risk of liver damage.

However, many people with arthritis or other chronic pain need greater relief, which NSAIDs may provide. In theory, celecoxib (*Celebrex*) and valdecoxib (*Bextra*), like their banished cousin rofecoxib (*Vioxx*), may be less likely to cause gastrointestinal bleeding than the other, older NSAIDs. But some research has raised concerns about celecoxib and valdecoxib, too. For now, at least, our medical consultants advise people with elevated cardiovascular risk to avoid those drugs; other people should take them with considerable caution and only after careful consultation with their physician.

One alternative is ibuprofen, since some research suggests it may be gentler on the stomach than most of the NSAIDs unrelated to *Vioxx*. Those who've had ulcers or bleeding or who have any gastrointestinal reactions to ibuprofen should consider taking it with a stomach protecting drug, such as misoprostol (*Cytotec*) or omeprazole (*Prilosec, Prilosec OTC*). And try to use the pills just to treat flare-ups, not continually to prevent them.

If NSAIDs don't control chronic pain, opioids may, though the risk of addiction with frequent use generally makes them a last resort. A better choice is often an antidepressant such as amitriptyline or an anticonvulsant such as gabapentin (*Neurontin*). They can substantially relieve the burning or shooting pain from certain common neurologic disorders, such as diabetic nerve damage, apparently by interfering with certain brain chemicals.

People with unresolved chronic pain despite treatment should ask for a referral to a pain clinic. Such facilities take a multidisciplinary approach, with neurologists, anesthesiologists, psychiatrists, and other specialists collaborating on a treatment plan that eases pain, avoids drug dependency, and helps people resume a normal life.

What You Can Do

- For our latest recommendations on pain-relieving drugs, go to our new health-letter Web site.
- For short-term relief of mild to moderate pain, use nonprescription drugs, such as acetaminophen or ibuprofen; for severe pain, see your doctor, who may prescribe an opioid.
- For chronic pain, try nondrug steps when possible and see your doctor, who may prescribe a treatment described in the accompanying table.
- Avoid celecoxib and valdecoxib if you have increased cardiovascular risk; if you don't, use those drugs with considerable caution. Consider taking ibuprofen plus a stomach-protecting medication if you need an NSAID but have elevated gastrointestinal risk.

Deep into Sleep

While researchers probe sleep's functions, sleep itself is becoming a lost art.

CRAIG LAMBERT

Not long ago, a psychiatrist in private practice telephoned associate professor of psychiatry Robert Stickgold, a cognitive neuroscientist specializing in sleep research. He asked whether Stickgold knew of any reason not to prescribe modafinil, a new wakefulness-promoting drug, to a Harvard undergraduate facing a lot of academic work in exam period.

The question resonated on several levels. Used as an aid to prolonged study, modafinil is tantamount to a "performance-enhancing" drug—one of those controversial, and often illegal, boosters used by some athletes. In contrast to wakefulness-producing stimulants like amphetamines, modafinil (medically indicated for narcolepsy and tiredness secondary to multiple sclerosis and depression) does not seem to impair judgment or produce jitters. "There's no buzz, no crash, and it's not clear that the body tries to make up the lost sleep," reports Stickgold. "That said, all sleeping medications more or less derange your normal sleep patterns. They do not produce normal sleep." Even so, the U.S. military is sinking millions of dollars into research on modafinil, trying to see if they can keep soldiers awake and on duty—in Iraq, for example—for 80 out of 88 hours: two 40-hour shifts separated by eight hours of sleep.

"No—no reason at all not to," Stickgold told the psychiatrist. "Not unless you think sleep *does* something."

When people make the unlikely claim that they get by on four hours of sleep per night, Stickgold often asks if they worry about what they are losing. "You get a blank look," he says. "They think that sleep is wasted time." But sleep is not merely "down time" between episodes of being alive. Within an evolutionary framework, the simple fact that we spend about a third of our lives asleep suggests that sleep is more than a necessary evil. Much transpires while we are asleep, and the question is no longer *whether* sleep does something, but exactly *what* it does. Lack of sleep may be related to obesity, diabetes, immune-system dysfunction, and many illnesses, as well as to safety issues such as car accidents and medical errors, plus impaired job performance and productivity in many other activities.

Although the modern era of sleep research started in the 1950s with the discovery of REM (Rapid Eye Movement) sleep, the field remained, well, somnolent until recently. Even 20 years ago, "The dominant paradigm in sleep research was that 'Sleep cures sleepiness,'" says Stickgold. Since then, researchers have developed a far more complex picture of what happens while we snooze. The annual meetings in sleep medicine, which only this year became a recognized medical speciality, now draw 5,000 participants. Harvard has long been a leader in the area. The Medical School's Division of Sleep Medicine, founded in 1997 and chaired by Baldino professor of sleep medicine Charles Czeisler, has 61 faculty affiliates. The division aims to foster collaborative research into sleep, sleep disorders, and circadian biology, to educate physicians and the lay public, to influence public policy, and to set new standards of clinical practice, aiming, as its website (www.hms.harvard.edu/sleep) declares, to create "a model program in sleep and circadian biology."

A Culture of "Sleep Bulimia"

Imagine going on a camping trip without flashlights or lanterns. As the sun sets at the end of the day, daylight gradually gives way to darkness, and once the campfire burns down, you will probably go to sleep. At sunrise, there's a similar gradient in reverse; from the beginning of time, human beings have been entrained to these cycles of light and dark.

Homo sapiens is not a nocturnal animal; we don't have good night vision and are not especially effective in darkness. Yet in an instant on the evolutionary time scale, Edison's invention of the light bulb, and his opening of the first round-the-clock power plant on Pearl Street in Manhattan in 1882, shifted our time-and-light environment in the nocturnal direction. At the snap of a switch, a whole range of nighttime activity opened up, and today we live in a 24-hour world that is always available for work or play. Television and telephones never shut down; the Internet allows you to shop, gamble, work, or flirt at 3 A.M.; businesses stay open ever-longer hours; tens of millions of travelers cross multiple time zones each year, worldwide; and with the growth of global commerce and communication, Wall Street traders may need to rise early or stay up late to keep abreast of developments on Japan's Nikkei exchange or at the Deutsche Bundesbank.

Number of Hours Slept per Night on Weekdays (past two weeks)

	1998	2001	2002	2005
Less than 6 hours	12%	13%	15%	16%
6 to 7.9 hours	51	49	53	55
8 or more hours	35	38	30	2
Mean (# of hours)	NA	7.0	6.9	6.8

Source: National Sleep Foundation

Consequently most of us now sleep less than people did a century ago, or even 50 years ago. The National Sleep Foundation's 2005 poll showed adult Americans averaging 6.8 hours of sleep on weeknights—more than an hour less than they need, Czeisler says. Not only how *much* sleep, but *when* people sleep has changed. In the United States, six to eight million shift workers toil regularly at night, disrupting sleep patterns in ways that are not necessarily amenable to adaptation. Many people get only five hours per night during the week and then try to catch up by logging nine hours nightly on weekends. "You can make up for *acute* sleep deprivation," says David P. White, McGinness professor of sleep medicine and director of the sleep disorders program at Brigham and Women's Hospital. "But we don't know what happens when people are chronically sleep-deprived over years."

"We are living in the middle of history's greatest experiment in sleep deprivation and we are all a part of that experiment," says Stickgold. "It's not inconceivable to me that we will discover that there are major social, economic, and health consequences to that experiment. Sleep deprivation doesn't have any good side effects."

All animals sleep. Fish that need to keep swimming to breathe sleep with half their brains while the other half keeps them moving. It is uncertain whether fruit flies actually sleep ("We can't put electrodes in their brains," says White), but they seem at least to rest, because for extended periods they do not move. When researchers stopped fruit flies from resting by swatting at them, the flies took even longer rest periods. When lab technicians added caffeine to the water that the flies drank, they stayed active longer—and also rested longer after the drug wore of, evidence that the caffeine had disrupted their resting patterns.

Sleeping well helps keep you alive longer. Among humans, death from all causes is lowest among adults who get seven to eight hours of sleep nightly, and significantly higher among those who sleep less than seven or more than nine hours. ("Those who sleep more than nine hours have something wrong with them that may be causing the heavy sleep, and leads to their demise," White notes. "It is not the sleep itself that is harmful.")

Sleep is essential to normal biological function. "The immune system doesn't work well if we don't sleep," says White. "Most think sleep serves some neurological process to maintain homeostasis in the brain." Rats totally deprived of sleep die in 17 to 20 days: their hair starts falling out, and they become hypermetabolic, burning lots of calories while just standing still.

There once was a fair amount of research on total sleep deprivation, like that which killed the rats. Doctors would keep humans awake for 48, 72, or even 96 hours, and watch their performance deteriorate while their mental states devolved into psychosis. For several reasons, such studies rarely happen any more ("Why study something that doesn't exist?" asks White) and researchers now concentrate on sleep *restriction* studies.

In this context, it is important to distinguish between acute and chronic sleep deprivation. Someone who misses an entire night of sleep but then gets adequate sleep on the following three days "will recover most of his or her normal ability to function," Czeisler says. "But someone restricted to only five hours of nightly sleep for weeks builds up a cumulative sleep deficit. In the first place, their performance will be as impaired as if they had been up all night. Secondly, it will take two to three weeks of extra nightly sleep before they return to baseline performance. Chronic sleep deprivation's impact takes much longer to build up, and it also takes much longer to recover." The body is eager to restore the balance; Harvard undergraduates, a high-achieving, sleep-deprived population, frequently go home for Christmas vacation and pretty much sleep for the first week. Stickgold notes that "When you live on four hours a night, you forget what it's like to really be awake."

"When you live on four hours a night, you forget what it's like to really be awake."

Sleep researcher Eve van Cauter at the University of Chicago exposed sleep-deprived students (allowed only four hours per night for six nights) to flu vaccine; their immune systems produced only half the normal number of antibodies in response to the viral challenge. Levels of cortisol (a hormone associated with stress) rose, and the sympathetic nervous system became active, raising heart rates and blood pressure. The subjects also showed insulin resistance, a pre-diabetic condition that affects glucose tolerance and produces weight gain. "[When] restricted to four hours [of sleep] a night, within a couple of weeks, you could make an 18-year-old look like a 60-year-old in terms of their ability to metabolize glucose," Czeisler notes. "The sleep-deprived metabolic syndrome might increase carbohydrate cravings and the craving for junk food."

Van Cauter also showed that sleep-deprived subjects had reduced levels of leptin, a molecule secreted by fat cells that acts in the brain to inhibit appetite. "During nights of sleep deprivation, you feel that your eating goes wacky," says Stickgold. "Up at 2 A.M., working on a paper, a steak or pasta is not very attractive. You'll grab the candy bar instead. It probably has to do with the glucose regulation going off. It could be that a good chunk of our epidemic of obesity is actually an epidemic of sleep deprivation."

Furthermore, "Many children in our society don't get adequate amounts of sleep," Czeisler says. "Contrary to what one might expect, it's common to see irritability and hyperactivity in sleep-deprived children. Is it really surprising that we treat them with wake-promoting drugs like Ritalin?" Schools and athletic

Unsound Sleep

The National Sleep Foundation's 2005 survey found that 75 percent of American adults experience symptoms of a sleep problem at least a few nights per week. Sleep clinics like Sleep Health Centers, a for-profit enterprise whose medical director, David P. White, supervises six sites with 32 beds in the Boston area, investigate many of the 84 types of sleep disorder that clinicians have identified. White, McGinness professor of sleep medicine, who directs the sleep disorders program at Brigham and Women's Hospital, explains that there are three main categories of sleep disorder: insomnias; disorders that make patients sleepy during the day, like narcolepsy or sleep apnea; and parasomnias, which include sleepwalking, sleep-talking, and REM behavior disorder.

Chronic insomnia may affect 10 percent of the population, but some Gallup polls indicate that as many as 40 percent have trouble sleeping on two or three nights per week. "Depression and anxiety states are the biggest cause of insomnia," White says. Besides treating the underlying problems and practicing good "sleep hygiene" (e.g., going to bed at a regular time, having no clock in the bedroom), one intervention is, paradoxically, sleep restriction. "A lot of insomniacs spend more and more time in bed—up to 14 hours a day. That's counterproductive," White says. "So you restrict them to the amount of time they can sleep: perhaps from 11 P.M. until 3 A.M. Get them to sleep well during that time and then build up from there."

In narcolepsy, which affects one in 2,000 people, components of REM sleep—being asleep, having muscular paralysis or weakness, and dreaming—affect people during waking hours. Research on narcoleptic Doberman dogs and genetically altered mice showed that animals unable to produce a protein called hypocretin were narcoleptic. The spinal fluid of humans who suffer from narcolepsy contains little or no hypocretin; hence treatment of narcolepsy may involve ways to enhance its production or replace it.

The most common problem that sleep clinics see is obstructive sleep apnea. "We're seeing an epidemic of sleep apnea," says Charles Czeisler, Baldino professor of sleep medicine. "It's related to overweight, and is especially prevalent in certain regions." Older, obese men are at higher risk. Sleep apnea affects individuals who may have a narrower passage of the upper throat; during sleep, muscles around this passage relax and close the passage partially or completely, stopping the flow of air into the lungs. This results in loud snoring, labored breathing, and even the cessation of breathing (apnea) for periods of more than 10 seconds. "It's important to breathe in the right amounts of oxygen and breathe out carbon dioxide, to keep the levels right," explains White, who trained in pulmonary medicine. "The mechanisms that control this don't work as well during sleep." Losing weight can help; in severe cases, sufferers may sleep wearing a special "continuous positive airway pressure" mask that keeps the passage open.

Parasomnias are a less common form of sleep disorder. In sleepwalking, something rouses the sleeper from deep (stage 3 or 4) sleep, and in a state somewhere between deep sleep and wakefulness, he or she can walk about or even drive a car for a period of 10 to 15 minutes. REM behavior disorder, which can be associated with degenerative brain disease, may last only seconds, but can be dangerous. "In REM sleep, all skeletal muscles are paralyzed, so that you can't act out your dreams," White explains. "But with REM behavior disorder, people can move."

---

programs press children to stay awake longer, and some children may be chronically sleep-deprived. Czeisler once took his daughter to a swim-team practice that ran from eight to nine o'clock at night, and told the coaches that this was too late an hour for children. "They looked at me like I was from another planet," he recalls. "They said, 'This is when we can get the pool.'"

Stickgold compares sleep deprivation to eating disorders. "Twenty years ago, bulimics probably thought they had the best of all worlds," he says. "They could eat all they wanted and never gain weight. Now we know that they were and are doing major damage to their bodies and suffering major psychological damage. We live in a world of sleep bulimia, where we binge on weekends and purge during the week."

"When you live on four hours a night, you forget what it's like to really be awake."

The Fatigue Tax

Lack of sleep impairs performance on a wide variety of tasks. A single all-nighter can triple reaction time and vastly increase lapses of attention. Sleep researcher David Dinges at the University of Pennsylvania studied such lapses using a "psychomotor vigilance task" on pools of subjects who had slept four, six, or eight hours nightly for two weeks. The researchers measured subjects' speed of reaction to a computer screen where, at random intervals within a defined 10-minute period, the display would begin counting up in milliseconds from 000 to one second. The task was first, to notice that the count had started, and second, to stop it as quickly as possible by hitting a key. It wasn't so much that the sleep-deprived subjects were slower, but that they had far more total lapses, letting the entire second go by without responding. Those on four hours a night had more lapses than those sleeping six, who in turn had more lapses than subjects sleeping eight hours per night. "The number of lapses went up and up for the whole two weeks," says David White, "and they hadn't plateaued at the end of the two-week study!"

There's fairly large individual variation in susceptibility to the cognitive effects of sleep deprivation: in one of Charles Czeisler's studies, somewhere between a quarter and a third of the subjects who stayed awake all night contributed two-thirds of the lapses of attention. "Some are more resistant to the impact of a single night of sleep loss," he says. "But they all fall apart after two nights without sleep." In a sleep-deprived state, says White, "Most of us can perform at a fairly low level. And a lot can run around sleep-deprived without it being obvious. But truck drivers, neurosurgeons, nuclear-plant workers—after six or eight hours, they have to put a second crew on and give them a break." Very few people are really immune to sleep deprivation: in Dinges's study, only one of 48 subjects had the same performance after two weeks of four hours' nightly sleep as on day one.

> "Your ability to do critical thinking takes a massive hit—you're knocking out the frontal-cortex functions."

Students often wonder whether to pull an all-nighter before an exam. Will the extra studying time outweigh the exhaustion? Robert Stickgold, who has studied sleep's role in cognition for the past 10 years, reports that it depends on the exam. "If you are just trying to remember simple facts—listing all the kings of England, say—cramming all night works," he explains. "That's because it's a different memory system, the declarative memory system. But if you expect to be hit with a question like 'Relate the French Revolution to the Industrial Revolution,' where you have to synthesize connections between facts, then missing that night of sleep can be disastrous. Your ability to do critical thinking takes a massive hit—just as with alcohol, you're knocking out the frontal-cortex functions."

"It's a version of 'sleeping on a problem,'" Stickgold continues. "If you can't recall a phone number, you don't say, 'Let me sleep on it.' But if you can't decide whether to take a better-paying job located halfway across the country—where you have all the information and just have to weigh it—you say, 'Let me sleep on it.' You don't say, 'Give me 24 hours.' We realize that it's not just time; we understand at a gut level that the brain is doing this integration of information as we sleep, all by itself."

Not only mental and emotional clarification, but the improvement of motor skills can occur while asleep. "Suppose you are trying to learn a passage in a Chopin piano étude, and you just can't get it," says Stickgold. "You walk away and the next day, the first try, you've got it perfectly. We see this with musicians, and with gymnasts. There's something about learning motor-activity patterns, complex movements: they seem to get better by themselves, overnight."

Stickgold's colleague Matthew Walker, an instructor in psychiatry, studied a simple motor task: typing the sequence "41324" as rapidly and accurately as possible. After 12 minutes of training, subjects improved their speed by 50 to 60 percent, but then reached a plateau. Those who trained in the morning and came back for another trial the same evening showed no improvement. But those who trained in the evening and returned for a retest the following morning were 15 to 20 percent faster and 30 to 50 percent more accurate. "Twenty percent improvement—what's that?" asks Stickgold, rhetorically. "Well, it's taking a four-minute mile down to three minutes and 10 seconds, or raising a five-foot high jump to six feet."

Bodily Rituals

So sleep is essential, but exactly why we go to sleep remains a mystery. Professor of psychiatry Robert McCarley, based at the VA Boston Healthcare System, has linked sleep to the brain neurochemical adenosine. Adenosine binds with phosphorus to create adenosine triphosphate (ATP), a substance that cells break down to generate energy. McCarley and colleagues inserted microcatheters into cat brains while keeping the cats awake for up to six hours—a long time for a cat. They found that rising adenosine levels in the basal forebrain put the cat to sleep; then, in the sleeping cat, adenosine levels fall again. In both cats and humans, the basal forebrain includes cells important for wakefulness, and adenosine turns these cells off, triggering sleep.

Like cats, when we are awake and active, we burn ATP, which breaks down to adenosine. Over time, adenosine levels build up, causing pressure for sleep. During sleep, many of the body's cells are less active and hence burn less ATP, so adenosine levels fall again, setting the stage for wakefulness.

A drug like caffeine, however, partially blocks adenosine receptors, so the brain doesn't perceive the actual adenosine level, and we don't get tired. In a world that values wakefulness and productivity over rest and recovery, caffeine has become, in dollar amounts, the second-largest commodity (after oil) traded in the world. Some consumers require ever-greater jolts—one 24-ounce Starbucks beverage packs a walloping 1,000-plus milligrams of caffeine. (A commonly used figure for one cup of coffee is 100 milligrams.)

The lab run by Putnam professor of neurology Clifford Saper has done related research, refining the location and functions of the "sleep switch," a group of nerve cells in the hypothalamus that turns of the brain's waking systems; conversely, the waking systems can turn of the sleep switch. "When you have a switch where either side can turn off the other, it's what electrical engineers call a 'flip-flop,'" Saper explains. "It likes to be in one state or the other. So we fall asleep, or wake up, quite quickly. Otherwise we'd be half asleep or half awake all the time, with only brief periods of being fully awake or asleep. But we're not—we are either awake or asleep."

The adenosine cycle at least partly explains the homeostatic drive for sleep—the longer we are awake, the greater our fatigue, and pressure to sleep builds up progressively. But circadian rhythms also profoundly affect sleep and wakefulness. Circadian cycles (from circa, meaning "about," and dies, a "day") are internal periodic rhythms that control many things like body temperature, hormone levels, sleep and wakefulness, digestion, and excretion. "The circadian cycles go way back in evolutionary time," Charles Czeisler says. "They are probably older than sleep."

Since the 1970s, Czeisler has established himself as one of the world's leading authorities on circadian cycles and the chronobiology of sleep and wakefulness. He has done groundbreaking work in the sleep laboratory at Brigham and Women's Hospital, where a special wing on one floor is shielded not only from sunlight, but from all external time cues. There, researchers can do exotic things like simulate the 708-hour lunar day or conditions on the International Space Station, where the sun rises and sets every 90 minutes. (Czeisler leads a sleep and chronobiology team that, under the auspices of NASA, researches human factors involved in space travel.)

Exotic light environments like space challenge human biology, partly because people differ from other mammals, which take short catnaps and rat naps throughout the day and night. In contrast, we have one bout of consolidated (unbroken) sleep, and one of consolidated waking, per day (or, in siesta cultures, two of each). In addition, "There is a very narrow window [in the daily cycle] in which we are able to maintain consolidated sleep," Czeisler says, "and the window gets narrower and narrower as we get older."

The origins of humans' consolidated sleep take us to the beginnings of terrestrial life, since even prokaryotes—one-celled organisms like bacteria, lacking a nucleus—have built-in 24-hour rhythms. It is not surprising that these biological clocks are so universal, as they reflect the entrainment of all living things to the primeval 24-hour cycles of light and darkness created by the rotation of Earth.

"The light and dark cycle is the most powerful synchronizer of the internal circadian clock that keeps us in sync with the 24- hour day," Czeisler says. As late as 1978, when he published a paper demonstrating this effect, many still believed that "social interaction was the most important factor in synchronizing physiological cycles—that we had evolved beyond light," he says. "But much of our subsequent research shows that our daily cycles are more like those of cockroaches than we want to believe. We are very sensitive to light."

Light strongly affects the suprachiasmatic nucleus (SCN), a biological clock in the anterior region of the hypothalamus that directs circadian cycles. All cells have internal clocks—even cells in a tissue culture run on 24-hour cycles. "They all oscillate like violins and cellos, but the SCN is the conductor that synchronizes them all together," Czeisler explains.

While the homeostatic pressure to sleep starts growing the moment we awaken, the SCN calls a different tune. Late in the afternoon, its circadian signal for wakefulness kicks in. "The circadian system is set up in a beautiful way to override the homeostatic drive for sleep," Czeisler says. The circadian pacemaker's signal continues to increase into the night, offsetting the build-up of homeostatic pressure and allowing us to stay awake well into the evening and so achieve our human pattern of consolidated sleep and wakefulness. (There is often a dip in the late afternoon, when the homeostatic drive has been building for hours but the circadian signal hasn't yet kicked in; Czeisler calls this "a great time for a nap.") The evolutionary benefit of consolidated sleep

Freud's Guesswork on Dreams

One of Sigmund Freud's great complaints about his mistreatment in life was that although he won a literary award for his famous book *The Interpretation of Dreams* (1900), it never received a scientific award. A century later, his peers' judgment has been vindicated. Freud's unscientific theory of dreams—based on self-analysis and a cherry-picked group of clinical anecdotes—has been demolished by the discoveries of sleep medicine. "I came into the field so far post-Freudian that Freud felt like someone with a goofy theory two centuries back," says Robert Stickgold, associate professor of psychiatry, who has studied dreams in sleep studies for years, often in collaboration with professor of psychiatry J. Allan Hobson. "The Greeks tried to explain thunder and lightning by creating gods; Freud tried to explain dreams by creating demons like the id and repressed desires," says Stickgold. "In general, Freud's dream theories have been remarkably resistant to scientific confirmation. He made a lot of observations that are quite prescient, but his attempt to build a model to explain them is completely wrong and there is no piece of it that holds up."

For example, Freud thought we dream to keep ourselves from being awakened. "That's absolutely false," says Stickgold. "Freud thought that as we sleep, with constraints on the id reduced, all these nasty Victorian desires well up, and if they were allowed to come into the conscious mind, they would be so distressing that the sleeper would wake up. So dreaming is all about disguising and transforming these desires to make them more acceptable to the conscious mind. Freud probably was assuming that people dream one or two times a night, for a few minutes—most people think that, since that's what we remember on waking. But since the 1960s, it's been clear that we dream most of the night—six hours out of eight hours of sleep. During the Rapid Eye Movement (REM) phases of sleep, which make up 15 to 20 percent of sleep time, we do have our most intense dreaming activity, but we dream in other sleep phases, too. If dreaming is all about repressed childhood desires, does everybody have the same amount of them?"

Another core tenet of Freud's dream theory is that a dream is the fulfillment of a wish. Stickgold reflects on this by describing a study using the game Tetris, a kind of geometrical puzzle. Subjects were taught to play the game, and in a sleep lab that night, 60 to 75 percent of them saw images from Tetris in their dreams. "Someone asked Mark Solms, a brilliant psychoanalyst who is trying to create a new field called neuropsychoanalysis—an oxymoron if I ever heard one—about the Tetris dream imagery. He said, 'Those are probably dreams about competition and winning'—in other words, wish fulfillments. But nobody dreamed about winning the game or competing!" Stickgold also wonders about a mother with a son in Iraq who has nightmares about her child being killed. "Maybe a Freudian can interpret that as wish-fulfillment," he says. "But I would take that as perverse, and blind adherence to an outdated model. Any dream can be interpreted as wish fulfillment, but there's no evidence that it is. In fact, there's tons of evidence against it."

Entering into the interpretation of dreams "gets very messy," Stickgold says. "If I could give the same dream to 10 analysts and they all said, 'This is about a wish for immortality,' then I could say, 'OK, at least they all agree on the same interpretation.' But they can't even do that."

and wakefulness is a subject of speculation; Czeisler says that long bouts of wakefulness may enable us to "take advantage of our greater intellectual capacity by focusing our energy and concentration. Frequent catnaps would interrupt that."

> ## "We don't know what happens when people are chronically sleep-deprived over years."
> —David White, McGinness professor of sleep medicine at the Sleep Health Center in Newton, Massachusetts

The circadian pacemaker's push for wakefulness peaks between about 8 and 10 P.M., which makes it very difficult for someone on a typical schedule to fall asleep then. "The period from two to three hours before one's regular bedtime, we call a 'wake maintenance zone,'" Czeisler says. But about an hour before bedtime, the pineal gland steps up its secretion of the hormone melatonin, which quiets the output from the SCN and hence paves the way for sleep.

Some years ago, melatonin supplements became popular as a natural sleeping pill, but as Czeisler's research has proven, light is a more powerful influence on the biological clock than melatonin. Mangelsdorf professor of natural sciences J. Woodland Hastings has shown that even a split-second of light exposure can shift the circadian cycle of a single-celled organism by a full hour. Light interferes with sleep, at least partly because it inhibits melatonin secretion and thus resets the biological clock. For this reason, those seeking a sound sleep should probably keep their bedroom as dark as possible and by all means avoid midnight trips to brightly lit bathrooms or kitchens; blue light, with its shorter wavelength—and its resemblance to the sunlit sky—has the most powerful resetting effect.

Light resets the pacemaker even in the case of some completely blind people, who generally lose circadian entrainment and suffer recurrent insomnia. "The eye has two functions, just as the ear does, with hearing and balance," says Czeisler. "The eye has vision, and also circadian photoreception." A subset of about 1,000 photosensitive retinal ganglion cells connects by a direct neural pathway to the SCN; these cells are sometimes active even in those who are blind to light. Exposure to bright light will decrease melatonin levels in some blind persons, and this subset, unlike other blind people, generally do not suffer from insomnia and are biologically entrained to the 24-hour day.

Disastrous Exhaustion

The human species, or much of it, anyway, apparently is trying to become simultaneously nocturnal and diurnal. Society has been squeezing the window for restful sleep ever narrower. (Czeisler likes to quote colleague Thomas Roth of the Henry Ford Sleep Disorders Center in Detroit, on the minimal-sleep end of the spectrum. "The percentage of the population who need less than five hours of sleep per night, rounded to a whole number," says Roth, "is zero.")

Czeisler has conducted several studies of medical interns, an institutionally sleep-deprived population who provide a hugely disproportionate fraction of the nation's healthcare services. Interns work famously long 80- and even 100-hour weeks; every other shift is typically 30 hours in duration. "On this kind of schedule, virtually everyone is impaired," he says. "Being awake more than 24 hours impairs performance as much as having a blood-alcohol level of 0.1 percent—which is legally drunk."

In addition to both acute and chronic sleep deprivation, interns sleep and wake in patterns that misalign with circadian cycles—being asked, for example, to perform with full alertness at 4 A.M. A fourth factor is that the human brain is "cold" and essentially impaired during the first half-hour after awakening—even more impaired, says Czeisler, than after 70 hours of sleeplessness. "It's a colossally bad idea to have an intern woken up by a nurse saying, 'The patient is doing badly—what shall we do?'" he says. "They might order 10 times the appropriate dose of the wrong med."

The intensity and growing technological advance of medical care only enhance the probability of errors under such conditions. Christopher Landrigan, assistant professor of pediatrics, led a study that compared interns working traditional schedules with those on an alternate schedule of fewer weekly hours and no extended (e.g., 30-hour) shifts in intensive-care units. The doctors on the tiring traditional schedule made 36 percent more serious medical errors, including 57 percent more nonintercepted serious errors, and made 5.6 times as many serious diagnostic errors.

> ## "Being awake more than 24 hours impairs performance as much as having a blood-alcohol level of 0.1 percent—which is legally drunk."

Some Harvard-affiliated teaching hospitals, like Brigham and Women's, where Czeisler works, are taking the lead in substantially reducing work hours for physicians and surgeons in training. Yet no rules limit the work hours of medical students (including those at Harvard Medical School), and at the national level, little has changed for interns and residents. Not long ago, the Accreditation Council of Graduate Medical Education, faced with the threat of federal regulation, enacted new rules limiting extended shifts to 30 hours (before the new rules, they averaged 32 hours), and capped work weeks at 80 hours (beforehand, the average was 72 hours)—with exceptions allowable up to 90 hours. "The new, self-imposed rules largely serve to reinforce the status quo," Czeisler says. "They haven't brought about fundamental change, and haven't changed the length of a typical extended shift, which is still four times as long as a normal workday. And those marathon shifts occur every other shift, all year, several years in a row during residency training."

The risks don't end when the doctors leave work. Research fellow in medicine Laura Barger led another group in a nationwide survey of interns that showed them having more than double the risk of a motor-vehicle crash when driving home after an extended shift. (They aren't alone: 60 percent of American adults drove while drowsy in the past year.)

The moral of much sleep research is startlingly simple. Your mother was right: You'll get sick, become fat, and won't work as well if you don't get a good night's sleep. So make time for rest and recovery. Stickgold likes to compare two hypothetical people, one sleeping eight hours, the other four. The latter person is awake 20 hours a day, compared to 16 hours for the first. "But if the person on four hours is just 20 percent less efficient while awake, then in 20 hours of waking he or she will get only 16 hours of work done, so it's a wash," he says. "Except that they are living on four hours of sleep a night. They're not gaining anything, but are losing a huge amount: you'll see it in their health, their social interactions, their ability to learn and think clearly. And I cannot believe they are not losing at least 20 percent in their efficiency."

Yet instead of encouraging restorative rest, many of our institutions are heading in the opposite direction. This fall, for example, Harvard will begin keeping Lamont Library open 24 hours a day, in response to student demand, and Harvard Dining Services has for several years offered midnight snacks. "These are the wrong solutions," says Stickgold. "This is like the Boston Police Department getting tired of drunk drivers killing people and setting up coffee urns outside of bars. At Harvard there is no limit on the amount of work students are assigned; you can take four courses and have three professors say, 'This is your most important course and it should take the bulk of your time.' Students are dropping to four hours of sleep a night, and the University sees it has to do something about it. But the way you deal with students overloaded with work is not by having dorms serve snacks at midnight and keeping the library open all night. Instead, you can cut back by one-third the amount of work you assign, and do that in every course without serious detriment."

Such are the prescriptions of sleep researchers, which differ radically from those of the society and the economy. The findings of the sleep labs filter only slowly into the mainstream, especially in areas like medical internships, where enormous financial pressures favor the status quo. Even at Harvard Medical School, in a four-year curriculum, only one semester hour is devoted to sleep medicine. For a sleep disorder like narcolepsy, the average time between symptom onset and diagnosis is seven years; for sleep apnea, four years. "Physicians aren't being trained to recognize sleep disorders," Czeisler says.

When all else fails, there is always the option of common sense. Sleep is quite possibly the most important factor in health, and neither caffeine nor sleeping pills nor adrenaline can substitute for it. "As it looks more and more like some of these processes occur exclusively during sleep and can't be reproduced while we are awake, the consequences of losing them look more and more terrifying," says Stickgold. "And that's the experiment we are all in the middle of, right now."

CRAIG A. LAMBERT '69, PhD '78, is deputy editor of this *Harvard Magazine.*

UNIT 10

Contemporary Health Hazards

Unit Selections

Key Points to Consider

- What diseases are most likely to have an environmental link?

- How does global warming increase the risk of disease?

- What health risks followed Hurricane Katrina?

Student Web Site

www.mhcls.com/online

Internet References

Further information regarding these Web sites may be found in this book's preface or online.

Centers for Disease Control: Flu
http://www.cdc.gov/flu

National Sleep Foundation
http://www.sleepfoundation.org

Center for the Study of Autism
http://www.autism.org

Food and Drug Administration Mad Cow Disease Page
http://www.fda.gov/oc/opacom/hottopics/bse.html

Environmental Protection Agency
http://www.epa.gov

Courtesy of Center for Disease Control

This unit examines a variety of health hazards that Americans must face on a daily basis and includes topics ranging from environmental health issues to newly emerging or reemerging infectious illnesses. During the 1970s and 1980s Americans became deeply concerned about environmental changes in our air, water, and food. While some improvements have been observed in these areas, much remains to be done as new areas of concern continue to emerge. In "Facing an Uncertain Future", Jennifer Fisher Wilson addresses issues related to health and the environment. Global warming may also be responsible for climatic changes including an increase in the number of weather disasters such as hurricanes. In the 2005 hurricane season, several notable storms affected the United States including Hurricane Katrina which left the residents of the Gulf Coast with a range of environmental health hazards. In "In Katrina's Wake", John Manuel dis-

cusses the health concerns faced by residents of the Gulf Coast following Hurricane Katrina. These include lack of potable water, untreated sewage, chemical spills, insect infestations, unsafe food, growth of toxic mold, and other sources of hazardous waste.

Newly recognized diseases such as Avian Flu, Severe Acute Respiratory Syndrome (SARS), AIDS, West Nile Virus, and Mad Cow Disease may have environmental relationships. Another disease that may have environmental relationships is autism though doctors truly don't know the exact cause. They do know, however, that autism cases continue to rise which may be due to better diagnoses or to an increase in whatever it is that is causing this vexing brain disorder that now affects one in 166 children in the United States.

While emerging diseases such as Avian Flu make headlines, other vintage viruses are making a comeback.

Mumps and whooping cough are both reemerging and affecting populations such as college students who tend to live in close quarters in college dormitories.

While this unit focuses on exogenous factors that influence our state of health, it is important to remember that health is a dynamic state representing the degree of harmony or balance that exists between endogenous and exogenous factors. This concept of balance applies to the environment as well. Due to the intimate relationship that exists between people, animals, and their environment, it is impossible to promote the concept of wellness without also safeguarding the quality of our environment, both physical and social.

'Vintage' Bugs Return

Mumps? Whooping cough? Rickets? What year is it?

MARY CARMICHAEL

Growing up in Peoria, Ill., in the 1950s, Lance Rodewald caught "measles and mumps and probably German measles," and though he doesn't remember suffering through any of them, his wife, Patricia, assures him they were all "absolutely miserable" experiences. She knows because she had them, too. Infectious diseases were a midcentury rite of passage. But as Rodewald grew up, he watched those childhood terrors retreat. Doctors started vaccinating widely in the '60s and '70s, and by the time he was old enough to have kids of his own, it seemed the only common illness left for American parents to worry about was chickenpox.

Scientists developed a vaccine for that as well. But even after his kids made it safely to adolescence, Rodewald, 52, didn't assume that the era of infectious disease in kids in the United States was over. As a pediatrician and director of the Centers for Disease Control's National Immunization Program, he had looked at the data—and seen that "all these diseases are just a plane ride away."

Or, in the case of the mumps, which is now tearing through the heartland for the first time in decades, nine plane rides away. That's how many connecting flights it took for just two infected airline passengers, one flying out of Arizona, the other from Iowa, to apparently kick-start a new eight-state epidemic that has so far sickened 1,165 people. The outbreak serves as a grim reminder that vaccines aren't perfect and that despite modern medicine's advances, germs commonly associated with the early 20th century are still very much in the world. Right now several of the mustiest-sounding diseases—whooping cough, anyone?—are spiking again. "When fewer people start getting diagnosed, there's a premature declaration of victory," says Kenneth Castro, of the CDC. "Then we let our guard down, and the diseases come back and bite us."

Public-health officials certainly weren't expecting to get "bitten" by mumps this year. Although the virus has been circulating in British kids since 2000, it hadn't caused much trouble in the United States since an outbreak in Kansas 18 years ago. The Midwest is the epicenter again, but the victims are primarily college students, not children. Once a childhood disease, the virus has now taken hold in university towns. That's partly because crowded dorms and cafeterias are breeding grounds for germs that are spread by sneezing and coughing. But there's also a factor unique to this generation of college students. In the late '80s, the measles/mumps/rubella vaccine was upgraded from one dose to two, and some of the last kids to get the less effective single-dose vaccine are in college now. Others haven't had any doses at all because some parents, fearing a purported link to autism, did not have their kids vaccinated. And even those who've had both doses aren't fully protected: the vaccine is 90, not 100, percent effective.

"Vaccine fatigue," as clinicians call it, may also explain the recent resurgence of another rare disease, whooping cough, or pertussis. Docs introduced a vaccine in the '40s, and by the '70s the disease was practically eradicated, with only a thousand or so cases per year. But as the disease's profile dwindled, parents were less careful about getting their kids the four to five necessary booster shots. Numbers started rising again in the '80s and '90s. In 2004, the most recent year for which there is full data, there were 25,800 cases. Rodewald hopes that a new adolescent booster vaccine introduced in June will put those numbers back on a downward trend.

As if they didn't have their hands full with mumps and whooping cough, doctors are also starting to worry about other blasts from the past. National statistics haven't been collected, but many papers in the medical literature argue that rickets—a vitamin deficiency long thought to be a relic of the 19th century—is increasing among African-American and Hispanic kids, particularly in the North. Doctors blame it on everything from an increase in breast-feeding (breast milk doesn't contain much vitamin D) to the overuse of sunscreen (the body needs ultraviolet light to produce the vitamin). Another vintage ailment, scarlet fever, the scourge of "Little Women" and "The Velveteen Rabbit," though easily treatable with antibiotics now, also endures. It infects hundreds of kids each year, but pediatricians will usually say those kids have "a symptom of strep throat," not scarlet fever, if only so as not to scare the parents. Finally, though tuberculosis is at a record low, a nasty drug-resistant strain has emerged. Seems like old times.

In Katrina's Wake

JOHN MANUEL

Hurricane Katrina has been called the most devastating natural environmental calamity in U.S. history. Visitors to the scene say the destruction is worse than anyone can imagine. Scientists also say that some perceived health threats have been overblown and others understated. Months after Katrina roared into the Gulf Coast, the environmental health implications of the storm are still being assessed.

Katrina presented residents of the Gulf Coast with a bewildering array of environmental health hazards. Aside from standing floodwater, hazards included a lack of potable water, sewage treatment, and electricity; chemical spills; swarms of insects (with anecodotal accounts of vermin and hungry domestic dogs); food contamination; disrupted transportation; mountains of debris; buildings damaged and destroyed; rampant mold growth; tainted fish and shellfish populations; and many potential sources of hazardous waste. Some impacts, such as deaths from drowning and injuries from cleaning up debris, have been relatively easy to determine. Others, such as post-traumatic stress disorder from the loss of homes and loved ones, may never be fully quantified.

In the weeks following the storm, federal agencies such as the NIEHS, the Centers for Disease Control and Prevention (CDC), and the Environmental Protection Agency (EPA), as well as state environmental and public health agencies, sent scientists to the region to begin assessing the environmental and human health impact of the disaster. Much of what they found was presented on October 20 at a meeting of the National Academies Institute of Medicine's Roundtable on Environmental Health Sciences, Research, and Medicine (commonly known as the EHSRT), supported by the NIEHS, the CDC, the EPA, Exxon-Mobile Corporation, the American Chemistry Council, and the Brita Water Research Institute. Still more information continues to emerge today. And much simply remains to be seen.

Katrina Hits

Katrina, rated as a Category 4 hurricane on the Saffir-Simpson scale, made landfall near New Orleans on 29 August 2005. Wind damage extended as far as 150 miles inland. Heavy rain battered the area, and the storm surge—measuring as high as 30 feet and sweeping several miles inland—breached several levees intended to protect New Orleans from the waters of Lake Pontchartrain. Water poured through the breaks in the days following the storm, covering approximately 80% of the city with water as deep as three meters. The American Red Cross estimates that more than 354,000 homes along the Gulf Coast were destroyed or damaged beyond repair by Katrina and, a month later, Hurricane Rita. Hundreds of small manufacturers or businesses using chemicals or fuels also were impacted.

Flooding, wind, and waves caused major damage to buildings and infrastructure whose integrity is key to the environmental health of the local citizenry. The EPA estimated that more than 200 sewage treatment plants in Louisiana, Mississippi, and Alabama were affected, with almost all the plants around New Orleans knocked out of action. Loss of power meant lift stations (which pump sewage uphill) could not work, causing sewage to overflow into houses and streets.

The region struck by Katrina and Rita is home to a large number of oil refineries and chemical plants. Prior to Katrina, the EPA had identified nearly 400 sites in the affected area as possibly needing cleanup because of their potential impact on human health. Following the storm, the U.S. Coast Guard reported numerous oil spills from refineries and tank farms in South Louisiana. A story in the September 30 *Boston Globe* reported that Katrina damaged 140 oil and gas platforms in the Gulf of Mexico, 43 seriously, including some that floated away or sank.

Across the Gulf Coast, more than 1.5 million people evacuated as the storm approached. More than 100,000 stayed behind in New Orleans, unwilling or unable to leave. As New Orleans flooded, thousands waded through chest-deep floodwaters to reach shelters or higher ground. Thousands more remained trapped in homes, hospitals, and nursing homes. Conditions in shelters rapidly became unsanitary. Many people were exposed to the elements for five days or more, living with little or no food, drinking water, or medicine. As of December 5, the death toll was reported at 1,071 in Louisiana, 228 in Mississippi, 14 in Florida, 2 in Alabama, and 2 in Georgia.

First Response

Numerous federal, state, and local agencies, as well as private individuals and relief groups, swung into action in the wake of the storm. Troops from the U.S. Army, Coast Guard, and

National Guard as well as state and local officials and private citizens rescued those they could. The Federal Emergency Management Agency (FEMA) was assigned the lead in disaster relief planning and administration, including provision of emergency food and shelter and contracting for debris removal. The Department of Health and Human Services (DHHS) declared a public health emergency in the Gulf states and directed the CDC to take appropriate action. The CDC deployed more than 600 professionals into the disaster zone, including specialists in public health nursing, occupational safety and health, laboratory science, medicine, epidemiology, sanitation, environmental health, disease surveillance, public information, and health risk communication.

The CDC also joined with the EPA to set up a joint task force to conduct an environmental health needs and habitability assessment to identify critical public health issues for the reinhabitation of New Orleans. This city was unique among the areas hit in that it was the only one left with standing water. Major urban areas in Mississippi and Alabama, while devastated, did not remain flooded.

In advance of the storm's arrival, the EPA had predeployed teams to the area, with the mission of guiding debris disposal, assisting in the restoration of drinking and wastewater treatment systems, and containing hazardous waste spills. Immediately after the storm, these teams used their 60 watercraft to help search-and-rescue efforts, rescuing about 800 people, according to EPA administrator Stephen Johnson. Five days after the storm, the EPA began testing floodwaters in New Orleans for biological and chemical contamination.

In coordination with the Louisiana Department of Environmental Quality (LDEQ), the EPA analyzed floodwaters for more than 100 hazardous pollutants such as volatile and semivolatile organic compounds, metals, pesticides, herbicides, and polychlorinated biphenyls. They also tested for biological agents such as *Escherichia coli.* Their testing revealed "greatly elevated" levels of *E. coli,* as much as ten times higher than EPA's recommended levels for contact. According to the EPA, agency scientists found levels of lead and arsenic at some sites in excess of drinking water standards—a potential threat given the possibility of hand-to-mouth exposure. The EPA posted these and other findings on its Hurricane Response 2005 website (http://www.epa.gov/katrina/), created after the storm.

Shortly after the hurricane struck, the U.S. Coast Guard began working with the EPA, the Louisiana state government, and private industries to identify and recover spilled oil along the coast. The team identified 6 major, 4 medium, and 134 minor spills totaling 8 million gallons. One of the most notorious spills occurred at the Murphy Oil Company plant, which dumped more than 25,000 barrels of oil into the streets of Chalmette and Meraux, Louisiana. As of December 7, the Coast Guard reported the recovery of 3.8 million gallons, with another 1.7 million evaporated, 2.4 million dispersed, and 100,000 onshore.

Meanwhile, the NIEHS was joining with Duke University Medical Center, the NIH, and the CDC to provide assistance with relief and recovery operations along the Gulf Coast, as well as working at home to establish a website on environmental health issues related to Katrina.

Floodwater Hazards

Kevin Stephens is director of the New Orleans Department of Health. He was in charge of interpreting the EPA data and advising citizens and responders about the health hazards presented by the floodwaters. "I struggled every day to determine what [the data] meant and what to tell our health workers and the public," he says. "What does 'not an immediate health hazard' mean when you have people wading through the water? What does 'not in excess of drinking water standards' mean? Is it a danger if you get your hands wet and touch your mouth?" Journalists claimed the floodwaters were a "toxic gumbo" of dangerous chemicals and microbes, raising fears that any contact was a health threaten.

These concerns prompted a team of scientists led by John Pardue, director of the Louisiana Water Resources Research Institute at Louisiana State University (LSU), to conduct its own study of the New Orleans floodwaters. The report, published 15 November 2005 in *Environmental Science & Technology,* stated categorically that, contrary to claims in the media, the floodwater was not a "toxic soup."

"Chemical oxygen demand and fecal coliform bacteria were elevated in surface floodwater, but typical of stormwater runoff in the region," the report said. "Lead, arsenic, and in some cases chromium exceeded drinking water standards, but with the exception of some elevated lead concentrations were generally typical of stormwater." The LSU study also found only low concentrations (less than 1%) of benzene, toluene, and ethylbenzene even in places where there was a visible oil sheen. "Collectively, these data indicate that Katrina floodwater is similar to normal stormwater runoff, but with somewhat elevated lead and VOC concentrations," the report concluded.

However, the LSU study was limited to two areas within the city of New Orleans, and the authors warned that conditions could be different elsewhere, particularly in Lake Pontchartrain, where floodwaters were being pumped. LSU and the University of Colorado are currently conducting studies of Lake Pontchartrain looking for a wide range of pathogens. The Colorado team is measuring aerosols created by pumping floodwater into the lake, while the LSU team is analyzing the lake water itself.

More Water Hazards

Still other threats were posed by water. As of December 9, the EPA reported that 99% of the waste treatment and water supply systems were back online, but some had been out of operation for weeks. At the October 20 EHSRT, Howard Frumkin, director of the National Center for Environmental Health and Agency for Toxic Substances and Disease Registry (NCEH/ATSDR), said that despite the percentage of sewage treatment plants already online at that point, the danger wasn't over. "We have no guarantees that sewage being flushed is getting to treatment plants," he said. "Raw sewage is going into the Mississippi River."

Though most water supply systems may be functioning again, the safety of distribution lines that were flooded can't yet be ensured either. "There are possible changes in pipe ecology due to the intrusion of contaminants," said Frumkin. "And we have additional concerns for homes on wells." Louisiana officials speaking at the roundtable said there are dozens of community water systems and tens of thousands of private wells that need to be tested for contamination.

Standing water poses a different threat, serving as a breeding ground for bacteria and mosquitoes. Even prior to Katrina, Louisiana had the highest number of reported cases of West Nile virus (66) of any state in the union, according to the CDC. West Nile virus can be transmitted to humans via mosquito bites, and the warm, wet weather following the storm was ideal for breeding of mosquitoes. The U.S. Air Force sprayed areas of standing water with pesticides to kill mosquito larvae. The CDC reported on its Update on CDC's Response to Hurricanes website that postspraying surveillance at ten sites found a 91% reduction in total mosquito density compared to prespraying surveillance results.

The Gulf Coast is also known for the presence of the bacterium *Vibrio vulnificus*. This relative of the pathogen that causes cholera thrives in brackish waters in warmer times of the year. Humans may become infected by eating contaminated seafood or through open wounds exposed to water. While not harmful to individuals in good health, it can be fatal to those with liver damage. Health officials at the roundtable reported counting 22 cases of illness induced by *V. vulnificus* following the storm, including 5 deaths.

In late September, the EPA launched the Ocean Survey Vessel *Bold* to conduct water quality testing in the river channels and nearshore waters of the Mississippi Delta. The agency monitored 20 areas to determine whether fecal pollution from flooded communities had spread into these waters. All 20 monitoring stations showed that, at the time, the water was safe for primary contact, including swimming. The EPA said on its website, however, that the data "should not be used to assess the safety of consuming raw or undercooked molluscan shellfish."

In the wake of the storm, Louisiana, Mississippi, and Alabama closed their shellfishing waters until testing could be done. On December 8, the three states issued a joint press release saying that fish and shellfish samples collected and analyzed since the hurricanes "show no reason for concern about the consumption of Gulf seafood." Louisiana and Alabama subsequently reopened their waters, while Mississippi's oyster reefs remain closed pending additional studies.

Toxicants in Sediment and Air

Health officials also anticipated a threat from contaminated sediment in the days and weeks following the storm. As floodwaters were pumped out of inundated areas, a dark sludge was found coating buildings, land, and pavement. *E. coli* was detected at elevated levels in many sediment samples taken from around New Orleans, implying the presence of fecal bacteria. The EPA has no standards for determining human health risks from *E. coli* in sediment, but warned people to limit exposure, and if exposed, to wash skin with soap and water.

The EPA was concerned, too, about the region's Superfund sites, which include former dump sites of pesticides and dioxins. The EPA identified 54 Superfund sites in the affected area.

Officials worried that at least some of these sites might have been compromised, releasing toxic chemicals into the land or water. Johnson reported at the EHSRT that as of October 20, the EPA had visually inspected all of the sites and sampled many. As of December 5, the EPA's posted test results for these sites indicated that none were compromised in a way that would present a human health hazard.

Elsewhere, as late as November 20, chemical testing of sediment samples in Louisiana's Orleans and St. Bernard Parishes indicated the continued presence of petroleum. However, the EPA's website states that exposures of emergency responders at these levels are not expected to cause adverse health effects as long as the proper personal protective equipment is worn, such as gloves and safety glasses. Volatile and semivolatile organic compounds, pesticides, and metals including aluminum were found, but at levels below what the ATSDR and CDC consider to be immediately hazardous to human health. However, the site continues, "EPA and ATSDR/CDC continue to recommend that residents avoid all contact with sediment deposited by floodwater, where possible, due to potential concerns associated with long-term skin contact."

The Natural Resources Defense Council (NRDC) and a host of local environmental groups paint a darker picture of the contamination situation. In a December 1 press release, the NRDC stated that tests it had conducted revealed "dangerously high levels" of industrial chemicals and heavy metals in the sediment covering much of New Orleans. For example, tests found arsenic levels in some neighborhoods that exceeded EPA safety limits by a factor of 30.

"We found arsenic and other cancer causing contaminants in sediment all across the entire city," said Monique Hardin, codirector of the New Orleans–based Advocates for Human Rights, at an NRDC press briefing. "We also found hot spots where there were some nasty surprises, such as banned pesticides." The groups urged the EPA to begin cleaning up or removing contaminated topsoil across the city and to conduct further testing in certain neighborhoods.

The NRDC also challenged the EPA's assertion that the flooded Superfund sites posed no threat. The December 1 press release stated that NRDC's own assessment of one of these sites, the New Orleans Agricultural Street Landfill Superfund Site, showed "visible leachate emerging from the site and spreading across the street and onto a local senior center's property. Sediment testing at this site found contamination as much as 20 times higher than the EPA soil cleanup standards for four [polycyclic aromatic hydrocarbons]."

LDEQ toxicologist Tom Harris responded in press reports that the NRDC's findings were fundamentally flawed because arsenic levels are naturally above the EPA's residential standard in Louisiana and elsewhere. "I have never personally seen soil samples come back below the residential screening level for arsenic," Harris told PlanetArk World Environmental News on December 5. "It's a naturally occurring [element] you can find everywhere." The state of Louisiana and the EPA continue to perform testing of sediment to determine when to give an all-clear to residents with respect to exposure to sediment.

The EPA has also addressed concerns about air quality in the Gulf region. According to Johnson, most of the agency's stationary air quality monitors were knocked out by Katrina. The EPA reinstalled the stationary monitors and employed their Airborne Spectral Photometrics Environmental Collection Technology to undertake airborne monitoring. The EPA also employed two Trace Atmospheric Gas Analyzer buses, self-contained mobile laboratories capable of continuous real-time sampling and analysis.

Air samples were tested for volatile priority pollutants such as benzene, toluene, and xylene, which are commonly found in gasoline, as well as other industrial solvents. The screening results indicated that chemical concentrations in most areas were below the ATSDR health guidelines of concern. The EPA stated on its website, "The low level of volatile pollutants is not surprising as contaminants may be bound in sediment. Monitoring data directly around Murphy Oil spill reveal some slightly elevated levels of benzene and toluene that are associated with petroleum release. Long-term exposure (a year or longer) at the levels measured would be required for health effects to be a concern."

Air may also play a role in an illness known as "shelter cough," or "Katrina cough." Shelter cough is presumed to be an allergic reaction to some particulate matter in the air, according to Stephens. However, despite the presence of shelter cough and earlier concerns about a wave of infectious diseases in the wake of Katrina, acute respiratory illness have made up only 8.7% of diagnoses between August 29 and September 24, according to the October 7 *Morbidity and Mortality Weekly Report*. "We have no evidence of infectious disease outbreaks," Stephens said at the EHSRT.

A Mountain of Debris

The amount of debris generated by Katrina is by all accounts staggering. FEMA estimates there are 39.9 million cubic yards of debris in Mississippi alone. Mark Williams, administrator of solid waste policy, planning, and grants at the Mississippi Department of Environmental Quality (MDEQ), says that state has enough space for the initial removal of debris to staging areas, but not for long-term deposition in landfills.

Jimmy Guidry, medical director of Louisiana's Department of Health and Hospitals, says Louisiana, too, lacks sufficient landfill space for all the debris: "We have more than three hundred thousand refrigerators that need to be disposed of. All these have freon in them." Guidry said at the roundtable that the Louisiana Department of Environmental Quality has approved dozens of temporary debris disposal sites, which will have to be carefully monitored.

Appliances can be recycled for metal content. Televisions and household computers pose a different problem. A single computer monitor contains 4.5 pounds of lead, and computer processing units contain trace metals that can leach out of unlined landfills.

As much as one-third of the debris is vegetative matter that can be burned or chipped for compost. The rest must be recycled or landfilled. Williams says burning of vegetative debris has been allowed in Mississippi for some months and is now largely complete. He adds, "EPA in conjunction with MDEQ has done some monitoring in the area [of controlled burns], which has indicated some elevated levels of formaldehyde and acrolein in certain areas." In the interest of minimizing air pollution, the EPA and MDEQ allowed only clean vegetative debris to be burned and strongly encouraged the use of air curtain destructors and other combustion units in the early stages of cleanup.

Williams says another daunting challenge was disposing of thousand of tons of food—chicken, fish, and beef—rotting in warehouses on the docks. Officials from Mississippi's Natural Resources Conservation Service said more than 6 million dead animals—poultry and livestock—had to be removed from farms in the affected area. Now officials are dealing with wastes in homes, including such items as propane tanks, household pesticides, and asbestos from roofing, insulation, and other home sources. The waste is taken to staging areas where hazardous waste is pulled out for disposal by the EPA. As of October 31, the EPA had collected an estimated 1 million pounds of household hazardous waste in Louisiana (the agency did not report on collections in other states).

Injury Protection

One of the major concerns officials have with regard to the handling and disposal of debris is the safety of workers. "We have a large number of workers coming to the Gulf seeking employment, and many of them are not properly trained and protected," says Max Kiefer, assistant director of emergency preparedness and response for the National Institute for Occupational Safety and Health (NIOSH). High-risk occupations include debris removal, levee rebuilding, residential refurbishment, and infrastructure rebuilding.

NIOSH is trying to keep workers apprised of health hazards. "We have assessed exposure to silica and metals during levee rebuilding, debris removal, and tasks involving the sediment," Kiefer said at the roundtable. "We also worried that people were wearing protective gear that may induce heat stress. After assessing certain tasks, we were able to downgrade our gear recommendations in light of that. Psychological stress on responders has been significant. But by far the biggest issue has been injuries—lacerations, falls, and trips." NIOSH is providing guidance for responders and providers on the CDC hurricane response website.

Private citizens also face significant risk of injury during cleanup. Officials talk of a "second wave" of injury following a natural disaster as citizens undertake to remove debris and repair buildings themselves. Will Service, the industrial hygiene coordinator with the North Carolina Office of Public Health Preparedness and Response, worked in a mobile hospital in Waveland, Mississippi, in the days following the storm. "We saw a lot of injuries from things like chain saws used during cleanup," Service says. "People are tired, their thinking isn't clear. They're doing things they don't normally do."

Illnesses and injuries associated with Katrina are being tracked by the CDC, with updates posted regularly on its website. Confirming what public health officials warned about a second wave of injuries, the most common diagnosis (26.2%) in reporting hospitals and clinics from September 8 to October 4 was injury. The major cause of injury was falling, followed closely by vehicle crash–related injuries (likely related to missing or nonfunctioning traffic signs and signals). Cutting and piercing injuries ranked third.

Coming Home to Hazards

Mold growth in houses damaged by Katrina is of enormous concern to health and housing officials. Estimates of the number of homes suffering water damage range in the hundreds of thousands. Claudette Reichel, an LSU professor of education and housing specialist, says that virtually every home that sustained flood damage will experience mold growth. "Houses that people were not allowed back into for weeks will all have mold, and that mold will have had time to multiply, spread, and get really thick," she says. Says Frumkin, "The magnitude of mold exposure in the Gulf region will in many instances greatly exceed anything we have seen before, adding to the concern and uncertainty regarding health effects."

How or even whether mold causes human health problems is disputed by public health professionals, but most acknowledge a connection. "It is a very difficult science, because there is no clear-cut dose–response threshold," Reichel says. "It is highly dependent upon the type of mold, whether the mold is producing a mycotoxin, the susceptibility of the patient, and the amount of exposure."

The CDC states that people who are sensitive to mold may experience stuffy nose, irritated eyes, or wheezing. People allergic to mold may have difficulty in breathing. People with weak immune systems may develop lung infections.

Health and housing officials advise homeowners and renters to throw out any furnishings, insulation, and bedding that may have gotten wet, to clean walls and floors with soap and water, to ventilate, and then to close up and dehumidify the home.

The CDC also reported a spike in post-Katrina carbon monoxide poisoning in the Gulf Coast in the October 7 *Morbidity and Mortality Weekly Report*. From August 29 to September 24, a total of 51 cases of carbon monoxide poisoning, including 5 deaths, were reported in Alabama, Louisiana, and Mississippi. After the hurricanes, many residents used gasoline-powered portable generators to provide electricity to their homes and businesses. These devices produce carbon monoxide, which can build up to fatal levels if run inside a living space or garage.

A number of other health issues loom as residents begin returning to New Orleans, where health care services aren't widely available, sewer and water services are still spotty, and structural inspections aren't complete. Residents have asked city officials for a health assessment to address their concerns about oil spills, mold contamination, and the possible long-term health effects related to mold and chemical exposures. "We are developing an assessment tool for this purpose, and we anticipate that it will be developed for the beginning of [2006]," says Stephens.

Many health care professionals worry that mental health may be the most serious longterm health issue resulting from Katrina. Hundreds of thousands of people across the Gulf region have had their homes destroyed. Thousands are still living in shelters. Many have no jobs, no health insurance, and no job prospects. "We are seeing a lot of symptoms of post-traumatic stress disorder," says Marty Allen, a psychologist with the Mississippi Department of Mental Health. "The trauma was not just the day of the storm. People are still being traumatized by living in tents, not having jobs, and having to walk for miles just to get food and water."

Lessons Learned?

What lessons have been learned from Katrina with respect to environmental health? Debate about how to protect Gulf Coast citizens from hurricanes and storm surge was ongoing before the storm and will continue with renewed intensity.

In Mississippi, Governor Haley Barbour enlisted the Chicago-based Congress for New Urbanism to come up with recommendations for rebuilding the Gulf Coast. The Congress sponsored a week-long Mississippi Renewal Forum in October attended by some of the nation's leading architects, engineers, and urban planners. Working with local leaders, the teams produced reports for 11 coastal towns impacted by the storm. Recommendations include improving the connectivity between towns by moving the CSX freight line north and transforming the abandoned right-of-way into a boulevard for cars and transit, connecting the Gulf region towns with high-speed rail, realigning and revising U.S. 90 to become a pedestrian-friendly "beach boulevard," and creating a Gulf Coast bikeway.

A similar process is under way in Louisiana under the auspices of the Louisiana Recovery Authority created by Governor Kathleen Blanco. The authority is developing short-, medium-, and long-range plans to guide the rebuilding of Louisiana in the wake of the hurricanes. At the authority's request, the American Association of Architects, in collaboration with the American Planning Association, presented the Louisiana Recovery and Rebuilding Conference on November 10–12. The authority has developed a 100-day plan that includes completion of an environmental evaluation of damages caused by the hurricanes and development of recommendations for how to proceed with reconstruction.

Discussion will center on how to protect New Orleans from further flooding and whether certain low-lying parts of the city should even be reoccupied. Such decisions will be made in the months and years to come. Meanwhile, environmental and public health officials have drawn some conclusions about how to better respond to events like Katrina.

Officials at the EHSRT agreed that communication in advance and in the wake of natural and man-made disasters is key. Fears and rumors of disease ran rampant in the days following Katrina. Citizens, the media, and even public health officials did not know which factors presented a genuine health threat and which did not. Federal agencies conducted testing and provided data, but people often did not know how to interpret those data with respect to the kinds of exposures they were encountering.

"The public health community must be actively involved and articulate key health issues," said Kellogg Schwab, an assistant professor at Johns Hopkins Bloomberg School of Public Health. "We must keep the message simple and focused. We must develop effective strategies to provide targeted timely results. We must provide concise and accurate public health information and advice."

Officials also agreed that responders must be properly trained and deployed, provided with proper protective gear and an effective communications system (land lines and cell phones were inoperative in much of the area for weeks after Katrina). Health officials must be able to assess the particular kinds of exposures that people have been subjected to and respond accordingly.

"Your response strategy for exposure varies with each event," said Paul Lioy, deputy director of the Environmental and Occupational Health Sciences Institute at Rutgers University. "The World Trade Center [collapse] was an instantaneous acute air exposure event like we'd never experienced. Katrina for the most part involved an acute water exposure event, but the exposure was over a longer period of time."

Lioy pointed out the need for a national review of the kind of standards and guidelines necessary to ensure that the correct information is given out to the public about immediate hazards versus long-term exposures and risks. "Comparison to general drinking water or ambient air quality standards are not sufficient for guiding the public or public officials during an acute exposure event," he said.

Most of all, roundtable participants agreed, Katrina represents a chance for officials across all levels of government to do things better—evacuation planning, urban design, communication, environmental monitoring, and involvement of citizenry, particularly minority and low-income residents. John McLachlan, director of the Tulane/Xavier Center for Bioenvironmental Research, said that preparing for disasters like Katrina requires the involvement of virtually every academic discipline. To that end, Tulane and Xavier are creating a Katrina Environmental Research and Restoration Network (KERRN) of researchers who share data and ideas across disciplinary, geographical, and institutional lines. Paraphrasing one of his colleagues, McLachlan stated, "This is the mother of all multidisciplinary problems."

From *Environmental Health Perspectives,* January 2006. Published by National Institute of Environmental Health Sciences. www.ehponline.org

Facing an Uncertain Climate

JENNIFER FISHER WILSON

Our climate is changing, and the results are increasingly disruptive. Droughts, dust storms, and wildfires are occurring more often in some areas, while others are plagued by an increasing number of intense rainstorms and hurricanes. Glaciers are melting, sea levels are rising, coasts are eroding, and heat waves are happening at historic rates, seriously threatening the survival of ecosystems and placing approximately 25% of all plant and animal species on the path to extinction by 2050.[1] Melting sea ice has shortened the season during which polar bears can search for food and has hindered their reproduction; the U.S. Fish and Wildlife Service is on the verge of deeming them the first mammals in danger of extinction because of global warming.

Human health is at stake, too. Research has linked climate change to a long list of health problems, including asthma, allergies, infectious diseases, heart disease, and cancer. The World Health Organization (WHO) has estimated that warming and precipitation trends already claim at least 150 000 lives annually worldwide and that this number will climb to at least 300 000 annually by 2030.

Nearly all scientists agree that the buildup of greenhouse gases in the atmosphere—particularly carbon dioxide from combustion of fossil fuels and forest burning—is warming the Earth and altering the natural climate and weather patterns in new and potentially perilous ways. Carbon dioxide levels are higher now than at any time in the past 800 000 years and are predicted to increase significantly in this century. The effects are likely to imperil health both directly (from extreme weather events, such as hurricanes, heat waves, or floods) and indirectly (from the disturbance of complex ecological processes, such as changes in patterns of infectious disease, freshwater supplies, and food availability).[2] A seminal report from the Intergovernmental Panel on Climate Change, a collaboration of more than 2000 scientists from 100 countries, predicted that the coming years would see an increase in extreme weather events as well as more climate variability and longer-term climate changes associated with rising water temperatures and changing ecosystems.[3] The fourth assessment report from the Intergovernmental Panel on Climate Change, which is due out in spring 2007, will review the evidence for the effects that climate change is already causing.

Just how much climate change will affect health is largely unknowable at this point, but scientists have warned that underestimating the potential threat could be dangerous. "Climate change is being realized more rapidly than scientists anticipated, and the impacts on health have already been greater than the experts projected for this decade. That doesn't happen very often," said R. Sari Kovats, MSc, an epidemiologist at the Public and Environmental Health Research Unit of the London School of Hygiene and Tropical Medicine. Kovats noted that different areas of the world will be affected in different ways depending on such factors as current disease burdens, socioeconomic status, and available public health resources.

While policymakers focus on ways to reduce or reverse the warming trend, doctors and public health workers should prepare to address the potential health effects. "A wealth of information already exists about the potential impacts of climate change on human health that can help inform decision making and public health interventions," said Joel Scheraga, PhD, director of global change research at the U.S. Environmental Protection Agency (EPA). "Tools that support public health officials can be developed, and decisions and actions can be taken, despite the existence of scientific uncertainties. Proactive decisions will yield public health benefits today, while at the same time increasing resilience to future climate change."

Linking Climate Change with Health

Although global warming has been studied for decades, researchers only truly began to assess the health impact in the 1990s. Research on the effects of such large-scale climate phenomena, such as El Niño, on diseases, such as malaria and cholera, demonstrated that large-scale climate processes could affect human health. The effects of local weather patterns on such diseases as malaria, encephalitis, dengue, and leptospirosis have been known for some time. However, in general, such effects were not carefully examined until climate change became apparent. In 1996, a joint effort of the WHO, the World Meteorological Organization, and the United Nations Environment Program produced the first book addressing this research.[4]

According to Kovats, who co-edited the 1996 report and various follow-up reports, many people did not take this issue seriously at first. However, she says, "the whole research area has developed rapidly in recent years," and the link has become more and more apparent. Many countries, including Canada, Japan, the Netherlands, the United Kingdom, and the United States, have now conducted reviews of the potential impact of climate change on the health of their populations and initiated the development of adaptive strategies for the future.

It is likely that the first significant and detectable impact on health will be alterations in the geographical range—particularly altitude—of certain vector species, according to Kovats. For instance, scientists have recently attributed changes in the northern limit of the disease-transmitting European tick in Sweden over the past 2 decades to a warming climate.[5] Recent malaria outbreaks in the highlands of East Africa and elsewhere may also stem from climate change. The major heatwave of 2003 in France—responsible for as many as 15 000 deaths—was arguably an impact of climate change as well, Kovats noted.[6]

Significant uncertainty still exists. Scheraga noted the lack of long-term, high-quality data sets and limited research about the probable health impacts associated with global climate change. Health is also affected by social, economic, political, and technology factors, as well as other environmental conditions, making it hard to winnow out the specific effects of climate change. "There certainly are health concerns associated with climate change . . . a wealth of information already exists about the potential impacts of climate change on human health that can help inform decision-making and public health interventions. [But] researchers cannot look at climate change's effects on a population in isolation, so it can be difficult to tell if a health outcome is due to climate change or another variable," Scheraga said. Even so, scientists have begun outlining the potential health risks brought about by climate change on the basis of available data.

Risks for the United States

Scientists hypothesize that people living in developed nations like the United States will be the least affected by the effects of climate change, in part because public health services and high living standards protect them. For instance, vigilant public health systems in North America or northern Europe make it unlikely that malaria will reestablish itself there. Last year's Hurricane Katrina disaster provided valuable information on how to better handle future severe weather events. People may also be more prepared for summer heat waves now that the National Weather Service has begun issuing severe heat advisories in addition to its usual severe storm warnings. These advisories have prompted the news media to disseminate specific tips on which groups are the most vulnerable during a heat wave and what precautions people should take.

Even with such public health strategies, however, scientists predict that Americans will still feel the effects of climate change in the coming decades. Extreme weather events are still unpredictable and dangerous, causing accidental injuries, outbreaks of infectious diseases, impaired mental health, and death even when preparations are in place.

It is also difficult to prepare for worsening air quality due to rising carbon dioxide levels. People with heart disease—already the leading cause of death in America—are particularly at risk from poor air quality. The particles that cause global warming, such as soot generated by vehicles, power plants, and forest fires, also cause air pollution—and these air pollutants pose the greatest risk for people who have heart disease. Gases found in polluted air, such as ozone, sulfur dioxide, and nitrogen dioxide, also contribute to heart disease.

Poor air quality also contributes to breathing difficulties. Already, the country has seen a 4-fold increase in the prevalence of asthma since 1980. "The combination of issues related to climate change and environmental change—carbon dioxide impact on plants, diesel particles, changes in the seasons, changes in ozone levels, dust storms coming across the Atlantic from African droughts—are most likely contributing to this tremendous increase in asthma," said Paul Epstein, MD, associate director of the Center for Health and the Global Environment at Harvard Medical School in Boston. Elevated carbon dioxide levels in particular trigger asthma and allergies by amplifying ragweed pollen production and fungal spore formation. Scientists at the U.S. Department of Agriculture determined that ragweed plants already produce twice as much pollen as they did 100 years ago. When ragweed plants were grown in conditions with twice the current ambient level of carbon dioxide, pollen production increased by more than 60%,[7] indicating that such production will continue to increase in the wild.

Other nuisance plants will also thrive with elevated carbon dioxide levels. Earlier this year, scientists showed that increased carbon dioxide resulted in increased photosynthesis, more efficient water use, more growth, and a larger population biomass of poison ivy. Moreover, the plants would produce a more allergenic form of urushiol, the compound that causes dermatitis in 80% of humans. Since contact with poison ivy is already one of the most widely reported ailments at poison centers in the United States,[8] an increase in the incidence and severity of this dermatitis would have significant effects.

Elevated carbon dioxide levels will also lead to increasing problems from disease-carrying ticks, mosquitoes (such as *Culex pipiens,* the common pest mosquito that carries West Nile virus), and rodents, all of which are likely to infest larger areas of the country as the climate becomes warmer. Epstein predicted that doctors would soon start to see more cases of *Borrelia burgdorferi* infection (Lyme disease) and linked increased weather variability to the emergence of West Nile virus, hantavirus, and other rodentborne diseases in the United States. In a recent article, he explained how climate changes directly influence the disease cycles: "*Culex pipiens* thrive in shallow pools of foul water that remain in drains during droughts. When dry springs yield to sweltering summers, viral development accelerates and, with it, the cycle of mosquito-to-bird transmission. During the hot summer of 2002, West Nile virus traveled across the country, infecting 230 species of animals, including 138 species of birds, along the way. Many of the infected birds of prey normally help to rein in rodent populations that can spread hantavirus, arenaviruses, and *Yersinia* and *Leptospira* bacteria, as well as ticks infected with *Borrelia burgdorferi*."[9]

Table. Known and Probable Health Hazards Resulting from Climate Variability and Change*

Temperature extremes, primarily more hot days, will lead to more daily deaths and disease events; some temperate countries will experience reduced winter deaths and disease events.

Floods will cause more injuries, deaths, infectious diseases, and mental health disorders.

Increased aeroallergen production due to a longer pollen season will lead to more hay fever and asthma; decreased aeroallergen production from shorter seasons of pollen circulation will reduce exposure in some regions.

Food poisoning (diarrheal disease), especially salmonellosis, will increase due to higher temperatures.

Waterborne infections, particularly cholera, might increase.

Vectorborne infections related to mosquitoes and ticks will tend to increase with warming and certain changes in rainfall patterns.

Regional crop yields may decrease in many low-latitude and low-rainfall regions while increasing in some places that are currently too cold for growing.

Fishery declines may lead to protein shortages in poor populations and possible increased contamination.

Rising sea levels may cause population displacement, lost livelihood, and exposure to coastal tidal surges and floods and may also lead to salinization of freshwater and coastal soil.

*Adapted from reference 11.

International Health Risks

According to the WHO, climate-sensitive diseases transmitted through insect or rodent vectors or through water pose a much larger threat to developing nations, where health standards are variable. Malaria, already one of the world's most serious and complex public health problems, is the disease most likely to be affected by climate change.[10] The countries at greatest risk from climate-triggered changes in malaria outbreaks are those at the fringes of its current distribution, including central Asia and Eastern Europe;[2] areas where lower temperatures limit malaria transmission, such as the highlands in East Africa, are also vulnerable. Climate change is less likely to affect malaria mortality and morbidity rates in lowland regions where the disease is already endemic, such as tropical African countries.

A warming climate would also increase the rates of dengue, a mosquitoborne disease that can lead to fatal hemorrhagic fever. The disease's prevalence has grown rapidly; dengue is now endemic in more than 100 countries, a vast increase from 9 countries before 1970. According to the WHO, dengue is spreading because the geographic distribution of the viruses that cause it and their mosquito vectors is expanding. Increasingly dense urban populations mean that more people come in contact with the vector, especially in areas favorable for mosquito

breeding. The largest increase in infection rates from climate change would probably occur at the northern and southern distribution limits of the virus, where mosquitoes are present but development of the virus is currently limited by lower temperatures.[2]

Both developing and developed nations are vulnerable to many threats from climate change. In a recent review for *Lancet*,[11] the authors, who are leaders in the field, assessed the available research and compiled a list of the known and probable global health hazards resulting from climate variability and change (Table). Another recent report, by economist Sir Nicholas Stern for the government of the United Kingdom, documented how continued climate change could bring hunger, water shortages, and coastal flooding to millions of people worldwide and seriously threaten global growth and development.[12]

Preparation and Adaptation

With the recognition that climate change is real, work has begun on developing strategies for coping. Many industrialized countries are already working to reduce their vulnerability to the health effects of climate change. According to Scheraga, examples of such anticipatory adaptation in the United States include building codes and zoning to prevent storm or flood damage; severe weather warning systems; improved disease surveillance and prevention programs; disaster preparedness; improved sanitation systems; wider use of protective technologies, such as sunscreen, water purification, and vaccinations; education of public health professionals and the public; and ongoing research to address key knowledge gaps in climate–health relationships.

For developing countries, the WHO and the United Nations Development Programme have launched a public health program that promotes climate adaptation strategies. A pilot project focuses on 7 countries, each of which faces different threats to health from climate change: Bhutan and Kenya (highland areas); Jordan and Uzbekistan (water-stressed areas); Barbados and Fiji (low-lying developing areas); and China, which has a broad range of health vulnerabilities. According to program director Diarmid Campbell-Lendrum, PhD, a scientist at the WHO Department of Protection of the Human Public Health and Environment, it's the first global project to work directly with developing countries to design and implement practical measures to protect health in a rapidly changing climate. "The range of health issues likely to be affected by climate change is extremely wide. Fiji islanders are worried about drought and diarrheal disease, but also about tropical cyclones and increases in dengue fever. Kenyans are worried about the spread of vectorborne diseases while the people of Uzbekistan are worried about an extended drought. We're only just starting to get hold of the dimensions of the problems and working out how we'll tackle them in ways that are important to the future of these countries," Campbell-Lendrum said.

Scientists who work in this field always note that how the climate will change in the future is not completely knowable.

The planet and its ecosystems might be more forgiving and adaptable than anticipated. Reality might fall short of the dire predictions of climate models. Government may rein in fossil fuel emissions and implement cleaner energy initiatives faster than expected. Even so, some climate change is likely—changes are occurring slowly, and carbon dioxide persists in the atmosphere for at least a century. At this point, the impact on human health is starting to hit home. "We all have to learn to cope," Campbell-Lendrum said, "because climate change is not going away anytime soon."

References

1. Thomas CD, Cameron A, Green RE, Bakkenes M, Beaumont LJ, Collingham YC, et al. Extinction risk from climate change. Nature. 2004;427: 145–8. [PMID: 14712274]

2. Kovats RS, Menne B, McMichael AJ, Corvalan C, Bertollini R, eds. Climate Change and Human Health: Impact and Adaptation. Geneva: World Health Organization; May 2000. Accessed at http: //whqlibdoc.who.int/hq/2000/WHO_SDE_OEH_00.4.pdf on 23 October 2006.

3. Houghton JT, Ding Y, Griggs DJ, Nogver M, van der Linden PJ, Dai X, et al., eds. Climate change 2001: The Scientific Basis. Cambridge, United Kingdom: Cambridge University Pr; 2001.

4. McMichael AJ, Haines A, Slooff R, Kovats RS, eds. Climate Change and Human Health. WHO document WHO/EHG/96.7. Geneva: World Health Organization; 1996.

5. Lindgren E, Tälleklint L, Polfeldt T. Impact of climatic change on the northern latitude limit and population density of the disease-transmitting European tick *Ixodes ricinus*. Environ Health Perspect. 2000;108:119–23. [PMID: 10656851]

6. Stott PA, Stone DA, Allen MR. Human contribution to the European heatwave of 2003. Nature. 2004;432:610–4. [PMID: 15577907]

7. Wayne P, Foster S, Connolly J, Bazzaz F, Epstein P. Production of allergenic pollen by ragweed (*Ambrosia artemisiifolia* L.) is increased in CO2-enriched atmospheres. Ann Allergy Asthma Immunol. 2002;88:279–82. [PMID: 11926621]

8. Mohan JE, Ziska LH, Schlesinger WH, Thomas RB, Sicher RC, George K, et al. Biomass and toxicity responses of poison ivy (*Toxicodendron radicans*) to elevated atmospheric CO2. Proc Natl Acad Sci U S A. 2006;103:9086–9. [PMID: 16754866]

9. Epstein PR. Climate change and human health. N Engl J Med. 2005;353:1433–6. [PMID: 16207843]

10. McMichael AJ, Campbell-Lendrum DH, Corvalän CF, Ebi KL, Githeko AK, Scheraga JD, et al. Climate Change and Human Health: Risks and Responses. WHO document WHO/WMO/UNEP 1996. Geneva: World Health Organization; 2003.

11. McMichael AJ, Woodruff RE, Hales S. Climate change and human health: present and future risks. Lancet. 2006;367: 859–69. [PMID: 16530580]

12. Stern N. Stern Review: The Economics of Climate Change. 30 October 2006. Accessed at www.sternreview.org.uk on 11 November 2006.

JENNIFER FISHER WILSON Science Reporter, *Annals of Internal Medicine*. E-mail: jenwilson@acponline.org.

HIV Apathy

New drugs have changed HIV from a terminal to a chronic illness. To counter complacency, health officials are pushing to make testing more widespread.

ZACH PATTON

On a rainy day last June, local officials in Washington, D.C., gathered under tents erected on a public plaza to be tested for HIV. The District of Columbia's health department was kicking off a sweeping new effort to encourage city residents to take action against the disease. With banners, music and mobile-testing units, officials hoped the launch event and the campaign would help raise local awareness about HIV—and help the city address its most pressing health concern.

Washington has the nation's highest rate of new AIDS cases, and the city's goal—HIV testing for every resident between the ages of 14 and 84, totaling over 400,000 people—was unprecedented in its scope. City officials said the campaign, which also included distributing an initial 80,000 HIV tests to doctors' offices, hospitals and health clinics, would enable them to get a better idea of how many residents are infected with HIV. And making such screenings routine, they hoped, would help erase the stigma against getting tested for the disease.

Six months later, though, the effort was faltering. Fewer than 20,000 people had been tested. Many of the HIV test kits expired before they were distributed, forcing the city to throw them away. Others were donated to the Maryland health department to use before they went bad. And the city still lacked a comprehensive plan for ensuring effective treatment for those residents who test positive for the disease.

It's not all bad news. The District nearly tripled the number of sites offering free HIV screenings, and the Department of Corrections began screening all inmates for HIV. And the city improved its disease-surveillance technique, recording information on behaviors and lifestyles, in addition to counting the number of new HIV cases.

But D.C.'s struggle to meet its goals underscores a challenge common to local health officials across the country. More than a million U.S. residents are infected with HIV, and one-quarter of them don't know it, experts estimate. Diagnosis rates of HIV have stabilized in recent years, but large cities continue to grapple with much higher rates. They're dealing with higher incidents of the risky behaviors—drug use and unprotected sex, particularly gay sex—that tend to spread the disease. But they're also trying to battle something less tangible: complacency. Antiretroviral drugs have largely changed HIV from a terminal illness into a chronic one. And the fears associated with AIDS have faded over the past 20 years. As health officials work to combat HIV, they're finding that their hardest fight is the one against apathy.

Testing Laws

The first test for the human immunodeficiency virus was licensed by the FDA in March 1985. It was quickly put into use by blood banks, health departments and clinics across the country. But HIV testing at that time faced some major obstacles, which would continue to thwart HIV policies for much of the following two decades. For one, it usually took two weeks to obtain lab results, requiring multiple visits for patients waiting to see if they had HIV. Many patients—in some places, as many as half—never returned for the second visit. Another barrier was that, at the time, a diagnosis of the disease was a death sentence. With no reliable drugs to slow the progression of HIV into AIDS, and with an attendant stigma that could decimate a person's life, many people just didn't want to know if they were HIV-positive. "The impact of disclosure of someone's HIV-positive status could cost them their job, their apartment and their social circle," says Dr. Adam Karpati, assistant commissioner for HIV/AIDS Prevention & Control for the New York City health department. "In a basic calculus, the value to the patient was questionable. Knowing their status could only maybe help them, but it could definitely hurt them."

Because of that stigma and the seriousness of a positive diagnosis, many cities and states developed rigorous measures to ensure that testing was voluntary and confidential, and that it included a full discussion of the risks associated with the disease. That meant requiring written consent in order to perform tests, and mandatory pre- and post-test counseling. "A lot of the laws were, appropriately, concerned with confidentiality and protecting people's rights," Karpati says.

Two major developments have since changed the method—and the purpose—of HIV testing. First, the development of antiretroviral drugs in the mid-1990s has lessened the impact of HIV as a fatal disease. And in the past two or three years, advancements in testing technology have effectively eliminated the wait time for receiving results. Rapid tests using a finger-prick or an oral swab can be completed in 20 minutes, meaning nearly everyone can receive results within a single visit.

Those changes, along with aggressive counseling and education about risk-prevention measures, helped stabilize the rate of HIV diagnosis. After peaking in 1992, rates of AIDS cases leveled off by 1998. Today, about 40,000 AIDS cases are diagnosed every year. Data on non-AIDS HIV infection rates are much harder to come by, but they seem to have stabilized as well.

The problem, however, remains especially acute in urban areas. While health experts take pains to stress that HIV/AIDS is no longer just a "big city" problem, the fact is that 85 percent of the nation's HIV infections have been in metropolitan areas with more than half a million people. "Urban areas have always been the most heavily impacted by the HIV epidemic, and they continue to be," says Jennifer Ruth of the Centers for Disease Control and Prevention. Intravenous drug use, risky sexual behavior and homosexual sex all contribute to higher HIV rates, and they are all more prevalent in urban areas. But cities face other complicating factors as well, including high poverty rates and residents with a lack of access to medical care, which exacerbate the challenges of HIV care.

Prevention Fatigue

Nowhere is that more evident than in Washington, D.C., where an estimated one in every 20 residents is HIV-positive. That's 10 times the national average. But that figure is only a rough guess. The truth is that health officials don't even know what the city's HIV rate is. Last year's campaign was supposed to change that. By setting a goal to test nearly all city residents, District health officials hoped to make HIV screening a routine part of medical care. In the process, the health department hoped it could finally get a handle on just how bad the crisis was. "We've had problems in the past, I'll be the first to say," says D.C. health department director Dr. Gregg A. Pane. "But we have galvanized interest and action, and we've highlighted the problem in a way it hasn't been before."

The effort stumbled, though. The Appleseed Center for Law and Justice, a local public advocacy group, has issued periodic report cards grading the District's progress on HIV. The most recent assessment, published six months into last

year's testing push, found mismanagement and a lack of coordination with the medical community. The District was testing substantially more people than it had been, but the number was still falling far short of officials' goal. "D.C. took a great step forward, but it takes more than just a report announcing it," says Walter Smith, executive director for the Appleseed Center. "You have to make sure there's a plan."

What D.C. did achieve, however, was a fundamental shift in the way health officials perceive the HIV epidemic. "This is a disease that affects everyone," says Pane. "It's our No. 1 public health threat, and treating it like a public health threat is the exact right thing to do."

That paradigm change has been happening in health departments across the country. Last year, the CDC made waves when it announced new recommendations for treating HIV as an issue of public health. That means testing as many people as possible, making HIV testing a routine part of medical care, and removing the barriers to getting tested. Washington was the first city to adopt the CDC's recommendations for comprehensive testing, but other cities have also moved to make testing more routine. San Francisco health officials dropped their written-consent and mandatory-counseling requirements for those about to be tested. New York City has been moving in a similar direction, although removing the written-consent rule there will require changing state law. Many health officials think that since testing has become so easy and social attitudes about the disease have shifted, the strict testing regulations adopted in the 1980s are now cumbersome. The protections have become barriers.

Officials also are moving away from "risk-assessment testing," in which doctors first try to identify whether a patient falls into a predetermined high-risk category. "What has evolved is that, with an epidemic, risk-based testing is not sufficient," says New York City's Karpati. "Now there's a general move toward comprehensive testing." Privacy advocates and many AIDS activists oppose the shift away from individual protections. Yes, the stigma isn't what it used to be, they say, but it still exists. HIV isn't like tuberculosis or the measles, so they believe health officials shouldn't treat it like it is.

But even if officials could strike the perfect balance between public health and private protection, there's another factor that everyone agrees is thwarting cities' efforts to combat HIV. Call it burnout or complacency or "prevention fatigue." In an age when testing consists of an oral swab and a 20-minute wait, and an HIV-positive diagnosis means taking a few pills a day, health officials are battling a growing sense of apathy toward the disease. "The very successes we've made in the past 20 years have hurt us, in a sense," Karpati says. "We don't have hospital wards full of HIV patients. We don't have people dying as much. There's a whole new generation of folks growing up who don't remember the fear of the crisis in the 1980s."

That casual attitude toward the disease can lead to riskier behavior and, in turn, more infections. With HIV and AIDS disproportionately affecting low-income residents, any increase in infections places an additional burden on governments. And while prescription drugs have made the disease more manageable, the fact is that 40 percent of the new HIV diagnoses in the nation are still made within a year of the infection's progressing to AIDS—which is usually too late for medicine to do much good. As cities try to fight HIV complacency through refined testing policies and a focus on comprehensive testing, residents will have increasingly widespread access to tests for the disease. But for health officials, the greatest challenge will be getting the right people to care.

ZACH PATTON can be reached at zpatton@governing.com

From *Governing,* February 2007, pp. 48–50. Copyright © 2007 by Congressional Quarterly, Inc. Reprinted by permission.

Test Your Knowledge Form

We encourage you to photocopy and use this page as a tool to assess how the articles in *Annual Editions* expand on the information in your textbook. By reflecting on the articles you will gain enhanced text information. You can also access this useful form on a product's book support Web site at *http://www.mhcls.com/online/*.

NAME: _____ DATE: _____

_____

TITLE AND NUMBER OF ARTICLE:

_____

BRIEFLY STATE THE MAIN IDEA OF THIS ARTICLE:

_____

LIST THREE IMPORTANT FACTS THAT THE AUTHOR USES TO SUPPORT THE MAIN IDEA:

_____

WHAT INFORMATION OR IDEAS DISCUSSED IN THIS ARTICLE ARE ALSO DISCUSSED IN YOUR TEXTBOOK OR OTHER READINGS THAT YOU HAVE DONE? LIST THE TEXTBOOK CHAPTERS AND PAGE NUMBERS:

_____

LIST ANY EXAMPLES OF BIAS OR FAULTY REASONING THAT YOU FOUND IN THE ARTICLE:

_____

LIST ANY NEW TERMS/CONCEPTS THAT WERE DISCUSSED IN THE ARTICLE, AND WRITE A SHORT DEFINITION: